TEEJAY PUBLISHERS

Int-2-Credit Maths Book IC1

Produced by members of the TeeJay Writing Group

T. Strang (Mathematics Dept - Clydebank High School)

J. Geddes (P.T. Mathematics - Renfrew High School)

J. Cairns (Mathematics Dept - Clydebank High School)

for Janice

D1438238

STUDENT BOOK
IC1

Our thanks go to Graeme Tripney and Donald Macaulay
for checking and typing the answers.

Contents

Mathematics 1

Mathematics 2

*   In both the Mathematics 1 and the Mathematics 2 contents lists given on these pages, the topics and exercises shown in **blue** represent the entire course content for **Intermediate 2** (Maths 1/2), as listed in the **National Course Specifications - course details Document**.

The topics and exercises shown in red (along with those in **blue**,) are those required to complete (two thirds) of the Standard Grade Credit Course as detailed in the **Standard Grade Arrangements Document**. (*The remaining third, along with revision, will be met in Book IC2*).

Pupils who intend to progress to Higher are encouraged to complete both the red and **blue** exercises.

Those pupils who have already completed a Standard Grade General Course and gained a 3 (or a 4 ?), or who followed the Intermediate 1 course and were awarded a grade A (or B ?) might be able to complete the Intermediate 2 course by simply choosing to tackle only the **blue** exercises. However, progress to Higher would then be considered very difficult with this "minimum" level of Mathematical competency.

Int-2-Credit Maths Book IC1

Mathematics 1

Decimals

unless stated

1. Do the following **mentally** :–

    (a) 36 × 100   (b) 304 × 30

    (c) 5800 ÷ 10   (d) 32 × 400

    (e) 147000 ÷ 700   (f) 10 × 2·37

    (g) 17·6 ÷ 10   (h) 100 × 0·123

    (i) 9·8 ÷ 100   (j) 6·8 + 4·7

    (k) 10 – 2·7   (l) 1 – 0·03.

2. Set down and find the following :–

    (a) $\begin{array}{r} 18\cdot7 \\ +\ 26\cdot93 \\ \hline \end{array}$ (b) $\begin{array}{r} 50\cdot1 \\ -\ 14\cdot94 \\ \hline \end{array}$

    (c) $\begin{array}{r} 13\cdot26 \\ \times\ 8 \\ \hline \end{array}$ (d) $8\overline{)13\cdot84}$

3. Write as a **decimal** :-

    (a) $\frac{3}{10}$ = ...   (b) $\frac{3}{4}$ = ...   (c) $\frac{2}{5}$ = ...

4. What does the **6** represent in :–

    (a) 5·651   (b) 0·062   (c) 10·036 ?

5. Share £87·66 equally amongst 6 people.

6. Round to 1 decimal place :–

    (a) 18·76   (b) 0·385

    (c) 0·4498   (d) 20·87.

7. £1 = 1·85 American dollars.
    How many dollars would I receive for £8 ?

8. If £5 = 6·80 Euros, how many Euros will I receive for £3 ?

9. Two bags of potatoes, each 1·8 kilograms in weight, are removed from a 5 kilogram sack.

    What weight of potatoes is left ?

Fractions and Percentages

10. Simplify these fractions as far as possible :-

    (a) $\frac{12}{18}$ (b) $\frac{20}{45}$ (c) $\frac{16}{48}$ (d) $\frac{36}{84}$.

11. Find the following :-

    (a) $\frac{2}{3}$ of 60   (b) $\frac{3}{4}$ of £120

    (c) $\frac{4}{5}$ of 35 kg   (d) $\frac{3}{10}$ of 1200.

12. Of the 180 adults living in Stewart Street, $\frac{8}{9}$ voted at the last election.

    How many of the adults did **not** vote ?

13. Do these **mentally** :-

    (a) 50% of £160   (b) 25% of £1200

    (c) 10% of £70   (d) $33\frac{1}{3}$% of 36p

    (e) 20% of £80   (f) 30% of £70

    (g) 1% of 5800   (h) 75% of 16 kg.

Ratios

14. Simplify these **ratios** :-

    (a) 4 : 8   (b) 27 : 36

    (c) 30 : 75   (d) 108 : 45.

15. The ratio of cassettes to cd's in a man's collection is 36 : 27.

    Simplify this ratio as far as possible.

16. The **ratio** of :-

    sprained ankles : sprained wrists

    in the Accident & Emergency Unit last week was :-

    3 : 5.

    If there were 15 sprained ankles, how many sprained wrists were there ?

Patterns

17. Fill in the next 3 terms in each of these patterns of numbers :–

    (a) 2, 6, 10, 14, ...   (b) 90, 83, 76, 69, ...

    (c) 4, 9, 16, 25, ...   (d) 1, 1, 2, 3, 5, 8, 13, ...

18. Find the 30th number in the pattern :–

    4, 7, 10, 13, 16, ...

19. List all the **Prime Numbers** less than 30.

20. A boy makes patterns with wooden bricks.

Pattern 1 **Pattern 2** **Pattern 3**

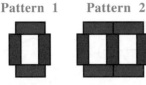 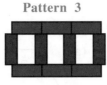

   4 bricks   7 bricks   .... bricks

(a) How many bricks are needed for each of the pattern numbers 3, 4 and 5 ?

(b) Describe in words (or symbols) a formula which will allow you to calculate the number of bricks needed, once you are given the pattern number.

(c) How many bricks are needed for pattern number 100 ?

Negative Numbers

21. What temperatures are represented on each of these thermometers ?

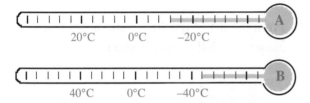

22. The temperature rose from $-18°C$ to $7°C$.

By how much had it risen ?

23. When a freezer was switched on, its temperature dropped by $35°C$.

If its temperature began at $10°C$, what was the final temperature ?

Algebra

24. What numbers must have gone "IN" the following number machines :–

(a)
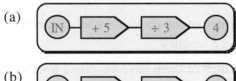

(b)
IN — × 4 — – 7 — 5

25. Solve the following **equations** for x :–

(a) $x - 4 = 11$ (b) $x + 5 = 14$

(c) $3x = 18$ (d) $2x = 13$

25. (e) $4x + 1 = 29$ (f) $3x - 5 = 19$

    (g) $3x + 3 = 3$ (h) $8x - 1 = 19$.

26. Choose all the numbers from the list :-

$$\{1, 2, 3, 4, 5, 6, 7, 8, 9, 10\}$$

which make these **inequalities** true :–

(a) $x < 4$ (b) $x \geq 5$

(c) $x - 3 > 6$ (d) $x + 2 < 7$.

Measurement and Estimation

27. The area of a girl's bedroom is known to be one of the following :-

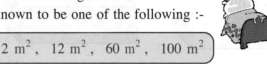

2 m^2, 12 m^2, 60 m^2, 100 m^2

Which is it most likely to be ?

28. Measure the length of the line AB in millimetres.

A ——————————————— B

29. How many kilograms are there in 5 tonnes ?

30. **Estimate** the volume of liquid in this container.

(*in millilitres*)

Capacity, when full, = 1 litre

31. Shown are the times of the winning horse and the last horse in a race.

By how much did the first horse beat the last horse ?

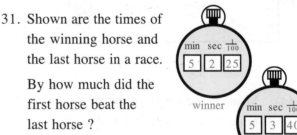
winner

last horse

32. Calculate the **area** of each of the following shapes :–

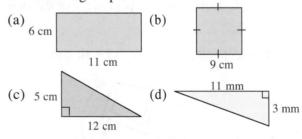

(a) 6 cm, 11 cm

(b) 9 cm

(c) 5 cm, 12 cm

(d) 11 mm, 3 mm

33. Calculate the **perimeters** of these shapes :–

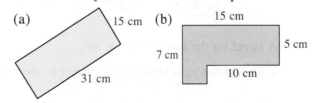

(a) 15 cm, 31 cm

(b) 15 cm, 7 cm, 5 cm, 10 cm

34. Calculate the following volumes (in cm^3) :–

(a)

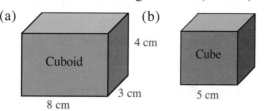

4 cm

Cuboid

3 cm

8 cm

(b)

Cube

5 cm

35. These 2 cuboids have the SAME volume.

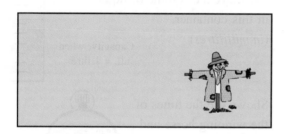

3 cm

4 cm

10 cm

? cm

5 cm

12 cm

Calculate the height of the green cuboid.

Scale Drawing

36. The scale of this drawing of a rectangular field is 1 cm to 25 metres.

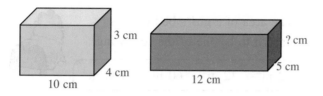

scale :- 1 cm = 25 metres

(a)   Measure the length of the rectangle which represents the field in this drawing.

(b)   Use the scale to determine the **real length** of the field in metres.

(c)   Calculate the real **perimeter** of the field.

37.   The scale on a map is :-   **1 : 10 000**.

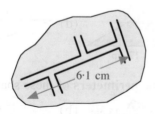

6·1 cm

A street on the map is 6·1 cm long.

Calculate the **real** length of the street in metres.

Quadrilaterals

38. Name these quadrilaterals :–

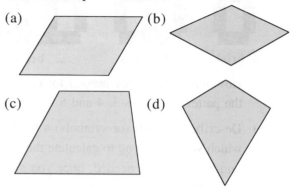

(a)   (b)

(c)   (d)

39. It is possible to **approximately** calculate the circumference of a circle if you know its diameter.

You simply multiply the diameter by :–
{2, 3, 4, 5 or 10}

Which one ?

40. From the list of quadrilaterals shown below, answer the following questions :–

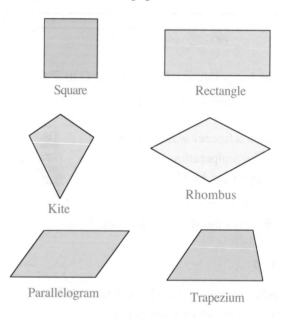

Square   Rectangle

Kite

Rhombus

Parallelogram   Trapezium

(*A sketch might help*).

(a)   Which of the above have all 4 sides the same length ?

(b)   Which of them have **exactly** 2 lines of symmetry ?

(c)   Which of them do **NOT** have $\frac{1}{2}$ turn symmetry ?

(d)   Which of them have their diagonals the same length ?

Drawing

41. (You will need **compasses**, a **protractor** and a **ruler** for this question.)

Shown below are sketches of 3 triangles. Construct (draw) them accurately.

(a)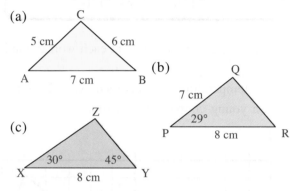

(b)

(c)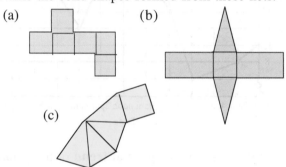

42. Shown are nets of 3 solid shapes. Name the solid shapes formed from these nets.

(a)

(b)

(c)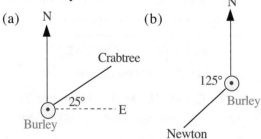

Bearings and Rotational Symmetry

43. Write down the **3 figure bearing** of each town from Burley.

(a)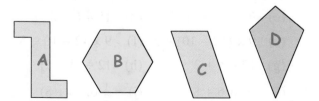

(b)

44. Which of the following shapes have **rotational** symmetry?

45. (a) Write down the coordinates of point A.

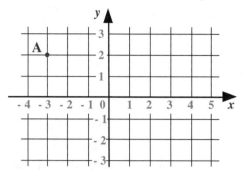

(b) Copy this diagram and plot the points :–
    B(4, -3) and C(-3, -1).

(c) Write down the distance, (in boxes), from A to C.

46. Copy this shape and rotate it by 180° around the "dot".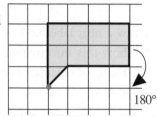

180°

47. 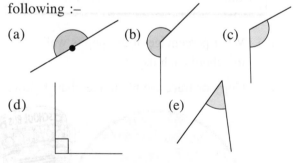 Make a neat copy of this shape on squared paper.

Show how to cover the surface with tiles **congruent** to this one.

Angles

48. State the "type" of angle in each of the following :–

(a)   (b)   (c)

(d)   (e)

49. **Calculate** the size of the angles p, q and r :–

(a)   (b)

(c)

50. Make a sketch of
this shape and fill
in the sizes of **ALL**
the angles.
(*Do not measure them*).

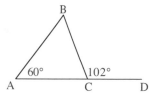

51.

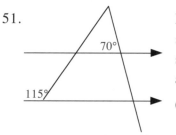

Make a sketch of this
shape and fill in the
sizes of **ALL** the
angles.

(*Do not measure them*).

Statistics

52. Draw a neat labelled **bar graph**
to show this information about
the make of calculators owned
by a group of pupils.

Make	Casio	Texas	Newton	Fuigi	Global
Number	8	13	5	10	4

53. The table below shows how a group of 3rd
year pupils travel to school.

Bus	45%
Car	10%
Train	20%
Walk	.....%

(a) What percentage of the pupils walk
to school each day ?

(b) Copy or trace the blank pie chart below.

(c) Complete and label it to show the
information from the table about
how pupils travel to school each day.

54. Five women discuss how much
money each of them spent on
a new dress for the Christmas
dance.

Jean – £80,   Sally – £45,   Kate – £55,

Beth – £60,   Liz – £110

Calculate the **mean** amount each woman paid.

55. The temperature was recorded every 2 hours
in a young couple's living room.

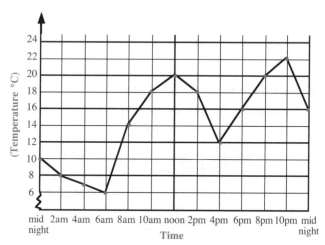

(a) Describe the general **trend** of the graph
over the 24 hour period.

(b) What was the :–

(i) maximum temperature ?

(ii) minimum temperature ?

(c) The central heating is switched on twice
daily. At what times (approx) ?

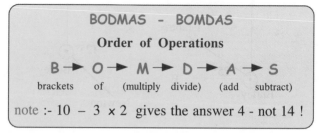

BODMAS - BOMDAS

Order of Operations

B → O → M → D → A → S

brackets   of   (multiply   divide)   (add   subtract)

note :- 10 – 3 x 2 gives the answer 4 - not 14 !

56. Try the following - check your answers !!

(a) 6 + 4 x 5   (b) (6 + 4) x 5

(c) 9 – 2 x 3   (d) 15 – 6 ÷ 3

(e) 9 x (12 – 10) ÷ 5   (f) 9 x 12 – 10 ÷ 5

(g) 12 ÷ 4 + 2   (h) 12 ÷ (4 + 2)

(i) $\frac{1}{2}$ of 6 + 8   (j) $\frac{1}{2}$ of (6 + 8)

Mental Percentages

By now, you should be able to find a **percentage** of a quantity using a calculator :-

Example :-   Find $17\frac{1}{2}$% of £160   =>

- $(17.5 \div 100) \times 160$ = £28·00
- 0.175×160 = £28·00

or

But - there are many percentage calculations which can to be done **MENTALLY**.

> 50% of 60p means
> **a half** of 60p
> (=> ÷ 2)

> $33\frac{1}{3}$% of 120 g means
> **a third** of 120 g
> (=> ÷ 3)

> 75% of £20 means
> **three quarters** of £20
> (=> ÷ 4 then × 3)

> 80% of 350 means
> **four fifths** of 350
> (=> ÷ 5 then × 4)

Exercise 1·1

1.   Make a COPY of these tables and complete :-

Percentage	50	25	75	$33\frac{1}{3}$	$66\frac{2}{3}$
Fraction	$\frac{1}{2}$				

Percentage	20	40	60	80	10	30	70	90
Fraction	$\frac{1}{5}$						$\frac{7}{10}$	

Learn the above percentage —> fraction conversions. You will need them here :-

2.   Find the following without a calculator :-

(a)   10% of £35   (b)   70% of £40

(c)   20% of £4·50   (d)   80% of 30p

(e)   25% of £1080   (f) $33\frac{1}{3}$% of £24

(g)   75% of £2·40   (h)   1% of £140

(i)   60% of £8000   (j)   50% of £30000

(k)   40% of £350   (l)   10% of 90p

(m) $66\frac{2}{3}$% of £12·60 (n)   90% of 20p

(o)   3% of £60   (p)   2·5% of £40.

3.   30% of the S4 pupils in Lochee Academy are left handed.

If there are 160 pupils in S4 in the school, how many are **not** left handed ?

4. $33\frac{1}{3}$% of the trees in an orchard are apple trees, 25% are banana trees and the rest of them are lemon trees.

If there are 480 trees in total in this orchard, how many are :-

(a)   apple   (b)   banana

(c)   lemon   (d)   not apple ?

> **Remember :-**   17% means $\frac{17}{100}$ = 0·17
>
>   8% means $\frac{8}{100}$ = 0·0̲8

5.   Write each of the following as a fraction **AND** as a decimal :–

(a)   32%   (b)   45%

(c)   51%   (d)   31%

(e)   78%   (f)   8%

(g)   12·5%   (h)   2·5%.

6.   Write these as fractions and **simplify** :–

(a)   35% = $\frac{35}{100}$ = $\frac{.....}{20}$

(b)   60% = $\frac{60}{100}$ = ...

(c)   55%   (d)   90%

(e)   15%   (f)   75%

(g)   4%   (h)   85%

(i)   5%   (j)   36%

(k) $2\frac{1}{2}$%   (l)   150%.

> **Remember** :- 17% of £420 means :-
>
> - $(17 \div 100) \times £420 = 71 \cdot 4 = £71 \cdot 40$
> - or $0 \cdot 17 \times £420 = 71 \cdot 4 = £71 \cdot 40$

7. Use your calculator to find the following :–

   (a) 8% of £40 = $(8 \div 100) \times 40$ = £......

   (b) 15% of £80   (c) 32% of £60

   (d) 48% of £3500   (e) 36% of £7·50

   (f) 75% of £26·40   (g) 95% of £4

   (h) 7% of £80   (i) 3% of £15

   (j) $17\frac{1}{2}$% of £240   (k) 6·8% of £300.

8. During a storm, the level of rain which ran into a barrel outside my front door was 140 mm.

   During the night the water level rose by another 35%.

   What was the level of rain water in the barrel when I woke in the morning ?

9. Only 55% of young eels are expected to survive the first few weeks of their young lives.

   In the River Lowis last year, 1·5 million eels were born.

   How many were expected to survive the early stages of their lives ?

10. Lanarewshire Town Council decided to increase council tax by 6·5% this year.

    The Thomsons of Glenview paid council tax totalling £780 last year.

    What should they expect to be paying in total this year ?

11. Before training, it took me 55 seconds to run 400 metres.
    After a training schedule, I knocked 12% off my time.

    How long did it then take to run the 400 m ?

12. A coat is priced £180.

    In a sale, it was reduced by 15%.

    What will the coat then cost ?

13. A plane was flying at 35 000 feet when it hit a storm.

    The pilot lowered the plane's altitude by 45%.

    At what height was the plane then flying ?

14. A standard jar of coffee holds 240 grams.

    In a special offer, an extra 12% is offered at no extra cost.

    How much coffee does the new jar then contain ?

15. The Scotia Bank offers its customers an interest rate of 4·5% p.a. on their savings.

    Jemma deposits £1200 in a new Scotia bank account and leaves it there for 1 year.

    > Special Savings Rate
    > 4·5% p.a.

    (a) What does the term "p.a." mean ?

    (b) How much interest will Jemma receive if she invests her £1200 in the account for 1 year ?

    (c) How much will her savings then be worth ?

16. Ted deposited £2500 with the Scotia Bank.

    (a) How much interest is Ted due if he leaves his savings there for 1 year ?

    (b) How much interest did Ted actually receive if he withdrew his savings after 6 months ?

17. Musa paid in £6000 to his building society special interest account where the annual interest rate was 4·2%.

    How much interest is Musa due if he removes all his money after a 9 month period ?

18. Who will get more interest :-

    Brian, who invests £4000 in the bank for 6 months if the annual rate is 5·2%

    or

     Nicole, who invest £3000 in her building society for 9 months where the annual interest rate is 4·6% ?

Expressing one Number as a Percentage of another Number

In many instances, you will be asked to express one number as a percentage of another one.

The process is quite simple and can be done using 3 steps as follows :-

Example :-   Davie scored **18 out of 25** in his Maths test.

=>   to find what 18 is, as a percentage of 25 :-

Davie
18 out
of 25
√

- write 18 as a fraction of 25   => $\frac{18}{25}$

- now do the "division"   => $18 \div 25$ $= 0{\cdot}72$

- finally, multiply this decimal by 100   => $0{\cdot}72 \times 100 = 72\%$

These 3 steps are used to show what one number is when expressed as a percentage of another.

Exercise 1·2

1. Copy the following and use your calculator to change each **fraction** to a **percentage** :–

    (a) $\frac{7}{50}$ = 7 ÷ 50

    = 0·..... = (0·.... × 100%) = ... %

    (b) $\frac{1}{5}$ = 1 ÷ 5

    = 0·..... = (0·.... × 100%) = ...%

    (c) $\frac{12}{50}$ (d) $\frac{20}{25}$ (e) $\frac{9}{20}$

    (f) $\frac{17}{20}$ (g) $\frac{23}{25}$ (h) $\frac{1}{8}$

    (i) $\frac{9}{25}$ (j) $\frac{7}{8}$ (k) $\frac{60}{80}$

    (l) $\frac{5}{8}$ (m) $\frac{13}{20}$ (n) $\frac{37}{74}$.

2. Change each of these marks to **percentages** :–

    (a) Julie scored 32 out of 40 ($\frac{32}{40}$)

    => 32 ÷ 40 = 0· ..... × 100% = ... %.

    (b) Francis scored 27 out of 50.

    (c) Ricky scored 30 out of 80.

    (d) Chic scored 6 out of 20.

3. Of the 240 pupils in 4th year, 192 of them were following the Credit Mathematics course.

    (a) What percentage were doing Credit ?

    (b) What percentage were NOT ?

4. Jamie managed to get 14 out of 18 in his test.

    What was Jamie's percentage mark ? (*Answer correct to 1 decimal place*).

5. Determine the following marks as percentages, giving each correct to 1 decimal place :-

    (a) Jilly scored 65 out of 80 in Maths.

    (b) Rebecca scored 27 out of 35 in French.

    (c) Alistair scored 40 out of 41 in Physics.

6. Lucy recorded her monthly test scores :-

    Aug - $\frac{10}{20}$ Sep - $\frac{30}{50}$ Oct - $\frac{26}{40}$

    Nov - $\frac{48}{80}$ Dec - $\frac{7}{10}$ Jan - $\frac{75}{100}$

    Feb - $\frac{54}{60}$ Mar - $\frac{20}{25}$ Apr - $\frac{24}{24}$

    May - $\frac{34}{40}$

    (a) Calculate Lucy's percentage scores over the 10 month period.

    (b) Draw a neat line graph to show Lucy's progress.

    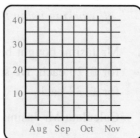

    (c) What was Lucy's average (**mean**) percentage mark ?

    (d) Describe the **trend** of her marks.

7. Nick sat a test out of 60. His score (*rounded to 1 decimal place*) was 82%.

    What must Nick's score have been ?

Percentage Profit and Loss

A shopkeeper buys an article for £A and sells it for £B. He will have made a :-

- **Profit** of £(B − A) as long as **B** is greater than **A**.
- **Loss** of £(A − B) as long as **A** is greater than **B**.

Generally, the shopkeeper is more interested in his **PERCENTAGE** profit.

—> he wants to know what his **profit** is, expressed as a **percentage** of what it **cost** him.

Example :-   Gerry the Grocer bought a barrel of 100 apples for £24·00
He packed them into bags of 10 and sold them all for £3·20 per bag.

(a)   Calculate his overall profit.

(b)   Express this as a percentage of what it cost Gerry.

(a)
Actual Profit :-	
Cost Price	£24·00
Selling Price = 10 × £3·20	£32·00
Profit = £32·00 − £24·00 =	£8·00

(b)
Percentage Profit :-

$$= \frac{\text{actual profit}}{\text{cost price}} \times 100\%$$

$$= (£8 \cdot 00 \div £24 \cdot 00) \times 100 = 33 \cdot 3\%$$

Exercise 1·3

1.   Susie bought a book for £15·00.
    Five years later, she sold it for £18·00.

    Calculate her percentage profit.

    Copy and complete :-

Original value	£15·00
New value	£18·00
Profit = £(18 − 15) =	£...·...
%age profit = (3 ÷ 15) × 100% =	.... %

   (*For the remainder of this exercise, set down
   all working using the 4 lines shown*).

2.   Mr Jasimi bought bicycles
    for £120 each. He sold them
    for £138 each.

    Calculate Mr Jasimi's percentage profit.

3.   For each of the following, calculate the profit
    and the percentage profit :-

    (a)   cost price - 80p,   selling price - 90p.

    (b)   cost price - £1500, selling price - £1950.

3.   (c)   cost price - £16000, selling price - £16480.

    (d)   cost price - 40p, selling price - £1·00.

4.   My PacaDell computer cost me £500 new.
    I sold it one year later for £350.

    Find how much I lost in the deal, and express
    this as a percentage of what it cost me.

5.   Calculate the loss and percentage loss each time.

    (a)   cost price - £160,   selling price - £112.

    (b)   cost price - £4000, selling price - £1260.

    (c)   cost price - 80p,   selling price - 10p.

6.   Davie's new Pickup
    cost him £12000.

    When he sold it 2 years
    later, he made a loss of 35%.

    How much must Davie have got for his Pickup ?

7.   Gerry the grocer wants to make a **40% profit**
    on the vegetables he sells.
    He bought a 50 kg sack of potatoes for £36
    which he then repacked into 5 kg bags.

    For how much will Gerry need to sell each bag ?

Compound Interest

You should already know that if money is left in a bank for up to a year, it gains INTEREST.

This is referred to as **Simple Interest** as is found by using percentages.

If you leave money in the bank for several years :-

> * the interest is found **for the first year year**
> * this is then **added** to the **previous balance**
> * the new interest for the next year is calculated
> * this is then added on again to the previous balance
> * ... and so on until all the interest has been calculated.

This is referred to as **COMPOUND INTEREST**.

Example :- Ailsa invests £800 in the Scotia Bank. Their **annual** rate was 4%.

Calculate the **compound interest** that builds up in the account.

First Year Balance	£800·00
1st Year Interest = 4% of £800·00	£32·00
Second Year Balance = £800·00 + £32·00	£832·00
2nd Year Interest = 4% of £832·00	£33·28
Third Year Balance = £832·00 + £33·28	£865·28
3rd Year Interest = 4% of £865·28	£34·61
=> Final Balance = £865·28 + £34·61	**£899·89**
=> Total Interest = £899·89 – £800·00	**£99·89**

Interest paid at 4% p.a.

Exercise 1·4

1. Andy leaves £1200 in his bank for 3 years.
   The annual rate of interest is 3%.

   Calculate how much **interest** Andy is then due.
   Copy and complete :-

1st Year Balance	£1200·00
1st Year Int = 3% of £1200·00	£.....·....
2nd Year Balance = £1200 + ...	£........·....
2nd Year Int = 3% of £.....·...	£.....·....
3rd Year Balance = £....... + ...	£........·....
3rd Year Int = 3% of £.....·...	£.....·....
Final Balance =	£........·....
Total Interest =	£.....·....

2. Nicki and Susan Dyer invested £480 in their building society account and left it there for two years. The annual interest rate was 3·5%.

   Calculate the **compound** interest that built up in their account over the 2 years.

3. Harry left his £25 000 Premium Bond winnings in a special savings account for 3 years.

   The annual rate of interest was 4·5%.

   How much were his savings then worth ?

4. Joan was told that if she left her savings of £2400 in the Scotia Bank for 5 years they would give her a special annual rate of 5·4%.

   How much would her £2400 be worth at the end of the 5 year period ?

5. Calculate the total compound interest due when the following investments are made :-

   (a) Colin deposited £360 in the bank for 3 years with an annual interest rate of 2·5%.

   (b) Alex put by £5000 in the bank for 2 years with an annual interest rate of 3·2%.

   (c) Tim paid in £600 to his bank and left it for 2 years. The annual interest rate was $3\frac{1}{2}$%.

6. An internet bank offered a tremendous interest rate of 9% per year on savings.
Jon and Ruth Williams invested their savings of £6000 in the internet bank.

(a) How much were their savings worth after :- (i) 1 year (ii) 2 years ?

(b) How many years would it take before their investment doubled in value ?

7.  Rebecca was advised to invest her £12000 life savings in a special High Interest Savings account, but she had to agree not to touch it for 4 years.

The interest rates for the 4 year period were 4·5%, 5%, 5·3% and 4·9% respectively.

(a) Calculate the value of her savings at the end of each year.

(b) What was the total interest that had accrued on her account ?

(c) Express this as a percentage of her original investment.

Depreciation and Appreciation

Most things you buy generally tend to **drop** or **DEPRECIATE** in value with time.

Example 1 :- A car, bought for £12000, depreciated by :-

- 15% during its 1st year,
- 20% in its 2nd year.
- 25% during its 3rd year.

What was its actual value after 3 years ?

Initial Value	£12000
1st Year depreciation = 15% of £12000	£1800
Second Year Value = £12000 – £1800	£10200
2nd Year depreciation = 20% of £10200	£2040
Third Year Value = £10200 – £2040	£8160
3rd Year depreciation = 25% of £8160	£2040
=> **Final** Value = £8160 – £2040	**£6120**

Some valuables, like paintings, diamond rings and "special" types of cars **rise** or **APPRECIATE**.

Example 2 :- A Jack Vetriano painting, bought for £5000, appreciated by :-

- 60% during its 1st year.
- 80% during in its 2nd year.

What was the painting worth after 2 years ?

Initial Value	£5000
1st Year appreciation = 60% of £5000	£3000
Second Year Value = £5000 + £3000	£8000
2nd Year appreciation = 80% of £8000	£6400
=> **Final** Value = £8000 + £6400	**£14400**

1. Jillian and Mike bought a dishwasher for £400. Its value **depreciated** by 20% every year.

   Calculate what it was worth after 3 years.
   Copy and complete :-

1st Year Value	£400
1st Year Dep. = 20% of £400	£....
2nd Year Value = £400 – £80	£.......
2nd Year Dep. = 20% of £....	£....
3rd Year Value = £.... – £....	£.......
3rd Year Dep. = 20% of £....	£....
=> Final Value = £.... – £....	£.......

2. Zak bought his first motorbike at the start of 2000 for £6400.

   It **depreciated** in value by 25% every year he owned it.

   What was the bike worth by the end of :-

   (a) 2000   (b) 2001   (c) 2002 ?

3.  The Wallaces paid £90 000 for their house 3 years ago.

   Because of a new motorway being built through their front lawn, they found that the house's value **dropped** by 5% the first year, 10% in the second and a further 20% in the third year.

   How much was their house then worth ?

4. A hot air balloon was drifting along at a height of 16 000 feet when it developed a leak.

   The balloon dropped by 8% every minute after that.

   What was the balloon's height after 3 minutes ?

5. Jules bought a Rolls Royce Silver Shadow and paid £48 000 for it.
   He discovered that the car **appreciated** in value by 6% during the first year he owned it and by 8% in its 2nd year.

   What was the car then worth ?

6. The cost of buying an average weekly shopping for a family of 4 generally rises each year.

   Choice meats

   The James' family spent about £150 per week in Tesdas in 2001.

   If the cost of living rose by 4% per year, what would they have paid for their weekly shop in

   (a) 2002   (b) 2003   (c) 2004 ?

7. The graph below shows the "**cost of living**" annual rise between 1990 and 1995.

   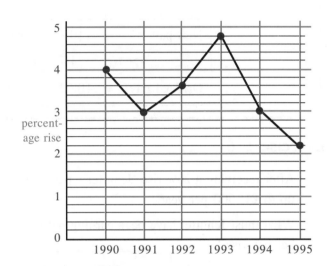

   (a) What was the cost of living rise in :-
   (i) 1991   (ii) 1993 ?

   (b) A new computer system cost £600 at the beginning of 1990. What would you expect to pay for it by the end of 1990 ?

   (c) A meal out for 4 cost on average £42 at the beginning of 1994. What would a similar meal cost by the end of 1994 ?

   (d) Greg and Sally paid £30 000 for their flat in January 1991.

   Estimate the value of the flat in January :-
   (i) 1992   (ii) 1993   (iii) 1994 ?

8. The pressure in a boiler is 120 poundals. A faulty valve causes the pressure to rise in the boiler by 12% every hour.

   The situation will become dangerous when the pressure reaches 200 poundals.

   If it continues to rise this way, during which hour will the boiler's pressure reach danger level ?

Percentage Problems – Working Backwards

Consider the following problem - solving it is **NOT** as easy as you think !

> **Problem** :- A man receives a 10% pay rise.
>
> His **new** weekly pay becomes £440.
>
> **Question** :- What must his **original** pay have been ?

What **NOT** to do ! :-   Do **NOT** simply find 10% of £440, (= £44), and subtract it => £396. **X**

Solution :-   Note that, after a 10% rise, the man was then earning **110%** of his original pay !

New pay	= 110%	=	....	£440
	=>	1%	= £440 ÷ 110 =	£4
Original pay	= 100%	=	£4·00 × 100 =	**£400**

* study this example carefully

Note :- the 3 steps

Exercise 1·6

1. After receiving a 20% rise, Jennifer's pay went up to £18 000 per year.

    What must Jennifer have been earning before her pay rise ?

    (*Hint* :- start with
=>	120%	= £18 000)
=>	1%	= £.........
=>	100%	= £.........

2. The painting I bought last year rose by 40% in value this year. It is **now** worth £560.

    How much must I have paid for the painting ?

3. Because of a fault in a thermostat, the temperature in an oven rises by 35% to 324°C.

    What was the temperature before the fault ?

4.  On his 14th birthday, Otis found he was 12% **taller** than he was on his previous birthday.

    He was 1·68 m tall on his 14th birthday.

    How tall was Otis on his 13th ?

5. When a speeding motorist overtook a police car, the police increased their speed by 60% to catch him.

    If the police car was then doing 80 mph, what was its speed before it accelerated ?

6. The bike I bought last year **dropped** in value by 20% this year.

    It is now only worth £160.

    How much must I have paid for the bike ?
    Copy and complete :-

    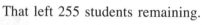
New value =	80%	(100% – 20%)	= £160
=>	1%	= £160 ÷ 80 =	£2
Old value =	100%	= 100 × £2	= £....

7. 15% of the maths students at Strathtay University dropped out of their course during their first year.
    That left 255 students remaining.

    How many students must there have been at the beginning of the year ?

8. When a window was left open for 10 minutes, the temperature dropped by 35% to 19·5°C.

    What was the temperature before the window was opened ?

9. When Donald sold his flat, he lost 3% of what he had originally paid for it.

    He only got £43 650 for his flat.

    What must Donald have paid for the flat when he bought it ?

Rounding - Significant Figures

A figure or digit in a number is "**significant**" if it gives some sense of QUANTITY & ACCURACY.

"**ZEROS**" can be complicated - when do we count them ? – when do we leave them out ?

If zeros are used only to show where the position of the decimal point is,
then they are NOT significant.

Example 1 :-

607 has .... <u>3</u> significant figures.   60·7 has .... <u>3</u> significant figures.

6·07 has .... <u>3</u> sig.figs.   0·607 has .... <u>3</u> sig.figs.

0·06070 has .... <u>4</u> sig. figs. (Front zero positions the decimal point, but trailing zero shows accuracy)

Example 2 :-

4386 rounded to 1 sig. fig. is   **4000**   39 264 rounded to 3 sig. figs. is   **39 300**

5·746 rounded to 3 sig. figs. is   **5·75**   0·008 317 rounded to 2 sig. figs. is   **0·0083**

Exercise 1·7

1. How many significant figures does each number have in the following context :-

    (a) There are **400** ten pences in forty pounds.

    (b) Approximately **70** boys attended the dance.

    (c) To the nearest million pounds, the football transfer fee was **£12 000 000**.

    (d) The altitude of Ben Nevis is **1344** metres.

2. Write down how many significant figures there are in each of these numbers :-

    (a) 41·0   (b) 9·00

    (c) 7·006   (d) 479

    (e) 70·1   (f) 25·80

    (g) 0·099   (h) 2·000 005

    (i) 0·000 80   (j) 6·000 003

    (k) 154·000   (l) 0·000 000 010.

3. Round each number to 1 sig. fig. :-

    (a) 53   (b) 478

    (c) 6478   (d) 22 364

    (e) 4499   (f) 4599

    (g) 1·96   (h) 0·426

    (i) 0·789   (j) 0·0021

    (k) 0·019   (l) 3 750 000

    (m) 0·000 785 (n) 79·99.

4. Round each number to 2 sig. figs :-

    (a) 809   (b) 7139

    (c) 30 700   (d) 181 129

    (e) 46·37   (f) 19·52

    (g) 7·192   (h) 0·339

    (i) 0·003 684 (j) 89·816.

5. Round each number to 3 sig. figs :-

    (a) 5841   (b) 25 081

    (c) 73 853   (d) 482 199

    (e) 15·826   (f) 12·817

    (g) 0·287 45   (h) 0·293 54

    (i) 0·001 677 (j) 0·049 999.

6. Find the weight of a set of 300 DVD's, if each DVD weighs 49 grams. (*Give your answer in grams to 2 sig. figs.*).

7. I deposited £25 531 in the Building Society, receiving an interest rate of 1·84% per annum.

    Calculate my interest for the year, correct to 2 sig. figs.

8. Miss Mace purchased a vacuum cleaner for £361·14 + V.A.T. at 17·5%.

    Calculate the V.A.T. correct to 4 sig. figs.

Pythagoras Theorem

Pythagoras came up with a simple rule which shows the connection between the three sides of any right angled triangle.

The **longest** side of a right angled triangle is called the **HYPOTENUSE**.

If the three sides are a cm, b cm and c cm (the hypotenuse), then Pythagoras' Rule says :-

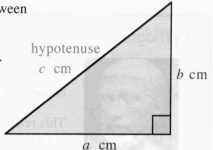

$$\Rightarrow \quad c^2 = a^2 + b^2$$

We can use this rule to calculate the length of the **hypotenuse** of a right angled triangle if we know the lengths of the two **smaller** sides.

Example 1 :- The two smaller sides of this right angled triangle are 12 centimetres and 16 centimetres.

To calculate the length of the hypotenuse, use **Pythagoras' Rule**.

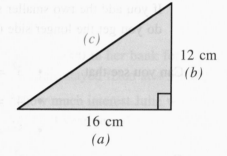

$$\Rightarrow \quad c^2 = a^2 + b^2$$
$$\Rightarrow \quad c^2 = 16^2 + 12^2$$
$$\Rightarrow \quad c^2 = 256 + 144 = 400$$

use your "√" button on the calculator

$$\Rightarrow \quad c = \sqrt{400} = \boxed{20 \text{ cm}}.$$

This is how you set down the working.

Exercise 2·1

1. Use **Pythagoras' Rule** to calculate the length of the hypotenuse in this triangle :-

$$c^2 = a^2 + b^2$$
$$\Rightarrow \quad c^2 = 15^2 + \ldots$$
$$\Rightarrow \quad c^2 = 225 + \ldots$$
$$\Rightarrow \quad c = \sqrt{\ldots} = \ldots$$

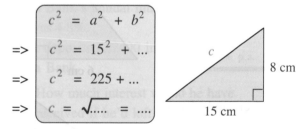

Copy and complete the working.

2. Use **Pythagoras' Rule** to calculate the length of the hypotenuse in the right angled triangle shown below.

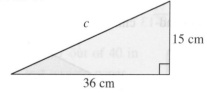

(*Show clearly your 4 lines of working*).

3. Use Pythagoras' Rule (referred to as **PYTHAGORAS' THEOREM**) to calculate the length of the hypotenuse in each of these 3 triangles :-

(a)

(b)

(c)

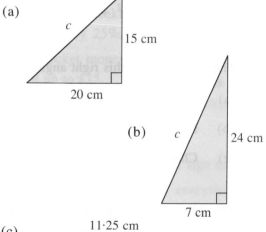

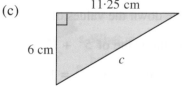

In most cases, the 3 sides are not exact values.

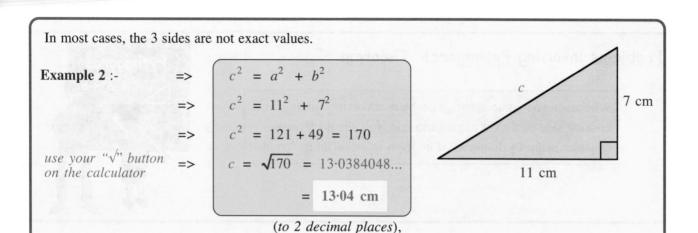

Example 2 :-

$$=> \quad c^2 = a^2 + b^2$$

$$=> \quad c^2 = 11^2 + 7^2$$

$$=> \quad c^2 = 121 + 49 = 170$$

use your "√" button
on the calculator $=>$ $\quad c = \sqrt{170} = 13 \cdot 0384048...$

$$= \boxed{13 \cdot 04 \text{ cm}}$$

(to 2 decimal places),

(For the remainder of this exercise, give your answers correct to 2 decimal places).

4. Use **Pythagoras' Theorem** to calculate the length of the hypotenuse in this triangle .

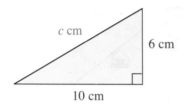

5. Use Pythagoras' Theorem to calculate the length of the hypotenuse in the right angled triangle shown .

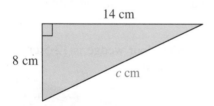

6. Calculate the length of the hypotenuse marked p cm.

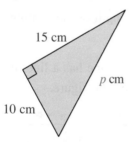

7. Calculate the length of the line marked q cm.

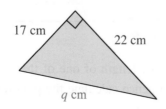

8. Calculate the length of the hypotenuse in this right angled triangle.

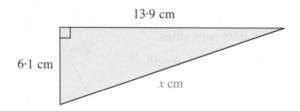

9. Sketch the following right angled triangles :-

Use **Pythagoras' Theorem** to calculate the length of the hypotenuse in each case.

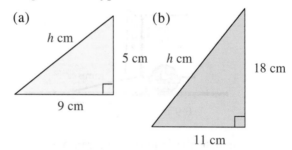

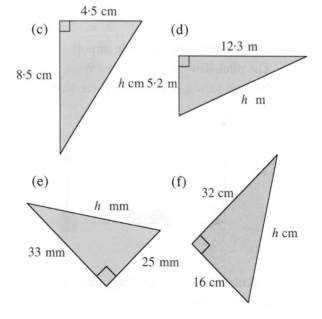

Problems involving Pythagoras' Theorem

Whenever you come across a problem involving finding a missing side in a right angled triangle, you should always consider using **Pythagoras' Theorem** to calculate its length.

Exercise 2·2

(The triangles in these questions are right-angled)

1. A strong wire is used to support a pole while the cement, holding it at its base, dries.

    Calculate the length of the wire.

    wire 7·5 m

    ← 4 m →

2. A ramp is used to help push wheelchairs into the back of an ambulance.

    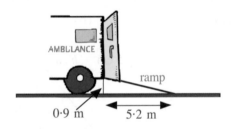

    Calculate the length of the ramp.

3. A plane left from Erin Isle airport.
    The pilot flew 175 kilometres West.
    He then flew 115 kilometres due North.

    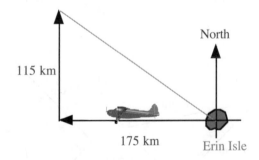

    Calculate how far away the plane then was from Erin Isle.

4. A cable is used to help ferry supplies onto a yacht from the top of a nearby cliff.

    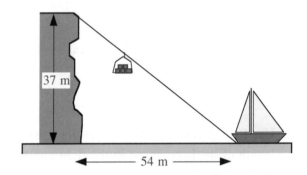

    Calculate the length of the cable used.

5. This wooden door wedge is 12·5 cm long. and 3·1 cm high.

    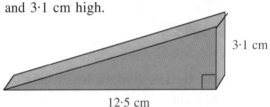

    Calculate the length of the sloping face.

6. This trapezium shape has a line of symmetry shown dotted on the figure.

    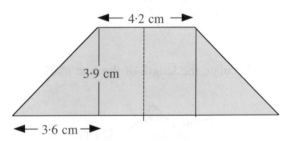

    Calculate the length of one of the sloping edges and hence calculate the **perimeter** of the trapezium.

7. A triangular corner unit (shown in yellow), is built to house a TV set.

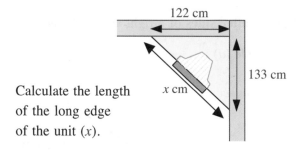

122 cm

133 cm

x cm

Calculate the length of the long edge of the unit (x).

8. A lawn in Edinburgh's Princes Street is in the shape of a rectangle 26 metres long by 14·5 metres wide.

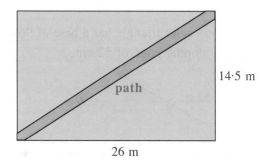

path

14·5 m

26 m

A path runs diagonally through the lawn.

Calculate the length of the path.

9.

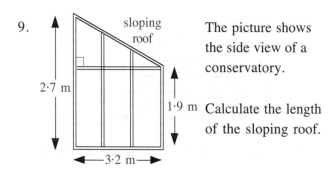

sloping roof

2·7 m

1·9 m

3·2 m

The picture shows the side view of a conservatory.

Calculate the length of the sloping roof.

10. The roof of a garage is in the shape of an isosceles triangle.

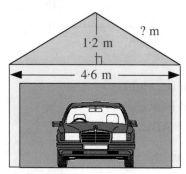

? m

1·2 m

4·6 m

Calculate the length of one side of the sloping roof.

11. Rhombus PQRS has its 2 diagonals, PR and QS, crossing at its centre C.

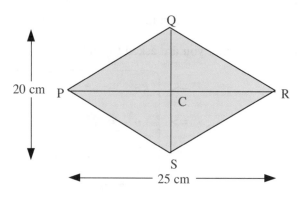

Q

20 cm   P   C   R

S

25 cm

Calculate the **PERIMETER** of the rhombus.

12. Two wires are used to support a tree in danger of falling down after a recent storm.

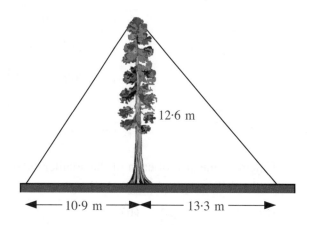

12·6 m

10·9 m   13·3 m

Calculate the **total** length of the support wires.

13. Calculate the **PERIMETER** of these 2 triangles.

(a)

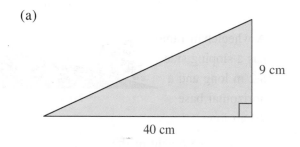

9 cm

40 cm

(b)

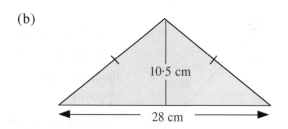

10·5 cm

28 cm

Calculating the Length of one of the Smaller Sides

You can use Pythagoras' Theorem to calculate one of the **smaller sides** of a right angled triangle.

This time, you are asked to find the length of the smaller side (a) :-

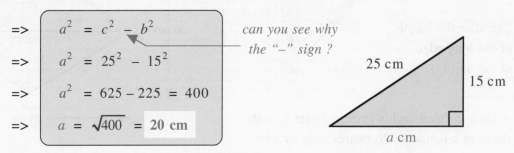

=> $\quad a^2 = c^2 - b^2$

=> $\quad a^2 = 25^2 - 15^2$

=> $\quad a^2 = 625 - 225 = 400$

=> $\quad a = \sqrt{400} = \boxed{20 \text{ cm}}$

can you see why the "–" sign ?

Exercise 2·3

1. Calculate the length of the side of this right angled triangle marked with a t.

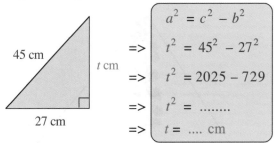

=> $t^2 = 45^2 - 27^2$

=> $t^2 = 2025 - 729$

=> $t^2 = \ldots\ldots$

=> $t = \ldots$ cm

2. Calculate the size of each of the smaller sides in the following right angled triangles.

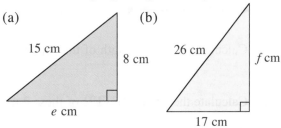

(a)   15 cm   8 cm e cm

(b)   26 cm f cm   17 cm

3. A wheelchair ramp has a sloping side 8·2 m long and a horizontal base 7·1 m long.

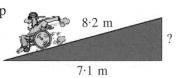

Calculate the height of the ramp.

4.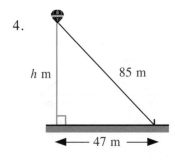

A helium balloon is tethered by a rope to the ground as shown opposite.

Calculate the height of the balloon.

5. This isosceles triangle has a base of 96 cm and a sloping edge of 52 cm.

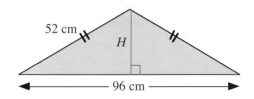

Calculate the **area** of the triangle.

6. Shown is the side view of a wooden bread tin.

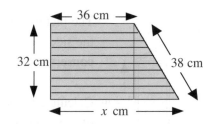

Calculate the length (x) of the base of the bin.

7.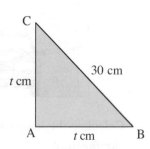

Calculate the **perimeter** of this right angled triangle.

8. Shown is a **right angled isosceles** triangle ABC.

Calculate the value of t.

Mixed Examples

In the following exercise, if you are asked to find :-

the hypotenuse	—>	use $c^2 = a^2 + b^2$.
the hypotenuse	—>	use $c^2 = a^2 + b^2$.
a shorter side	—>	use $a^2 = c^2 - b^2$.

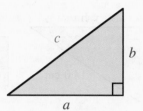

You must decide which formula you have to use.

Example 1 :-

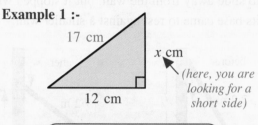

17 cm

x cm

12 cm

(here, you are looking for a short side)

$$x^2 = 17^2 - 12^2$$
$$x^2 = 289 - 144$$
$$x^2 = 145$$
$$x = \sqrt{145} = 12{\cdot}04 \text{ cm}$$

note

Example 2 :-

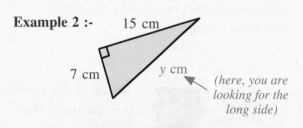

15 cm

7 cm

y cm

(here, you are looking for the long side)

$$y^2 = 15^2 + 7^2$$
$$y^2 = 225 + 49$$
$$y^2 = 274$$
$$y = \sqrt{274} = 16{\cdot}55 \text{ cm}$$

note

Exercise 2·4

1. Use the appropriate formula to find the value of *x* each time :–

(a)
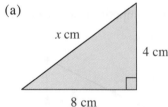
x cm   4 cm   8 cm

(b)
20 cm   9 cm   *x* cm

(c)
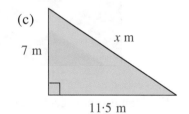
x m   7 m   11·5 m

(d)
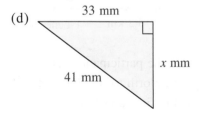
33 mm   *x* mm   41 mm

(e)
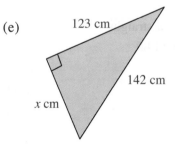
123 cm   142 cm   *x* cm

(f)
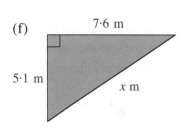
7·6 m   5·1 m   *x* m

2. Andy was answering this question in a class test.

His working was set down as shown :–

Why should Andy have known that his answer **had** to be **wrong**, by just comparing it to the length of the hypotenuse of the triangle ?

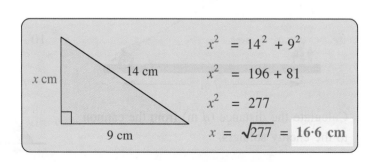

x cm   14 cm   9 cm

$$x^2 = 14^2 + 9^2$$
$$x^2 = 196 + 81$$
$$x^2 = 277$$
$$x = \sqrt{277} = 16{\cdot}6 \text{ cm}$$

3. **ONE** of the following two answers is known to be the **correct** value for y in this question.

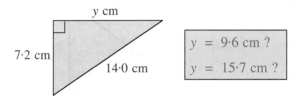

y cm

7·2 cm

14·0 cm

$y = 9 \cdot 6$ cm ?

$y = 15 \cdot 7$ cm ?

Without actually doing the calculation, say which one it must be and why the other is obviously wrong.

4.

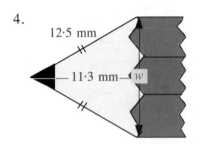

12·5 mm

11·3 mm — w

The tip of this pencil is in the shape of an isosceles triangle.

Calculate the width of the pencil (w).

5. This Scottish Flag is 2·35 metres long and 1·86 metres wide.

1·86 m

2·35 m

What length must each diagonal strip be?

6. A cannon ball was fired and flew in a straight line for 450 metres where it exploded 85 metres above the enemy lines.

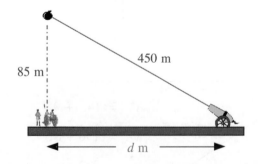

450 m

85 m

d m

Calculate the distance (d m) from the cannon to the enemy soldiers.

7. This warning sign is in the shape of an isosceles triangle.

Calculate the height of the sign.

48 cm

DANGER

44 cm

8. A ladder was leaning against a wall. It began to slide away from the wall, but it stopped when its base came to rest against a smaller wall.

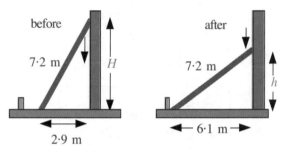

before

7·2 m

H

2·9 m

after

7·2 m

h

6·1 m

(a) Calculate the original height (H) of the top of the ladder above the ground.

(b) Calculate the new height (h) of the top of the ladder.

(c) By how many metres had the top of the ladder slipped ?

9. An orienteering competition was held over a triangular course.

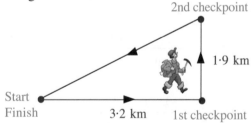

2nd checkpoint

1·9 km

Start Finish

3·2 km

1st checkpoint

From the start, the participants walk East to the 1st checkpoint, North to the 2nd one and then race back to the finishing line.

Calculate the overall distance of the event.

10.

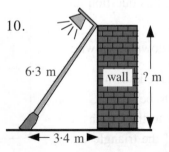

6·3 m

wall ? m

3·4 m

A lamppost fell over during a storm and came to rest with its top resting against the top of a wall.

Calculate the height of the wall.

Distances Between Coordinate Points

Consider the two coordinate points A(–3, –1) and B(5, 5).

They are plotted on the coordinate diagram opposite.

To **calculate** the distance from A to B :-

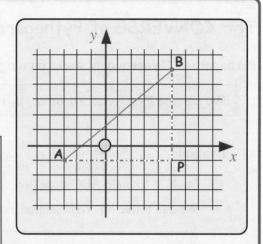

- draw in the 2 dotted lines to make a right angled triangle APB.

- write down the lengths of the two sides AP and BP.

- use Pythagoras' Theorem to calculate length of AB.

$$AB^2 = AP^2 + PB^2$$

$$AB^2 = 8^2 + 6^2$$

$$AB^2 = 64 + 36 = 100$$

$$AB = \sqrt{100} = \boxed{10 \text{ boxes}}$$

Exercise 2·5

1. (a) Make a copy of this coordinate diagram, showing the 2 points P(1, –1) and Q(4, 3).

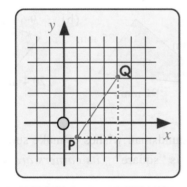

(b) By drawing in the 2 dotted lines, create a right angled triangle and use it to calculate the length of the line PQ.

2. (a) Draw a new coordinate diagram and plot the 2 points M(–4, 2) and N(8, 7)

(b) Create a right angle triangle in your figure and determine the length of the line MN.

3. Calculate the distance between the 2 points :-

R(–2, 0) and S(5, 4),

giving your answer correct to 2 decimal places.

4. For each pair of points below, calculate the length of the line joining them, giving your answer to 2 decimal places each time.

(a) F(2, –4) and G(–1, 5)

(b) U(6, –2) and V(0, 4).

5. Terry thinks triangle AST below is isosceles.

To prove it is, he has to find the lengths of the 2 lines AS and AT and show they are equal.

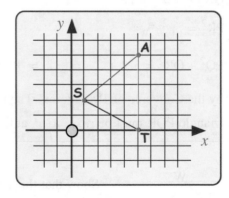

(a) Write down the length of the line AT.

(b) Calculate the length of the line AS.

(c) Was Terry correct ?

6. Prove that triangle LMN is isosceles where L(–2, 2), M(6, 8) and N(4, –6).

The CONVERSE of Pythagoras' Theorem

Pythagoras' Theorem only works on a right angled triangle.

> We can use Pythagoras Theorem "**in reverse**" to actually prove that a triangle **is** right angled.

Example :-

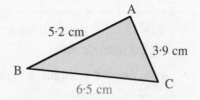

Look at triangle ABC opposite

We can prove it is right angled as follows :-

- Write down the 3 sides :- $AB = 5 \cdot 2$, $AC = 3 \cdot 9$, $BC = 6 \cdot 5$.

- **Square each side** :- $AB^2 = 27 \cdot 04$, $AC^2 = 15 \cdot 21$, $BC^2 = 42 \cdot 25$.

- **Add the two smaller** squares together :- $AB^2 + AC^2 = 27 \cdot 04 + 15 \cdot 21 = 42 \cdot 25$.

- Check if this is the same value as the largest square :- $AB^2 + AC^2 = 42 \cdot 25 = BC^2$.

- We say that, by the **CONVERSE of Pythagoras' Theorem**, the triangle is proven to be right angled at A.

Exercise 2·6

1. Check if this triangle is right angled at Q.

   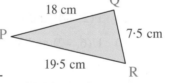

   Copy and complete :-

   - $PQ^2 = 18^2 = 324$,

   - $QR^2 = 7 \cdot 5^2 = \; \dots..$

   - $PR^2 = \dots.^2 = \; \dots.$

   - $PQ^2 + QR^2 = 324 + \dots. = \; \dots... = PR^2$

   - by the Converse of Pythagoras' Theorem, triangle PQR must be r....... a...... at Q

2.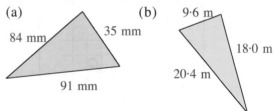

   Show that this triangle is **NOT** right angled.

   i.e. (*Show that* $UW^2 + VW^2 \neq UV^2$)

3. Decide which of the following is/are right angled triangles, and which is/are not :-

   (a)

   84 mm, 35 mm, 91 mm

   (b)

   9·6 m, 18·0 m, 20·4 m

4. A groundsman wishes to make sure the football pitch is "square" (*its corners are at 90°*).

   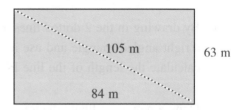

   To check, he measures the diagonal length. Is the pitch "square" ?

5. Has this flagpole been erected correctly, so that it is vertical ?

   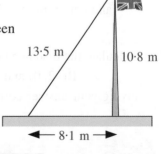

1. Calculate the lengths of the missing sides in the following right angled triangles :-

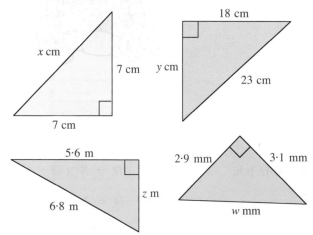

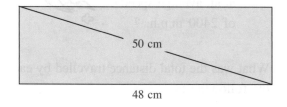

2. Shown is an isosceles triangle.

   (a) Calculate the height of the triangle.

   (b) Now calculate its **area**.

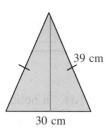

39 cm

30 cm

3. Calculate the **area** of the following rectangle :-

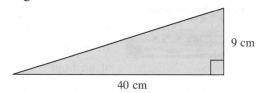

50 cm

48 cm

4. Calculate the **perimeter** of this right angled triangle :-

9 cm

40 cm

5. Calculate the value of x, which indicates the length of the sloping side of this trapezium.

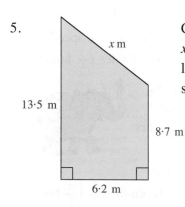

x m

13·5 m

8·7 m

6·2 m

6. This shape consists of a rectangle with an isosceles triangle attached to its end.

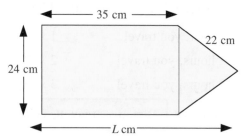

35 cm

22 cm

24 cm

L cm

   (a) Calculate the total length (L) of the figure.

   (b) Now calculate its area.

7. Shown are the points F(–5, –2) and G(4, 3).

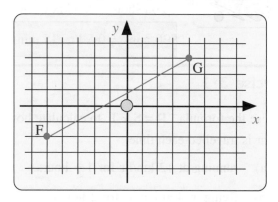

Draw a coordinate diagram, plot the two points and calculate the length of the line FG.

8. Draw a new set of axes, plot the 2 points M(–2, 6) and N(5, –3) and calculate the length of the line MN.

9. Prove that one of the following **IS** a right angled triangle and the other is **NOT**.

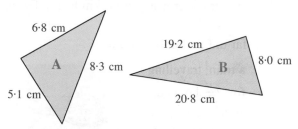

6·8 cm

A

8·3 cm

5·1 cm

19·2 cm

B

8·0 cm

20·8 cm

10. Prove that PQRS is a **rectangle** :-

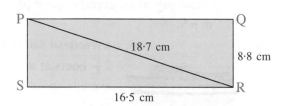

P   Q

18·7 cm

8·8 cm

S   R

16·5 cm

Distance Travelled

Let us imagine being in a car travelling at 70 km/hr.

in 1 hour, you travel　　　　$1 \times 70 = 70$ km.

in 2 hours, you travel　　　　$2 \times 70 = 140$ km.

in 3 hours, you travel　　　　$3 \times 70 = 210$ km.

In other words :-　　| **Distance (travelled) = Speed × Time** |　or, using letters :-　| $D = S \times T$ |

Example :-　　A light aircraft flies at a speed of 240 m.p.h.

How far will it travel in $2\frac{1}{2}$ hours ?

You should also know the following :-

| $D = S \times T$ |
| $\Rightarrow \quad D = 240 \times 2 \cdot 5$ |
| $\Rightarrow \quad D = 600$ miles |

| 30 mins = $0 \cdot 5$ hr;　15 mins = $0 \cdot 25$ hr;　45 mins = $0 \cdot 75$ hr. |

Exercise 3·1

1.　Use the formula　$D = S \times T$　to calculate how far is travelled each time :-

　(a)　running at 12 km/hr for $1\frac{1}{2}$ hours.

　(b)　flying at 400 km/hr for 2 hours.

　(c)　walking at 6 km/hr for $2\frac{1}{2}$ hours.

　(d)　strolling at 3·5 km/hr for $1\frac{1}{4}$ hours.

　(e)　driving at 40 m.p.h. for $1\frac{1}{4}$ hours.

　(f)　on a camel at 3·5 m.p.h. for 6 hours.

　(g)　speed-boating at 24 m.p.h. for $1\frac{3}{4}$ hours.

　(h)　in a truck cruising at 90 km/hr for $1\frac{1}{2}$ hrs.

2.　How far did the following travel :-

　(a)　a train, travelling for $2\frac{1}{2}$ hours at an average speed of 100 m.p.h. ?

　(b)　a $\frac{3}{4}$ hour jog, at an average speed of 12 m.p.h. ?

　(c)　 a riverboat sail lasting $2\frac{1}{4}$ hours at an average speed of 20 m.p.h. ?

2.　(d)　a helicopter flight for 15 minutes, at an average speed of 60 km/hr ?

　(e)　a rocket ship journey of 8 hours 30 mins at an average speed of 2400 m.p.h. ?

3.　What was the total distance travelled by each of the following :–

　(a)　a satellite, orbiting at an average speed of 3600 m.p.h., for $\frac{1}{4}$ of an hour ?

　(b)　 a motorboat, going at an average speed of 18 m.p.h., for quarter of an hour ?

　(c)　a coach, travelling at an average speed of 44 m.p.h. for 2 hours 15 minutes ?

　(d)　a train, travelling at an average speed of 120 km/hr for 45 minutes ($\frac{3}{4}$ hour) ?

　(e)　an elephant, walking at an average speed of 8 km/hr for 2 hours 45 minutes ?

　(f)　a yacht, sailing at an average speed of 16 km/hr for $1\frac{3}{4}$ hours ?

Speed - Calculation

I drove 150 miles, which took me 3 hours.

- in 3 hours, I travelled 150 miles.
- in 1 hour, I travelled $(150 \div 3) = 50$ miles.
- this means my speed was - 50 miles per hour.

(average speed)

In other words :-

$$\boxed{\text{Speed} = \text{Distance} \div \text{Time}}$$

or, using letters :-

$$\boxed{S = \frac{D}{T}}$$

Example :-

A train travels the 400 miles from Glasgow to London in 5 hours.

Calculate its (average) speed.

$$\boxed{\begin{array}{l} S = \dfrac{D}{T} \\[4pt] S = 400 \div 5 \\[4pt] S = \boxed{80 \text{ m.p.h.}} \end{array}}$$

Time - Calculation

I drove 240 km at an average speed of 40 km/hr.

To travel 40 miles takes 1 hour,

$\Rightarrow$ to travel 240 miles takes $240 \div 40 = 6$ hours.

In other words :-

$$\boxed{\text{Time} = \text{Distance} \div \text{Speed}}$$

or, using letters :-

$$\boxed{T = \frac{D}{S}}$$

Example :-

A coach travels the 260 miles from Edinburgh to Manchester at an average speed of 40 m.p.h.

How long will it take ?

$$\boxed{\begin{array}{l} T = \dfrac{D}{S} \\[4pt] T = 260 \div 40 \\[4pt] T = 6 \cdot 5 \text{ hrs} \\[4pt] = \boxed{6 \text{ hr } 30 \text{ mins}} \end{array}}$$

(note :- $6 \cdot 5$ hrs is **NOT** equal to 6 hr 5 mins or 6 hr 50 mins)

Exercise 3·2

1. Use the formula $S = \dfrac{D}{T}$ to find the average speed for these journeys :–

   (a) 200 miles travelled in 4 hours.

   (b) 161 km travelled in 7 hours.

   (c) 310 miles travelled in 5 hours.

2. Calculate the average speed for each of these journeys (*watch the units*) :–

   (a) 36 km travelled in 2 hours.

   (b) 350 metres travelled in 5 minutes.

   (c) 30 metres travelled in 6 seconds.

   (d) 56 km travelled in 4 days.

3. Calculate the average speed of the following :–

   (a) A plane flies 2020 miles in 5 hours.

   (b) A lorry covers 252 kilometres in 6 hours.

   (c) A train travels 30 km in $\frac{1}{2}$ hour.

   (d) A marathon runner runs 18 miles in $1\frac{1}{2}$ hrs.

   (e)  A snail travels 204 cm in 3 hours.

4. Use the formula $T = \dfrac{D}{S}$ to calculate the time taken for each of these journeys :–

   (a) on a motorcycle, 480 km at 120 km/hr.

   (b) on a bus, 225 miles at 50 m.p.h.

   (c) in a race, 1800 m at 30 m/sec.

   (d) flying, 375 miles at 250 m.p.h.

5. Change these times into hours and minutes :–

   (a) $2\frac{1}{2}$ hours   (b) $5\frac{1}{4}$ hours

   (c) $3\frac{3}{4}$ hours   (d) 8·25 hours

   > 1 hour 30 minutes is $1\frac{1}{2}$ or **1·5 hours.**
   >
   > 4 hour 15 minutes is $4\frac{1}{4}$ or **4·25 hours.**

6. Change the following times to both fractions of an hour and decimal form :–

   (a) 3 hours 30 mins.   (b) 2 hours 15 mins.

   (c) 5 hours 45 mins.   (d) 0 hour 15 mins.

7. Calculate the time taken for these journeys :-

   (a) on a train, 100 km at 80 km/hr.

   (b) sailing, 25 miles at 20 m.p.h.

Time - Distance - Speed Problems

In the previous 2 exercises, you learned how to use three formulae
to calculate the **speed**, the **distance** or the **time** for a journey.

The triangle opposite shows a simple way of remembering how
to use each of the three formulae. Try to memorise the diagram.

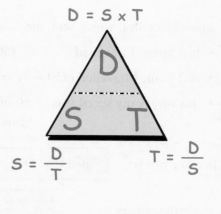

$$D = S \times T$$

$$S = \frac{D}{T} \qquad T = \frac{D}{S}$$

Example :-   David drove from his house to the coast,
a distance of 135 miles.

It took him 2 hrs 15 mins to do so.

Calculate David's average **speed**.

=>   From the triangle, we can see that $S = \dfrac{D}{T}$

=> $S = \dfrac{135}{2 \text{ hrs } 15 \text{ mins}} = \dfrac{135}{2 \cdot 25 \text{ hrs}} = \boxed{60 \text{ m.p.h.}}$

note

Exercise 3·3

1.   Calculate the missing quantity :-

(a)

Distance	Speed	Time
300 km	?	8 hours

(b)

Distance	Speed	Time
120 miles	40 mph	?

(c)

Distance	Speed	Time
?	29 mph	4 hours

(d)

Distance	Speed	Time
150 km	?	$2\frac{1}{2}$ hrs

(e)

Distance	Speed	Time
?	40 m/sec	$4\frac{1}{2}$ sec

(f)

Distance	Speed	Time
175 miles	100 mph	?

2.   Brian walked for half an hour and
covered a distance of 2700 m.

Calculate Brian's speed in :–

(a)   metres/hour

(b)   metres/minute.

3.      A plane flew 150 km at an
average speed of 300 km per hour.

For how long was it actually flying ?

4.   Paul and Paula towed their caravan and travelled
at an average speed of 42 km/hr.

The trip took $2\frac{1}{2}$ hours.

How far had they travelled ?

5.   A coach left Aberdeen at 1215 and arrived
at its destination at 1545.

If the coach travelled 210 miles, what was
its average speed ?

6.   A hill walker is crossing the valley at an average
speed of 8 km/hr.

How long will it take him to walk the whole
length of the valley which is 14 km long ?

7.   A satellite orbits the moon of a planet at
an average speed of 4800 km/hr.

It takes $2\frac{1}{4}$ hours to complete its orbit.

What is the length of the satellite's orbit ?

8.   It took old Mrs Broom 30 minutes
to walk the $1\frac{1}{2}$ miles to the post
office to collect her pension.

Now, with the aid of her electric
chair, she can do it in 15 mins.

(a)   Calculate Mrs Broom's walking speed.

(b)   How much **faster** does she travel in the
chair ?

Converting Hours & Minutess to Decimal Times

In a previous exercise you learned :- $\frac{1}{2}$ hour = 0·5 hr, $\frac{1}{4}$ hour = 0·25 hr and $\frac{3}{4}$ hour = 0·75 hr.

How would we enter **36 minutes** into our calculator as a decimal ?

Minutes => Decimals =>

36 minutes is $\frac{36}{60}$ of an hour = 36 ÷ 60 = $\boxed{0\cdot6 \text{ hr.}}$

27 minutes is $\frac{27}{60}$ of an hour = 27 ÷ 60 = $\boxed{0\cdot45 \text{ hr.}}$

3 hr 40 mins is $3 + \frac{40}{60}$ = 3 + (40 ÷ 60) = $\boxed{3\cdot6666... \text{ hr.}}$

Simple rule :- " To change minutes to a decimal of an hour => **divide by 60** ".

Exercise 3·4

1. You may use a calculator to change the following to decimals of an hour :–

    (a) $\boxed{48 \text{ minutes} = \frac{48}{60} \text{ hour } (= 48 ÷ 60) = ... \text{ hr}}$

    (b) 18 minutes   (c)   6 minutes

    (d) 54 minutes   (e) 24 minutes

    (f) 39 minutes   (g) 21 minutes

2. Use your calculator to change these times to decimal form :- (*answers to 2 decimal places*).

    (a) 10 minutes   (b) 17 minutes

    (c) 20 minutes   (d) 52 minutes

    (e) 50 minutes   (f) 70 minutes

3. Use your calculator to change the following times to decimal form :–

    (a) $\boxed{\begin{array}{l} 4 \text{ hours } 12 \text{ minutes } = 4 + \frac{12}{60} \\[4pt] \qquad\qquad\qquad\quad = 4 + (12 ÷ 60) = .. \text{ hr} \end{array}}$

    (b) 3 hr 48 mins   (c)   4 hrs 36 mins

    (d) 2 hrs 51 mins   (e)   2 hrs 57 mins

    (f) 1 hr 12 mins   (g)   5 hrs 6 mins

4 A helicopter flies at 120 km/hr for 24 minutes. How far does it fly in that time ? Show your working like this :-

$$\boxed{\begin{array}{l} D = S \times T \quad => D = 120 \times (\frac{24}{60}) \quad \text{(not } 120 \times 0\cdot24) \\[6pt] \qquad\qquad => D = 120 \times 0\cdot4 \quad \text{(calculator)} \\[6pt] \qquad\qquad\quad D = ... \text{ km} \end{array}}$$

5. Calculate the distances travelled here :–

    (a) A liner sailing at 15 mph for 36 minutes.

    (b) A cyclist travelling at 40 m.p.h. for 12 minutes.

    (c) A caravan pulled along at 30 km/hr for 21 minutes.

    (d) A jet plane flying at 450 mph for 20 minutes.

    (e) A hot air balloon travelling at 24 mph for 10 minutes.

6. Bob and Ted set off at the same time :–

    • Bob drives at 45 km/hr for 20 mins.

    • Ted drives at 60 km/hr for 12 mins.

    Who travels the further, Bob or Ted, and by how much ?

7. A train travels at 64 km/hr for 1 hour 24 mins. How far will it have travelled ?

    Show your working as follows :-

$$\boxed{\begin{array}{l} D = S \times T \quad = 64 \times (1 + \frac{24}{60}) \quad \text{calculator} \\[6pt] \qquad\qquad D = 64 \times (1\cdot4) \quad \text{(not } 1\cdot24) \\[6pt] \qquad\qquad D = ... \text{ km} \end{array}}$$

8. Calculate the distance travelled each time :-

    (a) A cargo plane flies at 280 m.p.h. for 2 hours 36 minutes.

    (b) A lorry is driven at 70 mph for 1 hour 18 minutes.

9. A bus travels a distance of 35 kilometres in 42 minutes. Calculate its speed in km/hr.

    Show your working like this :-

    $$S = \frac{D}{T} \qquad = 35 \div (42 \text{ mins})$$
    $$= 35 \div \left(\tfrac{42}{60}\right) \quad \text{(not } 35 \div (0{\cdot}42))$$
    $$= 35 \div 0{\cdot}7$$
    $$= \dots \text{ km/hr} \quad \text{(calculator)}$$

10. Find the average speed each time here :-

    (a) A police car travels 14 miles in 12 mins.

    (b) A fire engine travels 10 kilometres in 6 minutes.

    (c) A jet covers 240 miles in 45 mins.

    (d) A hovercraft sails 42 miles in 36 mins.

    (e) A submarine covers 54 km in 1 hour 21 minutes.

    (f) A truck driver travels 56 miles in 48 minutes.

    (g) A space ship flies 18 600 miles in 3 hours 6 minutes.

    (h) A train travels 80 miles through the countryside in 1 hour 20 minutes.

Converting Decimal Times back to Hours and Minutes

In the last exercise you learned a simple rule for changing hours and minutes to decimal form.

Rule 1 :-   "To change minutes to a decimal fraction => divide by 60".

If you have been using a calculator to find the time taken for a journey, it might appear as a decimal, like 0·35 hrs. There is an easy way of changing this to minutes.

Rule 2 :-   "To change decimals back to a minutes => multiply by 60".

Examples :-   Decimals to Minutes   =>

    0·8 hr. = (0·8 × 60) mins   = 48 minutes.

    0·35 hr. = (0·35 × 60) mins   = 21 minutes.

    2·3 hr. = 2 + (0·3 × 60) mins   = 2 hr 18 mins .

Exercise 3·5

1. Change the following calculator display times (*in decimal form (of an hour)*), to minutes :-

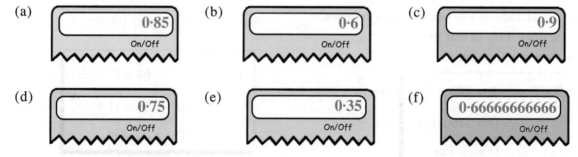

(a) 0·85 On/Off   (b) 0·6 On/Off   (c) 0·9 On/Off

(d) 0·75 On/Off   (e) 0·35 On/Off   (f) 0·66666666666 On/Off

2. If you wish to change **3·9 hours** into hours and minutes :–

   - Leave the hours as they are (**3 hours**)
   - Multiply the 0·9 by 60 => (**... minutes**)

3. Use the same technique to change the following times to hours and minutes :–

   (a)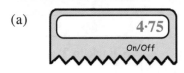
   3·2 hours = 3 hours + (0·2 × 60) mins
            = 3 hours ... minutes.

   (b) 5·5 hours   (c) 1·65 hours

   (d) 2·8 hours   (e) 3·85 hours

   (f) 4·7 hours   (g) 3·66666.. hrs

   (h) 1·8333333 hours   (i) 0·625 hours.

4. Write the following calculator (decimal) times in hours and minutes :-

   (a)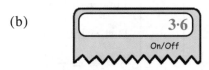
       4·75
       On/Off

   (b)
       3·6
       On/Off

   (c)
       1·333333333333
       On/Off

5. An ocean liner covers 66 miles at 20 mph.

   (a) Calculate the time taken in hours.

   $(T = \dfrac{D}{S})$ (*give answer as a decimal*).

   (b) Change your answer to hours and mins.

6. A cyclist travelled 37·4 kilometres at an average speed of 22 km/hr.

   (a) Calculate how long he took, (*as a decimal*).

   (b) How long did he take in hours and mins ?

7. Calculate the time taken (as a decimal) for each of the following, and then give your answer in hours and minutes :–

   (a) A tank crosses 92 miles of desert at an average speed of 40 mph.

   (b) A helicopter flies 18 kilometres at an average speed of 54 km/hr.

   (c) A sports car races 28 miles at an average speed of 80 m.p.h.

   (d) A canoeist paddles 13·5 miles at an average speed of 12 mph.

8. This map shows the 3 legs of an orienteering course. The average speed, as Bob covered the course, was 8 km/hr.

   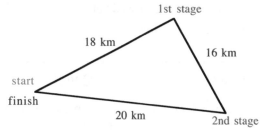
   1st stage
   18 km
   16 km
   start
   finish
   20 km
   2nd stage

   How long, in hours and minutes, should Bob take to walk between the :–

   (a) start and 1st stage ?

   (b) 1st and 2nd stages ?

   (c) start and finish ?

9. Jill ran 490 metres in 70 seconds.

   (a) What was her speed in metres per second ?

   (b) Here is how to convert Jill's speed from metres per second to km/hr :-

   - step 1 Change the speed to metres per minute, then metres per hour

     => 7 m/sec => 7 × 60 = 420 m/min

     => 420 × 60 => 25 200 metres/hour

   - step 2 Change the 25 200 metres to kilometres (÷ 1000)

     => 25 200 ÷ 1000 = ... km/hr

10. Change these speeds from m/sec to km/hr :-

    (a) 8 m/sec   (b) 15 m/sec

    (c) 200 m/sec   (d) 37·5 m/sec

    (e) 0·5 m/sec   (f) 1000 m/sec.

Time – Distance (Speed) Graphs

The graph opposite shows an outward journey from **P → Q → R → S**, then a return home from **S → T**.

We can answer questions about the journey from the graph, including finding the **speed** at various stages.

Can you see that after an hour, a stop of half an hour was made at Q ?

Can you also see that since the line RS is **steeper** than the line PQ, the speed was **greater** for that part ?

We can calculate the **SPEED** at various stages as follows :-

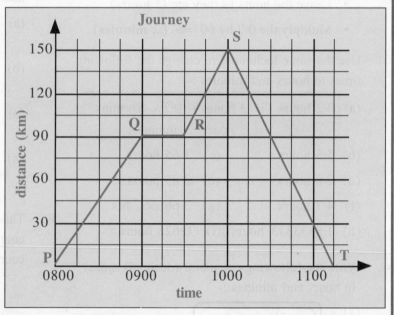

P to Q :-

Time = 1 hr

Dist = 90 km

$S = \dfrac{D}{T} = \dfrac{90}{1}$

= **90 km/hr**

Q to R :-

Time = $\frac{1}{2}$ hr

Dist = 0 km

$S = \dfrac{D}{T} = \dfrac{0}{0\cdot5}$

= **0 km/hr**

R to S :-

Time = $\frac{1}{2}$ hr

Dist = 60 km

$S = \dfrac{D}{T} = \dfrac{60}{0\cdot5}$

= **120 km/hr**

S back to T :-

Time = $1\frac{1}{4}$ hr

Dist = 150 km

$S = \dfrac{D}{T} = \dfrac{150}{1\cdot25}$

= **120 km/hr**

Exercise 3·6

1. Brian and his wife set off for a day's outing to Barnsby-on-Sea.

   They set out at 0900 along the motorway and stopped for coffee, before finishing the rest of their journey along the A25 road.

   (a) How long was the first part of their journey along the motorway ?

   (b) How long did they stop for coffee ?

   (c) When did they arrive in Barnsby ?

   (d) Calculate their speed :–

       (i) on the motorway.

       (ii) between 1100 and 1200.

       (iii) along the A25.

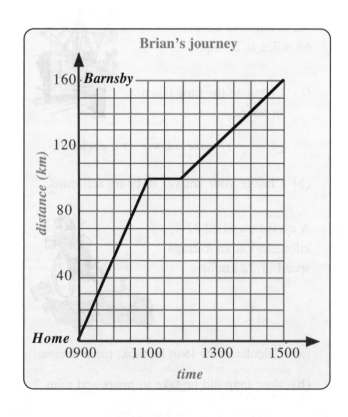

2. A helicopter flew from Struan to Bigly, dropped off supplies and returned to Struan.

(a) For how long was the helicopter on the ground at Bigly ?

(b) Calculate its speed for the outward flight to Bigly.

(c) It hit a "head wind" on the way back. Calculate the return speed.

(d) From your answers to (b) and (c), say whether the "head wind" slowed it down or helped it go faster.

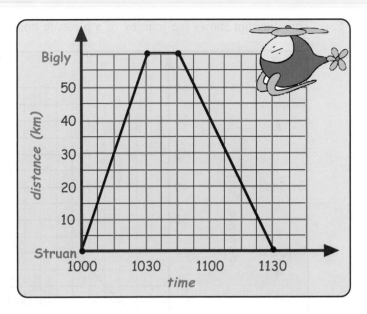

3. Gemma left Brioch Harbour in her dinghy at 10·00 am and set sail for Toule.

Anton left Brioch at 10·30 am in his small motor launch.

(a) Calculate Gemma's speed.

(b) Calculate Anton's speed.

(c) When did Anton's launch overtake Gemma's dinghy ?

(d) How far away from **Toule** were they when Anton overtook Gemma ?

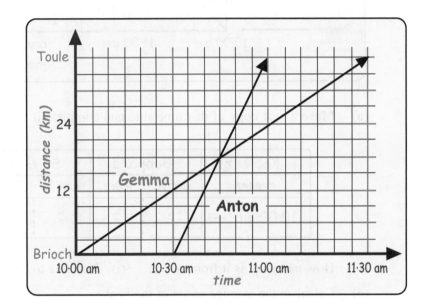

4. A goods train and a passenger train left 2 stations heading towards each other, one from London and one from Edinburgh.

The goods train was the slower of the two.

(a) Which line, A or B, represents the goods train's journey ? (*Explain why*).

(b) Calculate the :-

    (i) goods train's speed.

    (ii) passenger train's speed.

(c) At what time did the two trains pass ?

(d) At what time should train A reach London ?

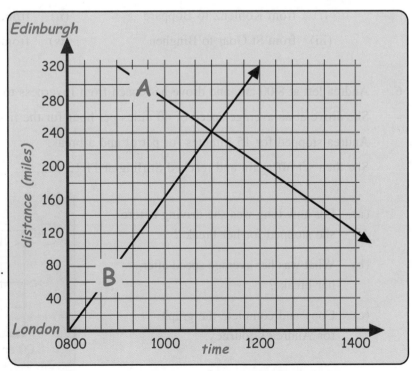

5. This diagram shows the journey of a pleasure boat on a Rhine cruise.

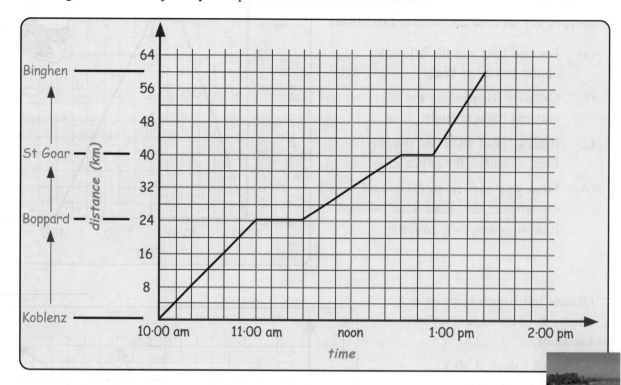

(a) Make a neat copy of this timetable and complete it for the pleasure boat's trip.

Koblenz	Boppard		St Goar		Binghen
depart	arrive	leave	arrive	leave	arrive
10·00 am →	?	?	?	?	?

(b) How many km is it from :–   (i) Koblenz to Boppard   (ii) St Goar to Binghen ?

(c) Calculate the average speed of the boat :–

    (i)   from Koblenz to Boppard   (ii)   from Boppard to St Goar

    (iii)   from St Goar to Binghen   (iv)   from Koblenz to Binghen.

6. Andrea left at 8·00 am, and drove her coach from Inverness to Stirling, 150 miles away.

She drove at an average speed of 40 miles per hour for the first 60 miles.

Andrea stopped for 15 minutes for petrol and a break.

She then set off again and reached Stirling at 11·15 am.

(a) For how long was she driving before she stopped for her break ?

(b) What was her average speed after her break ?

(c) Copy and complete the graph for Andrea's journey.

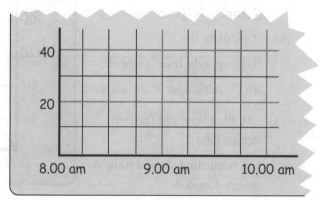

1. Use the diagram shown opposite to help
    choose the correct formula for each of the
    following questions :–

    (a) Bill flew his private jet at an average speed of 480 kilometres per hour for $1\frac{1}{2}$ hours.

         How far did Bill fly ?

    (b)  Phil drove his coach for $3\frac{1}{2}$ hours and covered
         a distance of 210 miles.

         What was Phil's average speed ?

    (c) Francis' train travelled at 120 km/hr on her journey through France.

         If the train travelled 150 km, how long did Francis's journey last ?

2. Use a calculator to change the following times to decimal form :–

    (a) 24 minutes   (b) 9 minutes   (c) 3 hrs 10 mins   (d) 2 hrs 51 mins.

3. Use a calculator to change the following to hours and minutes :–

    (a) 0·7 hour   (b) 0·35 hour   (c) 5·3 hours   (d) 1·65 hours.

4. (a) Alex took 18 minutes to cycle
         to his office, 3·6 miles away.

         What was Alex's average speed ?

    (b)  Steve's train travelled at an average speed of 64 km/hr.

         Mandy's train travelled at an average speed of 75 km/hr.

         If Steve's journey is 80 km long, and Mandy's is 100 km,
         whose trip took longer, and by how many minutes ?

5. Bob cycled to his friend Ted's house.

    When the rain came on, Ted's dad ran Bob home.

    (a) At what time did Bob leave his house ?

    (b) How far is Ted house from Bob's ?

    (c) What was Bob's average cycling speed ?

    (d) How long did Bob stay at Ted's ?

    (e) How long did it take Bob to get home ?

    (f) What was the average speed on the
         journey home ?

    (g) Bob's walking speed is half that of his
         cycling speed.

         How long would it take Bob to walk to
         Ted's house ?

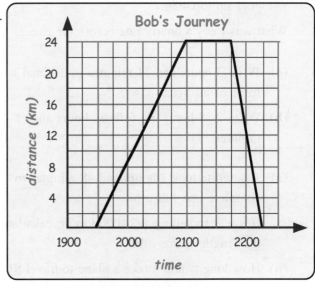

1. Write down the **simplest** fraction equivalent to :-

    (a) 20%   (b) 5%   (c) $66\frac{2}{3}$ (d) $12\frac{1}{2}$%

2. Gillian deposits £800 in her bank where the **annual** interest rate is 4·2%.

    How much will her savings be worth if she withdraws her money after 8 months ?

3. Gerald scored 52 out of 80 in his Maths test and 42 out of 60 in his Science test.

    In which subject did he do better ?

4. Martin's Mensware bought in gent's suits for £180 and sold them for £234.

    Calculate the profit on a sale, and express this as a percentage of the cost price.

5. George deposits his savings of £24 000 in Scotia Bank for 3 years. The annual rates of interest were 3·5%, 4·2% and 3·9% respectively.

    How much (compound) interest had built up in George's account by the end of the 3 years ?

6. A small iceberg weighs 50 000 kilograms. As it heats up, it loses 6% of its weight each day. What will it weigh at the end of 3 days ?

7. After getting a pay rise of 8%, Lucy's hourly rate goes up to £4·86.

    What was Lucy's hourly rate before the rise ?

8. (a) Write 3 hours and 24 minutes in decimal form of an hour.

    (b) Write 2·35 hours out fully in hours and minutes.

9. (a) A satellite took 2 hours and 48 minutes to complete one full orbit.

    If it was travelling at 24 000 km/hr, calculate the length of one orbit.

    (b) How long would it take a plane to travel 810 miles at a speed of 360 m.p.h. ?

10. Calculate the values of x and y in these right angled triangles :-

    (a)   (b)

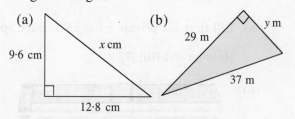

11. Shown is an isosceles triangle ABC.

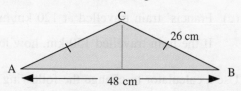

    Calculate its **AREA**.

12. Calculate the total length (L) of this shape :-

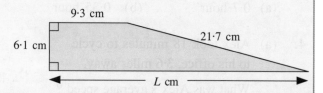

13. Plot the two points G(−4, 7) and H(6, −1) on a coordinate diagram and calculate the length of the line GH correct to 2 decimal places.

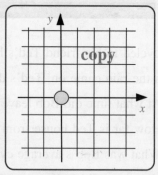

14. Prove that only one of the following is a **right angled triangle**. (*Show working*).

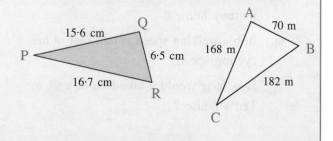

Turn off that Calculator...

1. Set down and find :-

   (a) $\begin{array}{r} 6000 \\ -\ 2189 \\ \hline \end{array}$
   (b) $\begin{array}{r} 397 \\ \times\ 9 \\ \hline \end{array}$
   (c) $\begin{array}{r} 1376 \\ \times\ 600 \\ \hline \end{array}$
   (d) $\begin{array}{r} 59 \\ \times\ 27 \\ \hline \end{array}$
   (e) $9\overline{)8073}$

   (f) 50^2
   (g) $66500 \div 70$
   (h) $30 - 9 \times 3$
   (i) $8 \times (9 + 5) - 7$
   (j) $34 - 18 \div 2.$

2. Set down and find :-

   (a) $\begin{array}{r} 5\cdot172 \\ -\ 1\cdot879 \\ \hline \end{array}$
   (b) $8 - 2\cdot457$
   (c) $9\overline{)43\cdot74}$
   (d) $\begin{array}{r} 3\cdot178 \\ \times\ 7 \\ \hline \end{array}$

   (e) $400 \times 0\cdot416$
   (f) $748 \div 200$
   (g) $\dfrac{7 \times 25\cdot4}{1000}$
   (h) $19\cdot6 \div 10000$

3. Change :-

   (a) 3720 m to km
   (b) 0·06 km to m
   (c) 54 cm to m
   (d) 3096 g to kg

4. Find :-
   (a) $\frac{3}{8}$ of 64
   (b) $\frac{4}{5}$ of 2000
   (c) $\frac{5}{9}$ of 1530

5. Simplify :-
   (a) $\dfrac{32}{48}$
   (b) $\dfrac{35}{49}$
   (c) $\dfrac{91}{105}$

6. Find :-
   (a) $\frac{3}{4} - \frac{1}{2}$
   (b) $3\frac{1}{2} + 2\frac{1}{4}$
   (c) $4 - 1\frac{1}{8}$
   (d) $3 \times 5\frac{1}{3}$

7. Express as a fraction :-
   (a) 80%
   (b) $12\frac{1}{2}\%$
   (c) $133\frac{1}{3}\%$

8. Find :-
   (a) 75% of £1600
   (b) 5% of £2400
   (c) $33\frac{1}{3}\%$ of £4·44

   (d) 40% of £150
   (e) $12\frac{1}{2}\%$ of £560
   (f) 3% of £4

9. Find :-
   (a) $28 + (-13)$
   (b) $141 + (-19)$
   (c) $(-29) + 15$

   (d) $(-18) + (-22)$
   (e) $14 - 20$
   (f) $(-9) - 32$
   (g) $14 - (-6)$

   (h) $(-11) - (-15)$
   (i) $0 - (-29)$
   (j) $(-6) - (-7)$
   (k) $(-2) - 3 - 4$

10. Find :-
    (a) $(-4) \times 13$
    (b) $8 \times (-21)$
    (c) $(-6) \times (-7)$
    (d) $(-15) \div 3$

    (e) $(-11)^2$
    (f) $210 \div (-7)$
    (g) $(-40) \div (-8)$
    (h) $\dfrac{(-4) \times (-12)}{(-6)}$

11. Convert to 24 hour format :-
    (a) 8·25 am
    (b) 7·45 pm
    (c) $\frac{1}{4}$ to midnight

12. How long is it from :-
    (a) 7·50 am to 2·25 pm
    (b) 2·43 pm to 7·16 pm ?

13. A show starts at 4·45 pm and lasts for two and three quarter hours. At what time does it end ?

14. (a) How far will a plane travel in 2 hours 20 minutes at an average speed of 360 m.p.h. ?

    (b) A train covered the 640 km from Glasgow to London in 5 hours.   Calculate its average speed.

Very Large Numbers

A number like 4700 can be written in a different way.

$$4700 = 470 \times 10 = 47 \times 10 \times 10 = 4 \cdot 7 \times 10 \times 10 \times 10 = 4 \cdot 7 \times 10^3.$$

$4 \cdot 7 \times 10^3$ is called the "Standard Form" of 4700.

It is also said to be in Scientific Notation when the number at the start, (the 4·7), lies between 1 and 10.

How to change a "normal" number into a number in Scientific Notation.

95800	–>	Step 1	move the decimal point until it comes between the 1st and the 2nd digits.	9·58
		Step 2	now count how many places the decimal point was moved (*4 places here*).	9·5800
		Step 3	finally, write this number, (the 4), as the power of 10.	$9 \cdot 58 \times 10^4$

Example :- Write 14 000 000 in scientific notation, $a \times 10^n$. $14\,000\,000 = 1 \cdot 4 \times 10^7$

Exercise 4·1

1. Write 6400 in scientific notation.

$$6400 \quad \Rightarrow \quad (6 \cdot 400) \quad \overset{3}{\Rightarrow} \quad 6 \cdot 4 \times 10^{\cdots}$$

2. Use the method shown above to write the following numbers in scientific notation :-

   (a) 73 (= $7 \cdot 3 \times 10^{\cdots}$)   (b) 516

   (c) 8540   (d) 6421

   (e) 7000   (f) 10000

   (g) 29000   (h) 34500

   (i) 9   (j) 60

   (k) 412000   (l) 658200

   (m) 87630   (n) 5000000

   (o) 4800000   (p) 3710000

   (q) 42000000   (r) 55500000

   (s) 300000000   (t) 453100000

Remember :-

25 million	=	25 000 000
1·86 million	=	1 860 000
$4\frac{1}{2}$ million	=	4 500 000

---

3. Write out each of the following in full, then change into scientific notation.

   (a) 3 million = 3000000 = $3 \cdot 0 \times 10^{\cdots}$

   (b) 2·5 million = 2 500 000 = ... $\times 10^{\cdots}$

   (c) 6·29 million = ... = ...

   (d) $9\frac{1}{2}$ million   (e) 3·6 million

   (f) $15\frac{1}{2}$ million   (g) 7·632 million

   (h) $44\frac{1}{4}$ million   (i) $50\frac{3}{4}$ million

   (j) Rovers sold their star player for £12·4 million.

   (k) The population of Iceland is two hundred and eighty five thousand.

4. Write the following decimal numbers in scientific notation.

   (a) 35·6   (b) 2·15

   (c) 250·1   (d) 462·55

   (e) 6470·5   (f) 82700·1

   (g) 200000·1   (h) 33·3333

Reversing the Process

How to change from Scientific Notation back to "normal" form.

Example :-   Write 3.85×10^4 in normal form.

3.85×10^4 —>   **Step 1**   Write down the 385 **without** the decimal point.

Step 2   Move the point (4) places to the right from where it was.

4 places

3.85×10^4 = $3\,8\,5\,0\,0$▼   = $38\,500$

(*Can you see why we need the two extra zero's ?*)

Further Example :- 3.852×10^7 = $38\,520\,000$

---

5. Each of the following is written in scientific notation, $a \times 10^n$.

    Change each back into **normal** form.

    (a) 2.3×10^2

    (b) 6.41×10^3

    (c) 8×10^5

    (d) 7.73×10^4

    (e) 9.102×10^3

    (f) 6.004×10^4

    (g) 4.913×10^6

    (h) 1.1×10^5

    (i) 8.71×10^7

    (j) 2.143×10^5

    (k) 1.9×10^8

    (l) 3.555×10^5

When large numbers appear on a scientific calculator, they sometimes do so in scientific notation form.

The calculator below shows the number .....

3.95×10^8

= $395\,000\,000$

6. What numbers are shown on these calculators :-

    (a)
    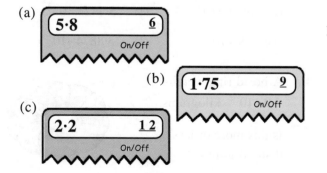

    (b)

    (c)

7. A cafe sells 7.73×10^5 litres of cola each year. Write this amount as a normal number.

8. Lottery Extra stands at £4.25×10^6. Write this amount as we would know it.

9. There are 3.156×10^7 seconds in a solar year. Write this number of seconds out fully.

10.  The distance from Neptune to the sun is 4.497×10^9 km. Write this in normal form.

11. The school vending machines made a profit of £8.105×10^3 last year. Write the profit in normal form.

12.  The population of China is 1.298×10^9. Write the population of China in normal form.

13. Chelsea paid Marseille £2.43×10^7 for a striker called Didier Drogba.

     Write this transfer fee in normal form.

Very Small Numbers

It is also possible to write very small numbers (decimal numbers) in **Scientific Notation**.

It is a process of moving the decimal point to a position just after the first **non-zero** whole number.

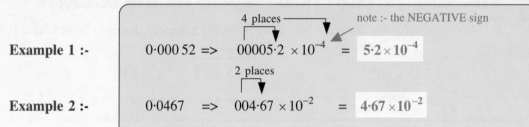

Example 1 :- $0.00052 \Rightarrow 00005.2 \times 10^{-4} = \boxed{5.2 \times 10^{-4}}$

4 places — note :- the NEGATIVE sign

Example 2 :- $0.0467 \Rightarrow 004.67 \times 10^{-2} = \boxed{4.67 \times 10^{-2}}$

2 places

Example 3 :- $0.0000093 = \boxed{9.3 \times 10^{-6}}$

Exercise 4·2

1. Write each of the following small numbers in scientific notation :-

    (a) 0·05   (b) 0·007

    (c) 0·9   (d) 0·0004

    (e) 0·00006   (f) 0·000001

    (g) 0·043   (h) 0·0097

    (i) 0·00035   (j) 0·000066

    (k) 0·00147   (l) 0·358

    (m) 0·000249   (n) 0·00000963

    (o) 0·000000003   (p) 0·000000000018

2. Rewrite each sentence, expressing the number in scientific notation.

    (a) The radius of the
         lead in a pencil is
         0·0012 m.

    (b)  The weight of a
         single eye-lash is
         0·00000024 kg.

    (c) Jenny Peters beat Alice Duff by 0·099
         seconds to win the race.

    (d) A thin film of grease is approximately
         0·000000755 mm thick.

    (e) There are 0·000114 years in an hour.

    (f) Pluto's mass is 0·0025 times that of the
         mass of the Earth.

Changing from a number in Scientific Notation, back to "normal" form.

Simply move the point **LEFT** to express the number in full.

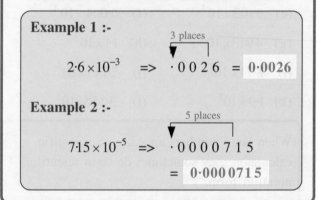

Example 1 :-

$2.6 \times 10^{-3} \Rightarrow .0026 = \boxed{0.0026}$

3 places

Example 2 :-

$7.15 \times 10^{-5} \Rightarrow .0000715$

5 places

$= \boxed{0.0000715}$

3. Write these numbers in **decimal** form :-

    (a) 5×10^{-2} (b) 3.4×10^{-3}

    (c) 4.7×10^{-3} (d) 9×10^{-6}

    (e) 8.01×10^{-4} (f) 3.002×10^{-3}

    (g) 4.775×10^{-6} (h) 6.283×10^{-5}

    (i) 1.111×10^{-2} (j) 5.442×10^{-3}

    (k) 9.9×10^{-7} (l) 3.8874×10^{-1}

4. A bread ring weighs
    5.9×10^{-2} kilograms.

    Is this more or less
    than 60 grams ?

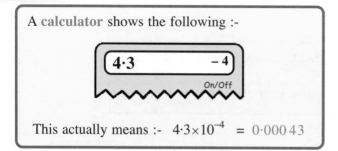

A **calculator** shows the following :-

4·3   − 4
On/Off

This actually means :- $4.3 \times 10^{-4} = 0.00043$

5. What do these readings mean ?

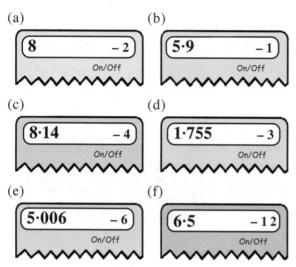

(a)

8   − 2
On/Off

(b)

5·9   − 1
On/Off

(c)

8·14   − 4
On/Off

(d)

1·755   − 3
On/Off

(e)

5·006   − 6
On/Off

(f)

6·5   − 12
On/Off

6. Write out in full :-

(a) 3×10^{-3}

(b) 7×10^{2}

(c) 2.5×10^{-2}

(d) 8.2×10^{3}

(e) 4.87×10^{4}

(f) 6.03×10^{-4}

(g) 7.123×10^{-6}

(h) 3.85×10^{5}

(i) 2×10^{-5}

(j) 7.009×10^{8}

7. Write in scientific notation :-

(a) 0·0006

(b) 49

(c) 9310

(d) 0·02

(e) 0·3

(f) 885000

(g) 0·089

(h) 1950000

(i) 0·00000055

(j) 69000000

8. Each of the following numbers can be written as
$a \times 10^{n}$, where a and n lie between 1 and 10.

Find the values of a and n in each case.

(a) The attendance at the Rugby
World Cup final in Australia
in 2003 was 82950.

8. (b) The distance from
the sun to Mars is
217 million kilometres.

(c) The average diameter of an human hair
is 0·00009 metres.

(d) The population of Alaska is 627000.

(e)  The average time taken
to blink is 0·4 seconds.

(f) 105 million people
voted in the last
election in the USA.

(g) A NASA space probe was recorded
travelling at a speed of 13650 mph.

(h) The thickness of a sheet of thin paper
is 0·000001 metres.

(i) A beam of light
travels 5 kilometres in
0·0000165 seconds.

(j) The stem of a rose is
0·009 metres thick.

(k)  A fast computer took
0·000085 seconds
to complete a calculation.

(l) A high speed train in Japan can reach a
top speed of 443·5 km/hr.

(m) An American **billion** is another name for a
"thousand million".

Write, in scientific notation :-

(i) 2 billion

(ii) 3·1 billion

(iii) 96 billion

(iv) $17\frac{1}{2}$ billion.

Scientific Notation and the Calculator

Your calculator is equipped to handle numbers in standard form (**scientific notation**).

Look for the (Exp) button (or the (EE) button) on your calculator.

Example 1 :- Calculate $6 \times (3 \cdot 25 \times 10^3)$ giving your answer in scientific notation.

In your calculator enter :-

The answer is **19 500**   In this case, the answer has not appeared in scientific notation.

You have to do this yourself as shown earlier. $1 \cdot 95 \times 10^4$.

Example 2 :-   Calculate $(1 \cdot 57 \times 10^{-5}) \div 7$

giving your answer in scientific notation, correct to 3 significant figures.

In your calculator enter :-

this might be different on your calculator

The answer may appear as $2 \cdot 242 \times 10^{-6}$.

It is then rounded to $2 \cdot 24 \times 10^{-6}$ (to 3 sig. figs).

Note :-   the answer may appear as 0·000 002 242.

(if it does, you have to change this into scientific notation and round).

Exercise 4·3

1. Use your scientific calculator to work out the following :-

   Answer in scientific notation.

   (a) $5 \times (4 \cdot 26 \times 10^5)$ (b) $6 \times (2 \cdot 97 \times 10^8)$

   (c) $9 \cdot 23 \times (3 \times 10^5)$ (d) $1 \cdot 4 \times (7 \cdot 5 \times 10^4)$

   (e) $2 \cdot 75 \times (6 \times 10^{-4})$ (f) $(8 \cdot 55 \times 10^{-7}) \times 2$

   (g) $3 \cdot 8 \times (4 \cdot 5 \times 10^{-8})$ (h) $(3 \cdot 7 \times 10^{-3}) \times 4 \cdot 4$

2. Work out the following, giving your answers in scientific notation, *(rounded to 3 significant figures when necessary).*

   (a) $(5 \cdot 8 \times 10^3) \div 9$ (b) $(8 \cdot 1 \times 10^7) \div 2$

   (c) $(3 \cdot 1 \times 10^5) \div 1 \cdot 9$ (d) $(4 \cdot 5 \times 10^2) \div 8 \cdot 8$

   (e) $3 \div (1 \cdot 27 \times 10^4)$ (f) $8 \div (3 \times 10^8)$

   (g) $5 \cdot 9 \div (8 \cdot 2 \times 10^{-3})$ (h) $7 \cdot 9 \div (2 \cdot 6 \times 10^{-8})$

3. Try these, answering in scientific notation :-

   (a) $(5 \cdot 8 \times 10^3) + 7$ (b) $(1 \cdot 5 \times 10^4) + 500$

   (c) $(9 \cdot 8 \times 10^3) - 40$ (d) $(4 \cdot 3 \times 10^{-2}) + 10$

   (e) $20 - (7 \cdot 5 \times 10^{-1})$ (f) $7000 - (6 \cdot 2 \times 10^3)$

   (g) $654 - (6 \times 10^2)$ (h) $0 \cdot 15 - (3 \cdot 8 \times 10^{-3})$

4. Do the following calculations :-

   Give your answers in "**normal**" form, rounded to 3 significant figures.

   (a) $(8 \cdot 2 \times 10^3) \times (3 \cdot 1 \times 10^2)$

   (b) $(5 \cdot 69 \times 10^4) \times (4 \cdot 7 \times 10^{-7})$

   (c) $(2 \cdot 8 \times 10^{10}) \div (5 \cdot 3 \times 10^{-3})$

   (d) $(5 \times 10^6) \div (8 \times 10^{-4})$

   (e) $(9 \cdot 1 \times 10^5)^3$

   (f) $(3 \cdot 2 \times 10^{-7}) \times (9 \times 10^6)^3$

In the following questions, always express each of your answers in **scientific notation**.

5. There are 3.156×10^7 seconds in a solar year. How many seconds are there in 5 solar years ?

6. The Lotto jackpot of $£8.4 \times 10^6$ was shared equally among 3 winners. How much did each receive ?

7. Last year, Robertsons Jam factory made a profit of $£7 \times 10^7$.

   This year they made $£1.2 \times 10^5$ more than that.

   How much profit was made this year ?

8. A carbon atom weighs 2.03×10^{-23} grams. What do 1000 carbon atoms weigh ?

9. The formula for the surface area of a sphere is

   $$\text{Area } = 4\pi r^2 \text{ , where } \pi = 3.14.$$

   A small electrically charged particle is spherical in shape, and has radius $r = 2.3 \times 10^{-8}$ cm.

   Calculate its surface area, giving your answer correct to 3 significant figures.

10.  Light travels at a speed of 3×10^5 km per second.

    How long would it take (in minutes and seconds) for a beam of light to travel from the sun to the Earth, a distance of 1.476×10^8 km ?

11. The planet Mars is at a distance of 2.3×10^8 km from the Sun.

    The speed of light is 3×10^5 km per second.

    How long does it take light from the Sun to reach Mars ?

    Give your answer to the nearest minute.

12. The new Hubble telescope, in orbit around the Earth, can now detect 3.8×10^{11} galaxies.

    If each galaxy has on average, 4.7×10^{13} visible stars, how many stars can the telescope detect ?

13. The total mass of argon in a flask is 5.23×10^{-2} grams.

    Given that the mass of a single atom of argon is 6.63×10^{-23} grams, find to 3 significant figures the approximate number of argon atoms in the flask.

14. A cyclotron produces high speed particles.

    A particle moving inside the cyclotron takes 9.4×10^{-23} seconds to travel 2.1×10^{-1} metres.

    Calculate the speed of the particle in metres per second.

15. The total number of visitors to The Modern House Exhibition was 1.425×10^5 .

    The exhibition was open each day from the 1st June to 14 September **inclusive**.

    Calculate the average number of visitors per day to the exhibition, to 3 significant figures.

16. The annual profit of a company was around $£3.2 \times 10^9$ during the year 2004. Approximately how much profit did the company make per second ?

17. The Aircraft Journal reported :-

    "The top airline's oldest jumbo jet has now flown 3.58×10^7 miles".

    (*This is equivalent to 150 trips from the earth to the moon*).

    Calculate the distance from the earth to the moon, giving your answer correct to 3 sig. figs.

1. Copy and complete :-

$$78\,300 = 7{\cdot}83 \times 10^{\cdots}\ .$$

2. Write each of these in **scientific notation** :-

(a) 860 $(= 8{\cdot}6 \times 10^{\cdots})$ (b) 7210

(c) 95 200 (d) 126 800

(e) 16·82 (f) 5 240 000

(g) 6 million (h) 243 million

(i) $5\frac{1}{2}$ million (j) $1\frac{3}{4}$ million

3. Copy and complete :-

$$0{\cdot}000\,623 = 6{\cdot}23 \times 10^{\cdots}$$

4. Write each of these in **scientific notation** :-

(a) 0·0036 (b) 0·0521

(c) 0·000 077 (d) 0·0008

(e) 0·989 (f) 0·000 000 42

5. Write out each of the following numbers in "**normal**" number form :-

(a) $5{\cdot}9 \times 10^3$ (b) $8{\cdot}08 \times 10^5$

(c) $7{\cdot}1 \times 10^2$ (d) $2{\cdot}81 \times 10^4$

(e) 4×10^6 (f) $3{\cdot}2 \times 10^9$

(g) $1{\cdot}001 \times 10^7$ (h) $3{\cdot}5 \times 10^{12}$

6. Write out each of the following numbers in "**decimal**" form :-

(a) $5{\cdot}8 \times 10^{-3}$ (b) $9{\cdot}9 \times 10^{-2}$

(c) $6{\cdot}2 \times 10^{-5}$ (d) $2{\cdot}3 \times 10^{-1}$

(e) 3×10^{-7} (f) 4×10^{-4}

7. Write in scientific notation :-

(a) 42000 (b) 0·0801

(c) 137 000 (d) 0·000 34

(e) 0·000 006 5 (f) $9\frac{1}{2}$ million

(g) 34 000 000 (h) 0·000 02

8. Re-write the following numbers out fully :-

(a) $7{\cdot}3 \times 10^6$ (b) $4{\cdot}9 \times 10^{-3}$

(c) $3{\cdot}61 \times 10^4$ (d) 8×10^{-5}

(e) 8×10^8 (f) $5{\cdot}5 \times 10^{-2}$

(g) $3{\cdot}03 \times 10^5$ (h) $4{\cdot}2 \times 10^{-1}$

9. Use your [EE] or [EXP] buttons to find the following :-

(*Give each answer in scientific notation*)

(a) $150 \times (3{\cdot}8 \times 10^8)$

(b) $(2{\cdot}31 \times 10^6) \times (1{\cdot}35 \times 10^5)$

(c) $(5{\cdot}4 \times 10^{13}) \times (2{\cdot}5 \times 10^{-4})$

(d) $(6{\cdot}8 \times 10^{15}) \div (4 \times 10^4)$

(e) $(5{\cdot}22 \times 10^8) \div (1{\cdot}8 \times 10^{-5})$

(f) $(3{\cdot}2 \times 10^{10})^2$

(g) $(1{\cdot}3 \times 10^{-4})^3$

(h) $\dfrac{(4{\cdot}2 \times 10^8) \times (2{\cdot}5 \times 10^7)}{(3 \times 10^{-4})}$

10. Calculate the **area** of this rectangle, and answer in scientific notation.

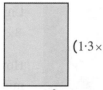

$(1{\cdot}3 \times 10^6)$ mm

$(6{\cdot}4 \times 10^5)$ mm

11.

Light travels at $2{\cdot}998 \times 10^8$ metres per second.

How far will a beam of light travel in :-

(a) an hour (b) a day (c) a year ?

12. The formula for the **volume** of a sphere is $V = \frac{4}{3}\pi r^3$. where r is its radius. ($\pi = 3{\cdot}14$)

Calculate the volume of the Earth which has a radius of $6{\cdot}4 \times 10^3$ km.

Circumference

Remember that the **perimeter**, or
the **circumference** of a circle
can be measured by the formula : –

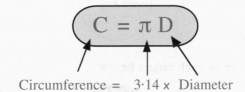

$$C = \pi D$$

Circumference = 3·14 × Diameter

(Your teacher will go over this with you if you have not met this before).

Example :- Calculate the **circumference** of this circle,
which has a diameter of 9 centimetres :-

=> $C = \pi D$

=> $C = 3·14 \times 9$

=> $C = 28·26$ cm

9 cm

Exercise 5·1

1. Calculate the **circumference** of a circle
    which has a diameter of 8 cm.

    Copy and complete : -

    => $C = \pi D$

    => $C = 3·14 \times 8$

    => $C = ...$ cm.

2. Calculate the circumference of each
    circle below : –
    (*Show 3 lines of working for each*).

    (a)   (b)

    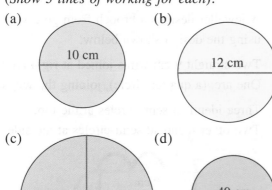

    10 cm   12 cm

    (c)   (d)

    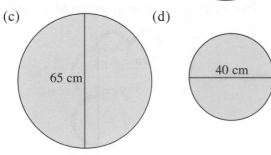

    65 cm   40 cm

    (e)   (f) A circle with
    diameter 1 cm.

    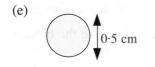

    0·5 cm

3. Find the circumference of each object below :–

    (a)   (b)

    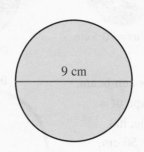

    70 60 cm

    diameter = 20 mm

    (c)   (d)

    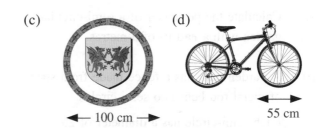

    ← 100 cm →   55 cm

Remember if you are given the **radius**
you need to **double** it to find the diameter.

4. Calculate the circumference of a circle
    with radius 10 cm.

    Copy and complete : –

    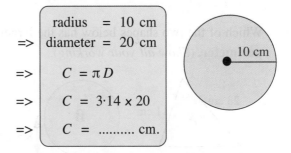

    => radius   = 10 cm
    => diameter = 20 cm

    => $C = \pi D$

    => $C = 3·14 \times 20$

    => $C = ...$ cm.

    10 cm

5. Calculate the circumference of each circle :-

(a)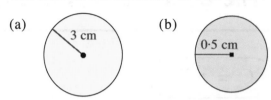
3 cm

(b)
0·5 cm

6. Find the **perimeter** of each object below :-

(a)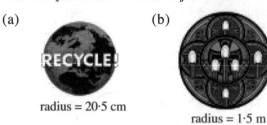
radius = 20·5 cm

(b)
radius = 1·5 m

7. A red wooden beam, in the shape of a semi-circle, has **diameter** 50 cm.

beam

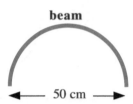

← 50 cm →

Calculate the length of the red wooden beam.

8. A semi-circular garden has a diameter of 8 metres.

Calculate the **perimeter** of the garden.

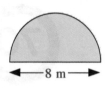
←8 m→

9. Calculate the perimeter of a semi-circular garden with a **radius** of 5 metres.

10. A garden path has a fence made from strips of metal rod bent into semi-circles.

Each semi-circle has a diameter of 20 centimetres.

metal rod

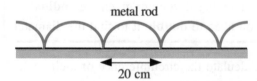

← 20 cm →

Find the length of metal rod needed to make the fence which has to be 5 metres long.

11. Which of the two shapes below has the larger **perimeter**. (*Show all your working*).

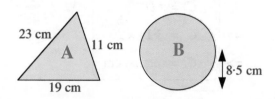
23 cm
A
11 cm
19 cm
B
8·5 cm

12. Calculate the **perimeter** of each shape below : –

(a)
2·5 m
3·3 m

(b)
20 mm

(c)
←———— 100 m ————→
25 m

(d)
←——— 15 cm ———→
10 cm

13. Push'n'Go Pram company have a large logo made from steel bars. The design consists of 2 straight bars each 2 metres long, two circular bars each with 1 metre diameter and a three quarter circular bar as shown.

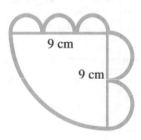
1 m

The bar costs £3 per metre.

Find the total cost of the bars required to make the logo.

14. A jeweller designs a brooch from gold wire using the design shown below.

Two straight 9 cm wires joined at right angles. One arc, (a quarter circle), joining the wires.

Three identical semi-circles at the top. Two other identical semi-circles at the side.

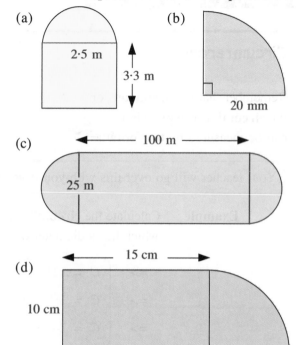
9 cm
9 cm

The gold wire costs £1·40 per centimetre.

Calculate the total cost to make the brooch.

Finding the Diameter

You can use the formula :- $C = \pi D$ to calculate the **diameter** of a circle if you know its circumference.

Example :– Find the diameter of a circle with circumference 94·2 cm.

$$C = \pi D$$

$$94·2 = 3·14 \times D$$

$$D = \frac{94·2}{3·14} = \boxed{30 \text{ cm}}$$

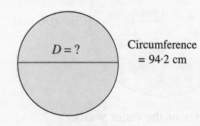

$D = ?$ Circumference = 94·2 cm

The formula needed to calculate the **diameter** is :–

Diameter $\longrightarrow$ $D = \dfrac{C}{\pi}$ $\longleftarrow$ Circumference

$\longleftarrow$ 3·14

Exercise 5·2

1. Find the diameter of a circle with a circumference of 21·98 cm.

    Copy and complete :–

    $$D = \frac{C}{\pi}$$

    $$\Rightarrow \quad D = \frac{21·98}{3·14}$$

    $$\Rightarrow \quad D = \text{........ cm}$$

    D

    Circumference = 21·98 cm

2. Calculate the diameter of each circle below :–
    (*Show 3 lines of working for each*)

    (a)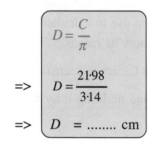

    C = 492·98 cm

    (b)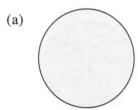

    C = 34·54 m

    (c)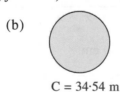

    C = 3·14 mm

    (d)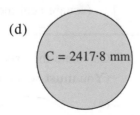

    C = 2417·8 mm

3. Find the diameter of a circle with circumference

    (a) 157 cm
    (b) 386·22 mm
    (c) 6280 m
    (d) 0·314 km

4. Write down the **radius** of each of the circles in question 3.

5. Find the **radius** of a circle with circumference 471 millimetres.

6. Find the radius of a circle which has **perimeter** 3 kilometres.
    (*Give your answer to the nearest metre*).

7. (*Give all answers to one decimal place*).

    (a) Determine the diameter of the tyre, given that its circumference is 200 centimetres.

    (b) Find the **diameter** of a circular button if its circumference is 8 centimetres.

    (c) The circumference of a large birthday cake is 0·5 metres.
    Determine the **radius** of the cake, in centimetres.

    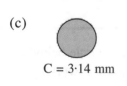

    (d) Find the **radius** of a circle with circumference :–

    (i) 18 cm
    (ii) 1056 m.

8. A small circular washer has an outer **circumference** of 30 millimetres.

   The hole has a radius of 1 millimetre.

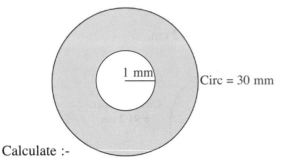

   Circ = 30 mm

   Calculate :-

   (a) the diameter of the outer washer.

   (b) the circumference of the hole.

9. A clock company uses a logo made from a large circle and two squares.

   (*The large square is twice as wide as the small one*).

   The logo needs red trim.

   Find the total length of red trim needed if the circle has a circumference of 3 metres.

   (*Answer to the nearest centimetre*).

Area of a Circle

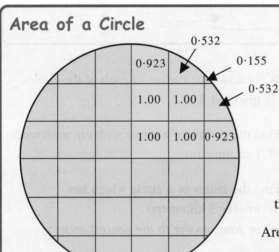

0·532

0·923

0·155

0·532

| 1.00 | 1.00 | |
| 1.00 | 1.00 | 0·923 |

The **blue** area (quarter circle) has been put onto a square centimetre grid and the area for each part has been measured and is given in the diagram.

The total shaded area (*quarter circle*) is **7·065 cm²**

This means the total area of the circle is :-

$$7·065 \times 4 = 28·26 \text{ cm}^2$$

There is a formula (or rule) we can use to calculate the area of a circle as long as you know its radius.

Area generally uses two measurements (... cm x ... cm)

We find that if we calculate $r \times r$ (or r^2), and multiply it by π, we also get an answer of **28·26 cm²**

(*which is the same value as we found by measuring !*)

To find the area of a circle we can use :- $\pi \times r \times r$ **or** $\boxed{A = \pi r^2}$

$$Area = \pi \times r \times r$$

Example :- Calculate the area of a circle with radius 40 cm.

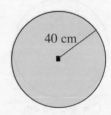

40 cm

$A = \pi r^2$

=> $A = 3·14 \times 40 \times 40$

=> $A = 5024 \text{ cm}^2$ (square centimetres)

Exercise 5·3

1. Find the **area** of a circle with radius 4 cm.

   Copy and complete :–

   $A = \pi r^2$

   => $A = 3·14 \times 4 \times 4$

   => $A = \text{.......} \text{ cm}^2$

2. Calculate the **area** of each circle below :– (You **must** set down 3 lines of working).

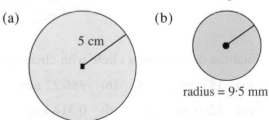

   (a)

   5 cm

   (b)

   radius = 9·5 mm

3.   Find the area of each object below : -

(a)   (b)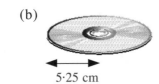

radius of light
= 27 cm

5·25 cm

4.   Find the area of each circle below : –
       (*Remember you must use the* radius)

(a)    (b)

17 cm

2 m

5.   (a)   Find the area of a circular poster
             with **diameter** 60 centimetres.

       (b)   Find the area of a
             circular place-mat,
             whose radius is
             13 centimetres.

       (c)   Find the area of a circular rug with
             diameter 2·2 metres.

       (d)   A knight's circular
             shield shown
             has a radius
             of 0·25 metres.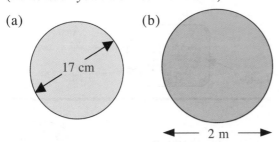

             Find the area of the shield.

       (e)   A circular serving plate has a diameter
             of **half a metre**.

             Calculate the area of the plate.

6.   A square metal machine plate with side 35
       centimetres has a circular hole cut from it.

       Find :–

       (a)   the area of the plate.

       (b)   the area of the hole.

       (c)   the area of steel
             plate remaining.
             (*shown shaded*).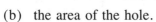

35 cm

7.   Two semi-circular mirrors of radius
       60 centimetres are placed side by side
       on a light blue frame as shown.

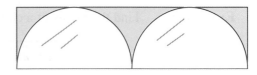

       Find the area of light blue frame **not** covered
       by the mirrors.

8.   (a)   Find the area of a circular glass panel
             with **diameter** 100 centimetres.

       (b)   A circular field has a **diameter** of 1 km.

             Find the area of the field.

9.   A garden is in the shape of a semi-circle.

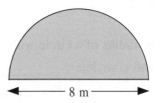

8 m

       Find the area of the garden.

10.   A garden is designed as shown using a square
       of side 6 metres and four semicircles.

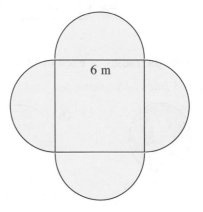

6 m

       Find the total area of the garden.

11.   A cylindrical snake tank has a circular base
       with diameter 75 centimetres.

       The base has to be treated
       with a special paint which
       costs 2·5p per square
       centimetre.

       Find the cost of painting the base of the tank.

Finding the Radius given the Area

You can use the formula :- $A = \pi r^2$ to calculate the **radius** of a circle if you know its area.

Example :- Find the radius of a circle with area 78·5 cm².

$$A = \pi r^2$$

$$78\cdot5 = 3\cdot14 \times r^2$$

$$r^2 = 78\cdot5 \div 3\cdot14 = 25$$

$$r = \sqrt{25} = \boxed{5 \text{ cm}}$$

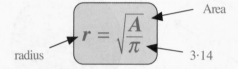

Area = 78·5 cm²

A special formula, which can be used
to calculate the radius, given the area, is :-

$$r = \sqrt{\frac{A}{\pi}}$$

Area

radius   3·14

Exercise 5·4

1. Find the radius of a circle with area 314 cm².

   Copy and complete :-

   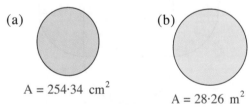

   $$r = \sqrt{\frac{A}{\pi}} \quad \Rightarrow \quad r = \sqrt{\frac{314}{3\cdot14}}$$

   $$\Rightarrow \quad r = \sqrt{\ldots\ldots} \text{ cm}$$

   $$\Rightarrow \quad r = \ldots\ldots \text{ cm}$$

2. Calculate the radius of each of these :-

   (Show 3 lines of working for each)

   (a) A = 254·34 cm²

   (b) A = 28·26 m²

   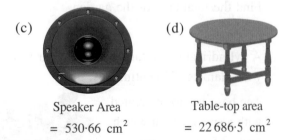

   (c) Speaker Area
   = 530·66 cm²

   (d) Table-top area
   = 22 686·5 cm²

3. Calculate the **radius** of a circle with an area
   of 628 square centimetres.

4. Calculate the **diameter**
   of the circle shown.

   A = 1256 cm²

5. Calculate the **diameter** of a circle with area :-

   (a) 4710 cm²   (b) 2041·785 cm².

6. Circular biscuits, each
   with an **area** of 78·5 cm²,
   are baked on a rectangular
   tray 100 centimetres by
   80 centimetres as shown.

   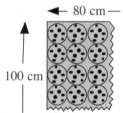

   ← 80 cm —

   100 cm

   What is the **maximum** number of biscuits
   that can be baked, like this, on one tray ?

7. Bart has a square piece of card which has an
   area of 400 cm².

   Explain why he cannot cut out a circular piece
   from it with an area of 325 cm².

8. A cylinder with a base area of 113·04 cm²
   fits **exactly** into a box with a square base.

   Calculate the lengths
   of the sides of the base.

   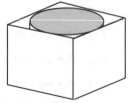

9. A circle has area 1384·74 square centimetres.
   Calculate the **perimeter** of the circle.

A Mixture of Problems

Remember :– when finding :–

the area of a **semi-circle** .... find the area of the whole circle and half it.

the area of a **quarter circle** ...find the area of the whole circle and divide by four.

a **composite** area .... find the area of each part and add them together.

Exercise 5·5

1. Find the area of each shape :–

(a)

(b)

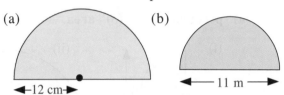

–12 cm–

— 11 m —

(c)

(d)

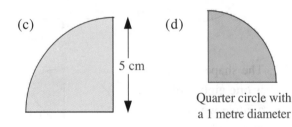

5 cm

Quarter circle with
a 1 metre diameter

2. For each of the three shapes below, find :–

(i)   its area   (ii)   its perimeter.

(a)

(b)

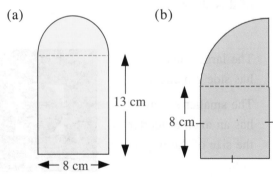

13 cm

8 cm

← 8 cm →

(c)

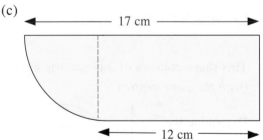

←——— 17 cm ———→

←—— 12 cm ——→

3. A circle has **circumference** 157 centimetres.
Calculate the **area** of the circle.

4. A circle has an area of 11683·94 cm² .
Calculate the **perimeter** of the circle.

5. The semi-circular garden shown below has a
diameter of 12 metres.

A semi-circular brick pathway **one metre wide**
partly surrounds the grass lawn.

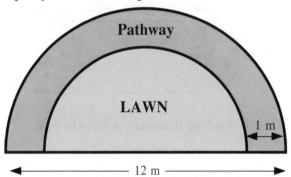

Pathway

LAWN

1 m

←———————— 12 m ————————→

Find the perimeter of : –

(a)   the grass lawn   (b)   the brick path.

6. A company logo uses five circles, each
with a **circumference** of 100 cm, which
overlap as shown.

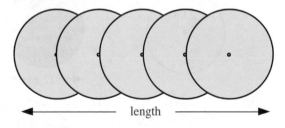

←——————— length ———————→

Find the total length of the company logo.

7. A **semi-circle** has an area of 401·92 cm² .
Calculate the perimeter of the semi-circle.

8. A quarter circle has an
area of 854·865 cm² .

Calculate the perimeter
of the quarter circle.

Area = 854·865 cm²

1. Calculate the **circumference** of each circle below. *(Show 3 lines of working)* :–

   (a)

   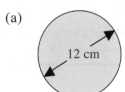

   12 cm

   (b)

   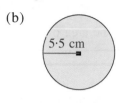

   5·5 cm

2. Calculate the **perimeter** of each shape below :–

   (a)

   ◄— 11 m —►

   (b)

   5 cm

   (c)

   ◄——— 150 m ———►

   20 m

   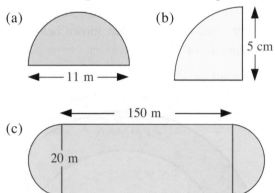

3. (a) Find the **diameter** of a circle with :–

   (i) circumference 20·41 cm

   (ii) perimeter 4·71 km.

   (b) Find the **radius** of a circle with circumference 329·7 mm.

4. Calculate the **area** of each of these :–
   (Show at least 3 lines of working)

   (a)

   5 cm

   (b)

   ◄— 12 m —►

   (c)

   ◄— 40 m —►

   (d)

   1 cm

   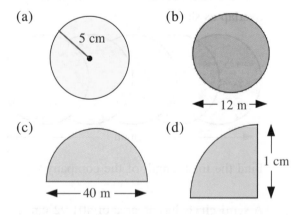

5. Find the **area** of a circle with :–

   (a) 15 cm radius   (b) 23 cm diameter.

6. Calculate the :–

   (a) **radius** of a circle with area 7·065 m^2.

   (b) **diameter** of a circle with area 0·785 mm^2.

7. A yellow square with side 8 centimetres has four identical quarter circles cut out from each corner as shown.

   Determine the yellow area.

   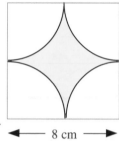

   ◄— 8 cm —►

8. For each of the blue shapes below, find the :–

   (a) **perimeter**   (b) **area**.

   (i)

   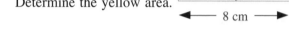

   10 cm

   (ii)

   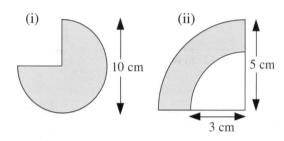

   5 cm

   3 cm

9. The shape shown is **one eighth** of a circle which has a radius of 6 centimetres.

   Calculate the area of this shape.

   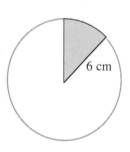

   6 cm

10. The large square has side 2 metres.

    The smaller square has an **area** a quarter the size of the larger area.

    Calculate the total red area.

    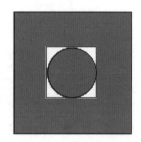

11. This shape consists of 3 concentric circles (*with the same centre*).

    Determine the combined areas which are shaded pink.

    3 m   1 m   2 m

Gradients

We can measure how steep a hill or road is, or how steeply a ladder is resting against a wall.

This is called the **slope** or the GRADIENT of the hill or ladder.

The **gradient** of a hill is usually written as a **fraction**.
(*It can be given as a decimal or as a percentage*).

Hill Street has a **gradient** of **1 in 10**.

This is written as   **gradient = $\frac{1}{10}$**

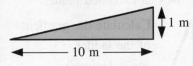

This means that for every 10 metres moved across (**horizontally**), the road rises by 1 metre (**vertically**).

How to Calculate the GRADIENT of a hill.

Example :–   New Street rises by 4 metres.
It is 80 metres (horizontally)
from one end to the other.

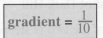

Gradient = 4 metres in 80 metres

=>   **gradient = $\frac{4}{80}$ = $\frac{1}{20}$**

Can you see that $\frac{1}{20}$ is **smaller** than $\frac{1}{10}$? –> this means New Street is **less** steep than Hill Street.

Definition :–   **Gradient = $\frac{\text{vertical distance}}{\text{horizontal distance}}$**

Exercise 6·1

1.   Look at this picture of Dunn Street.

(a)   Calculate its **gradient** like this :–

Copy :–

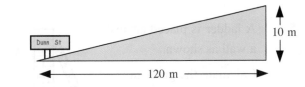

Gradient = $\frac{\text{vertical distance}}{\text{horizontal distance}}$

=> gradient = $\frac{10}{120}$ => gradient = $\frac{?}{?}$ (*simplify the fraction $\frac{10}{120}$*)

(b)   Compare the **gradient** of Dunn Street with that of Hill Street and New Street.

Which of the three is the :–   (i)   steepest   (ii)   least steep ?

2. Look at each hill shown.

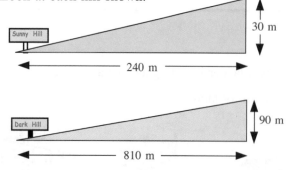

Sunny Hill
30 m
240 m

Dark Hill
90 m
810 m

(a) Calculate the **gradient** of each hill.

(b) Compare the **gradient** of Sunny Hill with that of Dark Hill.

Which of the two is steeper ?

3. Four hills have gradients,

$$\frac{8}{50}, \quad 0{\cdot}24, \quad 19\% \quad \text{and} \quad 0{\cdot}2.$$

Write the gradients in order, (steepest first).
(Hint : change them all to decimals)

4. Two car ramps are shown below.

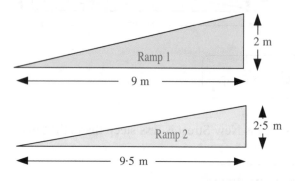

Ramp 1
2 m
9 m

Ramp 2
2·5 m
9·5 m

(a) Calculate the gradient of each ramp.

(b) Change each gradient to a decimal.

(c) Compare the gradients to find which ramp is the steeper.

5. A ladder is placed against a wall as shown.

Calculate the gradient of the ladder.

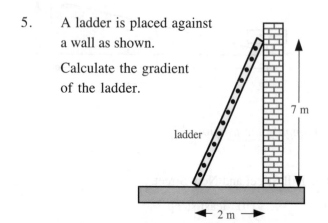

7 m

ladder

2 m

6. Two ladders are placed against a wall shown.

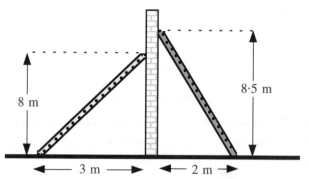

8 m

8·5 m

3 m

2 m

For safety reasons, a ladder must have a gradient with a value between **4** and **5**.

Which of the ladders shown above is/are safe ?

7. A fire engine uses an extended ladder.

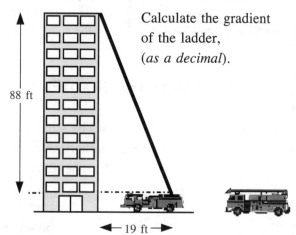

Calculate the gradient of the ladder, (*as a decimal*).

88 ft

19 ft

8. A ramp, with vertical height of 2 metres, has a gradient of 0·25.

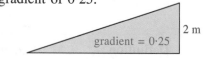

2 m
gradient = 0·25

Calculate the **horizontal** distance.

9. A cable car travels from a base point to the top of a mountain as shown.

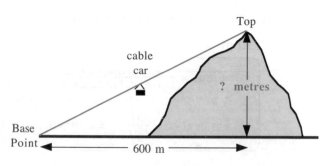

Top

cable car

? metres

Base Point

600 m

If the gradient of the cable is 0·4, calculate the **height** of the mountain.

Finding the Gradient of a Line from a Coordinate Diagram

The gradient of a line can be found from a coordinate (or Cartesian) diagram.

Any 2 given points on a straight line can be used to form a right angled triangle.
Vertical and horizontal **changes** can be found, using points on the line, and the formula used as before.

Example :-

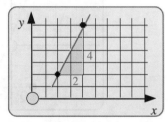

Pick any two coordinates - P(2, 1) and Q(8, 4) and form a right-angled triangle as shown.

Horizontal change is 6.

Vertical change is 3.

$$Gradient = \frac{vertical\ distance}{horizontal\ distance} = \frac{3}{6} = \frac{1}{2}$$

Exercise 6·2

1. Copy and complete the calculation to find the **gradient** of the line shown.

   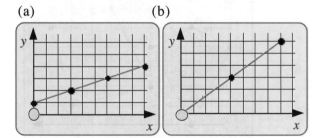

   Horizontal dist = 2.

   Vertical dist = 4.

   $$Gradient = \frac{vertical\ distance}{horizontal\ distance} = ... = ...$$

2. Calculate the gradient of each line in the Cartesian diagrams below :–

   (a)   (b)

   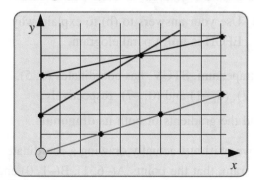

3. The diagram shows three coloured lines.

   Find the gradient of each line.

4. Plot each set of points and calculate the gradient of the line passing through each set.

   (a) (1, 1), (2, 2), (3, 3)

   (b) (0, 2), (2, 3), (6, 5)

   (c) (0, 0), (1, 4), (2, 8)

5. The line AB is shown in a Cartesian diagram.

   (a) Write down the coordinates of :–

        (i) A   (ii) B.

   (b) By writing down the horizontal and vertical distance from A to B, calculate the gradient of the line AB.

   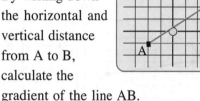

6. Calculate the gradient of each line below:–

   (a)   (b)

   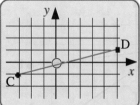 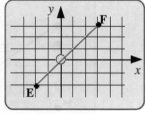

7. Each set of points represents a straight line. Calculate the gradient of each :–

   (a) (–2, 1), (1, 4)   (b) (–4, 2), (6, 4)

   (c) (–1, –2), (2, 4)   (d) (–4, –3), (5, 0)

   (e) (–12, –61), (4, 3).

Example :–   Find the **gradient** (m) of the line CD.

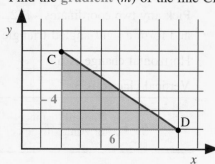

Vertical change is – 4
Horizontal change is 6.

$$\textit{Gradient } (m_{CD}) = \frac{\text{vertical distance}}{\text{horizontal distance}} = \frac{-4}{6} = \frac{-2}{3}$$

$$m_{CD} = -\frac{2}{3}$$

8. Copy and complete the calculation to find the gradient of the line shown.

Vertical change is ....

Horizontal change is ...

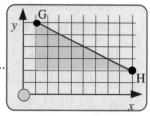

$$m_{GH} = \frac{\text{vertical distance}}{\text{horizontal distance}} = \frac{-?}{8} = -\frac{?}{?}$$

9. Calculate the gradient of each line in the Cartesian diagrams below :–

(a)   (b)

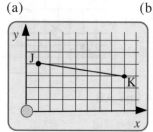

10. (a) Calculate the gradient of each line below.

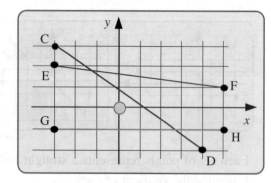

(b) Notice the gradient of line GH.

What can you say about the gradient of **ALL** horizontal lines ? Explain.

11. (a) Calculate the gradient of each **parallel** line.

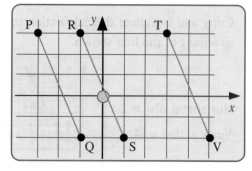

(b) What can you say about the gradient of lines which are **parallel** to each other ?

12. (a) Find :–   (i) m_{AB} (ii) m_{BC}
              (iii) m_{CD} (iv) m_{AD}

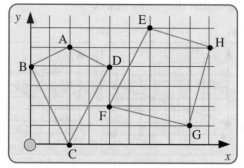

(b) Find the gradient of each side of EFGH.

(c) Use your answers to (b) to explain why EFGH is **not** a parallelogram.

13. A trapezium, STUV, has coordinates (0, 5), (2, 7), (6, –1) and (0, –7) respectively.

Find the gradients of both its **diagonals**.

14. Prove, **without** actually drawing a coordinate diagram, that the points A(–6, 1), B(–1, 0) and C(4, –1) all lie on the same straight line.

The Equation of a Line - a formula

Consider the equation $y = 2x$.

A table of values can be constructed

x	-1	0	1	2
y	-2	0	2	4

and the points plotted.

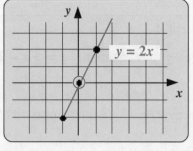

The formula connecting the points on this line can be written as

$$y = 2x$$

It is called the **equation of the line**.

Can you see that the gradient is 2 ?

Consider the equation $y = 2x + 3$.

A table of values can be constructed

x	-1	0	1	2
y	1	3	5	7

and the points plotted.

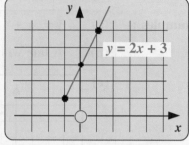

The formula connecting the points on this line can be written as $y = 2x + 3$

(The y-coordinate of any point on the line is 2 times the x-coordinate **plus** 3).

Can you see that the gradient is also 2 ?
Can you see that it cuts the y-axis at 3 ?

Exercise 6·3

1. (a) Copy and complete the table for $y = 3x$.

x	-1	0	1	2
y	-3	...	...	...

    (b) Draw a set of axes, plot the 4 points, join them up and label the line $y = 3x$.

    (c) Calculate, or write down the gradient (m) of the line.

2. For each of the following :–

    (i) construct a table using 4 points.
    (ii) plot the points on a Cartesian diagram.
    (iii) write down the gradient of the line formed.

    (a) $y = 4x$ (b) $y = x$

    (c) $y = \frac{1}{2}x$ (d) $y = -x$

    > Any straight line through the origin will have its equation $y = mx$ where m is the gradient.

3. Write down the **gradient** of each line below :–

    (a) $y = 6x$ (b) $y = \frac{1}{5}x$

    (c) $y = -12x$ (d) $y = 0{\cdot}5x$

4. (a) Copy and complete the table for the equation $y = 3x + 1$.

x	-1	0	1	2
y	-2	...	...	...

    (b) Draw a set of axes, plot the 4 points, join them up and label the line $y = 3x + 1$.

    (c) Calculate, or write down the gradient (m) of the line.

    (d) Where does this line cut the y-axis ?

5. For each of the lines below :–

    (i) construct a table using 4 points.
    (ii) plot the points on a Cartesian diagram.
    (iii) write down the gradient of each line.
    (iv) write down where the line cuts the y-axis.

    (a) $y = 4x - 1$ (b) $y = -2x + 3$

    (c) $y = \frac{1}{2}x + 3$ (d) $y = -x - 4$

6. For the line $y = 5x + 2$,

    (a) write down its gradient.

    (b) write down where it meets the y-axis.

The Equation of a Straight Line

The equation of any line (a linear equation) takes the form :–

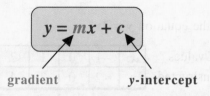

$$y = mx + c$$

gradient   y-intercept

Where m represents the **gradient** of the line
and c represents the **y-intercept**. (*where it cuts the y-axis*).

Examples :–

(a) $y = 3x + 4$ has gradient 3 and y-intercept 4.

(b)   A line with y-intercept –2 and gradient $\frac{3}{4}$ has equation $y = \frac{3}{4}x - 2.$

(c)

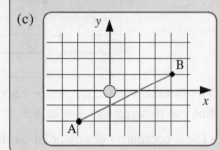

$m_{AB} = \frac{3}{6} = \frac{1}{2}$ y-intercept is –1

=>   Equation of line AB is $y = \frac{1}{2}x - 1$

Exercise 6·4

1. Write down the **gradient** and **y-intercept** in each of these equations :–

   (a) $y = 3x + 2$ (b) $y = 5x - 3$

   (c) $y = x + 1$ (d) $y = -2x + 5$

   (e) $y = \frac{1}{2}x + 2$ (f) $y = -\frac{1}{3}x - 1$

   (g) $y = 0·5x + 9$ (h) $y = -0·1x + 2$

   (i) $y = 4 + 2x$ (j) $y = 15 - x$

2. Write down the **y-intercept** of the line given by the equation :- $y = 4x.$

3. Write down the **equation** of each of these lines :–

   (a) $m = 2$, and the y-intercept is 3.

   (b) $m = 4$, and the y-intercept is – 2.

   (c)   y-intercept is 6, and the gradient is 4.

   (d)   gradient is – 2, and it passes through (0, 3).

   (e)   gradient is $\frac{1}{3}$, and it passes through (0,–1).

   (f) $m = 12$ and line passes through the origin.

4. Line AB cuts the y-axis at the point (0, 4) and is **parallel** to a line with equation $y = 2x - 3$.

   (a)   Write down the **gradient** of the line AB.

   (b)   Write the equation of this line AB.

5. For each of the six lines below,

   (i)   calculate its gradient

   (ii)   write down its y-intercept

   (iii)   write the equation of the line.

   (a)   (b)

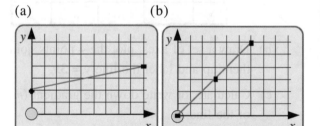

   (c)   (d)

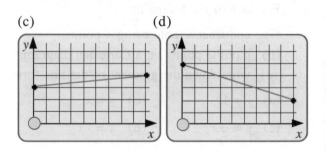

   (e)   (f)

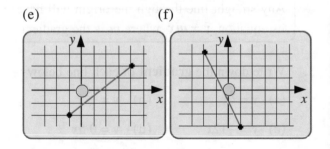

6. The line shown has equation $y = mx + c$.

    (a) Write down the value of c.

    (b) Calculate the gradient.

    (c) Write down the **equation** of the line.

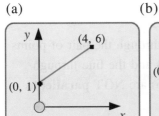

10. Which of the two lines below is steeper ?
    (*Careful!*)

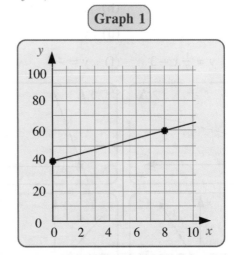

7. Write down the equation of each line below :–

    (a)

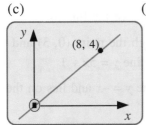

    (b)

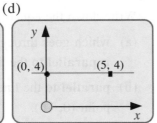

    (c)

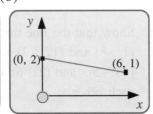

    (d)

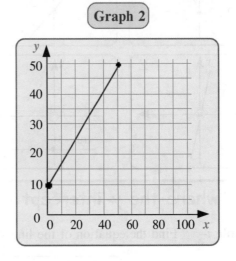

8. The line AB passes through points A(0, 2) and B(4, 4).

    (a) Show the line AB on a Cartesian diagram.

    (b) Calculate the gradient of this line.

    (c) Write down its y-intercept.

    (d) Write down the equation of the line AB.

11. Write down the equation of each of the four lines below :–

    (a)

    (b)

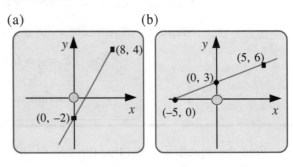

9. Find the **equation** of the line shown below.

    (*Hint : look at the scale on each axis carefully*).

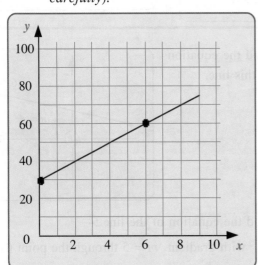

    (c)

    (d)

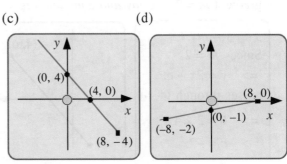

12. Match each of the following equations with their corresponding graphs shown below :-

(a) $y = 3x$ (b) $y = 2x - 1$

(c) $y = -5x$ (d) $y = -x - 1$

(e) $y = \frac{1}{2}x + 3$ (f) $y = -5$

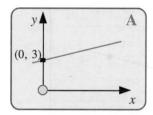
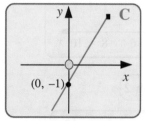
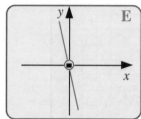
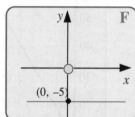

13. Find the equation of the line passing through each set of points below :-

(a) C(0, 1), D(4, 5) (b) E(0, 5), F(6, 6)

(c) G(–2, 6), H(0, –2) (d) J(0, –5), K(3, 4)

14. Show that the line through the pair of points (0, 1), (4, 7) and the line through (0, –3) and (4, 3) are **parallel** to each other
(*Remember : parallel lines have equal gradients*)

15. Show that the line through the pair of points (1, –8) and (12, –3) and the line through (–5, –5), and (21, 6) are **NOT parallel** to each other.

16. Write down the equation of the line :–

(a) which goes through the point (0, 3) and is **parallel** to the line $y = 5x + 1$

(b) **parallel** to the line $y = -x$ and lies on the point (0, –6).

Lines where the y-intercept is not known

Example :–   Find the equation of the line with gradient $m = \frac{1}{2}$ through P(6, 10).

Step 1 :   Start with $y = mx + c$

Step 2 :   Let $m = \frac{1}{2}$ => $y = \frac{1}{2}x + c$

Step 3 :   Substitute $x = 6$ and $y = 10$ into the equation.

=> $10 = \frac{1}{2} \times 6 + c$ => $c = 7$.

=> Equation of line is $y = \frac{1}{2}x + 7$

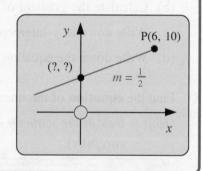

17. Find the equation of the line through (4, 6) with gradient $m = 2$. (*Copy and complete the steps*).

$y = mx + c$
Since $m = 2$,
=> $y = 2x + c$.
passes through (4, 6)
=> $6 = 2 \times 4 + c$
=> $c = -2$.
=> Equation is :–

$y = ... x - ....$

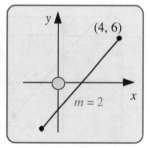

18. Find the equation of this line.

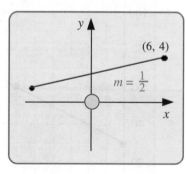

19. Find the equation of the line :–

(a) with gradient $m = 5$ through the point (3, 1).

(b) through the point (–1, –11) with $m = -\frac{1}{2}$.

The General Equation of a Straight Line

The equation of any line can be written in the form $Ax + By + C = 0$.

This is called the **General Equation** of a line.

The General Equation can be **re-arranged** so that
the gradient and y-intercept are easier to obtain.

Example :- Find the gradient and y intercept of the line

$$5y - 2x + 1 = 0.$$

> $5y - 2x + 1 = 0$
>
> => $\quad 5y = 2x - 1$
>
> => $\quad y = \frac{2}{5}x - \frac{1}{5}$
>
> => $m = \frac{2}{5}$ and y-intercept is $(0, -\frac{1}{5})$

Exercise 6·5

1. The equation of a line is given by :-

    $$2x + 3y - 1 = 0.$$

    Copy and complete the calculation below to
    find the **gradient** and the **y-intercept**.

    > $2x + 3y - 1 = 0$
    >
    > => $\quad 3y \quad = -.... + ...$
    >
    > => $\quad y \quad = - ....$
    >
    > $m = ...$ and the y-intercept is ....

2. Find the gradient and y-intercept of the
    equation :-

    $$4y - 6x + 3 = 0.$$

    Copy and complete :

    > $4y - 6x + 3 = 0$
    >
    > => $\quad 4y \quad = ... - ....$
    >
    > => $\quad y \quad = - ....$
    >
    > $m = ...$ and the y-intercept is ....

3. Find the gradient and the y-intercept of each
    of the lines defined by the equations below :–

    (a) $2x + 4y + 6 = 0$ (b) $x + 2y - 1 = 0$

    (c) $3y - 3x + 1 = 0$ (d) $2y - 6x + 4 = 0$

    (e) $2x + y = 16$ (f) $3x + y + 1 = 0$

    (g) $3y + 3 = x$ (h) $2y + 8 = \frac{1}{2}x$

4. The equation of a line is given by :-

    $$4x + 2y - 8 = 0.$$

    (a) Re-arrange the equation into the form

    $$y = mx + c.$$

    (b) Draw this line on a Cartesian diagram.
    (*Hint - construct a table of values*).

5. Draw each of the lines with equations given
    below on Cartesian diagrams.

    (a) $2x + y + 1 = 0$ (b) $4x + 2y + 6 = 0$

    (c) $3x + 3y = 9$ (d) $2y - 4x - 2 = 0$

6. Determine the gradient and the y-intercept of
    the line :-

    $$x - y + 2 = 0$$

    (Hint : *be careful with negative y-value*).

7. Find the gradient and y-intercept of each of
    these lines with equations :–

    (a) $3y = 9x + 15$ (b) $4y = 2x - 1$

    (c) $6x + 3y = 15$ (d) $4x + 2y - 8 = 0$

    (e) $2y + \frac{1}{2}x - 3 = 0$ (f) $5x - 4y + 1 = 0$

8. Find the gradient and y-intercept of the line
    with equation $x - 2y = 4.$

Linear Equations in everyday use

A linear equation is usually written as $y = mx + c$, but other letters can be used to form a linear equation.

$y = ax + b$ and $P = mt + c$, could also represent straight lines.

Example :–

Bob earns £4 per hour.
A table can be drawn to show his earnings.

A graph can be plotted using h (hours) and P (pay) in place of x and y.

Other values can be found from the table or a formula can be made.

Gradient = 4 and the P-intercept is 0.

=> $\boxed{P = 4h}$

hours (h)	0	1	2	3	4
Pay (£P)	0	4	8	12	16

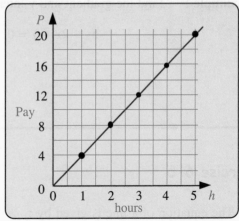

note :– $y = 2x^2 + 1$ and $y = -5x^{\frac{3}{4}}$ 4 are **NOT** linear.
Can you see why not ?

Exercise 6·6

1. Write down which of these are linear equations.

   (a) $P = 7t + 2$ (b) $y = x^2 + 3$

   (c) $s = -3t$ (d) $3t + 4w + 2 = 0$

   (e) $2h - t^2 = 4$ (f) $x = 3y - 1$

2. Maggie earns £6 an hour.

   (a) Copy and complete the table of values.

hours (h)	0	1	2	3	4
pay (£P)	0	6	...	...	...

   (b) From the table, plot 5 points on a Cartesian diagram.

   (c) Find the gradient m and P - intercept.

   (d) Write a formula representing the line.

   (e) Use your formula to find how much Maggie would earn in :–

   (i) 8 hours   (ii) $12\frac{1}{2}$ hours ?

   (f) How many hours would Maggie have to work to earn £72 ?

   (*hint : set up an equation and solve it*)

3. Mr. Jenkins earns £9·50 an hour.

   (a) Use a table of values to construct a line graph involving P and h.

   (b) Write a formula representing the line.

   (c) Use your formula to find how much he would earn in 6 hours ?

   (d) How many hours he would need to work to earn £218·50 ?

4. A painter can paint a fence at a rate of 3 metres per hour.

   (a) Use a table of values to construct a line graph. (Use L for length and H for hours).

   (b) Write a formula representing the line.

   (c) Use your formula to find how long it would take to paint a 45 metre fence.

5. Jennifer can make 7 paper roses every hour.

   (a) Construct a line graph to represent this information using t (time) and R (roses).

   (b) Write a formula and use it to find how long it would take to make 35 roses.

Example :– Pete the plumber charges a call-out fee **plus** an hourly charge.

The line graph shows the relative costs where t is the time and C the cost.

The call-out fee is £20 (0 hours work)

=> The y-intercept is 20.

The hourly charge is £10 per hour.

=> The gradient (m) = 10.

The equation of the line is

$$C = 10t + 20$$

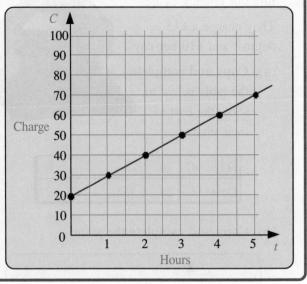

6. (a) Use the above formula $(C = 10t + 20)$ to calculate the total cost of :–

   (i) 4 hours work   (ii) $9\frac{1}{2}$ hours work.

   (b) If the charge is £80, form an equation (in t) and **solve** it to find the time taken.

7. Jack the joiner charges a call-out fee plus an hourly rate. Jack's charges are represented by the line graph below :–

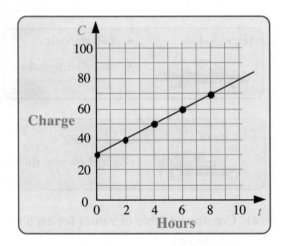

   (a) Write down the :–
       (i) call-out fee   (ii) hourly rate.

   (b) Calculate the :–
       (i) gradient   (ii) y-intercept.

   (c) Make a formula to represent the line.

   (d) Use your formula to find the cost for :–

       (i) 7 hours   (ii) $9\frac{1}{2}$ hours work.

   (e) Use your formula to find how long would it take for a job costing £55.

8. Eric, an electrician, charges a call-out fee of £20 and charges £5 (C) for every hour (h).

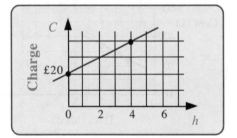

   (a) Write down a formula for the charge £C for h hours worked.

   (b) Calculate the cost for 5 hours worked.

9. The graph below shows a kite dropping from a height (H) of 100 metres to the ground at a steady rate (given in seconds s).

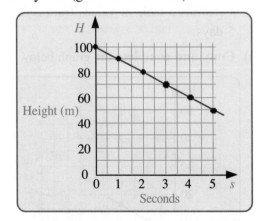

   (a) Determine the **gradient** of the line.

   (b) Write a formula to represent this line.

   (c) Use your formula to find the height of the kite after 5 seconds.

   (d) Use your formula to calculate how long it would take for the kite to land.

10. The "**Bouncy Company**" hire out bouncy castles.

They charge a £15 deposit and £10 per day.

(a) **Copy and complete** the table below to show the cost of their charges.

Days (d)	1	2	3	4
Cost (£C)	25	35	...	...

(b) **Copy and complete** the graph.

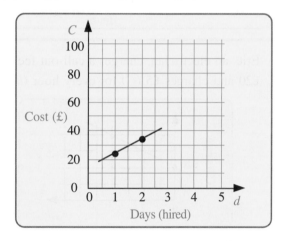

(c) Write a formula in terms of C and d.

(d) What will it cost to hire it for a week ?

11. A Carpet Cleaning firm hires out industrial cleaners. They charge a £5 deposit and a daily hire charge of £6.

(a) Construct a table of values from zero up to 5 days.

(b) **Copy and complete** the graph below.

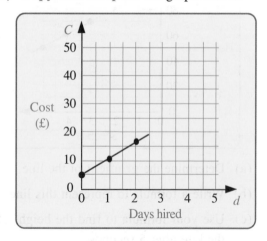

(c) Devise a formula and use it to find the length of hire for a £59 charge.

12. For each case below, develop a linear formula to represent the given information :–

(a)  Paul the plumber charges a call-out fee (F) of £60 plus a working rate of £20 per hour (h).

(b) A bicycle hire company's charges (£C) consists of a £10 deposit plus £5 per day (d) rental.

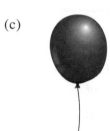

(c)  A balloon filled with helium starts at a height (H) of 20 feet.

Every hour (t) the balloon loses 2 feet in height.

(d) A living room begins from a temperature (T) of – 6°C and heats up at a steady rate of 4°C every hour (h).

13. Two "car-hire" companies advertise their charges as shown :–

Hire-A-Car :-
• £40 deposit
• and £10 per day.

Car Rent Co :-
• £10 deposit
• and £20 per day.

(a) Construct a table of values for each of the companies.

(b) Draw two lines on the same diagram to represent each company's charges.

(c) After how many days is the cost the same for each company ?

(d) Write a formula for each company to represent their hire charges.

(e) Which company would you use for a :–

(i) 3 day hire   (ii) fortnight hire ?

Finding the Equation of a Line given any two points on it.

Example :– The points A(1, 3) and B(3, 7) lie on a straight line.

Find the equation of the straight line through A and B.

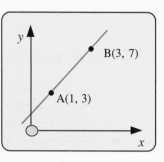

Step 1 : Sketch the line.

Step 2 : Find the gradient. $m = \dfrac{\text{vertical}}{\text{horizontal}} = \dfrac{4}{2} = 2$

Step 3 : Find the y-intercept   Substitute A(1, 3) and $m = 2$ into

$$y = mx + c$$
$$\Rightarrow \quad 3 = 2 \times 1 + c \qquad \Rightarrow c = 1$$

Step 4 : Use gradient and
y-intercept to write
down the formula.

$m = 2$ and the y-intercept is 1

$\Rightarrow$ Equation of line is $\boxed{y = 2x + 1}$

Exercise 6·7

1. The points C(2, 5) and D(8, 8) lie on a line.

    Copy and complete the calculations below to
    find the equation of the line through CD.

    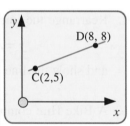

    $m = \dfrac{\text{vertical}}{\text{horizontal}} = ...$

    Using C(2, 5) and
    $m = ...$ gives
    $\Rightarrow \quad 5 = ... \times .... + c$
    $\Rightarrow \quad c = ...$
    $m = ...,$ y-intercept is ...
    $\Rightarrow \quad y = ... x + ...$

2. Determine the equation of each line below :–

    (a)

    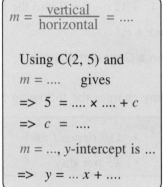

    (b)

    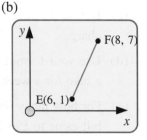

    (c)

    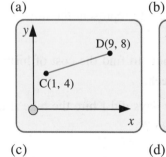

    (d)

    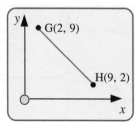

3. Determine the equation of each line :–

    (a)

    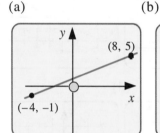

    (b)

    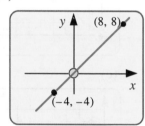

    (c)

    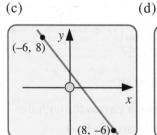

    (d)

    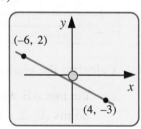

4. Determine the equation of the line through
    each set of points below :–

    (a) (–3, 2), (2, 7)   (b) (–1, –4), (–1, 9)
    (c) (–10, 4), (–4, –5) (d) (–1, 16), (1, –16).

5. A line passes through the points (–36, 6) and
    (–16, 21).
    The line also passes through the point (a, 24).

    (a) Determine the equation of the line.

    (b) Find the value of a.

1. Calculate the **gradient** of this ramp.

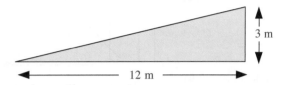

3 m

12 m

2. The gradient of four ramps are given below :–

car ramp   20%,   garage ramp   0·15,

skateboard ramp $\frac{1}{2}$,   bike ramp   0·3.

List the ramps in order, **steepest** first.

3. Calculate the gradient of each line below :–

(a)   (b)

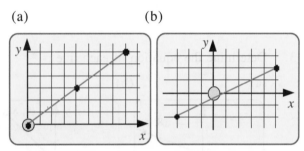

(c)   (d)

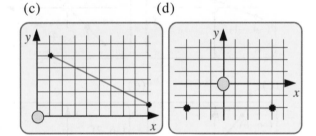

4. Calculate the gradient of :–

(a) the line AB which passes through the points A(–2, –1) and B(3, 4).

(b) the line CD which passes through the points C(–6, 5) and D(4, –5).

5. Write down the **gradients** and the **y-intercepts** of these lines :–

(a) $y = 2x + 7$ (b) $y = 1 - x$.

6. Write down the **equation** of each of the following lines :–

(a) $m = 3$, and its y-intercept is –2.

(b)   gradient of -1, through the point (0, –2).

(c) $m = -5$ and passing through the origin.

7. Find the equation of each line below :–

(a)   (b)

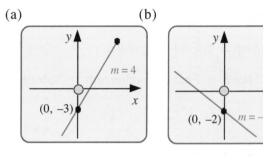

8. Find the equation of this line.

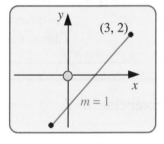

9. Write down the gradient and y-intercept of :–

(a) $2y + 6x - 2 = 0$ (b) $3x + 4y = 0$.

10. Rearrange the line $4y + 12x - 6 = 0$ into the form

$$y = mx + c,$$

and show the line on a Cartesian diagram.

11. A Bike Hire company charges the following :–

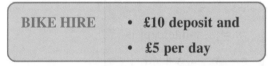

BIKE HIRE   •   **£10 deposit and**

•   **£5 per day**

(a) Construct a table of values for 1 to 5 days.

(b) Plot the 5 points on a Cartesian diagram.

(c) Devise a formula to represent the hire charges.

(d) Use your formula to find the cost of hiring a bike for a week.

(e) For how many days did I hire the bike if my bill came to £95 ?

12. Find the equation of this line.

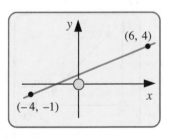

1. In which test did David do better ?

    French - $^{20}/_{25}$, German - $^{27}/_{36}$.

2. Ruth left £2400 in the bank for 3 years where her savings grew with a **compound interest** rate of 4·5% p.a. Calculate how much Interest she was due. (*Show all working*).

3. A **light year** is the **distance** a particle of light would travel in 1 year. Its value is

    $$9 \cdot 46 \times 10^{15} \text{ metres.}$$

    The Star, Bellea, is $2 \cdot 1 \times 10^4$ light years away. How far away is Bellea (in metres) ?

4. This barn is 14 m wide.

    From the ground to the bottom of the roof of the house is 6 m.

    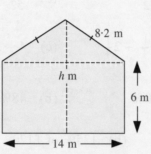

    The sloping roof is 8·2 m long.

    Calculate the height (h m) of the barn.

5.

    Prove that this **is** a right angled triangle.

6. Calculate the **circumference** of this circle with diameter 22 cm.

7.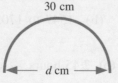

    Calculate the **perimeter** of this shape ?

8. A 30 cm plastic ruler is bent into the shape of a semi-circle.

    Calculate the diameter of the semi-circle formed.

9. 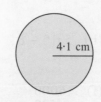 Calculate the **area** of this circle with a radius of 4·1 cm.

10. Calculate the gradient of the line joining the 2 points A(–1, 3) and B(5, –1).

    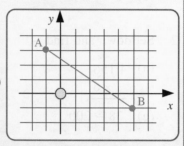

11. Write down both the **gradient** and the *y*-intercept of each of these two lines :-

    (a) $y = \frac{1}{2}x - 2$ (b) $3y + 2x - 6 = 0$

12. Write down the **equation** of this line.

    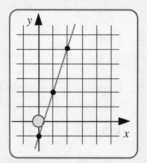

13. Make a neat sketch of the following lines showing all the important points :-

    (a) $y = \frac{2}{3}x + 2$ (b) $y = -2x - 3$.

14. Write down the equation of this line :-

    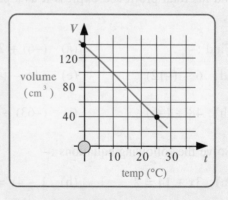

15. (a) It took Billy from 9·10 am till 11·22 am to drive the 99 miles from his home to the airport. Calculate Billy's average speed.

    (b) How long would it take a plane to fly 320 km at an average speed of 240 km/hr ? (*Answer in hours and minutes*).

Turn off that Calculator...

1. Set down and find :–

   (a) 413
   $\times 62$

   (b) $5016 \div 8$

   (c) 312×400

   (d) 30^2

   (e) 7^3

   (f) 6000
   $- 529$

   (g) $18 - 5 \times 3$

   (h) $7\overline{)5054}$

2. Set down and find :–

   (a) $4\cdot156$
   $\times 6$

   (b) $17\cdot2 + 8\cdot876$

   (c) $9\overline{)833\cdot58}$

   (d) $17\cdot43 \times 600$

   (e) $38 \div 200$

   (f) $9 - 8\cdot279$

   (g) $\frac{2}{1000}$

   (h) $30\cdot4 \div 4000$

3. Find :–
   (a) $\frac{7}{8}$ of 120
   (b) $\frac{3}{7}$ of 560
   (c) $\frac{9}{11}$ of 880

4. Simplify :–
   (a) $\frac{28}{49}$
   (b) $\frac{16}{72}$
   (c) $\frac{13}{52}$
   (d) $\frac{65}{85}$

5. Find :–
   (a) $\frac{1}{3} + \frac{1}{3}$
   (b) $3\frac{1}{4} + 2\frac{1}{4}$
   (c) $4 - 1\frac{2}{3}$
   (d) $2 \times 5\frac{1}{5}$

6. Express as a simple fraction :–
   (a) 60%
   (b) 48%
   (c) $2\frac{1}{2}\%$

7. Find :–
   (a) $66\frac{2}{3}\%$ of £180
   (b) 125% of £120
   (c) $2\frac{1}{2}\%$ of 360 g

   (d) 5% of 600 ml
   (e) 15% of £640
   (f) 11% of £9

8. Express :–
   (a) 42 as a percentage of 60
   (b) 15 as a percentage of 45.

9. A shopkeeper bought a box of a dozen toilet rolls for £3·00. He sold them at 35p each.
   Find his total profit and express it as a percentage of the cost price.

10. Find :–
    (a) $(-6) + 21$
    (b) $(-7) - 13$
    (c) $(-30) + 19$

    (d) $6 - (-12)$
    (e) $-15 - (-8)$
    (f) $(-8) \times (-6)$
    (g) $(-200)^2$

    (h) $48 \div (-6)$
    (i) $(-63) \div (-7)$
    (j) $\frac{11 - (-14)}{(-5)}$
    (k) $-3(-10 - (-8))$

11. Solve the following equations :–

    (a) $3x + 14 = 2$
    (b) $1 - 4x = -19$
    (c) $5x - 5 = 5$
    (d) $10 - x = x$

12. How long is it from :–

    (a) 9·55 am to 12·37 pm
    (b) 1547 to 1702 ?

13. Change to hours and minutes :–   (a) 0·3 hours   (b) 2·45 hours   (c) $1\frac{2}{3}$ hours.

Adding and Subtracting Integers

* **Positive** and **Negative** whole numbers, along with **Zero** are called the set of **INTEGERS**.

A thermometer is an extremely useful way of looking at integers and it can also be useful in helping with integer calculations.

Example 1 :- To find $(-2) + 5$ =>
- picture the **first** number, (-2)
- then move (**up**) by 5 => $\boxed{3}$

Example 2 :- To find $5 - 9$ =>
- picture the **first** number, (5)
- then move (**down**) by 9 => $\boxed{-4}$

Example 3 :- To find $2 + (-7)$ =>
- picture the **first** number, (2)
- then move (**down**) by 7 => $\boxed{-5}$

Example 4 :- To find $(-1) + (-4)$ =>
- picture the **first** number, (-1)
- then move (**down**) by 4 => $\boxed{-5}$

Example 5 :- Similarly, in Algebra, ...
To find $4x + (-9x)$ =>
- picture the **first** term, $(4x)$
- then move (**down**) by $9x$ => $\boxed{-5x}$

10°C

5°C

0°C   +5

3

−2

−5°C

−10°C

Exercise 7·1

1. Write down each question first, then the answer.

(a) $7 + 12$ (b) $18 + 19$

(c) $0 + 52$ (d) $9 + (-6)$

(e) $5 + (-1)$ (f) $8 + (-8)$

(g) $3 + (-8)$ (h) $4 + (-14)$

(i) $0 + (-16)$ (j) $(-4) + 13$

(k) $(-7) + 7$ (l) $(-2) + 13$

(m) $(-8) + 7$ (n) $(-11) + 8$

(o) $4 + (-12)$ (p) $(-7) + (-2)$

(q) $(-10) + (-10)$ (r) $(-15) + (-16)$

(s) $(-18) + 4$ (t) $(-25) + (-12)$

(u) $(-40) + 70$ (v) $(-44) + (-21)$

(w) $20 + (-55)$ (x) $(-1·7) + (-4·3)$

2. Do the following subtractions :-

(a) $14 - 9$ (b) $23 - 23$

(c) $1 - 2$ (d) $4 - 6$

(e) $7 - 10$ (f) $3 - 11$

2. (g) $0 - 17$ (h) $(-1) - 6$

(i) $(-8) - 3$ (j) $(-12) - 8$

(k) $(-1) - 16$ (l) $0 - 43$

(m) $17 - 37$ (n) $(-12) - 15$

(o) $200 - 700$ (p) $(-62) - 18$

(q) $0 - 65$ (r) $(-14) - 14$

(s) $3 - 21$ (t) $(-15) - 40$

(u) $(-3) - 3$ (v) $(-67) - 23$

3. Set down and calculate the following :-

(a) $7 - 12$ (b) $5 - 13$

(c) $(-3) + 12$ (d) $(-6) - 7$

(e) $5 - 17$ (f) $(-3) - 14$

(g) $(-20) - 35 + 15$ (h) $(-17) - 13 + 20$

(i) $(-20) + 35 - 5$ (j) $(-10) + 9 - 2$

(k) $(-24) + 24 - 1$ (l) $32 - 52 + 20$

(m) $(-104) + 102 - 1$ (n) $102 - 104 + 1$

4. Copy each question, then write down the answer.

   (a) $3x + 7x$ (b) $2x + (-7x)$ (c) $4a - a$ (d) $(-a) + 4a$

   (e) $(-y) + (-3y)$ (f) $(-2y) - 7y$ (g) $7m - 9m$ (h) $(-12m) + 15m$

   (i) $0 - 4p$ (j) $(-4p) - 4p$ (k) $(-4p) + 4p$ (l) $(-6x) - 6x + 6x$

   (m) $3x + 7x - 4x$ (n) $3x + (-6x) + x$ (o) $(-3x) - 8x + 9x$ (p) $(-4x) - 4x - 4x$

   (q) $4a - 2b + a - b$ (r) $6a + 2b - a - 3b$ (s) $(-a) - 5b + 6a + b$ (t) $(-3a) - 7b - 7a - 3b$

5. Write down the **value** of each expression by replacing the letters x and y with their **stated** values.

   (a) $5 - x$, $x = 8$ (b) $11 + x$, $x = -6$ (c) $y - 7$, $y = -3$

   (d) $7 - y$, $y = 13$ (e) $(-9) + x$, $x = 17$ (f) $(-x) + 3$, $x = 1$

   (g) $x - y$, $x = -10$, $y = 2$ (h) $x + y$, $x = 7$, $y = -12$ (i) $y - x$, $y = -1$, $x = 9$.

6. George is flying his kite from his bedroom window.

   The height h metres of a kite above the window ledge, after t seconds,

   is given by the formula :- $h = t - 10$.

   (a) Calculate the height after :-   (i) 20 seconds   (ii) 10 seconds   (iii) 5 seconds.

   (b) Explain (in words) the meaning of each answer.

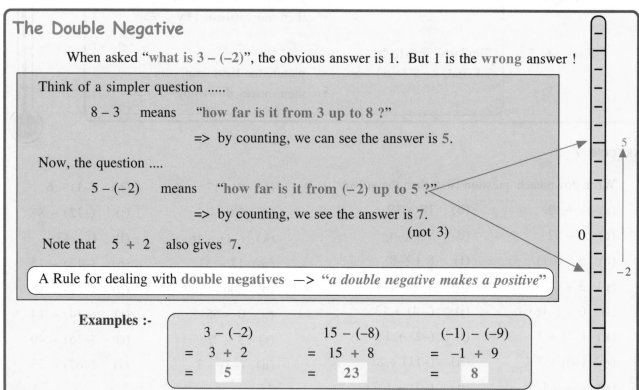

The Double Negative

When asked "what is $3 - (-2)$", the obvious answer is 1. But 1 is the **wrong** answer !

Think of a simpler question .....

   $8 - 3$ means   "how far is it from 3 up to 8 ?"

   => by counting, we can see the answer is 5.

Now, the question ....

   $5 - (-2)$ means   "how far is it from (-2) up to 5 ?"

   => by counting, we see the answer is 7.
                                          (not 3)

Note that $5 + 2$ also gives **7**.

A Rule for dealing with **double negatives** —> *"a double negative makes a positive"*

Examples :-

   $3 - (-2)$ $15 - (-8)$ $(-1) - (-9)$

   $= 3 + 2$ $= 15 + 8$ $= -1 + 9$

   $= \boxed{5}$ $= \boxed{23}$ $= \boxed{8}$

Exercise 7·2

1. Copy and complete the following :-

   (a) $4 - (-1)$ (b) $6 - (-8)$
        $= 4 + 1$ $= 6 + 8$
        $=$ .... $=$ ....

   (c) $7 - (-3)$ (d) $25 - (-10)$
        $= 7 + ...$ $= ... + ...$
        $=$ .... $=$ ....

2. Show two steps in obtaining the answer to :-

   (a) $(-4) - (-3)$ (b) $(-8) - (-9)$

   (c) $(-5) - (-2)$ (d) $(-6) - (-13)$

   (e) $(-10) - (-15)$ (f) $(-13) - (-7)$

   (g) $(-2·5) - (-3·5)$ (h) $(-0·6) - (-1·4)$

   (i) $(-7) - (-7)$ (j) $(-40) - (-41)$

   (k) $(-40) - (-39)$ (l) $(-39) - (-40)$

3. Simplify these algebraic expressions :-

(a) $4x - (-2x)$ (b) $7x - (-9x)$

(c) $0 - (-8x)$ (d) $3p - (-5p)$

(e) $7q - (-10q)$ (f) $5m - (-12m)$

(g) $9y - (-14y)$ (h) $30y - (-10y)$

(i) $(-2x) - (-7x)$ (j) $(-3k) - (-8k)$

(k) $(-7g) - (-7g)$ (l) $(-w) - (-2w)$

(m) $(-6n) - n$ (n) $(-6a) - (-11a)$

(o) $(-x) - (-5x)$ (p) $(-7b) - (-7b)$

4. **A Mixture.** Simplify :-

(a) $(-1) + 7$ (b) $(-3) - 8$

(c) $2 - (-5)$ (d) $(-14) + 17$

(e) $(-25) + 25$ (f) $3 - 17$

(g) $0 - 12$ (h) $(-7x) + 15x$

(i) $8a - (-14a)$ (j) $(-3) - (-9)$

(k) $6 - (-6)$ (l) $(-32b) + 52b$

(m) $5x - (-6x)$ (n) $(-2p) + 9p$

(o) $14a - (-a)$ (p) $(-3t) - 11t$

(q) $c - (-c)$ (r) $0 - (-21e)$

(s) $103 - (-98)$ (t) $24f - 84f$

(u) $(-7t^2) + 15t^2$ (v) $(-7t^2) - 15t^2$

(w) $(-5000) + 4900$ (x) $(-7\tfrac{1}{4}) - 9\tfrac{1}{4}$

5. In this question, $a = -1$, $b = -3$ and $c = -5$.
Determine the value of :-

(a) $a + b$ (b) $a - b$

(c) $b - c$ (d) $b + c$

(e) $a - c$ (f) $c + a$

6. Replace the letters in each expression with their stated values and evaluate the expression :-

(a) $7 - x$, $x = 9$ (b) $9 + y$, $y = -3$

(c) $15 - z$, $z = -7$ (d) $d - 3$, $d = -6$

(e) $g + 8$, $g = -4$ (f) $-w + 4$, $w = 4$

(g) $7 - k$, $k = 8$ (h) $-2 - x$, $x = -3$

(i) $a + b$, $a = -6$, $b = -1$

(j) $c - d$, $c = -6$, $d = -1$

(k) $h - j$, $h = -2$, $j = -7$

(l) $-k - m$, $k = -1$, $m = -4$

7. Simplify :-

(a) $5a + 4a + a$ (b) $7c - 5c - c$

(c) $p + 2p - 3p$ (d) $4w + 4w - (-4w)$

(e) $(-g) - g - g$ (f) $(-m) - m - (-m)$

(g) $x + 2x + y - 2y$ (h) $3p - p + q - 4q$

(i) $2a + b - (-2a) - b$ (j) $p^2 - p + p^2 - (-p)$

(k) $x^2 - (-4y^2) + z^2 - (-x^2) + y^2 - (-6z^2)$

Multiplication and Division of Integers

Since $3 \times 7 = 21$, then obviously $3 \times (-7)$ **cannot** also be 21.

$3 \times (-7)$ means "3 lots of -7" = -21

Examples :-

$4 \times (-2)$ =	-8	$6 \times (-8)$ =	-48
$(-10) \times 7$ =	-70	$(-9) \times 9$ =	-81

Similarly :-   Since $24 \div 6 = 4$, then obviously $(-24) \div 6$ **cannot** also be 4.

$(-24) \div 6$ = "-24 shared by 6" = -4.

Also $18 \div (-6) = -3$ and $36 \div (-2) = -18$

> If you **multiply** or **divide** two integers, where one of them is **positive** and one of them is **negative** => the answer is always **negative**.

Examples :-

$(-8) \div 2$ =	-4	$(-36) \div 9$ =	-4
$80 \div (-8)$ =	-10	$63 \div (-7)$ =	-9

1.   Write down each of the following and find the answers :–

(a) 2 × (–5)   (b) 7 × (–7)   (c) 3 × (–9)   (d) 5 × (–5)

(e) (–8) × 4   (f) (–9) × 5   (g) (–11) × 6   (h) (–10) × 3

(i) 7 × (–8)   (j) 8 × (–1)   (k) 4 × (–11)   (l) 7 × (–9)

(m) 4 × (–2a)   (n) (–5y) × 4   (o) (–2p) × 10   (p) 5x × (–9x)

(q) (–20) ÷ 2   (r) (–27) ÷ 3   (s) (–42) ÷ 6   (t) (–35) ÷ 5

(u) (–36) ÷ 9   (v) (–42) ÷ 7   (w) (–64) ÷ 8   (x) (–20a) ÷ 10

2.   Simplify, by doing the calculation in the brackets first :-

(a) (5 × 10) ÷ 2   (b) (4 × (–10)) ÷ 5   (c) 8 × (–1) × 3   (d) (–8) × 5 ÷ 4

(e) (8 + (–1)) × 3   (f) 9 × (3 – 8)   (g) ((–5) – 7) ÷ 3   (h) (10 – 7) × (–9)

(i) ((–2) – 8) × 7   (j) (3 + (–12)) ÷ 9   (k) ((–12) – 9) ÷ 7   (l) ((–19) – 20) ÷ 3

Multiplication and Division – the Double Negative

=>   **Remember :-**   since 3 × (–5) = –15 => (–3) × (–5) **cannot** also be –15 !

=>   the only other possiblilty is that   (–3) × (–5) = 15   (i.e. +15)

RULE 1:-   "when **two negatives** are **multiplied** => the answer is **positive**"

Examples :-   (–2) × (–5) = 10   (–7) × (–6) = 42   (–9) × (–10) = 90

RULE 2:-   "when **two negatives** are **divided** => the answer is **positive**"

Examples :-   (–14) ÷ (–2) = 7   (–35) ÷ (–7) = 5   (–72) ÷ (–8) = 9

3.   Find :-

(a) (–2) × (–8)   (b) (–3) × (–4)   (c) (–9) × (–6)   (d) (–8) × (–7)

(e) (–4) × (–10)   (f) (–9) × (–9)   (g) (–1) × (–17)   (h) (–10) × (–3)

(i) (–1) × (–1)   (j) (–30) × (–3)   (k) (–5) × (–50)   (l) (–200) × (–10)

(m) (–20) ÷ (–4)   (n) (–18) ÷ (–2)   (o) (–32) ÷ (–8)   (p) (–55) ÷ (–11)

(q) (–54) ÷ (–9)   (r) (–42) ÷ (–6)   (s) (–60) ÷ (–6)   (t) (–120) ÷ (–4)

(u) (–91) ÷ (–7)   (v) (–240) ÷ (–6)   (w) (–800) ÷ (–10)   (x) (–213) ÷ (–3)

4. Simplify :-

(a) $(3 \times (-12)) \div 9$

(b) $((-2) \times (-8)) \div 4$

(c) $7 \times (-2) \times (-5)$

(d) $4 \times (-7) \div (-14)$

(e) $(-9) \times (-4) \div (-12)$

(f) $(-7) \times 8 \div (-28)$

(g) $(3 + (-8)) \times (-4)$

(h) $(-9) \times (3 - 8)$

(i) $((-17) + (-1)) \div (-3)$

(j) $(-6) \times (-3) \times (-2)$

(k) $(-3a) \times (-7a)$

(l) $(-4p) \times (-5p) \times (-2p)$

(m) $(-4)^2$

(n) $(-7)^2$

(o) $(-10y)^2$

(p) $10 \times (-1)^2$

(q) $(-1)^3$

(r) $(-2)^4$

(s) $(-2)^3 + (-3)^2$

(t) $(-1)^4 - (-1)^3$

(u) $(-x)^2 - (-x)^2$

(v) $(-3p) - (-5p)$

(w) $(-8a) - (-8a)$

(x) $3ab - (-7ab)$

5. $w = 2$, $x = 0$ and $y = -3$. Calculate the values of the following :-

(a) wxy

(b) $w + x + y$

(c) $w^2 + x^2 + y^2$

(d) $wx + xy + yw$

(e) $w + x - y$

(f) $2w^2 + 2y^2$

(g) $w^3 + y^3$

(h) $3w^2 - y^2$

(i) $(w + y)(w - y)$

(j) $(w - y)^2$

(k) $(wxy)^2$

(l) $(-3w) \div y$

6. Simplify the following expressions :-

(a) $a \times b$

(b) $a \times (-b)$

(c) $(-a) \times b$

(d) $(-b) \times (-a)$

(e) $y \times y$

(f) $2y \times 3y$

(g) $(5x)^2$

(h) $p \times p^2$

(i) $(-w)^2$

(j) $(-2t) \times (-20t)$

(k) $(xy)^2$

(l) $w^2 \times y^2$

(m) $-w^2 \times y^2$

(n) $25p \div 5p$

(o) $25a \div (-5a)$

(p) $12ab \div (-2a)$

(q) $(-12a^2) \div 6a$

(r) $(-xy) \div (-y)$

7. Vorgin Rail calculates its profit (£P) per journey by using the formula :-

$$P = 50n - 3000$$

n is the number of passengers on the train.

(a) What is the profit when there are 100 passengers on a Vorgin Rail train ?

(b) Comment on the company's profit when only 20 passengers are on a train.

(c) How many passengers does Vorgin need on a train to "break even" ?

Remember Remember.....?

1. Simplify :–

   (a) $6 + (-7)$ (b) $(-8) + (-10)$ (c) $(-17) + (21)$ (d) $30 - 75$

   (e) $(-8) - 9$ (f) $(-12) - 1$ (g) $(-12) - 15 - 6$ (h) $(-3) + 9 + 6$

   (i) $7 - 12 - 5$ (j) $(-3) + (-2) + 10$ (k) $103 + 109 - 2$ (l) $(-200) - 400 - 10$

2. Simplify these algebraic expressions :-

   (a) $4x + 9x$ (b) $x + (-6x)$ (c) $8a - a$ (d) $(-y) + 7y$

   (e) $(-3b) - 5b$ (f) $(-8e) + 17e$ (g) $(-5m) - 5m$ (h) $(-2x) - 5x + 9x$

   (i) $2x + 9x - 10x$ (j) $5c + (-8c) + 2c$ (k) $(-7w) - 7w - 7w$ (l) $5a + 7b - a - 2b$

3. If $x = 6$ and $y = -4$, write down the value of :-

   (a) $3 - x$ (b) $7 + y$ (c) $x - 14$ (d) $y + 20$

   (e) $(-x) + 15$ (f) $(-x) + y$ (g) $x + y$ (h) $y - x$

4. Simplify :–

   (a) $7 - (-1)$ (b) $17 - (-3)$ (c) $(-4) - (-6)$ (d) $(-7) - (-1)$

   (e) $(-9) - (-10)$ (f) $(-15) - (-15)$ (g) $5x - (-3x)$ (h) $0 - (-11x)$

   (i) $(-4x) - (-5x)$ (j) $(-9x) - (-x)$ (k) $-(-4x) - (-x)$ (l) $(-8x^2) - (-8x^2)$

5. $p = -2$, $q = -1$ and $r = -3$. Find the value of :-

   (a) $p + q$ (b) $p - q$ (c) $q - r$ (d) $q + r$

   (e) $p - r$ (f) $r + p$ (g) $(-p) - r$ (h) $-(-r) + q$

6. Work out the answers to the following :–

   (a) $3 \times (-3)$ (b) $(-7) \times 5$ (c) $9 \times (-1)$ (d) $(-20) \times 0$

   (e) $5 \times (-2a)$ (f) $(-7y) \times 3$ (g) $2x \times (-3x)$ (h) $(-40) \div 4$

   (i) $(-50x) \div 5$ (j) $(-18p) \div 9$ (k) $(-15m) \div 3m$ (l) $7 \times (-1) \times 4$

   (m) $((-5) - 1) \times 8$ (n) $((-17) - 13) \div 3$ (o) $(-7) \times (-10)$ (p) $(-40) \times (-5)$

   (q) $(-35) \div (-7)$ (r) $(-90) \div (-9)$ (s) $5 \times (-2) \times (-4)$ (t) $((-19) + (-9)) \div (-7)$

   (u) $(-2a) \times (-6a)$ (v) $(-7)^2$ (w) $(-2)^6$ (x) $(-4)^2 - (-2)^3$

7. $a = 5$, $b = 0$ and $c = -2$. Calculate the values of :-

   (a) abc (b) $a + b + c$ (c) $a^2 + b^2 + c^2$

   (d) $ab + bc + ca$ (e) $a^2 + b - c$ (f) $4a^2 + 2c^2$

   (g) $a^3 + c^3$ (h) $a^2 - 5c^2$ (i) $(a + c)(c - a)$

Revision - Areas

The formulae for calculating the **areas** of quadrilaterals, circles and triangles should already be known :-

SQUARE	RECTANGLE	RHOMBUS	KITE
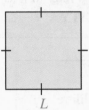	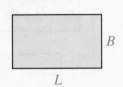	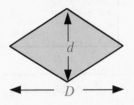	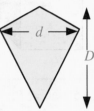
Area $= L^2$	Area $= L \times B$	Area $= \frac{1}{2}D \times d$	Area $= \frac{1}{2}D \times d$

PARALLELOGRAM	TRIANGLE	CIRCLE	TRAPEZIUM
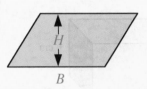	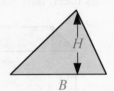		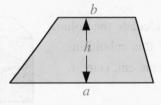
Area $= B \times H$	Area $= \frac{1}{2}B \times H$	Area $= \pi r^2$	Area $= \frac{1}{2}h(a + b)$

Exercise 8·1

1. Use the appropriate formula from the above to calculate the **areas** of the following figures :-

(a)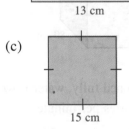
13 cm

(b) 6 cm, 5 cm (circle)

(c)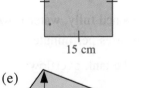
15 cm

(d) 8 cm, 17 cm (rhombus)

(e)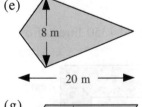
8 m, 20 m

(f) 11 mm, 14 mm (triangle)

(g)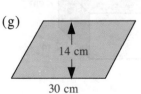
14 cm, 30 cm

(h)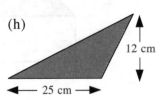
12 cm, 25 cm

2. Calculate the **area** of each figure by splitting it into shapes whose areas you can find easily :-

(a) 9 cm, 10 cm, 7 cm, 16 cm

(b) 12 cm, 6 cm, 7 cm, 4 cm, 4 cm

(c) 9 cm, 5 cm, 8 cm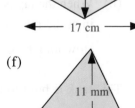

(d) 11 cm, 15 cm, 7 cm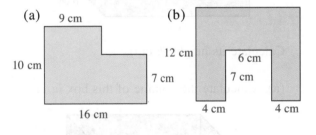

(e) 6 cm, 6 cm, 20 cm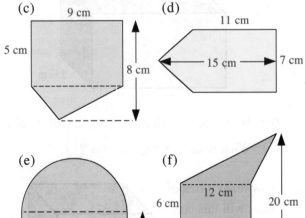

(f) 12 cm, 20 cm, 6 cm

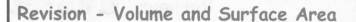

Revision - Volume and Surface Area

The formulae for calculating the **volume** and **surface area** of a cube and cuboid should already be known.

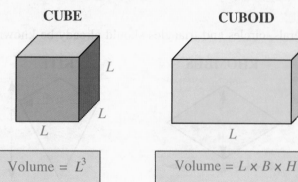

CUBE

Volume = L^3

S.A. = $6 \times L^2$

CUBOID

Volume = $L \times B \times H$

S.A. = $2(LB + LH + BH)$

CAPACITY

When you talk about the volume of a **liquid** quantity, you refer to it as its **CAPACITY**.

NOTE

$1 \text{ cm}^3 = 1$ millilitre (ml)

$1000 \text{ ml} = 1$ **litre**

Exercise 8·2

1. Calculate the volume of this cuboid in cubic cm, (cm^3).

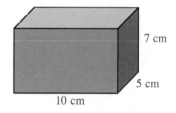

7 cm
5 cm
10 cm

2. The volume of this shallow block is 126 cm^3.

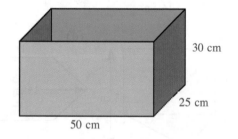

h cm
6 cm
7 cm

Calculate its height (*h* cm).

3. (a) Calculate the volume of this box in cm^3.

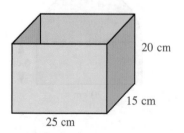

30 cm
25 cm
50 cm

(b) How many millilitres of liquid will it hold ?

(c) What is its **capacity** in litres ?

4. How many litres of water will this box hold when it is only **half** full ?

20 cm
15 cm
25 cm

5. This metal tank holds 67·2 litres when full.

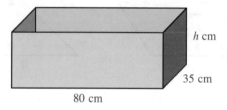

h cm
35 cm
80 cm

(a) How many millilitres is this ?

(b) Calculate the height, *h* cm, of the tank.

6. (a) Calculate the volume of this tank in cm^3.

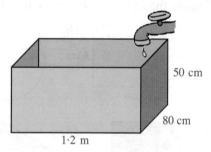

50 cm
80 cm
1·2 m

(b) When the tap is opened fully, water flows in at the rate of 6 litres per minute.

How long before the tank overflows ?

7. This tank is built to hold 1350 litres of oil.

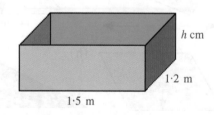

h cm
1·2 m
1·5 m

Calculate the height of the tank.

8. Shown is a cube with each of its sides 1 metre, or 100 cm long.

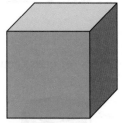

1 metre = 100 cm

(a) Calculate its volume in cubic metres (m^3).

(b) Now, calculate its volume in cm^3. (100 × 100 × ...).

(c) Hence, copy and complete the statement :-

$$1\,m^3 = \ldots\ldots\ldots cm^3.$$

9. A cube measures 200 cm by 200 cm by 200 cm.

(a) Calculate its volume in cm^3.

(b) Now write down its volume in m^3.

10. Calculate the volume of this concrete block in both cubic centimetres and cubic metres.

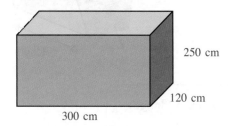

250 cm

120 cm

300 cm

11. This "podium" is created using concrete.

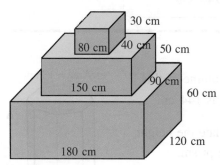

30 cm

80 cm   40 cm   50 cm

150 cm

90 cm

60 cm

180 cm

120 cm

(a) Calculate the total volume in cm^3.

(b) How many cubic **metres** of concrete were used to make the podium ?

12. Look at this cuboid.

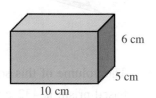

6 cm

5 cm

10 cm

(a) Calculate the area of its front face.

(b) By calculating the area of each of its other 5 faces, write down the **total surface area** of the cuboid.

13. This cuboid measures 15 cm by 12 cm by 8 cm.

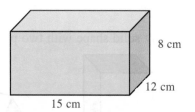

8 cm

12 cm

15 cm

Calculate its total surface area in cm^2.

14. Use the formula :-

S.A. = 2(LB + LH + BH),

to calculate the surface area of this cuboid.

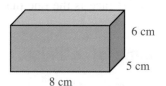

6 cm

5 cm

8 cm

15. This metal box is made from aluminium sheeting.

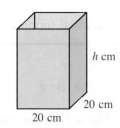

12 cm

10 cm

25 cm

The sheeting costs 3·2p per cm^2 to produce.

(a) Calculate the total surface area.

(b) Calculate the cost of the aluminium sheeting needed to make it.

16. An open topped metal container is to be manufactured to hold exactly **12 litres** of oil.

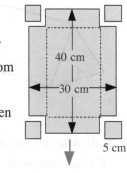

h cm

20 cm

20 cm

(a) Calculate the height of the metal box.

(b) Calculate the area of sheet metal which would be required to make the (open topped) container.

17. From a rectangular piece of card measuring 30 cm by 40 cm, four squares of side 5 cm are removed from the corners.

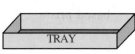

40 cm

30 cm

5 cm

The remaining piece is then folded and glued to make the shallow tray shown.

Calculate both the volume and the surface area of the tray.

TRAY

Prisms

A **PRISM** is any solid shape with two parallel **congruent** faces (or ends) generally in the shape of polygons.

Examples :-

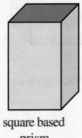

square based
prism

triangular
prism

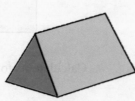

hexagonal based
prism

pentagonal
prism

The **RED** face is the one that runs right through the shape, (top to bottom, left to right or front to back).

Volume of a Prism

It is very easy to calculate the volume of a prism, as long as you know the **area** of the **congruent** face.

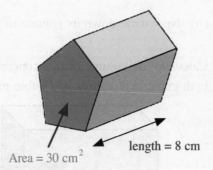

> **VOLUME** (prism) = **Area** (of end face) **× length**
> **or**
> **VOLUME** (prism) = **Area** (of base) **× height**

length = 8 cm

Area = 30 cm²

For this pentagonal prism,

$$\begin{aligned} \text{Volume} &= \text{Area} \times \text{length} \\ &= 30 \text{ cm}^2 \times 8 \text{ cm} \\ &= \boxed{240 \text{ cm}^3} \end{aligned}$$

* The usual formula is :- $\boxed{V = A \times h}$

Exercise 8·3

1. The area of the top of this square based prism is 24 cm². Its height is 6 cm.

   Calculate its **volume**.

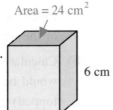

Area = 24 cm²

6 cm

2.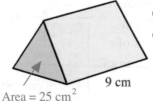

   Area = 25 cm²

   9 cm

   Calculate the volume of this triangular prism.

3. Calculate the volume of this hexagonal based prism.

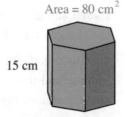

Area = 80 cm²

15 cm

4. The volume of this prism is 144 cm³.

   Calculate the height of the prism.

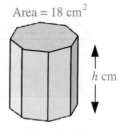

Area = 18 cm²

h cm

5.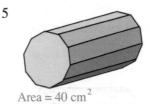

   Area = 40 cm²

   The volume of this prism is 1040 cm³.

   Calculate the length of the prism.

6. The volume of this square based prism is 432 cm³.

   Calculate the length of each **side** of its base.

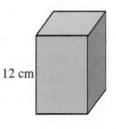

12 cm

7. This is a (right angled) triangular prism.

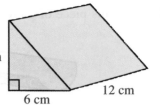

(a) Calculate the **area** of the pink triangular face.

(b) Now calculate the **volume** of the prism.

8.

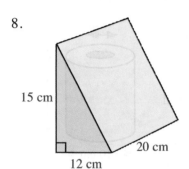

Calculate the volume of this prism in a similar way.

9. The yellow face of this prism is an isosceles triangle.

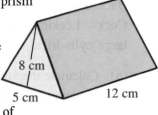

The base of the triangle is 5 cm and its height is 8 cm.

(a) Calculate the area of the yellow triangular face.

(b) Now calculate the **volume** of the prism.

10. The volume of this prism is 510 cm³.

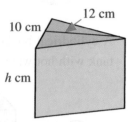

The isosceles triangle on top has base 10 cm and height 12 cm.

Calculate the height of the prism.

A Special Prism - the Cylinder

If the common face of a prism is a **CIRCLE**, then the prism is called a **CYLINDER**, and there is a special formula for calculating its volume.

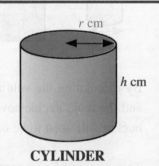

Volume = **Area** (of base) × **height**   => $V = \pi r^2 h$

CYLINDER

Example :-   Calculate the volume of this cylindrical tin can.

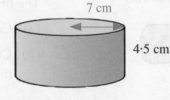

$$V = \pi r^2 h$$
$$V = 3.14 \times 7 \times 7 \times 4.5$$
$$V = 692.37 \text{ cm}^3$$

Exercise 8·4

1. Calculate the **volume** of this cylinder with base radius 8 cm and height 10 cm.

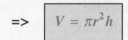

2.

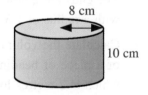

Calculate the volume of this cylinder.

3. The **diameter** of the base of this cylinder is 12 cm.

(a) Write down its radius.

(b) Calculate its volume.

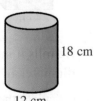

4. These two cylindrical cans are to be filled with soup. Which one will hold more ?

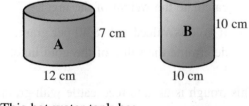

5. This hot water tank has base diameter 60 cm. It is 80 cm tall.

How many **litres** of water will it hold when full.

(*Find volume in ml first*).

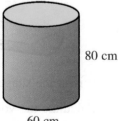

6. Backsters cook up their
   Cock-a-Leekie soup in a
   large cylindrical pot.   50 cm

   (a) Calculate the volume
       of soup if the pot is full.

       40 cm

   (b) Each tin holds $\frac{1}{2}$ litre.

       How many tins can be
       filled from the pot ?

7. A cylindrical bucket is used to fill a rectangular
   tank with hot water.

   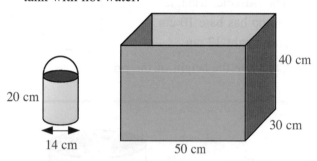

   40 cm

   20 cm

   30 cm

   14 cm   50 cm

   By calculating the volume of both the bucket
   and the tank, decide how many times the
   bucket will need to be used to fill the tank.

8. This section of pipe forms part of a sewer.

   9 cm

   1·5 metres

   How many litres of water will it hold ?

9. This small gold ingot is cylindrical.

   (a) Calculate its volume in cm^3 .   1·5 cm

   (b) If 1 cm^3 of gold weighs 19·3 grams,   1 cm
       calculate the weight of the ingot.

   (c) If gold is valued at £18·40 per gram,
       determine the value of the gold ingot.

10. This trough is used to feed cattle with grain.

    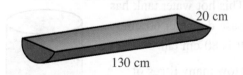

    20 cm

    130 cm

    It is in the shape of a half-cylinder.

    Calculate the volume of grain it can hold.

    (Hint - *find the volume of the whole cylinder*).

11. This piece of gutter is 3·5 metres long.

    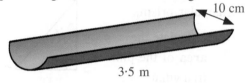

    10 cm

    3·5 m

    If caps are fitted on the ends, how much water
    will the gutter hold when full ? (*in litres*).

12. This toilet roll has a
    hollow cardboard
    tube in its middle.

    Calculate the volume of
    the actual toilet paper
    surrounding the tube.

    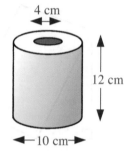

    4 cm

    12 cm

    ←10 cm→

13. This metal block has 4 identical cylindrical holes
    drilled out of it as shown.

    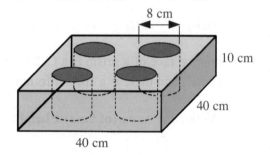

    8 cm

    10 cm

    40 cm

    40 cm

    The **diameter** of each circle is 8 cm.

    (a) Calculate the volume of one of the holes.

    (b) Calculate the volume of the metal block
        remaining after the holes have been drilled.

14. George uses wooden beading as an edging
    round the skirting of his newly laid floor.

    The ends are quarter circles,
    with a radius of 1·5 cm.

    Calculate the volume
    of a piece of beading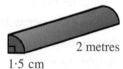
    which is 2 metres long.   1·5 cm   2 metres

15. Timmy has a cube of plasticine of side 4 cm.

    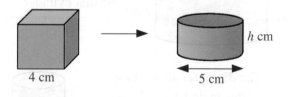

    h cm

    4 cm   5 cm

    He rolls it into a cylinder as shown with a base
    diameter of 5 cm.

    Calculate the **height** (h) of the cylinder formed.

Pyramids and the Cone

A **PYRAMID** is any solid shape with a polygon as its base and triangular sides with a common vertex.

Examples :-

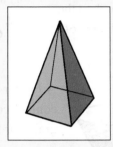

square based
pyramid

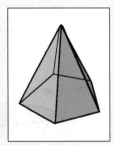

pentagonal based
pyramid

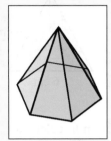

hexagonal based
pyramid

circular based
pyramid

Volume of a Pyramid

It is possible to calculate the volume of a pyramid,
as long as you know the **area** of the base.

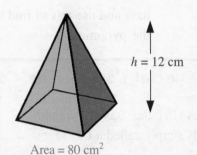

$h = 12$ cm

> **VOLUME** (pyramid) = $\frac{1}{3}$ × **Area** (of base) × **height**

Area = 80 cm^2

For this square based pyramid,

$$
\begin{aligned}
\text{Volume} &= \tfrac{1}{3} \times \text{Area} \times \text{height} \\
&= \tfrac{1}{3} \times 80 \text{ cm}^2 \times 12 \text{ cm} \\
&= \tfrac{1}{3} \times 960 \text{ cm}^3 \;=\; \boxed{320 \text{ cm}^3}
\end{aligned}
$$

Exercise 8·5

1. The area of the base of this
   square based pyramid is 13 cm^2.
   Its height is 9 cm.

   Calculate its **volume**.

   9 cm

   Area = 13 cm^2

2.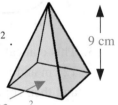

    7·5 cm

    Area = 20 cm^2

    Calculate the volume of this
    triangular based pyramid.

3. Calculate the volume
   of this hexagonal
   based pyramid.

   7·2 cm

   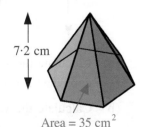

   Area = 35 cm^2

4. The base of this pyramid
   is a square with each
   side 7 cm.

   It is 12 cm tall.

   Calculate its volume.

   12 cm

   7 cm

5. Shown are two cartons used to hold popcorn.

   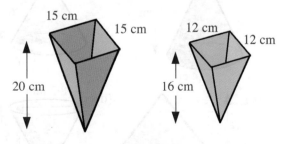

   15 cm

   15 cm

   20 cm

   12 cm

   12 cm

   16 cm

   How much **more** does the big one hold than
   the small one ?

6. The base of this pyramid is an **equilateral triangle** with its sides 6 cm long.

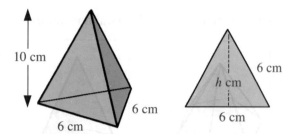

(a) Use Pythagoras' Theorem to calculate the height (h cm) of the equilateral triangle.

(b) Now calculate the area of the triangular base and use this to find the volume of the pyramid.

Special Case - The Cone

A **Circular Based** Pyramid is simply called a **CONE**.

The formula for its volume is :-

$$V = \tfrac{1}{3}\pi r^2 h$$

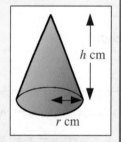

7. The radius of the base of this cone is 5 cm and its height is 9 cm.

Copy and complete :-

Volume $= \tfrac{1}{3}\pi r^2 h$

=> $V = 3\cdot14 \times 5 \times 5 \times 9 \div 3$

=> $V = \dots\dots cm^3$

8. Calculate the volumes of these cones :-

(a)

(b)

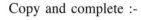

(c)

(d)

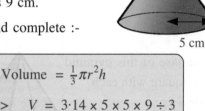

(diameter =) 16 cm

9. The **volume** of this cone is 400 cm³.

(a) Calculate the **area** of its base.

(b) Now calculate the height (h cm) of the cone.

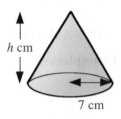

10. 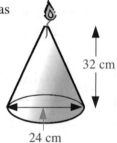 A farmer uses this conical container to hold grain for his cattle.

Calculate the weight of grain in the full container, if 1 m³ of grain weighs 750 kilograms.

11. This glass conical oil lamp has a base **diameter** of 24 cm and is 32 cm tall.

How many litres of oil will the lamp hold when full ?

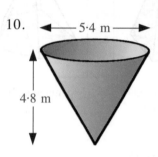

12. 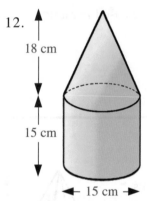 This shape consists of a conical tower on top of a cylindrical base.

By calculating the volume of base and top, determine the volume of the whole shape.

13. This conical paper cup has a top diameter of 12 cm and is 16 cm tall. It was filled with water and then some of the water was poured out.

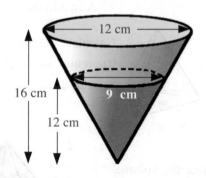

(a) Calculate the volume of water in the paper cup when it was full.

(b) Calculate the volume of water poured out.

Curved Surface Area of a Cylinder

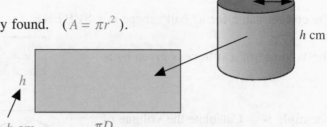

The top of a cylinder is a circle and its area is easily found. ($A = \pi r^2$).

The **curved** bit is more difficult :-

Imagine the "label" of a tin of soup cut
and opened out to reveal - a **rectangle**.

- The "breadth" of the rectangle this time is h cm.

- The "length" is in fact the **circumference** of the top circle => $L = \pi D$ (can you see this ?)

    => This means that the **curved surface area** is given by :- $C.S.A. = \pi Dh$

    => (nearly there !) - Since $D = 2 \times r$, => $\boxed{C.S.A. = 2\pi rh}$ is the formula used.

Example :- Find the curved surface
area of this cylinder :-

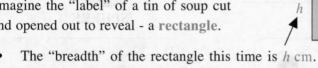

$$C.S.A. = 2\pi rh$$
$$=> C.S.A. = 2 \times 3 \cdot 14 \times 7 \times 5$$
$$=> C.S.A. = \boxed{219 \cdot 8 \text{ cm}^2}$$

Exercise 8·6

1. Calculate the C.S.A.
   of this cylinder with
   base radius 8 cm and
   height 10 cm.

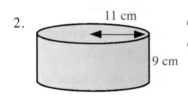

2. 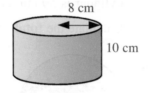 Calculate the C.S.A.
   of this cylinder.

3. The **diameter** of the base
   of this cylinder is 40 cm.

   (a) Write down its radius.

   (b) Calculate its C.S.A.

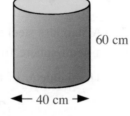

4. 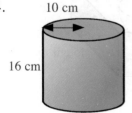 This cylinder has top radius
   10 cm and height 16 cm.

   (a) Calculate the area of
       the **top** surface.

   (b) Calculate the C.S.A.
       of the cylinder.

   (c) Now calculate the **Total Surface Area** of
       the cylinder. (*top, bottom and curved bit*).

5. Which of these two cylinders has the larger **total**
   surface area (T.S.A.) ?

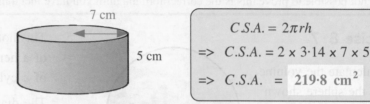

6. This **open topped** can is made
   out of aluminium sheeting.

   Calculate the area of
   aluminium sheeting
   needed to make it.

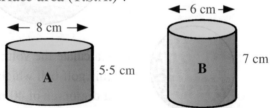

7. A paddling pool is made out of rigid plastic.

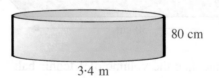

   Calculate the total area of plastic required.

8. (Hard) This is
   the label off a
   tin of soup.

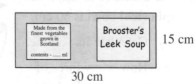

   Calculate the **volume** of the tin of soup.

Volume of a Sphere

The correct name for a "ball" shape is a **SPHERE**.

The volume* of a sphere is given by :-

$$V = \frac{4}{3}\pi r^3$$

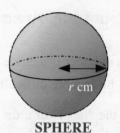

SPHERE

Example :- Calculate the volume of this football which has a **diameter** of 30 cm.

30 cm

$D = 30$ cm $\Rightarrow r = 15$ cm

$V = \frac{4}{3}\pi r^3$

note

$V = 4 \times 3{\cdot}14 \times 15 \times 15 \times 15 \div 3$

$V = \boxed{14\ 130\ \text{cm}^3}$

* It is not possible to prove this is the correct formula until you have met a mathematical topic called Integral Calculus.

Exercise 8·7

1. Calculate the volume of the sphere shown with radius 12 cm.

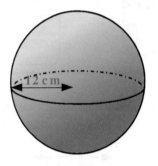

12 cm

2.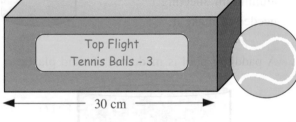

Calculate the volume of this golf ball which has a **diameter** of 40 mm.

3. This box is **tightly packed** with 3 tennis balls.

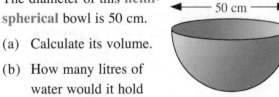

Top Flight
Tennis Balls - 3

30 cm

Calculate the volume of 1 tennis ball.

4. The diameter of this **hemi-spherical** bowl is 50 cm.

50 cm

(a) Calculate its volume.

(b) How many litres of water would it hold when full ?

5. This hot water tank consists of a hemi-sphere on top of a cylinder.

The diameter of both the cylinder and hemi-sphere is 60 cm and the cylinder is 50 cm tall.

Calculate the **total** volume.

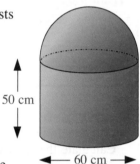

50 cm

60 cm

6. This large metal shape is used to advertise Monty's Ice-Cream Shop.

36 cm

42 cm

It consists of a hemi-sphere on top of a cone.

Calculate the volume of the metal shape.

7. A stainless steel ashtray is made by drilling out a hemi-sphere from a square based cuboid.

The diameter of the hemi-sphere is 8 cm.

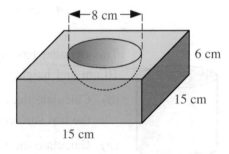

8 cm

6 cm

15 cm

15 cm

(a) Calculate the volume of the ashtray.

(b) Calculate the weight of the ashtray given 1 cm^3 of stainless steel weighs 8·03 grams.

Remember Remember.....?

1. For the cuboid shown below, calculate its

   (a) volume

   (b) surface area.

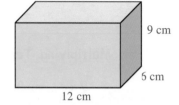

9 cm

6 cm

12 cm

2.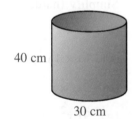

   30 cm

   80 cm

   1·2 m

   How many **litres** will this tank hold when full?

3. Calculate the volume of each of these prisms :-

   (a) Area = 55 cm²

   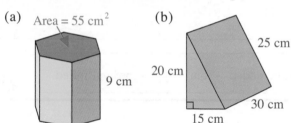

   9 cm

   (b)

   25 cm

   20 cm

   15 cm

   30 cm

4. Calculate the volume of this tank in cm³ and write down its **capacity** in litres.

   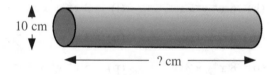

   40 cm

   30 cm

5. When this pipe is filled with oil, it holds 5 litres.

   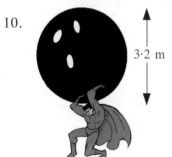

   10 cm

   ? cm

   (a) How many millilitres is this ?

   (b) Calculate what the pipe length must be.

6. Calculate the volume of each of these pyramids.

   (a)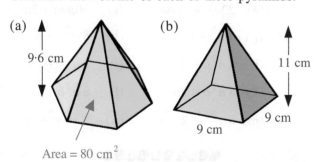

   9·6 cm

   Area = 80 cm²

   (b)

   11 cm

   9 cm

   9 cm

7. 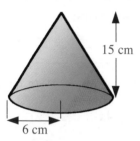 Calculate the volume of this cone.

   15 cm

   6 cm

8. This shape is formed from a cone and a cylinder.

   Calculate its volume.

   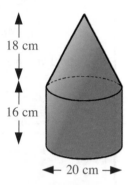

   18 cm

   16 cm

   20 cm

9. For the metal cylinder shown below, calculate :-

   (a) the area of the top

   (b) the curved surface area

   (c) the total surface area.

   14 cm

   12 cm

10.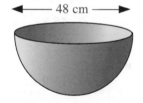

    3·2 m

    This statue is used to advertise "Townend Bowling Club".

    Calculate the volume of the sphere used in the sign.

11. Calculate the **capacity** (in litres), of this bowl.

    48 cm

12.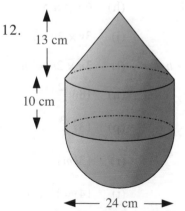

    13 cm

    10 cm

    24 cm

    This shape consists of a cone on top of a cylinder on top of a hemi-sphere.

    Calculate the **total** volume of the shape.

Multiplication in Algebra

Examples :-

Collecting Like Terms (a reminder)	Multiplying Terms

$x + x + x + x \quad = \quad 4x$

$7a - 4a \quad = \quad 3a$

$6p + q - p + 8q \quad = \quad 5p + 9q \quad$ (NOT $= 14pq$)

$10 + 2m - 6 \quad = \quad 4 + 2m \quad$ (NOT $= 6m$)

$b^2 + b^2 + b^2 \quad = \quad 3b^2 \quad$ (NOT b^6)

$9 \times c \quad = \quad 9c$

$a \times 3 \quad = \quad 3a$

$x \times x \quad = \quad x^2 \quad$ (NOT $2x$)

$5p \times 6p \quad = \quad 30p^2 \quad$ (NOT $30p$)

$2m \times 5n \quad = \quad 10mn$

$5a^2b \times 4ab \quad = \quad 5 \times a \times a \times b \times 4 \times a \times b$

$= \quad 20a^3b^2$

Note :- "unlike" terms, like $2x$ and $3y$, **cannot** be added - but they **can** be multiplied.

Exercise 9·1 - Revision Work

1. Simplify by collecting like terms :-

(a) $3m + 9m$

(b) $p + p - p + p$

(c) $5x + x + 7x + x$

(d) $3b + c - b + 6c$

(e) $v + w + v - w$

(f) $5g - 2r + 5g - r$

(g) $9a^2 + h^2 - 8a^2 - 2h^2$

(h) $x^2 - 5y^2 + 3x^2 + 5y^2 - 4x^2$

2. Simplify by multiplying :-

(a) $15 \times c$

(b) $u \times 18$

(c) $t \times t$

(d) $p \times p \times 6$

(e) $s \times 9 \times s$

(f) $3y \times 2k$

(g) $18 \times c \times 4$

(h) $6 \times p \times 5$

(i) $6a \times 9a$

(j) $3v \times 2v \times 7$

(k) $3 \times h \times h \times h$

(l) $3n \times 2n \times 8n$

(m) $3p \times 5p$

(n) $(8w)^2$

(o) $(2k)^3$

(p) $(3f)^3$

(q) $(2xy)^2$

(r) $(3km)^3$

(s) $(2mn)^4$

(t) $(4vw)^2 \times vw$

3. Simplify (harder) :-

(a) $4x \times 2y$

(b) $5x^2 \times 3y$

(c) $6x \times 4y^2$

(d) $7xy \times y$

(e) $2xy \times x$

(f) $8x^2y \times x$

(g) $9xy^2 \times y$

(h) $3x^2y \times x^2$

(i) $12x^2y \times y^2$

(j) $10x^2y^2 \times y$

(k) $6x^2y^2 \times x$

(l) $3x^2y^2 \times xy$

(m) $4xy \times 4xy$

(n) $3x^2y \times 2xy^2$

(o) $8x^2y \times 3xy$

(p) $5x^2y^2 \times 2x^2y^2$

4. Try these divisions :-

(a) $12b \div b$

(b) $30c \div 10c$

(c) $16pq \div 8p$

(d) $3gh \div h$

(e) $22vw \div 11vw$

(f) $30lmn \div 3lm$

(g) $4x^2 \div x$

(h) $8a^2b \div b$

(i) $8a^2b \div a$

(j) $8a^2b \div 2a$

(k) $8a^2b \div 2b$

(l) $8a^2b \div 2ab$

(m) $8a^2b \div 2a^2b$

(n) $3x^2y^2 \div xy$

Removing Brackets and Simplifying

Examples :-

1. $3(a + 4)$
$= 3a + 12$

2. $4(2x - 3y)$
$= 8x - 12y$

3. $c(c + 5)$
$= c^2 + 5c$

4. $5m(2m - 7n)$
$= 10\,m^2 - 35mn$

5. $-3(x + 6)$
$= -3x - 18$

6. $-7(y - 1)$
$= -7y - 7 \times -1$
$= -7y + 7$
(Note the double
negative = +ve)

7. $2(x + 3) - 5$
$= 2x + 6 - 5$
$= 2x + 1$

8. $4(3v + 2w) - 7w$
$= 12v + 8w - 7w$
$= 12v + w$

9. $3(x + 5) + 2(x - 3)$
$= 3x + 15 + 2x - 6$
$= 5x + 9$

10. $3(2a + 4) - 3(a - 1)$
$= 6a + 12 - 3a + 3$
$= 3a + 15$

11. $8 - 2(x + 1)$
$= 8 - 2x - 2$ [not $6(x + 1)$!]
$= 6 - 2x$

Exercise 9·2

1. Multiply out the brackets :-

(a) $2(b + 4)$ (b) $5(a + 1)$ (c) $8(d - 6)$ (d) $9(1 - g)$

(e) $3(m + n)$ (f) $7(c - t)$ (g) $11(3 + y)$ (h) $30(x - 5)$

(i) $3(6p + 1)$ (j) $5(3 - 4q)$ (k) $8(11x - 7y)$ (l) $a(b + 7)$

(m) $g(h - 10)$ (n) $x(6 + x)$ (o) $k(3e + 8g)$ (p) $4u(10u - v)$

(q) $3(4a + 7b + 2)$ (r) $9(p + q - 4r)$ (s) $6(3 - 5f - 2g)$ (t) $x(x - y - 9z)$

(u) $-5(a + 1)$ (v) $-x(3 + x)$ (w) $-g(6g - 1)$ (x) $-x(7y - 11x)$

2. Multiply out the brackets and collect like terms :-

(a) $2(q + 4) + 3$ (b) $3(e + 1) + 6$ (c) $5(t + 4) + 2$

(d) $6(u + 2) - 7$ (e) $4(p + 2) - 7$ (f) $3(s + 6) - 20$

(g) $2(f + 4) + 8f$ (h) $9(h + 1) + h$ (i) $4(k + 5) - 3k$

(j) $6(z + 2) - 2z$ (k) $10(5 + c) - 3c$ (l) $7b + 7(b + 2)$

(m) $8m + 9(m - 1)$ (n) $5w + 2(4w + 3)$ (o) $7r + 4(3r - 2)$

(p) $5y + (y - 1)$ (q) $6a + 10(a + 3p)$ (r) $g + 10(5g + 2h)$

(s) $20x + 2(5x - 15y)$ (t) $80v + 10(7v + n)$ (u) $7 + 2(q + 1)$

(v) $8(5w - 3e) - 36w$ (w) $3 + 2(x - 1)$ (x) $12 - 2(x - 5)$

3. Simplify :-

(a) $3(m + 2) + 4(m + 1)$ (b) $5(b + 2) + 2(b + 4)$ (c) $8(c + 1) + 3(c + 6)$

(d) $4(k - 1) + 2(k + 5)$ (e) $6(g - 2) + 3(g + 4)$ (f) $2(a - 6) + 7(a + 2)$

(g) $3(4 + p) + 7(1 - p)$ (h) $9(1 - u) + 3(1 + u)$ (i) $10(2y + 3) + 2(3y - 11)$

(j) $2(8t - 2) + 5(2t + 4)$ (k) $6(4 - 5e) + 7(2 + 4e)$ (l) $3(2x + 4y) + 5(3x - y)$

4. Simplify :-

(a) $5(x + 1) - 2(x + 2)$ (b) $8(x + 2) - 7(x + 2)$ (c) $4(x + 6) - 3(x + 7)$

(d) $4(2x + 1) - 3(x + 2)$ (e) $7(3x + 4) - 4(x + 6)$ (f) $8(x + 3) - 6(x - 1)$

(g) $9(x + 1) - 6(x - 2)$ (h) $10(1 + 2x) - 10(1 - x)$ (i) $2(2 - x) - 6(1 - x)$

(j) $x(x + 1) + 5(x - 1)$ (k) $x(x + 3) - 5(x + 1)$ (l) $x(8x - 2) - 2(3x - 8)$

5. Simplify :-

(a) $9 - 2(y + 4)$ (b) $6 - 6(p - 1)$ (c) $8 - (d - 1)$

(d) $7 + 6(h + 2)$ (e) $2 + 9(2 - c)$ (f) $12 - 2(1 - u)$

(g) $10(b - 2) - 1$ (h) $-2(n - 1) + 8$ (i) $m + 3(m - 20)$

(j) $x - (100 - x)$ (k) $7k - 2(k + 11)$ (l) $4w - 2(1 - 5w)$

Multiplying Out "Double Brackets"

Look at this pair of brackets (double brackets) ---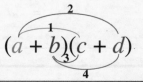

To multiply out the double brackets, follow these steps :-

- multiply the two **first** terms in each bracket $a \times c$ (1)   *write the answer*
- multiply the two **outside** terms in each bracket $a \times d$ (2)   *write the answer*
- multiply the two **inside** terms in each bracket $b \times c$ (3)   *write the answer*
- multiply the two **last** terms in each bracket $b \times d$ (4)   *write the answer*

- Now write your four answers as an expression and **gather like terms** to finish.

$$(a + b)(c + d) = ac + ad + bc + bd$$

Example 1 :-

$(x + 3)(x - 4)$

$= x^2 - 4x + 3x - 12$

$= x^2 - x - 12$

Example 2 :-

$(x - 2)(x - 5)$

$= x^2 - 5x - 2x + 10$

$= x^2 - 7x + 10$

Example 3 :-

$(2x + 1)(x - 3)$

$= 2x^2 - 6x + x - 3$

$= 2x^2 - 5x - 3$

Exercise 9·3

1. Multiply out the brackets and simplify :-

(a) $(x + 3)(x + 1)$ (b) $(x + 5)(x + 3)$ (c) $(x + 2)(x + 4)$ (d) $(x + 3)(x + 4)$

(e) $(p + 5)(p + 5)$ (f) $(p + 6)(p + 1)$ (g) $(p + 2)(p + 3)$ (h) $(x + 1)(2x + 1)$

(i) $(x + 2)(3x + 1)$ (j) $(x + 3)(2x + 6)$ (k) $(2a + 4)(2a + 4)$ (l) $(3y + 1)(3y + 1)$

(m) $(2m + 1)(4m + 3)$ (n) $(5m + 2)(5m + 1)$ (o) $(8g + 2)(2g + 3)$ (p) $(4 + x)(x + 5)$

(q) $(3 + 2x)(6 + 3x)$ (r) $(10w + 1)^2$ (s) $(3x + 4)^2$ (t) $(2y + 8)^2$

2. Multiply out and simplify :-

(a) $(x-3)(x-2)$ (b) $(x-2)(x-1)$ (c) $(x-3)(x-4)$ (d) $(p-4)(p-4)$

(e) $(5-p)(p-5)$ (f) $(p-1)(p-1)$ (g) $(x-1)(2x-3)$ (h) $(x-2)(4x-2)$

(i) $(x-2)(5x-1)$ (j) $(x-3)(2x-3)$ (k) $(2a-3)(2a-3)$ (l) $(2a-3)(4a-1)$

(m) $(2m-1)(2m-5)$ (n) $(2-3c)(6-2c)$ (o) $(5x-1)(5x-1)$ (p) $(2w-1)^2$

3. Expand the brackets and simplify :-

(a) $(x+5)(x-2)$ (b) $(y-1)(y+4)$ (c) $(a-2)(a+3)$ (d) $(b+2)(b-1)$

(e) $(m-5)(m+3)$ (f) $(3+n)(1-n)$ (g) $(x+3)(2x-1)$ (h) $(a-4)(5a+1)$

(i) $(u-2)(3u+4)$ (j) $(3x+5)(3x-5)$ (k) $(7a+1)(2a-2)$ (l) $(4h-3)(5h+2)$

(m) $(x+y)(x+2y)$ (n) $(x+y)(x-2y)$ (o) $(x-y)(x+2y)$ (p) $(x-y)(x-2y)$

(q) $(a+b)(3a+4b)$ (r) $(2p+q)(p-2q)$ (s) $(5+2x)(2+x)$ (t) $(2-a)(1-a)$

(u) $(5-b)(3+2b)$ (v) $(p-q)(q+p)$ (w) $(1-y)(1+9y)$ (x) $(1-4k)(1-5k)$

4. These are slightly harder :-

(a) $(x+2)(x^2+1)$ (b) $(x+3)(x^2+5)$ (c) $(x-2)(x^2+3)$ (d) $(x-4)(2x^2+3)$

(e) $(2x+1)(x^2-2)$ (f) $(5x-3)(2x^2+3)$ (g) $(x^2+3)(x^2+4)$ (h) $(x^2-2)(x^2+5)$

(i) $(x+y)(x^2+y^2)$ (j) $(2x-y)(x^2-y^2)$ (k) $(x^2-y^2)(3x+2y)$ (l) $(x^2-y^2)(x^2+y^2)$

5. Calculate the area of each of these rectangles, in terms of the letters used :-

(a)

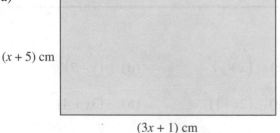

$(x+5)$ cm

$(3x+1)$ cm

(b)

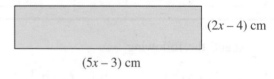

$(2x-4)$ cm

$(5x-3)$ cm

(c)

$(x+y)$ cm

$(3x+y)$ cm

(d)

$(5a+2b)$ cm

$(3a-2b)$ cm

Multiplying Out "Harder Double Brackets" - Using RAINBOWS

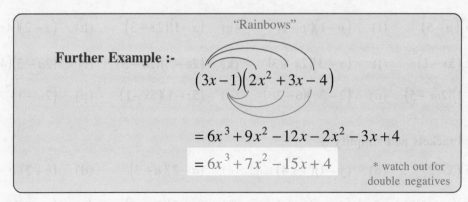

"Rainbows"

Further Example :-

$$(3x-1)(2x^2+3x-4)$$

$$= 6x^3+9x^2-12x-2x^2-3x+4$$

$$= 6x^3+7x^2-15x+4$$

* watch out for double negatives

6. Simplify :-

(a) $(x+2)(x^2+4x+1)$

(b) $(x+1)(x^2+5x-2)$

(c) $(x-1)(x^2+x-3)$

(d) $(2a+1)(3a^2+5a+2)$

(e) $(3p-2)(2p^2-p-4)$

(f) $(4y+5)(2y^2-3y+3)$

Squaring Brackets - a Quick Method

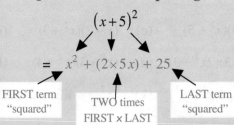

Present

$$(x+5)^2$$

$$= (x+5)(x+5)$$

$$= x^2+5x+5x+25$$

$$= x^2+10x+25$$

Quick Method for Squaring

$$(x+5)^2$$

$$= x^2+(2\times 5x)+25$$

FIRST term "squared"

TWO times FIRST × LAST

LAST term "squared"

$$= x^2+10x+25$$

Further Example :-

$$(x-4)^2$$

$$= x^2-(2\times 4x)+16$$

$$= x^2-8x+16$$

7. Expand the following :-

(a) $(x+3)^2$

(b) $(x+7)^2$

(c) $(x+y)^2$

(d) $(y-2)^2$

(e) $(y-6)^2$

(f) $(x-y)^2$

(g) $(2x+1)^2$

(h) $(3x+4)^2$

(i) $(4a-1)^2$

(j) $(2b-10)^2$

(k) $(x+3y)^2$

(l) $(a-7b)^2$

(m) $(2x-3h)^2$

(n) $(4v-5w)^2$

(o) $(x^2+2)^2$

(p) $(y^2-4)^2$

(q) $\left(p+\dfrac{1}{p}\right)^2$

(r) $\left(q-\dfrac{1}{q}\right)^2$

(s) $\left(2x-\dfrac{1}{2x}\right)^2$

(t) $\left(5x-\dfrac{1}{5x}\right)^2$

8. Calculate the area of each square in terms of x (and/or y) :-

(a)

(3x + 2) cm

(b)

(5x – 1) cm

(c)

(3x + 6y) cm

Multiplying Out Brackets, Tidying Up and "CUBING"

Example 1 :–

$$(x+2)^2 - x^2 - 12$$
$$= x^2 + 4x + 4 - x^2 - 12$$
$$= \boxed{4x - 8}$$

Example 2 :–

Danger !

$$(2a+3)(3a-1) - (a+1)^2$$
$$= 6a^2 - 2a + 9a - 3 - [a^2 + 2a + 1] \quad \text{Careful}$$
$$= 6a^2 + 7a - 3 - a^2 - 2a - 1 \quad \text{careful with negative signs}$$
$$= \boxed{5a^2 + 5a - 4}$$

Example 3 :– (Cubing)

$$(x+2)^3$$
$$= (x+2)(x+2)^2$$

using quick method of squaring

$$= (x+2)(x^2 + 4x + 4)$$

using the now familiar "rainbow method"

$$= x^3 + 4x^2 + 4x + 2x^2 + 8x + 8$$
$$= \boxed{x^3 + 6x^2 + 12x + 8}$$

Exercise 9·4

1. Expand the brackets and simplify :–

   (a) $(x-3)^2 - x^2 + 15$

   (b) $(x+4)(x+3) - x^2 + 2$

   (c) $(a-4)(a-3) - a^2 + 13$

   (d) $(b+1)^2 - b^2 - 3$

   (e) $(x+4)^2 - (x+1)(x+6)$

   (f) $(x+1)(x+2) - (x-1)^2$

   (g) $(2y+4)(3y+1) + (y+1)(2y-4)$

   (h) $(5p-1)(2p+3) + (2p-2)(4p-1)$

   (i) $(2x-3)(5x-1) + (3x-1)(x-1)$

   (j) $(3x+5)(2x-4) + (2x-3)^2$

   (k) $(2g+5)^2 + (4g-2)^2$

   (l) $(2q+4)(3q+1) - (q+1)(4q+1)$

   (m) $(5x+3)(2x-4) - (3x-1)(2x+1)$

   (n) $(4x-1)(6x-3) - (3x-2)(4x-5)$

   (o) $(6x-2)(2x+4) - (3x+3)^2$

   (p) $(3x-6)^2 - (2x+4)^2$

   (q) $a^2 - (a-5)^2 - 50$

   (r) $24 - (3-w)^2 - 15 + w^2$

   (s) $2(x+5)^2 - 3(x-4)^2$

   (t) $5(2x-3)^2 - 6(x-2)^2$

2. Expand :–

   (a) $(x-2)^3$

   (b) $(x+1)^3$

   (c) $(a-1)^3$

   (d) $(x+3)^3$

   (e) $(k-3)^3$

   (f) $(2x+1)^3$

   (g) $(3x-2)^3$

   (h) $3(m+4)^3$

   (i) $2(x-5)^3$

   (j) $(a+b)^3$

   (k) $(p-q)^3$

   (l) $(2x-2y)^3$

Factorising Algebraic Expressions - "The Common Factor"

Earlier, when we multiplied out the brackets, $4(2x + 3)$, we obtained :- $8x + 12$

If we **start** with the expression $8x + 12$, we can **reverse** the process

$=>$ and we can see, from above, that we obtain $4(2x + 3)$.

When you are given the algebraic expression, $8x + 12$ and you are asked :–

"What is the HIGHEST factor of the two terms, $8x$ **and** 12 ?" $=>$ Answer is 4.

Now take the 4 outside a set of brackets $=>$ $4(\ldots\ldots)$

and decide what goes in the bracket so that when multiplied, you obtain $8x + 12$.

Example :- $8x + 12$

$= \boxed{4(2x + 3)}$ This is called "**FACTORISING**" the expression.

* Note - In the above example, the "4" is the **highest common factor**" (**h.c.f.**)

> *You must always use the h.c.f. if the expression is to be factorised FULLY !*

Further Examples :-

Factorise fully :-
1. $5x + 10$
2. $12a - 16b$
3. $pq + pr$
4. $12x - 18x^2$

Check answers by removing the brackets

$= \boxed{5(x + 2)}$ $= \boxed{4(3a - 4b)}$ $= \boxed{p(q + r)}$ $= \boxed{6x(2 - 3x)}$

5 is *h.c.f.*   4 is *h.c.f.* p is *h.c.f.* $6x$ is *h.c.f.*

Exercise 9·5

1. **COPY and complete :-**

   (a) $5a + 5b = 5(\ldots\ldots)$
   (b) $2x + 8y = 2(\ldots\ldots)$
   (c) $6g + 4h = 2(\ldots\ldots)$

   (d) $pq + pr = p(\ldots\ldots)$
   (e) $cd + c = c(\ldots\ldots)$
   (f) $mn + n^2 = n(\ldots\ldots)$

   (g) $vw^2 + v = v(\ldots\ldots)$
   (h) $3ab + 3ac = 3a(\ldots\ldots)$
   (i) $8x + 12y = 4(\ldots\ldots)$

   (j) $40b - 16a = 8(\ldots\ldots)$
   (k) $4cd - 8d = 4d(\ldots\ldots)$
   (l) $6p + 21p^2 = 3p(\ldots\ldots)$

2. Factorise the following, by considering the highest common factor in each case :-

   (a) $5a + 25$
   (b) $3x + 12$
   (c) $9p - 36$
   (d) $11v + 11w$

   (e) $6p - 6q$
   (f) $10c - 20h$
   (g) $7m - 28$
   (h) $12n + 60$

   (i) $4x + 6y$
   (j) $14u - 21v$
   (k) $20x - 25y$
   (l) $4r - 32u$

   (m) $9s + 24$
   (n) $22u - 11$
   (o) $24x - 56y$
   (p) $18a + 12c$

3. Factorise fully :-

   (a) $5b + bc$
   (b) $7x - vx$
   (c) $pq + pr$
   (d) $a^2 + 6a$

   (e) $8t - t^2$
   (f) $c^2 - 4c$
   (g) $4xm + 4xn$
   (h) $5ad - 10ae$

   (i) $17rs - 17s$
   (j) $3y^2 + 7y$
   (k) $12x^2 - 20xy$
   (l) $6q^2 + q$

   (m) $6d + 14d^2$
   (n) $a - 13a^2$
   (o) $3y^2 - 24cy$
   (p) $24mn + 32n^2$

4. Completely factorise :-

   (a) $a^2 + 4ab - 7a$
   (b) $8xy - 8xz + x$
   (c) $p^3 + p^2$
   (d) $4d^3 - 16d$

   (e) $a^2c + ac^2$
   (f) $18rs^2 - 30rs$
   (g) $8x^2 - 12xa$
   (h) $\frac{1}{5}gh + \frac{1}{5}hj$

Factorising Algebraic Expressions - "The Difference of Two Squares"

When expanding brackets, we discovered that .... $(a-b)(a+b) = a^2 + ab - ab - b^2 = a^2 - b^2$.

In reverse, when we factorise $a^2 - b^2$ we obtain the answer $(a+b)(a-b)$.

An algebraic expression of the form $a^2 - b^2$ is known as "a Difference of Two Squares" - obviously because both terms are **squares** and also the appearance of a **minus** sign.

Examples :-

Factorise :- 1. $x^2 - 9$ 2. $49 - x^2$ 3. $4x^2 - 25y^2$

     $= (x-3)(x+3)$ $= (7-x)(7+x)$ $= (2x)^2 - (5y)^2$

                                                     $= (2x - 5y)(2x + 5y)$

Exercise 9·6

1. Factorise, using the difference of two squares :-

(a) $x^2 - 4$ (b) $a^2 - 16$ (c) $b^2 - 25$ (d) $x^2 - 1$

(e) $1 - k^2$ (f) $49 - w^2$ (g) $64 - h^2$ (h) $100 - x^2$

(i) $a^2 - b^2$ (j) $w^2 - v^2$ (k) $4a^2 - 1$ (l) $x^2 - 25y^2$

(m) $36 - 49p^2$ (n) $81a^2 - 4b^2$ (o) $121v^2 - 100w^2$ (p) $64p^2 - 81q^2$

(q) $1 - 16a^2$ (r) $25 - 81x^2$ (s) $49 - 4k^2$ (t) $1 - 144y^2$

Consider this **example :-**   Factorise $3x^2 - 48$ It is a "difference", but NOT of two squares !

                               $= 3(x^2 - 16)$ By **removing the common factor**,

                               $= 3(x-4)(x+4)$ we now have a **difference of two squares**.

2. Factorise these fully :- (*difficult !*)

(a) $2x^2 - 18$
     $= 2(x^2 - 9)$
     $= ....$

(b) $3p^2 - 3$
     $= 3(p^2 - ...)$
     $= ....$

(c) $5a^2 - 80$
     $= 5(...^2 - ...)$
     $= ....$

(d) $6v^2 - 24$
     $= 6(... - ...)$
     $= ....$

(e) $4g^2 - 16$ (f) $7x^2 - 7y^2$ (g) $6v^2 - 150u^2$ (h) $10a^2 - 90b^2$

(i) $19x^2 - 19y^2$ (j) $aw^2 - av^2$ (k) $\pi m^2 - \pi n^2$ (l) $kp^2 - 36kq^2$

(m) $kp^2 - 9kq^2$ (n) $d^3 - 4d$ (o) $27x^3 - 48x$ (p) $a^4 - 1$

(q) $1 - k^4$ (r) $p^4 - q^4$ (s) $1 - 16y^4$ (t) $3d^4 - 48$

3. Shown is a square with side 5 centimetres inside a square of side k centimetres.

(a) Prove that the **pink** area can be expressed as :- $(k-5)(k+5)$ cm^2.

(b) Find the area when $k = 8·5$.

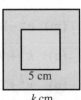
5 cm

k cm

Factorising Trinomials (or Quadratic Expressions)

Remember the "Rainbows" ?　　$(x+2)(x+3) = x^2+5x+6$

Now we examine how to reverse the process and **FACTORISE** x^2+5x+6 to obtain $(x+2)(x+3)$.

Example :-　　Factorise x^2+5x+6

- Draw up a small table

- In the front part of the table put the factors of the x^2.

x	
x	

- In the back part of the table put some* factors of the 6.

x	1	6	2	3
x	6	1	3	2

- Now, take it in turn to **multiply diagonally** with the x's and **add** looking for the middle term (in this case the $5x$)

x	1	6	2	3
x	6	1	3	2

$6 \times x + 1 \times x = 7x$　*no use.*

..... keep choosing factors until you find the ones which work - you may be lucky early !

x	1	6	2	3
x	6	1	3	2

$2 \times x + 3 \times x = 5x$　*Yes !*

=> x^2+5x+6 factorises to give $(x + 2)(x + 3)$

Examples :- Factorise ....

1.　　$x^2 + 3x - 10$

x	10	-10	2	-2
x	-1	1	-5	5

$= (x-2)(x+5)$

2.　　$x^2 - 9x + 20$

x	-10	-20	-4
x	-2	-1	-5

$= (x-5)(x-4)$

*must use **negatives** because of the $-9x$!*

Exercise 9·7

1.　Factorise these trinomials :-

(a)　$x^2 + 2x + 1$　$= (x + ...)(x + ...)$

(b)　$a^2 + 3a + 2$　$= (a + ...)(a + ...)$

(c)　$k^2 - 7k + 10$　$= (k - ...)(k - ...)$

(d)　$d^2 - 9d + 14$　$= (d - ...)(d - ...)$

(e)　$x^2 - 2x + 1$

(f)　$b^2 - 6b + 9$

(g)　$c^2 - 9c + 18$

(h)　$w^2 - 11w + 24$

(i)　$x^2 + 3x - 4$

(j)　$n^2 + n - 6$

(k)　$p^2 + 2p - 15$

(l)　$q^2 + 3q - 18$

(m)　$x^2 - 3x - 4$

(n)　$r^2 - 6r - 7$

(o)　$y^2 - 4y - 12$

(p)　$h^2 - 8h - 20$.

2.　Factorise the following quadratic expressions :-

(a)　$x^2 - 5x - 6$

(b)　$x^2 + 8x + 15$

(c)　$x^2 - 4x - 5$

(d)　$x^2 - 11x + 18$

(e)　$y^2 - 2y - 15$

(f)　$y^2 + 7y - 8$

(g)　$y^2 - 9y + 14$

(h)　$y^2 + 8y + 12$

(i)　$a^2 - 14a + 49$

(j)　$a^2 - 10a - 11$

(k)　$a^2 + a - 30$

(l)　$a^2 - 9a + 20$

(m)　$c^2 - 8c + 15$

(n)　$c^2 + 4c - 21$

(o)　$c^2 - 6c - 27$

(p)　$c^2 - 10c + 16$

(q)　$k^2 + 9k - 10$

(r)　$k^2 - 8k - 9$

(s)　$k^2 - 2k - 35$

(t)　$k^2 + 2k - 24$

(u)　$v^2 + 2v - 8$

(v)　$v^2 - 13v + 30$

(w)　$v^2 - v - 12$

(x)　$v^2 - 13v + 40$

Factorise :- 1. $3x^2 + 5x - 2$

$= (3x-1)(x+2)$

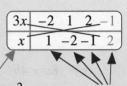

factors of $3x^2$ factors of -2

Multiply **diagonally** and **add** to obtain **$5x$**

2. $6x^2 + 13x + 2$

=> try $3x$ and $2x$

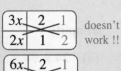

doesn't work !!

=> try $6x$ and $1x$

$2 \times 6x + 1 \times x = 13x$ *Yes* !

factors are $(6x+1)(x+2)$

3. Factorise the following and check each answer mentally.

(a) $2x^2 + 5x + 3$ (b) $2a^2 + 7a + 3$ (c) $6y^2 + 7y + 2$ (d) $3g^2 + 14g + 15$

(e) $12k^2 - 8k + 1$ (f) $2b^2 - 7b + 3$ (g) $8c^2 - 14c + 5$ (h) $3x^2 - 2x - 8$

(i) $3a^2 - 5a - 2$ (j) $5p^2 + 4p - 1$ (k) $2m^2 + m - 1$ (l) $3q^2 - 2q - 1$

(m) $8c^2 + 2c - 3$ (n) $8n^2 + 10n - 3$ (o) $12w^2 - 11w - 5$ (p) $4c^2 + 12c + 9$

(q) $24k^2 + 2k - 1$ (r) $1 + 3x - 18x^2$ (s) $15 - 7y - 2y^2$ (t) $x^2 + 8xy + 12y^2$

(u) $p^2 - 10pq + 24q^2$ (v) $b^2 + 3bc + 2c^2$ (w) $a^2 - 5ab - 14b^2$ (x) $2u^2 - 5uv - 3v^2$

(y) $9g^2 + 6gh - 8h^2$ (z) $9\sin^2\theta - 12\sin\theta + 4$.

Exercise 9·8   *Miscellaneous Exercise on Factorisation*

ORDER OF FACTORISATION :-

- *Look for Common Factor(s) and put them outside the bracket(s).*
- *Watch for a Difference of Two Squares.*
- *Complete the factorisation of any Trinomial which remains.*

Factorise fully :-

1. $6x + 36y$ 2. $p^2 - 49$ 3. $y^2 + 6y + 9$ 4. $k^2 - k$

5. $v^2 - v - 6$ 6. $1 - a^2$ 7. $de + dh - dj$ 8. $3c^2 - 12$

9. $m^2 - 8m$ 10. $q^2 - 2q + 1$ 11. $b^2 - 1$ 12. $b^2 - b$

13. $b^2 - b - 2$ 14. $2t^2 - 18$ 15. $2x^2 - 32x$ 16. $a^3 - a^2$

17. $2p^2 + 3p - 5$ 18. $9n^2 + 6n + 1$ 19. $81 - x^2$ 20. $50 - 2c^2$

21. $18y - 6y^2$ 22. $81 - 4b^2$ 23. $2k^2 - k - 1$ 24. $14x^2 + 42y^2$

25. $14m^2 - 56n^2$ 26. $16x^2 - 8x + 1$ 27. $3p^2q - 9pq^2$ 28. $1 - 2u + u^2$

29. $3x^3 - 27x$ 30. $6a^2 + 5a - 6$ 31. $4x^2 + 4x - 8$ 32. $10w - 40w^3$

33. $ak^2 - am^2$ 34. $2x^2 - 7x - 15$ 35. $p^7 - p^6 - p^5$ 36. $x^4 - 81$

1. Simplify :-

   (a) $24 \times x$ (b) $g \times g$ (c) $8a \times 4b$ (d) $(5p)^2 \times 2$

   (e) $4mn \times m$ (f) $3xq^2 \times q$ (g) $20c \div c$ (h) $12x^2y \div 3y$.

2. Multiply out the brackets :-

   (a) $5(a + 2)$ (b) $4(2 - 6r)$ (c) $a(9 + a)$ (d) $-2x(3x - 6y)$.

3. Simplify :-

   (a) $3(x + 1) + 7$ (b) $9(y + 4) - 8y$ (c) $10 - 3(a - 2)$

   (d) $4(w + 1) + 5(w + 2)$ (e) $10(1 - d) + 2(4 + d)$ (f) $7(2 - 3q) - 3(4 - 8q)$

   (g) $20 - 5(u + 3)$ (h) $8 - 2(1 - k)$ (i) $6m - 2(1 - 4m)$

4. Multiply out the brackets and simplify :-

   (a) $(a+7)(a+2)$ (b) $(b-3)(b-6)$ (c) $(c-2)(c+9)$ (d) $(2d+3)(6d+1)$

   (e) $(1-3e)(5-2e)$ (f) $(2y+3)(7y-1)$ (g) $(2k-5)^2$ (h) $\left(m+\dfrac{2}{m}\right)^2$

   (i) $(n+1)^3$ (j) $(2s-3)^3$ (k) $(x+2)(x+5)-x^2-10$

   (l) $(2x-1)(4x-2)-(3x+1)(x+1)$ (m) $(2y-1)(3y^2+4y-3)$

5. Factorise fully :-

   (a) $4a + 24$ (b) $21a - 28b$ (c) $cd + cg$ (d) $2b^2 - 10b$

   (e) $n^3 - n^2$ (f) $24k^2h + 36kh^2$ (g) $r^2 - 100$ (h) $5q^2 - 20$

   (i) $w^2 - 10w - 16$ (j) $2m^2 + 7m + 6$ (k) $5b^2 - 27b + 10$ (l) $x^2 - xy - 2y^2$

   (m) $6x^2 + 7xy - 3y^2$ (n) $x^2 - 14xy + 49y^2$ (o) $1 - 25a^2$ (p) $9n^2 - 9n - 18$

   (q) $3p^2 - 48p$ (r) $7a^3b - 21ab$ (s) $17st^2 - 17su^2$ (t) $x^4 - 2x^2y^2 + y^4$

6. Shown is a picture of two rectangles :-

   - the larger has sides $(2k + 5)$ centimetres and $(k + 4)$ centimetres.
   - the smaller rectangle is separated from the larger by a **one centimetre** border all round.

   Write down an expression in x for :-

   (a) the length of the pink rectangle.

   (b) the breadth of the pink rectangle.

   (c) the area of the pink rectangle.

   (d) the area shown in yellow.

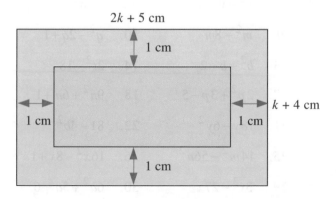

1. List Jimmy's Test scores in order, highest first.

   January - $\frac{42}{60}$, February - $\frac{26}{40}$, March - $\frac{32}{50}$.

2. The Dooleys invested $1200 in the Bank of the U.S.A., where the annual interest rate was 4·5%.

   Calculate the (**compound**) interest due if they withdrew their savings 3 years later.

3. Due to a fault, the pressure in a boiler rose by 20% **to** 300 poundals.

   What was the pressure before the fault arose ?

4. The altitude (height) of triangle ABP is shown dotted. Calculate the length of side BP (x).

   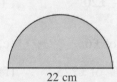

   30 cm · · · x cm

   A · · 24 cm · · T · 8 cm · B

5. Prove that a triangle, LMN, with sides :-

   LM = 12·5 cm, MN = 30 cm and LN = 32·5 cm,

   is right angled at point M.

6. Write, in **scientific notation**, the number 0·0064.

7. Determine the value of $\dfrac{(6\cdot 8 \times 10^5) \times (2\cdot 5 \times 10^7)}{8\cdot 5 \times 10^{-3}}$.

8. Calculate the **perimeter** of this semi-circle.

   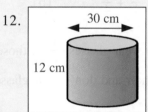

   22 cm

9.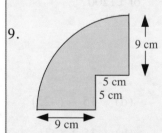

   9 cm

   5 cm
   5 cm

   9 cm

   Shown is a quarter circle, with a square removed from its corner.

   Calculate its area .

10. **Copy** the following and simplify :-

    (a) $9 - (-3)$ (b) $(-2) - (-11)$

    (c) $(-9x) - (-x)$ (d) $(-6x^2) - (-6x^2)$

    (e) $(-8y) \times 4$ (f) $3x \times (-5x)$

    (g) $(-40x) \div 8$ (h) $(18p) \div (-9)$

    (i) $5 \times (-2) \times 6$ (j) $(-42) \div (-7)$

    (k) $(-3) \times (-2) \times (-4)$ (l) $(-6a) \times (-7a)$

11. When the burner in a furnace was switched off, the temperature began to drop slowly.

    This is shown in the graph below.

    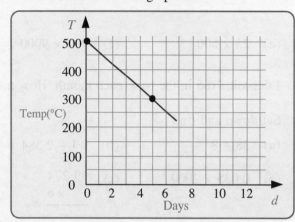

    (a) Write down the equation of the line.

    (b) Use your equation to determine when the furnace temperature will reach 20°C.

12. (a) Calculate the volume of this cylinder.

    30 cm

    12 cm

    (b) How many litres of water would it hold when full ?

13. Multiply out the brackets and tidy up terms :-

    (a) $(x + 3)(2x - 5)$ (b) $(3x - 1)^2$

    (c) $(x + 2)^3$ (d) $(x + 3)^2 - (x + 2)^2$

14. Factorise fully :-

    (a) $7a + 28$ (b) $6b^2 - 9b$

    (c) $m^3 - m^2$ (d) $r^2 - 100$

    (e) $4x^2 - 25y^2$ (f) $5t^2 - 45$

    (g) $x^2 - 10x + 16$ (h) $2y^2 + 9y + 10$

    (i) $7w^2 - 17w + 6$ (j) $x^2 - xy - 12y^2$

15. (a) If a truck travelled at an average speed of 72 m.p.h., what distance would it cover in 2 hours 36 minutes ?

    (b) Drew arranges to meet an important client in Euston Station at 11·45 am.

    He sets off from home at 6·30 am, and travels the 480 km by train at an average speed of 90 km/hr.

    Will he meet his client on time ? (*Explain*).

1. Set down and find :-

   (a) 263×25

   (b) $9 \overline{\smash{\big)}\,7533}$

   (c) 5×72

   (d) 3420×8

   (e) 25×500

   (f) 700×9000

   (g) $70400 \div 80$

   (h) $8000 - 964$

2. I deposit £185 in the bank each month. How much will I have deposited after 1 year ?

3. Set down and find :-

   (a) $38 \div 8$

   (b) $9 \cdot 1 - 2 \cdot 384$

   (c) $20 - 9 \cdot 749$

   (d) $54 \div 300$

   (e) $0 \cdot 035 \times 2000$

   (f) $19 \cdot 274 \times 6$

   (g) $19 \cdot 2 - 11 \cdot 93 + 16 \cdot 174$

   (h) $8 \overline{\smash{\big)}\,17 \cdot 344}$

4. Find :–

   (a) $\frac{4}{5}$ of 330

   (b) $\frac{3}{4}$ of 84

   (c) $\frac{2}{7}$ of 2100

5. Simplify :–

   (a) $\frac{10}{15}$

   (b) $\frac{24}{27}$

   (c) $\frac{34}{51}$

   (d) $\frac{19}{76}$

6. Find :–

   (a) $\frac{1}{2} + \frac{3}{4}$

   (b) $7 - 2\frac{1}{4}$

   (c) $4 \times 2\frac{1}{4}$

   (d) $\frac{1}{2}$ of $\frac{1}{2}$

7. Of 180 pupils, $\frac{5}{6}$ do not wear glasses. $\frac{2}{3}$ of those without glasses have brown hair.

   How many have brown hair and don't wear glasses ?

8. VAT is charged (at $17\frac{1}{2}\%$) on luxury goods.   (= $10\% + 5\% + 2\frac{1}{2}\%$).

   Calculate the final cost of the following items if these are the pre–VAT prices :–

   (a) Widescreen T.V. — £240

   (b) P.C. game — £20

   (c) Speakers — £36

9. Find :–

   (a) 25% of £6·40

   (b) 70% of £6

   (c) 3% of £32·00

   (d) 15% of £60

   (e) $33\frac{1}{3}\%$ of £225

   (f) $2\frac{1}{2}\%$ of £1200

10. I deposit £1600 in the bank. I receive 4% interest **per annum**.

    How much will I have in my bank account after 6 months ?

11. Find :–

    (a) $(-6) + 13$

    (b) $(-17) - 12$

    (c) $7 + (-24)$

    (d) $15 - (-25)$

    (e) $(-79) - (-19)$

    (f) $(-3) \times 15$

    (g) $(-11)^2$

    (h) $35 \div (-7)$

    (i) $(-5) \times (-3)^2$

    (j) $\dfrac{(-10) \times 4 \times (-6)}{5 \times (-8)}$

    (k) $-6((-2) - (-5))$

    (l) $(-70) \div (-2)$

12. The temperature fell from 19°C at noon to – 17°C at midnight. By how much had it fallen ?

13. Today is 13th June. My birthday was 3 weeks ago. On what date was my birthday ?

Finding an Arc Length

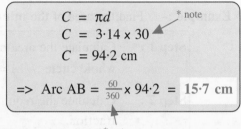

An **ARC** is a part, (or fraction), of the circumference of a circle.

    Arc AB, (the **red** part), is called the **minor** arc.

    Arc AB, (the **blue** part), is called the **major** arc.

Example :–   Find the length of the **minor** arc AB.

Step 1 :   Calculate the full circumference $C = \pi d$
Step 2 :   Find the required fraction of the circumference.

$$C = \pi d \quad \text{* note}$$
$$C = 3{\cdot}14 \times 30$$
$$C = 94{\cdot}2 \text{ cm}$$

$$\Rightarrow \text{ Arc AB} = \tfrac{60}{360} \times 94{\cdot}2 = \mathbf{15{\cdot}7 \text{ cm}}$$

        * note

The **major arc** AB is found in the same way by multiplying the circumference by the fraction $\tfrac{300}{360}$.

Exercise 10·1

1. Copy and complete the calculation to find the length of the **minor arc** of the circle shown :-

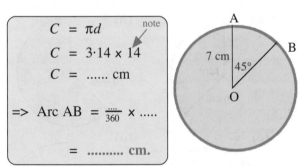

$$C = \pi d \quad \text{note}$$
$$C = 3{\cdot}14 \times 14$$
$$C = \text{...... cm}$$

$$\Rightarrow \text{ Arc AB} = \tfrac{....}{360} \times .....$$

$$= .... \text{ cm.}$$

2. Find the length of each **minor arc** :–

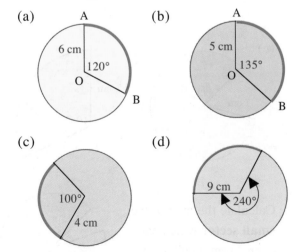

   (a)   (b)   (c)   (d)

3. Find the length of the **major arc** in question 2(a).

Sometimes the words **minor** or **major** are not used.

4. Calculate the **arc length** in each of these :–

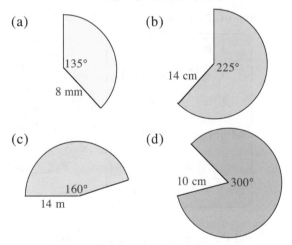

   (a)   (b)   (c)   (d)

5. Calculate the **perimeter** of each shape :-

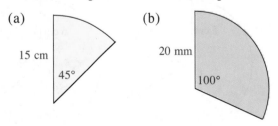

   (a)   (b)

6. The shape trapped between two radii and an arc is called a **sector** of a circle.

Calculate the **perimeter** of a sector which is a fifth of a circle with diameter 5 centimetres. (*A sketch would help*).

Finding the Area of a Sector

A **sector** is a part, (or a fraction) of the **area** of a circle.
The **sector** is the part trapped between the two radii and the arc.

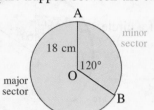

Shown is sector AOB

Sector AOB, (the **pink** part), is called the **minor** sector.

Sector AOB, (the **blue** part), is called the **major** sector.

Example :–   Find the area of the **minor** sector.

> **Step 1 :**   Calculate the area of the whole circle :- $A = \pi r^2$
>
> **Step 2 :**   Calculate the required fraction.

$$A = \pi r^2$$
$$A = 3 \cdot 14 \times 18 \times 18$$
$$A = 1017 \cdot 36 \text{ cm}^2$$
$$\Rightarrow \text{ Minor sector AOB} = \tfrac{120}{360} \times 1017 \cdot 36$$
$$= \boxed{339 \cdot 12 \text{ cm}^2}$$

The area of the **major sector** AOB is found in the same way, by multiplying by the fraction $\frac{240}{360}$.

Exercise 10·2

1. Copy and complete the calculation to find the area of the minor sector of this circle :-

    > $A = \pi r^2$
    >
    > $A = 3 \cdot 14 \times 10 \times 10$
    >
    > $A = \text{ .... cm}^2$
    >
    > Minor sector AOB
    >
    > $= \frac{\text{....}}{360} \times \text{ ......}$
    >
    > $= \text{ .... cm}^2.$

    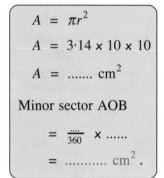

2. Find the area of each **minor** sector :–

    (a)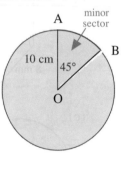

    (b)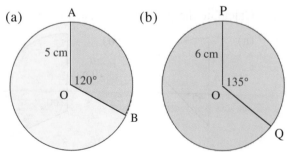

3. (a) Find the area of the **major** sector in question 1.

    (b) Find the area of the **major** sector in question 2(a).

4. Calculate the **area** of each sector :–

    (a)   (b)

    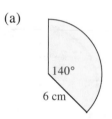

    140°

    6 cm

    20 mm   230°

    (c)   (d)

    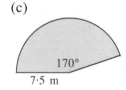

    170°

    7·5 m

    12·5 cm   40°

    (e)   (f)

    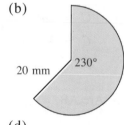

    7 cm   300°

    8·7 cm

    105°

5. Calculate the area of the **small sector** which has been "removed" from the circle shown.

    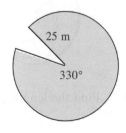

    25 m

    330°

Mixed Exercise 10·3

(Answer to 2 decimal places where necessary).

1. For each shape below, find :–

   (i) the arc length (ii) the sector area.

   (a)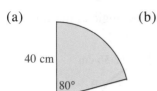

   40 cm
   80°

   (b)

   135°
   5·5 mm

2. The **net** of a wizard's hat is shown.

   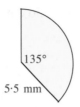

   40 cm
   100°

   Calculate the area of material needed to make the hat.

3. An **eighth** of a circular pizza, with diameter 40 cm, is heated in a microwave.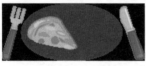

   Calculate the area of the top of the pizza piece.

4. A clock pendulum is 35 centimetres long.

   It swings though an angle of 40° as shown.

   40°
   35 cm

   Calculate the distance through which the end of the pendulum swings.

5. Part of a hairpin bend on a racetrack forms the sector of a circle.

   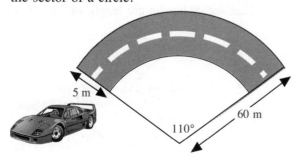

   5 m
   60 m
   110°

   Calculate :–

   (a) the outside length of this part of the track.

   (b) the inside length of this part of the track.

6. Find the perimeter of the shape below. (Shown in red).

   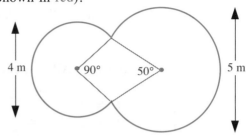

   4 m   90°   50°   5 m

7. A logo is made from three different shapes.

   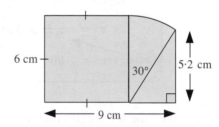

   6 cm
   30°   5·2 cm
   9 cm

   - a square of side 6 centimetres,
   - a right angled triangle,
   - a sector of a circle .

   Calculate :–

   (a) the **perimeter** of the logo.

   (b) the **area** of the logo.

8. The **red** shaded area shown is called a **segment** of the circle.

   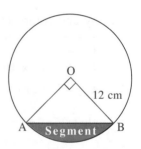

   O
   12 cm
   A   Segment   B

   (a) Calculate the **area** of the sector OAB.

   (b) Now calculate the area of the right angled triangle OAB.

   (c) Finally, find the area of the **red** segment.

9. This shape consists of a sector of a circle with 2 identical right angled triangles.

   Calculate its **area**.

   (You will need to calculate the radius first).

   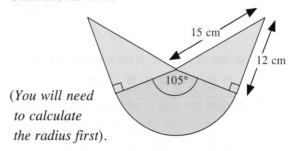

   15 cm
   12 cm
   105°

Finding the Angle at the Centre, given the Arc Length

You can rearrange the formula, $\boxed{\textbf{Arc length} = \frac{\text{angle}}{360} \times \boldsymbol{\pi d}}$ to help you find the **angle** at the centre.

Example :– If the arc length AB of a circle, radius 12 cm, is 12·56 cm, find the angle at the centre.

$C = \pi d$ note
$C = 3\cdot14 \times 24$
$C = 75\cdot36$ cm

=> Angle at centre ($x°$) is given by :-

$x = \frac{12\cdot56}{75\cdot36} \times 360°$

note $x = \boxed{60°}$

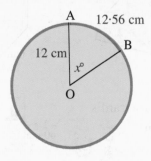

A   12·56 cm
B
12 cm
$x°$
O

If you are given the arc length, then the formula needed to calculate the **centre angle** is :–

$$\text{Angle } (x°) = \frac{\text{arc length}}{\text{circumference}} \times 360°$$

Exercise 10·4

1. The minor arc length AB is 6·28 centimetres. Calculate the size of the angle at the centre.

Copy and complete :–

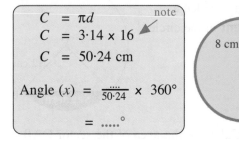

$C = \pi d$ note
$C = 3\cdot14 \times 16$
$C = 50\cdot24$ cm

Angle $(x) = \frac{......}{50\cdot24} \times 360°$

$= .....°$

A   6·28 cm
B
8 cm
$x°$
O

2. For each of the 2 sectors shown below, calculate the size of the angle at the centre :–

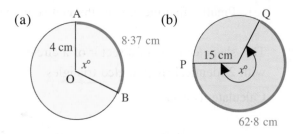

(a)
A
4 cm
8·37 cm
$x°$
O
B

(b)
Q
15 cm
P
$x°$
62·8 cm

3. A sector of a circle, with a **diameter** of 25 cm, has an arc length of 39·25 cm.

Calculate the size of the angle at the centre.

4. Find the angle at the centre of each sector :–

(a)
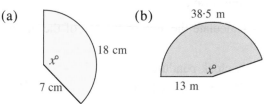
18 cm
$x°$
7 cm

(b)
38·5 m
$x°$
13 m

(c)
18 cm
$x°$
70 cm

(d)
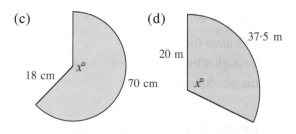
37·5 m
20 m
$x°$

5. This sector has an arc length of 241·78 mm.

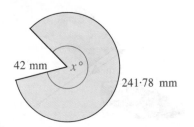

42 mm
$x°$
241·78 mm

(a) Find the size of the angle at the centre.

(b) Calculate the area of the blue sector.

Finding the Angle at the Centre given the Area

You can rearrange the formula $\boxed{\text{Area of Sector} = (\frac{\text{angle}}{360}) \times \pi r^2}$ to help find the **angle** at the centre.

Example :– Find the angle at the centre, given that the area of the minor sector AOB is 75·36 cm^2 .

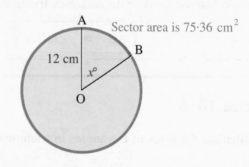

$$A = \pi r^2$$
$$A = 3·14 \times 12 \times 12$$
$$A = 452·16 \text{ cm}^2$$

Angle at centre is found as follows :-

$$\Rightarrow \quad \text{angle } (x°) = \frac{75·36}{452·16} \times 360$$

$$x = \boxed{60°}$$

The formula needed to calculate the **angle at the centre**, given the sector area is :–

$$\boxed{\text{Angle} = \frac{\text{area of sector}}{\text{area of circle}} \times 360°}$$

Exercise 10·5

Give each angle correct to one decimal place.

1. The area of the minor sector AOB is 1·57 cm^2
   Calculate the size of angle x.
   Copy and complete :–

   $$A = \pi r^2$$
   $$A = 3·14 \times 2 \times 2$$
   $$A = 12·56 \text{ cm}^2$$
   $$\text{Angle } (x) = \frac{1·57}{\text{........}} \times 360°$$
   $$= \text{......}°$$

2. Find the size of angle x and angle y :–
   (a)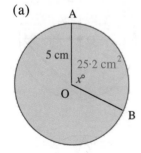
   (b)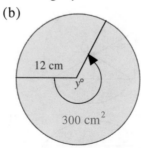

3. The sector of a circle, with a radius of 5 cm, has an area of 65·5 cm^2 .

   Calculate the angle at the centre of the sector.

4. Find the angle at the centre of each sector :–

   (a)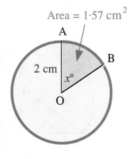
   (b)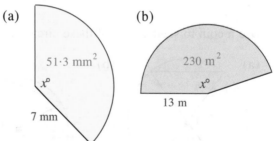

   (c)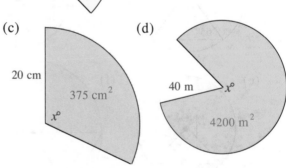
   (d)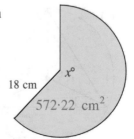

5. The sector shown has an area of 572·22 cm^2 .

   (a) Find the size of the angle at the centre.

   (b) Find the length of the **major** arc.

Angles formed inside Circles - Isosceles Triangles

Any line joining two points on the circumference of a circle is call a **chord**.

A **diameter** is a special chord.

If the two points, A and B, are joined by a chord **AB**, then the triangle formed must be an **isosceles** triangle.

$$\angle OAB = \angle OBA$$

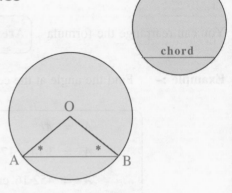

Exercise 10·6

1. Calculate the sizes of the angles in triangle OAB shown opposite.

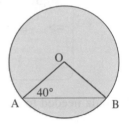

2. Find the missing angles in each of these :–

(a)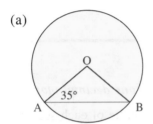

(b)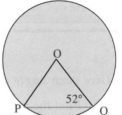

(c)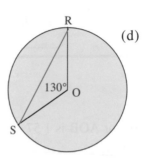

(d)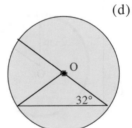

3. Use a coin to sketch each of these circles and fill in all the missing angles :–

(a)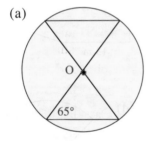

(b)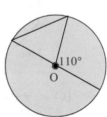

(c)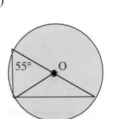

(d)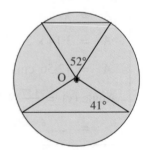

(e)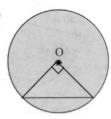

(f)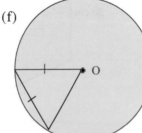

(g)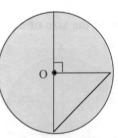

(h)

(i)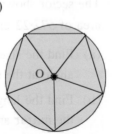

(j)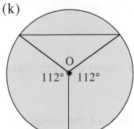

(k)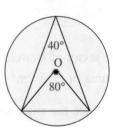

(l)

A **perpendicular bisector** is a line which cuts another line **in half** and does so at **right angles** to the first line.

For the diagram shown, the **chord AB** is now cut into two parts AC and CB, (both 4 cm long), by the line OC.

OC is the **perpendicular bisector** of the chord AB.

Can you see that triangle OCB is a right angled triangle ?

This means that you can use **Pythagoras' Theorem** to find the length of OC.

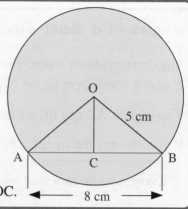

4. Use **Pythagoras' Theorem** to calculate the length of OC in the above diagram.

Copy and complete :-

$$OC^2 = OB^2 - CB^2$$
$$OC^2 = 5^2 - 4^2$$
etc.

5. Use Pythagoras' Theorem to calculate the length of OC, to the nearest millimetre, in each diagram below :–

(a)   (b)

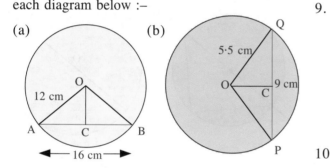

6. Calculate the value of x in each of these :–

(a)   (b)

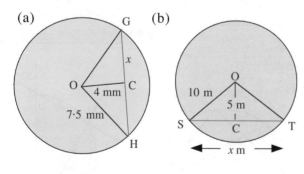

7.

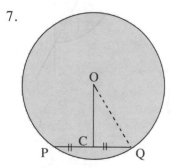

In this circle, chord PQ is 10 cm and the line OC is 12 cm long.

Calculate the **area** of the circle.

8. A horizontal pipe has some water in it to a depth (CD).

The surface AB is 24 cm.

The radius OB of the circle is 15 cm.

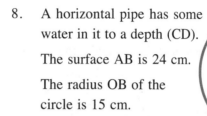

(a) Calculate the length of the line OC.

(b) Now write down the depth of the water CD.

9. A tunnel entrance has centre C and a circular arc of radius 8 metres.

Calculate the height of the tunnel entrance.

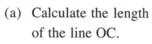

10.

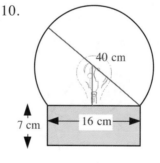

The picture shows a glass lamp, consisting of part of a spherical globe on top of a cylindrical base.

(a) Calculate the length of the red line.

(b) Calculate the total height of the lamp.

11. A clown's face is drawn using a segment of a circle, with an isosceles triangular hat.

• The Radius = 26 cm
• Line OC = 10 cm
• Side TB = 40 cm.

(a) Calculate the length of the base AB of triangle ATB.

(b) Calculate the total height of the face and hat.

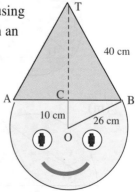

Angles in a Semi-Circle

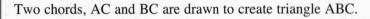

The diagram shows a semi-circle with diameter AB and a 3rd point
C drawn somewhere on the circumference of the semi-circle.

Two chords, AC and BC are drawn to create triangle ABC.

If you measure the size of ∠ACB, it **always turns out to be 90°**, (*as long as C is on the circumference*) !

Every triangle in a semi-circle, formed like this, with the diameter as base, is a right angled triangle.

Exercise 10·7

1. Calculate the values of *a, b, c, d* and *e* in each of the following :–

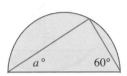 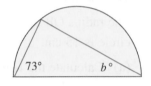 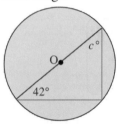 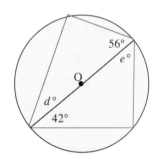

2. Sketch each of the following (*a coin might help*) and fill in all the missing angles :-

(a) 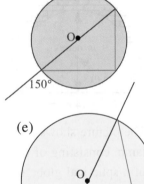   (b) 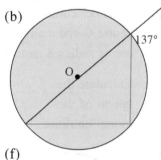   (c) 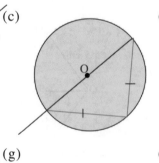   (d)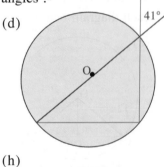

(e) 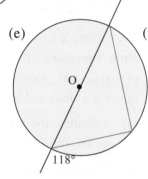   (f) 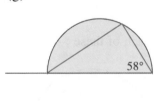   (g)   (h)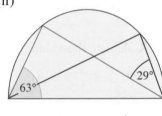

(i) 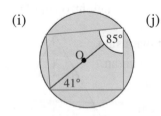   (j) 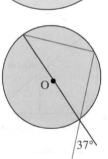   (k) 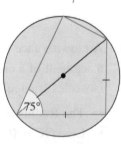   (l)

(m) 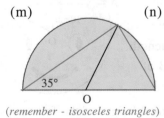   (n) 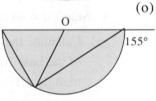   (o)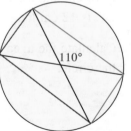

(*remember - isosceles triangles*)

Because we have right angle triangles formed in semi-circles, we can once again use **Pythagoras' Theorem** to find a unknown lengths.

3. Calculate the length of the diameter AB shown in the semi-circle below :-

Copy and complete :–

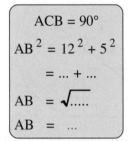

$$ACB = 90°$$
$$AB^2 = 12^2 + 5^2$$
$$= ... + ...$$
$$AB = \sqrt{.....}$$
$$AB = ...$$

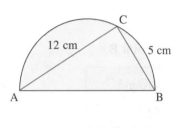

4. Calculate the value of x for each of these :–

(a)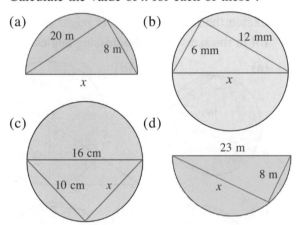

20 m
8 m
x

(b)
12 mm
6 mm
x

(c)
16 cm
10 cm x

(d)
23 m
8 m
x

5. Calculate the **perimeter** of quadrilateral PQRS, where PR is a diameter of the circle.

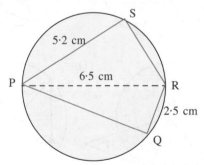

S
5·2 cm
P   6·5 cm   R
2·5 cm
Q

6. Calculate the **area** of this circle, which has EF as its diameter.

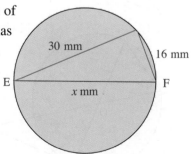

30 mm
16 mm
E
x mm
F

7. An entrance to a tunnel, through which water flows, is in the shape of a semi-circle.

Two wooden beams are used to support it while work is being carried out on the tunnel.

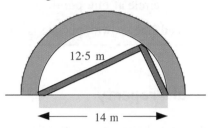

12·5 m

14 m

Calculate the length of the smaller beam.

8. A semi-circular swimming pool has a diameter of 20 metres.

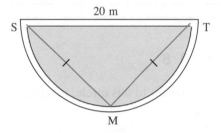

20 m
S   T
M

Lucy swims from T to M, then from M to S. Josh walks directly from T to S.

How much further has Lucy travelled than Josh ?

9. Ryan looks at this sketch of a semi-circle with diameter PQ.

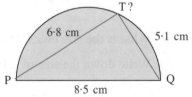

T ?
6·8 cm   5·1 cm
P   8·5 cm   Q

He is not sure whether the point T actually lies **on** the circumference.

Use the **Converse of Pythagoras' Theorem** to decide if T lies on the circumference or not.

10. The **circumference** of this circle, with diameter UV, is 125·6 cm, and chord UW = 32 cm.

(a) Calculate the size of the circle's diameter.

(b) Calculate the length of the chord VW.

(c) Calculate the total area of the **pink** segments.

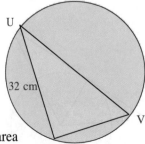

U
32 cm
V
W

Tangents to a Circle

A **tangent** is a line which, even if extended, would only ever touch a circle **at one point.**

Only the **red** line shown opposite is a **tangent.**

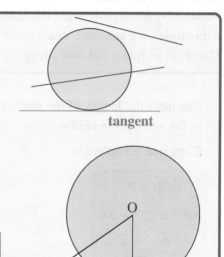

tangent

A Special Property

The diagram shows a tangent, AB, meeting the circle at point B.

If we draw a radius (OB) to this point of contact B, it is found that the radius and the tangent are **at right angles.** (∠ABO = 90°)

O

A   B

Exercise 10·8

1. PA is a tangent to this circle, meeting it at the point A.

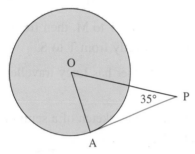

O

35°   P

A

   (a)   What is the size of ∠PAO ?

   (b)   Write down the size of ∠POA.

2. Write down the values of *a*, *b*, ... *g*.

3. Sketch the following, (*a coin might help*), and fill in the sizes of all the missing angles.

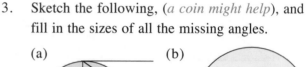

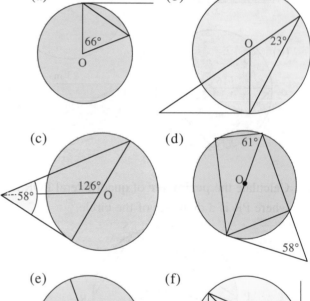

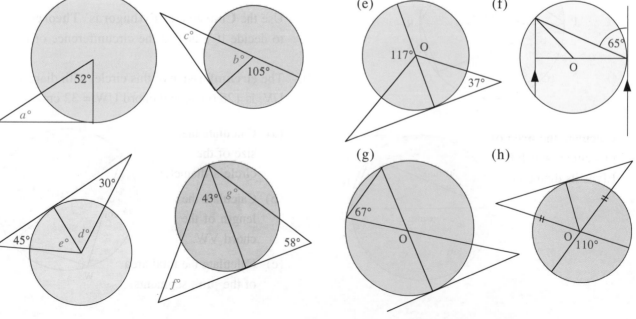

Pythagoras (again !)

Again, because right angle triangles are formed, **Pythagoras' Theorem** can be used to find missing lengths.

The distance from O to A can be calculated as shown :-

$$OA^2 = 24^2 + 10^2$$
$$OA^2 = 576 + 100$$
$$OA^2 = 676$$
$$OA = \sqrt{676} = 26 \text{ mm}$$

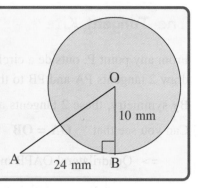

4. Calculate the distance from P to the centre of the circle C.

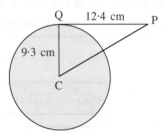

5. Determine the lengths of the **red** lines.

(a) (b)

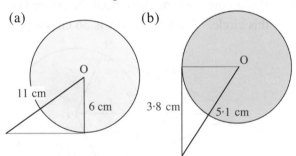

6. 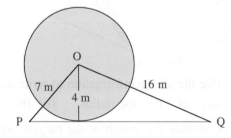 Calculate the **area** of this circle.

7. Determine the length of the tangent PQ.

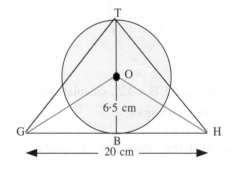

8. Determine the length of the line PA.
   (*Hint :- find the length of PO first*).

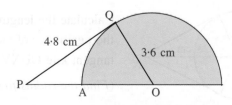

9. BA is a diameter of this semi-circle and is extended to point S.
   ST is a tangent meeting the semi-circle at the point T.

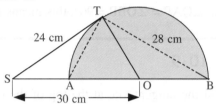

   (a) Calculate the size of radius OT.

   (b) Now find the length of the chord AT.

10. The diagram shows a wheel, centre O, with a radius of 6·5 centimetres.

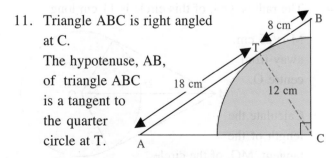

   GH is a tangent and diameter BT is a line of symmetry for the whole figure.

   A **red** wire is stretched from G to O to H.
   A **blue** wire is stretched from G to T to H.

   By how much is the blue wire longer than the red one ?

11. Triangle ABC is right angled at C.
    The hypotenuse, AB, of triangle ABC is a tangent to the quarter circle at T.

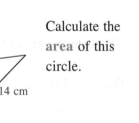

    Calculate the **perimeter** of triangle ABC.

The Tangent Kite

From any point P, outside a circle, it is possible to draw 2 tangents PA and PB to the circle.

By symmetry, these 2 tangents are **equal** in length.

Can you see that **OA = OB** and **PA = PB** ?

=> Quadrilateral OAPB must be a **KITE**.

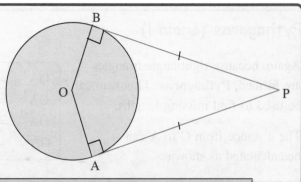

=> When a kite is formed from tangents, it is referred to as a **TANGENT KITE**, and this kite has the special property that its 2 equal angles are both **right angles** (90°).

Special Property of Tangent Kite

Since ∠OAP = ∠OBP = 90°, this means that => | ∠AOB + ∠APB = 180°

Exercise 10·9

1. Look at the tangent kite at the top of the page. If ∠APB = 55°, calculate the size of ∠AOB.

2. Make a neat sketch of this tangent kite.

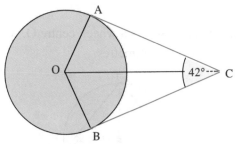

Given that ∠ACB = 42°, calculate the sizes of all the missing angles.

3. Write down the values of *a*, *b*, *c* and *d*.

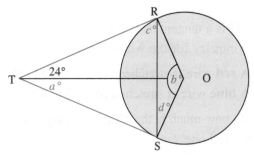

4. The radius, OG, of this circle is 11 cm long.

M is 25 cm away from centre O.

Calculate the length of the tangent, MG, of the circle.

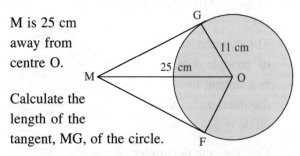

5. P is a point, 39 cm away from the centre O of this circle. The tangent PN is 36 cm long.

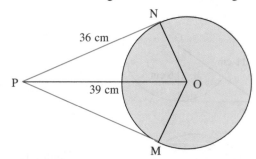

Calculate the **area** of the circle with centre O.

6. Diameter PQ = 20 cm and QC = 18 cm.

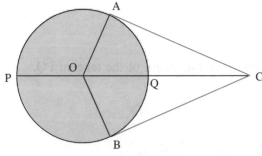

(a) Use the above information to write down the sizes of (i) the radius (ii) the line OC.

(b) Calculate the length of the tangent AC.

7. The **circumference** of this circle is 60 cm and the distance from O to X is 23 cm.

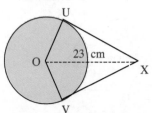

Calculate the length of the **perimeter** of the tangent kite OUXV.

(*Find the radius first !*)

Remember Remember..... ?

(Answer to 3 significant figures where necessary).

1. Calculate the arc length in each of these :–

   (a)
   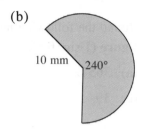
   15 m 45°

   (b)
   10 mm 240°

2. Calculate the area of each sector in question 1.

3. Find the angle at the centre of each sector :–

   (a)

   $x°$ 9 cm
   Arc length is 21·195 cm.

   (b)
   15 cm $x°$
   Arc length is 26·17 cm.

   (c)
   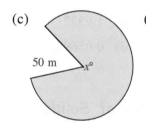
   50 m $x°$
   Area of sector is 6542 m².

   (d)
   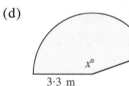
   $x°$ 3·3 m
   Area of sector is 15·2 m².

4. Calculate the value of x, y, z and w :–

   (a)
   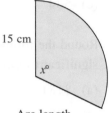
   O 88° $x°$

   (b)
   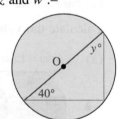
   O 40° $y°$

   (c)
   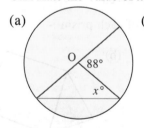
   $z°$ O 80°

   (d)
   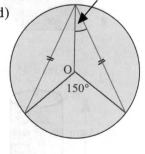
   $w°$ O 150°

5. Calculate the value of x for each of these :–

   (a)
   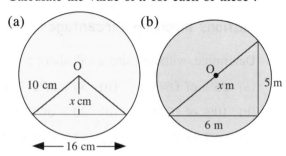
   O 10 cm x cm ← 16 cm →

   (b)
   O x m 5 m 6 m

   (c)
   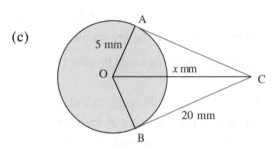
   A 5 mm O x mm C 20 mm B

6. A company logo consists of a **circle** with a **right angled triangle** removed from it as shown below.

   (a) Calculate the total **green** area.

   A gold trim is fitted around the edges of the triangle and the circle.

   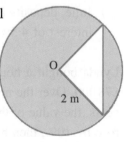
   O 2 m

   (b) Calculate, **to the nearest centimetre**, the length of gold trim needed.

7. A path runs around part of a circular lawn. which has a diameter of 15 metres.

   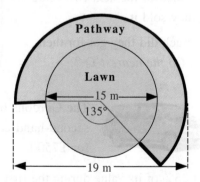
   Pathway Lawn 15 m 135° 19 m

   Calculate :–

   (a) the total perimeter of the path.

   (b) the area covered by the path.

Outcome 1 - Using Percentages

Calculations involving Percentages

1. Determine, without using a calculator :-

   (a) 25% of £64·00 (b) 50% of £17·50

   (c) 10% of £9·40 (d) 20% of £7·50

   (e) 70% of £800 (f) $33\frac{1}{3}$% of £240

2. When Brian was 10, he was 1·20 metres tall. Over the next year he grew taller by 12·5%.

   How tall was Brian when he was 11 ?

3. For each of the following, calculate the total amount in their account at the end of the stated period, after (**compound**) interest had been added.

   (a) Sue, deposits £600 for 3 years at a rate of interest of 3% per annum.

   (b) Julie, deposits £1150 for 2 years at a rate of interest of 4·5% per annum.

4. Lynda bought a house for £78 000. Over the next two years, the value of the house rose by 10%, then by 20%.

   How much was the house then worth ?

5. A young couple bought a house for £42 500. It **appreciated** in value by 9% p.a. for the next two years until they sold it.

   How much did they get for their house, (*to the nearest £*) ?

6.  The Gordons bought a second-hand car for £7500.

   It lost 25% of its value during the first year, 20% during the second year and 10% during the third year.

   How much was the car worth after 3 years ?

Rounding to Significant Figures

7. Round the following numbers to **one significant figure** (1 sig. fig.).

   (a) 3657 (b) 29 846

   (c) 39 (d) 749.

8. Round the following numbers to **two significant figures** (2 sig. figs.).

   (a) 4286 (b) 43 884

   (c) 534 (d) 855.

9. Round the following numbers to **three significant figures** (3 sig. figs.).

   (a) 8181 (b) 64 729

   (c) 6088 (d) 147 499.

10. Round to **3 significant figures** :-

    (a) 6·858 (b) 19·337

    (c) 0·23478 (d) 0·05697.

Outcome 2 - Volumes of Solids

Volume of a Prism

11. For each of the following prisms, the area of the base or end face is given.

    Calculate the **volume** of each prism :-

    (a) Area = 15 cm^2

    8 cm

    (b) Area = 8·5 cm^2

    5 cm

    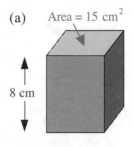

    (c) Area = 45 cm^2

    11 cm

    (d) Area = 21·5 cm^2

    7 cm

    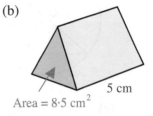
    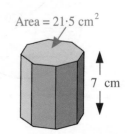

12. This time, you must calculate the **green** area first, then find the **volume** of each prism.

(a)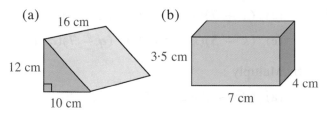
16 cm
12 cm
10 cm

(b)
3·5 cm
4 cm
7 cm

13. Calculate the volume of each of these **cylinders** (to 3 significant figures) :-

(a)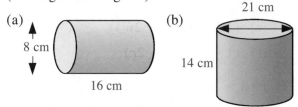
8 cm
16 cm

(b)
21 cm
14 cm

14. **Remember :-**

$$1 \text{ cm}^3 = 1 \text{ ml} ; \quad 1000 \text{ cm}^3 = 1000 \text{ ml} = 1 \text{ litre}$$

How many litres of oil will this tank hold ?

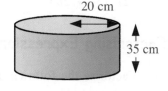
20 cm
35 cm
$V = \pi r^2 h$

Volume of a Cone

15. Calculate the volume of each of these **cones** :-

(a)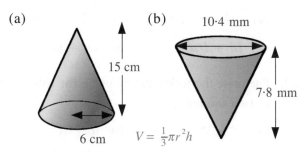
15 cm
6 cm
$V = \frac{1}{3}\pi r^2 h$

(b)
10·4 mm
7·8 mm

Volume of a Sphere

16. Calculate the volume of the **sphere** and the **hemi-sphere** (to 3 significant figures) :-

(a)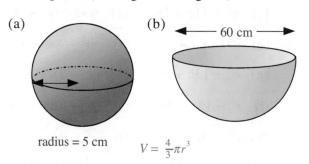
radius = 5 cm
$V = \frac{4}{3}\pi r^3$

(b)
60 cm

Outcome 3 - Linear Relationships

Gradient of a Straight Line

17. Find the **gradient** of each line using the formula :-

$$\text{gradient} = \frac{\text{vertical distance}}{\text{horizontal distance}}$$

(a)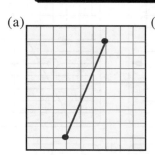

(b)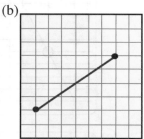

18. Plot each of the following pairs of points on a coordinate diagram and calculate the **gradient** of each line.

  (a) A(5, 2), B(11, 6) (b) E(−4, −5), F(1, 5).

19. Calculate the **gradient** of each line.
(*This time, each has a negative value*).

(a)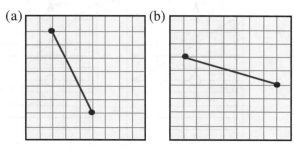

(b)

20. Calculate the **gradients** of the lines joining the following points :-

  (a) R(3, 10), S(10, 3) (b) W(−1, 6), V(1, −2)

  (c) M(−3, −6), N(0, −3).

Sketching Lines of the form $y = mx + c$

21. Determine three points on each of the following lines and make neat sketches of the lines.

  (a) $y = 2x + 3$ (b) $y = 3x − 1$

  (c) $y = x − 5$ (d) $y = \frac{1}{2}x + 2$

  (e) $y = −2x − 1$ (f) $y = −4x + 1$

Determining the Equation of a given Line from its Graph

22. • Calculate the gradient of each line.
    • Note where each cuts the y-axis.
    • Write down the equation of each line as :-

$$y = mx + c.$$

(a) 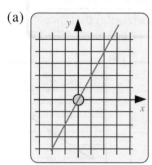 (b)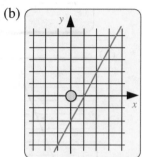

(c) 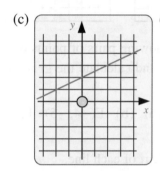 (d)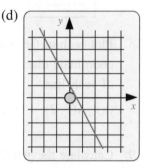

(e) 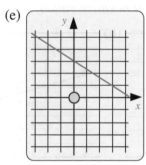 (f)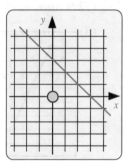

(each box stands for 1 unit in the above diagrams)

Outcome 4 - Algebraic Operations

Multiplying Expressions involving Brackets

23. Write the following without brackets :-

    (a) $8(x + 5)$ (b) $5(p + 2)$

    (c) $3(a - 6)$ (d) $9(w - 3)$

    (e) $6(3n - 2)$ (f) $d(f + 6)$

    (g) $g(4g + 5h)$ (h) $w(31 - 3w)$

24. Write the following without brackets :-

    (a) $4(a + b - 3)$ (b) $y(y^2 + 4)$

    (c) $5(e - f + 11)$ (d) $d(3 - d^2)$

25. Multiply out these brackets :-

    (a) $(x + 3)(x + 5)$ (b) $(x + 8)(x + 2)$
    (c) $(x + 7)(x - 1)$ (d) $(h - 3)(h + 4)$
    (e) $(k - 5)(k - 5)$ (f) $(q - 7)(q + 3)$

26. Multiply :-

    (a) $(4x + 3)(2x - 5)$

    (b) $(6e - 5)(2e + 3)$

    (c) $(3t - 2)(3t + 5)$

    (d) $(5 - a)(6 - a)$

    (e) $(10 - w)(3 + 2w)$

    (f) $(1 - 5r)(3 - 2r)$

27. Find :-

    (a) $(x + 4)^2$ (b) $(y + 3)^2$
    (c) $(w - 2)^2$ (d) $(e + 10)^2$
    (e) $(3x + 1)^2$ (f) $(5a - 2)^2$
    (g) $(3a + 2b)^2$ (h) $(4t - s)^2$

Factorising Expressions

28. Factorise the following by taking out the highest common factors :-

    (a) $8a + 8b$ (b) $5t + 5s$
    (c) $10u - 10v$ (d) $9d - 6e$
    (e) $10a + 15b$ (f) $12m - 8n$
    (g) $bt + bu$ (h) $xn - xm$

29. Factorise the following by using the difference of two squares :-

    (a) $x^2 - 25$ (b) $a^2 - 81$
    (c) $36 - w^2$ (d) $e^2 - f^2$

30. Factorise the following expressions :-

    (a) $x^2 + 7x + 10$ (b) $w^2 + 10w + 16$
    (c) $g^2 + 11g + 18$ (d) $w2 - 4w + 4$
    (e) $d^2 - 8d + 16$ (f) $m^2 - 8m + 12$
    (g) $b^2 - 13b + 36$ (h) $y^2 - 2y + 1$
    (i) $t^2 - 15t + 50$ (j) $f^2 + 16f + 15$
    (k) $r^2 - 3r - 10$ (l) $e^2 - 4e - 12$
    (m) $z^2 + z - 20$ (n) $c^2 + 5c - 14$

Outcome 5 - Properties of Circles

The Length of an Arc

31. In each diagram, calculate the length of the **arc** of the sector.

(a)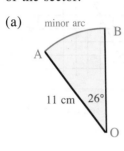
minor arc

(b)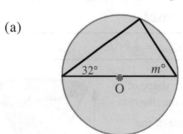
major arc

The Area of a Sector

32. Calculate the area of each **green** sector (*to the nearest square centimetre*).

(a)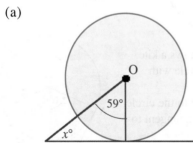

(b)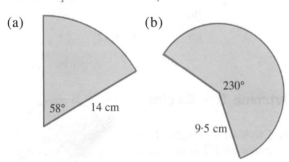

Properties of a Circle

33. Copy the diagrams below and fill in the sizes of the angles marked with the letters x and y.

(a)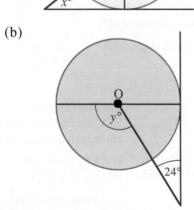

(b)

34. Calculate the length of the line marked x.

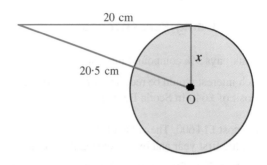

35. Calculate the sizes of the angles marked m and n.

(a)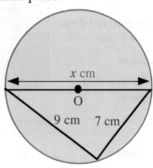

(b)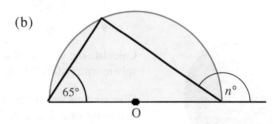

36. In the diagram below, calculate x, correct to 1 decimal place.

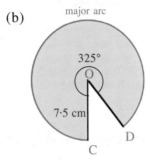

37. Write down the size of the angle marked $t°$ where PQ and PR are tangents to the circle.

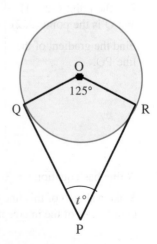

Specimen N.A.B. -Maths 1

Outcome 1 - Using Percentages

1. Scotia Bank pays 5% compound interest per annum.

   How much interest would be received after two years
   on a deposit of £640 in Scotia Bank ?   (5)

2. A new car cost £14 600. The value of the car depreciated
   by 15% in the first year and by 9% during the second.

   Calculate the value of the car after 2 years.   (5)

Outcome 2 - Volumes

$$V_{sphere} = \frac{4}{3}\pi r^3, \qquad V_{cone} = \frac{1}{3}\pi r^2 h, \qquad V_{cylinder} = \pi r^2 h$$

3. A container is in the shape of
   a cone as shown in the diagram.

   Calculate the volume of the
   container.   (2)

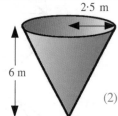
2·5 m
6 m

4.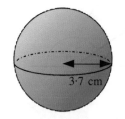
3·7 cm

   Calculate the volume of a
   sphere with radius 3·7 cm.

   Give your answer correct to
   two significant figures and
   state the units clearly.   (4)

5. A tin of soup is in the shape
   of a cylinder.

   The radius of the base is 3·2 cm
   and its height is 9·5 cm.

   Calculate its volume.

   Give your answer correct to
   3 significant figures.   (3)

   3·2 cm
   9·5 cm

Outcome 3 - Lines

6. P is the point (−2, −1)
   and Q is the point (3, 2),

   Find the gradient of the
   line PQ.

   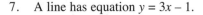

   (2)

7. A line has equation $y = 3x - 1$.

   Make a sketch of this line on blank paper showing the
   coordinates of the intercept on the y-axis.   (2)

8. Find the equation
   of this straight
   line in the diagram
   in terms of x and y.

   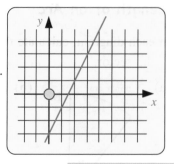
   (3)

Outcome 4 - Algebra

9. Simplify :-   (a) $a(5a + 2b)$ (1)

              (b) $(x + 3)(x - 2)$ (2)

10. Factorise :-   (a) $x^2 - 8x$ (1)

               (b) $a^2 - b^2$ (1)

               (c) $x^2 + 8x + 12$ (2)

Outcome 5 - Circles

11. Calculate the length of the
    minor arc PQ in this circle
    with radius 17 cm.

    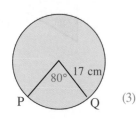
    80°   17 cm
    P   Q   (3)

12.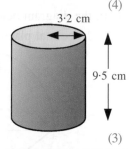
    7·5 cm   50°   B
    A

    Calculate the area of the
    pink sector of the circle
    shown.   (3)

13. The diagram shows a kite
    AOBT and a circle with
    centre O.
    AT is a tangent to the circle
    at A and BT is a tangent to
    the circle at B.

    (a)   State the size of angle OBT.   (1)

    (b)   Find the size of angle ATB.   (2)

    O
    130°
    A   B
    T

14. V

    S   T

    The diagram shows triangle
    STV inscribed in a semi -
    circle with diameter ST.

    If ∠VST = 68°, find
    the size of ∠VTS.   (1)

Int-2-Credit Maths Book IC1

Mathematics 2

Trigonometry - an Introduction

Trigonometry is one topic in mathematics that helps you calculate the size of an unknown side in a right angled triangle. (Pythagoras Theorem is another).

It can also help calculate the size of an unknown angle in a right angled triangle.

Look at the following 3 right angled triangles. They all have TWO things in common.

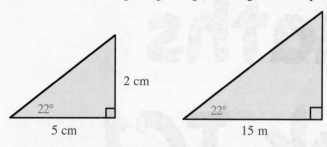
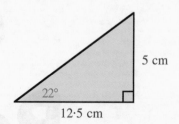

- They all have an angle in common (*in this case 22°*).

- When you divide the vertical side by the horizontal side in each case, you obtain the same answer.

$$\frac{2}{5} = 0\cdot4, \qquad \frac{6}{15} = 0\cdot4, \qquad \frac{5}{12\cdot5} = 0\cdot4.$$

For every Right Angled Triangle (*with an angle of 22°*), it is always true that when you divide the vertical side of the triangle by the horizontal side, you get an answer of 0·4.

This number, 0·4 has a special name here - It is called the "TANGENT of 22°" or "tan 22°" for short.

The Tangent (and the Naming of the Sides in a Right Angled Triangle)

Instead of vertical and horizontal, we use 3 names to describe the sides of a right angled triangle :-

hypotenuse	- the longest side
opposite	- directly **across from** the angle
adjacent	- right **next to** the angle

The Tangent is defined as follows :-

$$\Rightarrow \qquad \text{Tangent of angle A} = \frac{\text{opposite}}{\text{adjacent}}$$

or $$\tan A = \frac{\text{opp}}{\text{adj}}$$ for short.

From the above triangles we saw :- $\tan 22° = \frac{2}{5} = 0\cdot4$, $\tan 22° = \frac{6}{15} = 0\cdot4$, $\tan 22° = \frac{5}{12\cdot5} = 0\cdot4$.

Note :- Every angle from 0° to 90° has its own tangent value.

These values can be found using a SCIENTIFIC CALCULATOR.

Exercise 11·1

1. Use the **tangent** (or tan) button on a scientific calculator to find the following tangents and give your answer correct to **3 decimal places** :-

   (a) tan 23°   (b) tan 47°   (c) tan 54°   (d) tan 85°

   (e) tan 55°   (f) tan 16°   (g) tan 4°   (h) tan 64°

   (i) tan 83°   (j) tan 45°   (k) tan 65·3°   (l) tan 3·5°

2. Check with your calculator that tan 22° really is 0·40 (to 2 decimal places).

3. Look at this right angled triangle with ∠G = 58°.

   (a) What is the length of the "**opposite**" side ?

   (b) What is the length of the "**adjacent**" side ?

   (c) Divide :-   (opposite ÷ adjacent) to get => tan 58°.

   (d) Look up tan 58° on your calculator
       to check you get the same answer.

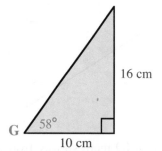

16 cm

G 58°

10 cm

Using Trigonometry to Calculate the Opposite Side

You can use your calculator, along with **tangents**, to quickly and easily calculate the length of the **opposite** side of a right angled triangle as long as you already know the **angle** and the **adjacent side**.

Example :–

The right angled triangle shown has angle P = 25° and adjacent side = 8 cm.

Calculate the length of the **opposite side**.

$$\tan P = \frac{\text{opp}}{\text{adj}}$$

$$\Rightarrow \quad \tan 25° = \frac{x}{8}$$

$$\Rightarrow \quad 0·466... = \frac{x}{8}$$

$$\Rightarrow \quad x = 8 \times 0·466... = 3·7304.....$$

$$\Rightarrow \quad x = 3·7 \text{ cm } (\textit{to 1 decimal place})$$

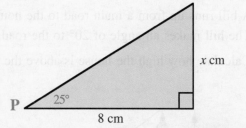

x cm

P 25°

8 cm

TOA

Exercise 11·2

1. Make a sketch of this right angled triangle and use the method shown above to calculate the size of the **opposite** side.

$$\tan C = \frac{\text{opp}}{\text{adj}}$$

$$\Rightarrow \quad \tan 65° = \frac{x}{15}$$

$$\Rightarrow \quad 2·........ = \frac{x}{15}$$

$$\Rightarrow \quad x = ... \times ....$$

$$\Rightarrow \quad x = ... \text{ cm} \quad (\textit{to 1 decimal place})$$

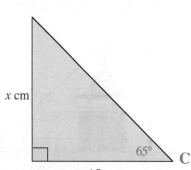

x cm

65°

C

15 cm

2. Sketch each of these right angled triangles and use **tangents** to calculate the length of the opposite side (x cm) in each case, to 1 decimal place :-

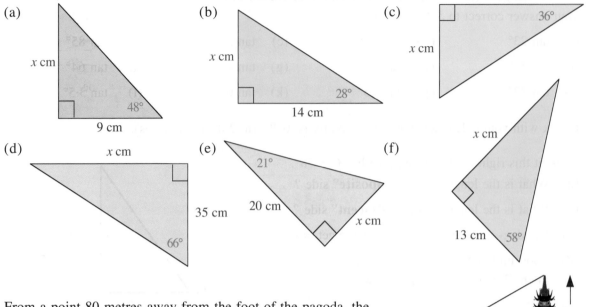

(a) x cm, 48°, 9 cm

(b) x cm, 28°, 14 cm

(c) 7·8 cm, 36°, x cm

(d) x cm, 35 cm, 66°

(e) 21°, 20 cm, x cm

(f) x cm, 13 cm, 58°

3. From a point 80 metres away from the foot of the pagoda, the angle of elevation of the top is measured as 35°.

   Calculate the height of the pagoda.

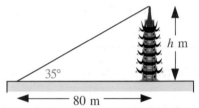

35°, 80 m, h m

4.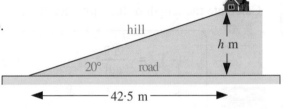

   18°, 25 metres, h m

   The angle of elevation of the top of a tree from a point 25 metres from its foot is 18°.

   Calculate the height of the tree.

5. A hill runs up from a main road to the house at the top. The hill makes an angle of 20° to the road.

   Calculate how high the house is above the road.

   hill, 20°, road, 42·5 m, h m

6. h m, 32°, 200 m

   From the far end of a bridge, the angle of elevation of a belfry is 32°.

   If it is 200 metres from the far end of the bridge to the foot of the belfry, how high is the belfry ?

7. From the top of a cliff, a small boat is observed at an angle of depression of 19°.

   If the boat is 120 metres from the foot of the cliff, find the height of the cliff.

   19°, h m, 120 metres

8.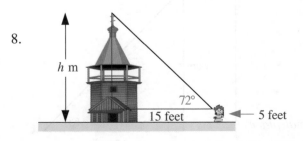

   h m, 72°, 15 feet, 5 feet

   A girl, who's eyes are 5 feet above ground-level, is attempting to measure the height of this tower.

   She is standing 15 feet from the tower looking to the top at an angle of 72° to the horizontal.

   How high is the tower ?

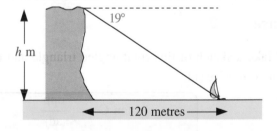

Calculating an Angle using the Tangent

Qu. Imagine you already know that **tan A = 0·9**.

How can you work backwards to find the size of ∠A ?

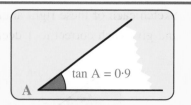

Ans. You press **two** buttons [shift] [tan] along with **0·9** and the answer **42** appears.

(In some calculators it is [2nd] [tan] and in others it is [Inv] [tan])

* check with your teacher

Example :-

The right angled triangle shown has sides AB = 8 cm and BC = 5 cm.

Calculate the size of angle BAC.

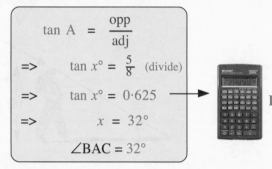

$$\tan A = \frac{opp}{adj}$$

$$\Rightarrow \quad \tan x° = \frac{5}{8} \quad (divide)$$

$$\Rightarrow \quad \tan x° = 0·625$$

$$\Rightarrow \quad x = 32°$$

$$\angle BAC = 32°$$

PRESS your 2 buttons NOW

TOA

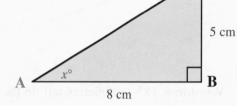

Exercise 11·3

1. Check which buttons you need to press on **YOUR** calculator and find the sizes of the angles A, B, C ..... to the nearest degree :-

   (a) tan A = 0·466   (b) tan B = 1·483

   (c) tan C = 0·249   (d) tan D = 0·105

   (e) tan E = 1   (f) tan F = 0·781

   (g) tan G = $\frac{2}{5}$ (h) tan H = $\frac{3}{14}$

   (i) tan I = $\frac{9}{4}$ (j) tan J = $\frac{23}{2}$

2. Make a sketch of this right angled triangle and use the method shown above to calculate the size of ∠RPQ to 1 decimal place.

   $$\tan P = \frac{opp}{adj}$$
   $$\Rightarrow \quad \tan x° = \frac{10}{25}$$
   $$\Rightarrow \quad \tan x° = ...$$
   $$\Rightarrow \quad x = ... \quad (to\ 1\ dec.\ place)$$
   $$\angle RPQ = ...$$

   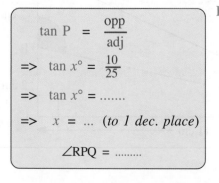

3. Do the same for the following triangles. Calculate the sizes of angles y° and z° (*to 1 decimal place.*)

   (a)
   $$\tan A = \frac{opp}{adj}$$
   $$\Rightarrow \quad \tan y° = \frac{4}{9}$$
   $$\Rightarrow \quad \tan y° = ...$$
   $$\Rightarrow \quad y = ...$$

   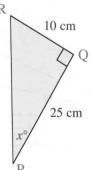

   (b)
   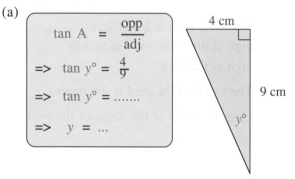

   $$\tan B = \frac{opp}{adj}$$
   $$\Rightarrow \quad \tan z° = \frac{4·2}{.....}$$
   $$\Rightarrow \quad \tan z° = ...$$
   $$\Rightarrow \quad z = ...$$

4. Sketch each of these right angled triangles and use **tangent** to calculate the size of angles *a, b, ... f.* and give each correct to 1 decimal place :-

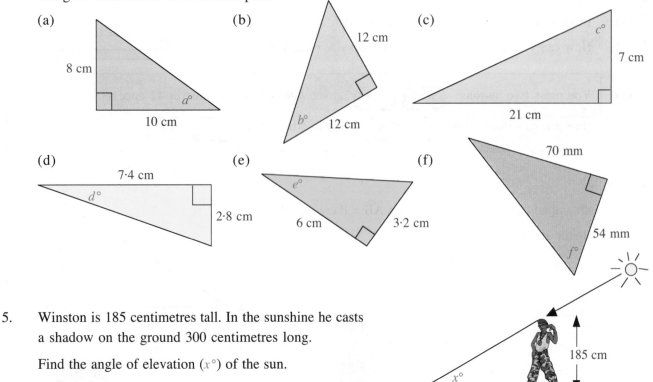

(a)

8 cm

10 cm

a°

(b)

12 cm

12 cm

b°

(c)

c°

7 cm

21 cm

(d)

7·4 cm

d°

2·8 cm

(e)

e°

6 cm

3·2 cm

(f)

70 mm

54 mm

f°

5. Winston is 185 centimetres tall. In the sunshine he casts a shadow on the ground 300 centimetres long.

Find the angle of elevation (*x°*) of the sun.

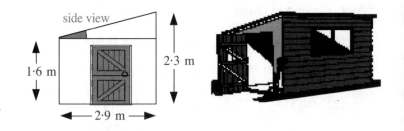

185 cm

x°

300 cm

6.

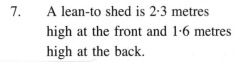

100 ft

x°

35 ft

What is the angle of elevation of the top of a bell tower 100 feet high, from a point on level ground 35 feet from the base of the tower ?

7. A lean-to shed is 2·3 metres high at the front and 1·6 metres high at the back.

The width of the shed is 2·9 metres.

Find the angle of the slope of the roof.

side view

1·6 m

2·3 m

2·9 m

8. Triangle ADC is right angled at C.

(a) Use trigonometry to calculate the size of ∠BDC.

(b) Calculate the size of angle ∠ABD.

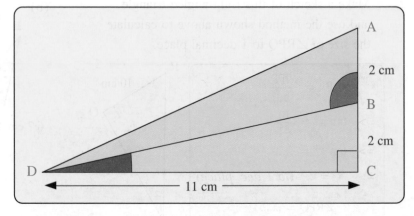

A

2 cm

B

2 cm

D

C

11 cm

The Sine Ratio

In a similar way to the tangent ratio, where you worked with the opposite and the adjacent sides of a right angled triangle, there is another trig ratio, called the **Sine Ratio** where you again work with 2 sides, – this time the **opposite** and the **hypotenuse**.

For every given angle (**A**) in a right angled triangle, the **sine of A°** (or **sin A°** for short) is defined as :-

$$=> \quad \text{Sine of angle A} = \frac{\text{opposite}}{\text{hypotenuse}}$$

or $\boxed{\text{Sin A} = \frac{\text{opp}}{\text{hyp}}}$ for short.

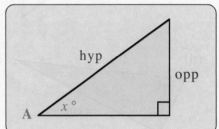

Example 1 :-

The right angled triangle below has

- angle Q = 25° and
- hypotenuse = 8 cm.

Calculate the length of the **opposite side**.

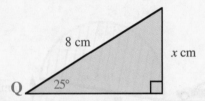

$$\sin Q = \frac{\text{opp}}{\text{hyp}}$$

$$=> \quad \sin 25° = \frac{x}{8}$$

$$=> \quad x = 8 \sin 25° = 3 \cdot 3809.....$$

$$=> \quad x = 3 \cdot 4 \text{ cm } (\textit{to 1 dec. place})$$

SOH

Example 2 :-

The right angled triangle below has sides

$$BC = 5 \text{ cm and } AC = 8 \text{ cm.}$$

Calculate the size of **angle BAC**.

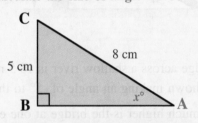

$$\sin A = \frac{\text{opp}}{\text{hyp}}$$

$$=> \quad \sin x° = \frac{5}{8}$$

$$=> \quad \sin x° = 0 \cdot 625 \rightarrow \boxed{\text{shift}}$$

$$=> \quad x = 38 \cdot 7° \leftarrow \boxed{\text{sin}}$$

$$\angle BAC = 38 \cdot 7°$$

Exercise 11·4

1. Check which buttons you need to press on **YOUR** calculator, if you don't already know. Write down the following :-

    (a) sin 50°   (b) sin 30°

    (c) sin 60°   (d) sin 84°

    (e) sin 7°   (f) sin 28·5°

    (g) sin 19·8°   (h) sin 72°

    (i) sin 89·9°   (j) sin 90°

2. Use your calculator to determine the sizes of angles A, B, C, ... (*to 1 decimal place*).

    (a) $\sin A = \frac{2}{5}$ (b) $\sin B = \frac{3}{14}$

    (c) $\sin C = \frac{4}{9}$ (d) $\sin D = \frac{24}{25}$

    (e) $\sin E = \frac{1}{8}$ (f) $\sin F = \frac{2}{11}$

    (g) $\sin G = \frac{17}{34}$ (h) $\sin H = \frac{1}{4}$

    (i) $\sin I = \frac{2 \cdot 5}{7 \cdot 5}$ (j) $\sin J = \frac{6 \cdot 4}{10 \cdot 9}$

3. Sketch each of these right angled triangles and use **sine** to calculate the length of the opposite side (*x* cm) in each case, (*to 1 decimal place*) :-

(a)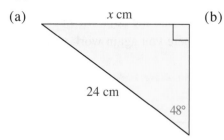
x cm
24 cm
48°

(b)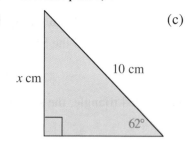
10 cm
x cm
62°

(c)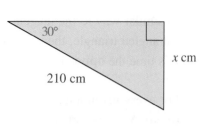
30°
210 cm
x cm

(d)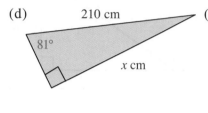
210 cm
81°
x cm

(e)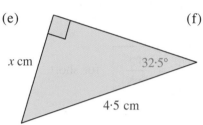
x cm
32·5°
4·5 cm

(f)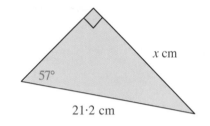
x cm
57°
21·2 cm

4.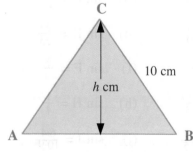
3·5 m
h m
30°

A plank is 3·5 metres long, and lies at an angle of 30° to the ground.

It is just touching the top of a wall.

Calculate the height (*h* metres) of this wall.

5. A bridge across a shallow river is 10·5 metres long.
It is shown making an angle of 5° to the horizontal.

How much higher is the bridge at one end than it is at the other at this stage ?

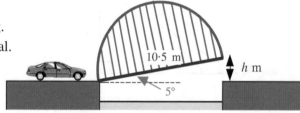
10·5 m
h m
5°

6.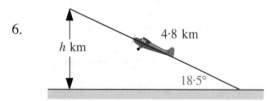
h km
4·8 km
18·5°

An aeroplane takes off in a straight line at an angle of 18·5° to the horizontal and flies for 4·8 km on this path.

What height is the plane at that point ?

7. The angle of slope of a roof is 52°.

If the sloping part is 8 metres long, how high is the apex above the foot of the roof ?

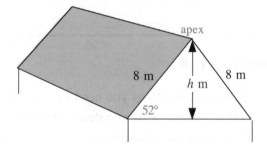
apex
8 m
h m
8 m
52°

8. Triangle ABC is an **equilateral** triangle of side 10 cm.

(a) Write down the size of ∠BAC.

(b) Calculate its height (*h* cm), **using trigonometry**.

(c) Now check your answer using **Pythagoras' Theorem**.

C
10 cm
h cm
A   B

9. Sketch each of these right angled triangles and use **sine** to calculate the size of angles $a, b, c.....f$.
   (*Answer correct to 1 decimal place*).

(a)

4 cm

10 cm

$a°$

(b)

7·5 cm

5 cm

$b°$

(c)

$c°$

12·8 cm

2·4 cm

(d)

300 mm

$d°$

250 mm

(e)

8·9 m

$e°$

10·4 m

(f)

1·25 km

2 km

$f°$

10. A kite is flying at a height of 80 metres and is attached to a taut string 100 metres long.

Find the angle between the string and the ground.

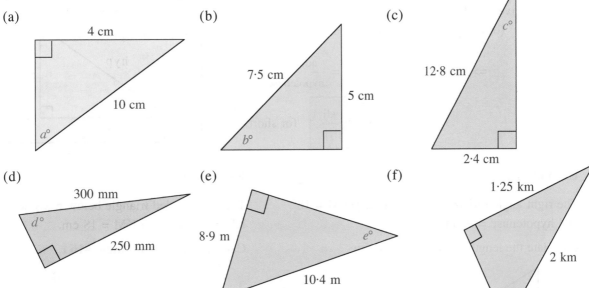

80 m   100 m

?

11.

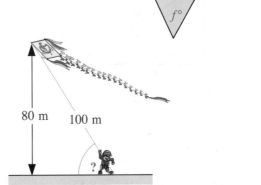

65 m   275 m $x°$

A funicular railway is 275 metres long and the difference between the height from the top to the bottom is 65 metres.

Find the angle of inclination between the railway and the ground.

12. The hand-rail of a staircase is 12 metres long. Its lower end is 1·4 metres above ground and its upper end 4·6 metres above ground.

Find the angle between the hand-rail and the horizontal.
(*Draw a sketch to show the required angle*).

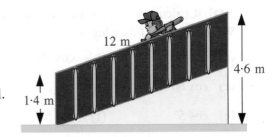

12 m

4·6 m

1·4 m

13. Two vertical columns are 12·4 metres and 18·1 metres in height. A wire, stretched from top to top, is 22·2 metres long.

Find the angle of the slope of the wire.
(*Draw a sketch to show the required angle*).

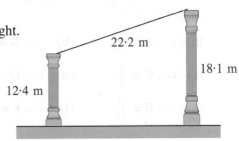

22·2 m

18·1 m

12·4 m

The Cosine Ratio

For every given angle (A) in a right angled triangle, the
cosine of A° (or cos A° for short) is defined as :-

$$\Rightarrow \quad \text{Cosine of angle A} = \frac{\text{adjacent}}{\text{hypotenuse}}$$

or $\boxed{\text{Cos A} = \dfrac{\text{adj}}{\text{hyp}}}$ for short.

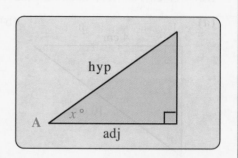

Example 1 :-

The right angled triangle below has angle M = 18°
and hypotenuse = 9 cm.

Calculate the length of the adjacent side.

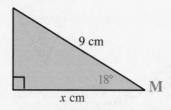

$$\cos M = \frac{\text{adj}}{\text{hyp}}$$

$$\Rightarrow \quad \cos 18° = \frac{x}{9}$$

$$\Rightarrow \quad x = 9 \cos 18° = 8{\cdot}559.....$$

$$\Rightarrow \quad x = 8{\cdot}6 \text{ cm (to 1 decimal place)}$$

CAH

Example 2 :-

The right angled triangle below has sides
KL = 14·5 cm and KM = 18 cm.

Calculate the size of angle MKL.

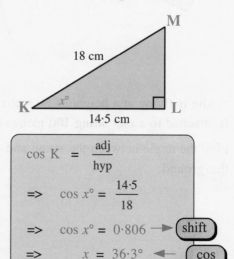

$$\cos K = \frac{\text{adj}}{\text{hyp}}$$

$$\Rightarrow \quad \cos x° = \frac{14{\cdot}5}{18}$$

$$\Rightarrow \quad \cos x° = 0{\cdot}806 \rightarrow \boxed{\text{shift}}$$

$$\Rightarrow \quad x = 36{\cdot}3° \leftarrow \boxed{\text{cos}}$$

$$\angle \text{MKL} = 36{\cdot}3°$$

Exercise 11·5

1. Check which buttons you need to press on
   YOUR calculator, if you don't already know.
   Write down the following :-

   (a) cos 40°   (b) cos 80°

   (c) cos 60°   (d) cos 30°

   (e) cos 5°   (f) cos 52·5°

2. Use your calculator to determine the sizes of
   angles A, B, C, ...

   (a) $\cos A = \frac{4}{5}$ (b) $\cos B = \frac{5}{14}$

   (c) $\cos C = \frac{1}{9}$ (d) $\cos D = \frac{21}{25}$

   (e) $\cos E = \frac{2}{11}$ (f) $\cos F = \frac{7}{8}$

3. Sketch each of these right angled triangles
   and use **cosine** to calculate the length of the
   adjacent side (x cm) in each case.
   (*to 1 decimal place*).

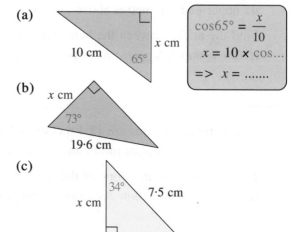

(a)

$$\cos 65° = \frac{x}{10}$$
$$x = 10 \times \cos...$$
$$\Rightarrow x = ...$$

(b)

(c)

4. The diagonal of this rectangle ABCD is
    25 centimetres long.

    Calculate the length of the side DC.

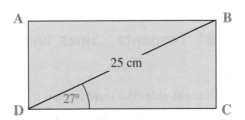

5.

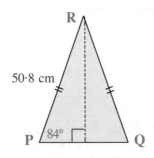

A yacht is moored to the quay wall by a rope
4·5 metres long. When the rope is taut, it makes
an angle of 53° with the surface of the sea.

How far is the yacht from the quay wall ?

6. This umbrella has a cord joining the end
    of the handle to one of the "prongs" of
    the cover.

    Calculate the length of the handle shown (x).

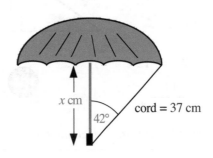

7.

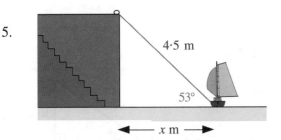

Triangle PQR is isosceles with

   •   side PR = 50·8 cm.

   •   ∠RPQ is 84°.

Calculate the length of side PQ.

8. A new floodlight has to be held in place
    overnight to enable its concrete base to dry.
    It is secured by two strong metal wires
    The longer wire is 39 metres in length and
    is attached to the ground 30 metres from
    the base of the floodlight.

    Calculate the angle this wire makes with the ground.

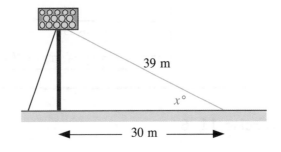

9.

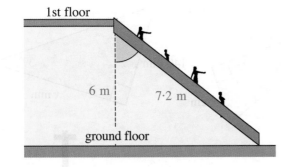

An escalator connects the 1st floor to the ground
floor 6 metres below.

   (a) If the escalator is 7·2 metres long, calculate the size
        of the angle between the escalator and the vertical.

   (b) Write down the size of the angle between the
        escalator and the ground floor.

10. Triangle KLM is **isosceles** with sides ML = 240 mm
    and MK = 74 mm.

    Calculate the size of angle MKL.

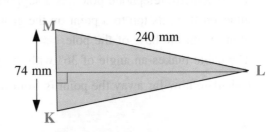

A Mixture of Tangents, Sines and Cosines - Trickier Examples

Finding :-

      1. the **adjacent** side of a right angled triangle using **tan**.

      2. the **hypotenuse** of a right angled triangle using **sin**.

      3. the **hypotenuse** of a right angled triangle using **cos**.

Example 1 :-

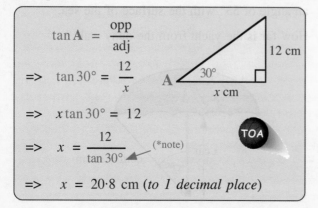

$$\tan A = \frac{opp}{adj}$$

$$\Rightarrow \quad \tan 30° = \frac{12}{x}$$

$$\Rightarrow \quad x \tan 30° = 12$$

$$\Rightarrow \quad x = \frac{12}{\tan 30°} \quad \text{(*note)}$$

$$\Rightarrow \quad x = 20·8 \text{ cm } (to\ 1\ decimal\ place)$$

Example 2 :-

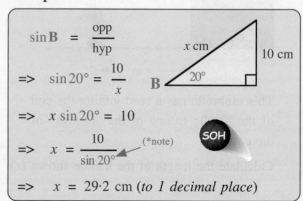

$$\sin B = \frac{opp}{hyp}$$

$$\Rightarrow \quad \sin 20° = \frac{10}{x}$$

$$\Rightarrow \quad x \sin 20° = 10$$

$$\Rightarrow \quad x = \frac{10}{\sin 20°} \quad \text{(*note)}$$

$$\Rightarrow \quad x = 29·2 \text{ cm } (to\ 1\ decimal\ place)$$

Example 3 :-

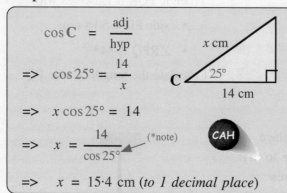

$$\cos C = \frac{adj}{hyp}$$

$$\Rightarrow \quad \cos 25° = \frac{14}{x}$$

$$\Rightarrow \quad x \cos 25° = 14$$

$$\Rightarrow \quad x = \frac{14}{\cos 25°} \quad \text{(*note)}$$

$$\Rightarrow \quad x = 15·4 \text{ cm } (to\ 1\ decimal\ place)$$

* note :-

When the missing length, (the x), appears on the **bottom** of the fraction, you end up "swapping" it with the *sin*, *tan* or *cos*.

Exercise 11·6

1.   Use **tangent** to calculate the length of the **adjacent side** in each case, (*to 1 decimal place*) :-

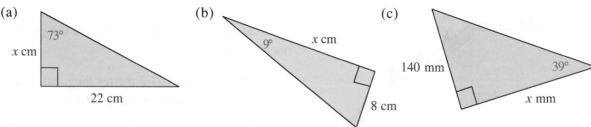

(a)   73° x cm   22 cm

(b)   9° x cm   8 cm

(c)   140 mm   39° x mm

2.   Use **tangent** in this question.

The 5·9 metre telephone pole has a support cable attached from its top to a point on the ground, along from the base of the pole.

The cable makes an angle of 36° with the ground.

Calculate how far away the point is from the pole.

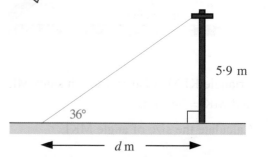

3. Use **sin** to calculate the length of the **hypotenuse** in each case, (*to 1 decimal place*) :-

(a)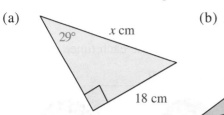

(b)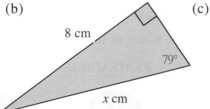

(c)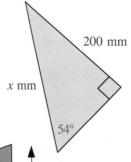

4. Use **sin** in this question.

The angle between the sloping roof on this house and the horizontal is 23°.
From the ceiling of the room to the top of the roof is 1·2 metres.

What is the length of the sloping roof ?

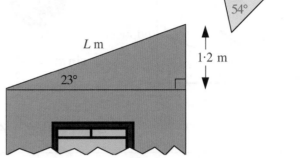

5. Use **cos** to calculate the length of the **hypotenuse** in each case, to 1 decimal place :-

(a)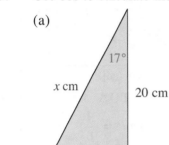

(b)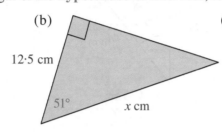

(c)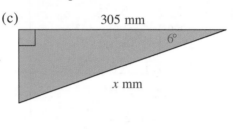

6. Use **cos** in this question.

A pencil lies with its end just resting against a book.

The point of the pencil sits on a table 14·5 cm from the binding of the book.

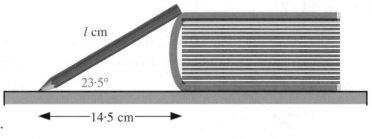

If the angle between the pencil and the table top is 23·5°, calculate the length of the pencil.

7.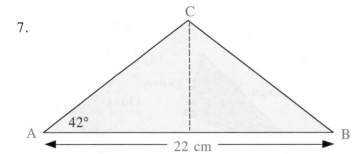

Shown is an **isosceles** triangle with

- ∠BAC = 42°
- base AB = 22 cm.

Calculate the **perimeter** of triangle ABC.

8. PQRS is a trapezium with

- ∠QPS and ∠RSP = 90°
- ∠PQR = 125°
- PS = 8·4 cm

Calculate the length of the sloping line QR.

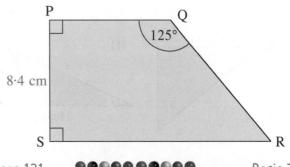

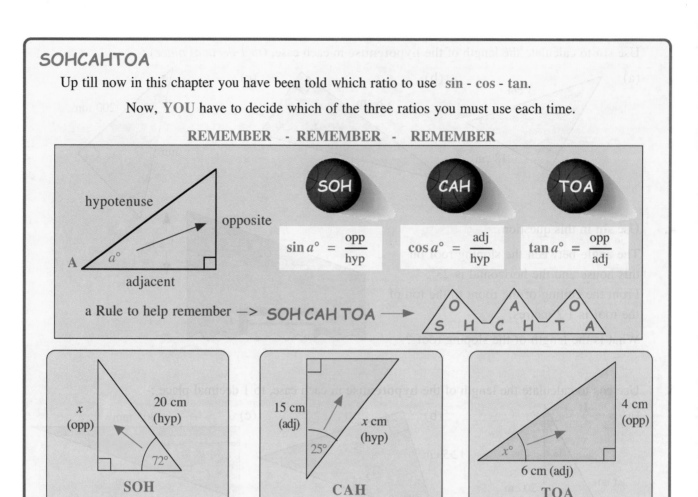

SOHCAHTOA

Up till now in this chapter you have been told which ratio to use sin - cos - tan.

Now, **YOU** have to decide which of the three ratios you must use each time.

REMEMBER - REMEMBER - REMEMBER

$$\sin a° = \frac{opp}{hyp}$$

$$\cos a° = \frac{adj}{hyp}$$

$$\tan a° = \frac{opp}{adj}$$

a Rule to help remember $\rightarrow$ **SOH CAH TOA** $\rightarrow$

SOH

$$\sin 72° = \frac{x}{20}$$

CAH

$$\cos 25° = \frac{15}{x}$$

TOA

$$\tan x° = \frac{4}{6}$$

Exercise 11·7

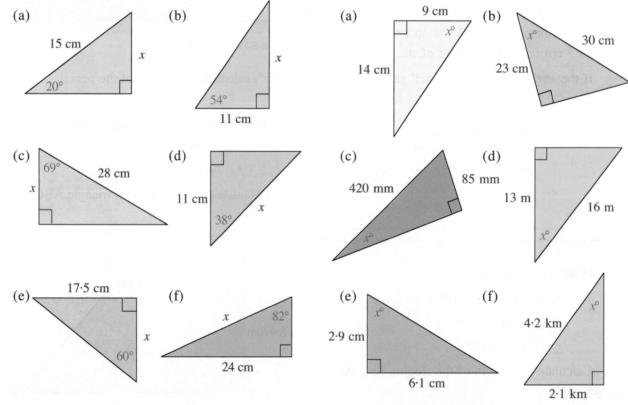

1. Choose your ratio from **SOHCAHTOA** to find the value of *x* in each case, (*to 1 decimal place*).

   (a) 15 cm, 20°, *x*

   (b) *x*, 54°, 11 cm

   (c) 69°, 28 cm, *x*

   (d) 11 cm, 38°, *x*

   (e) 17·5 cm, 60°, *x*

   (f) *x*, 82°, 24 cm

2. Choose the correct ratio to find the size of angle *x*° in each case, (*to 1 decimal place*).

   (a) 9 cm, *x*°, 14 cm

   (b) *x*°, 30 cm, 23 cm

   (c) 420 mm, 85 mm, *x*°

   (d) 13 m, 16 m, *x*°

   (e) *x*°, 2·9 cm, 6·1 cm

   (f) 4·2 km, *x*°, 2·1 km

3. The angle of elevation from the ground to the top of an apartment block is 42·5°.
The angle is measured at a point 43 metres from the block.

Calculate the height, h metres, of the apartment block,
correct to 1 decimal place.

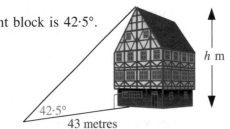

42·5°
43 metres

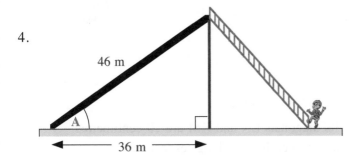

4.

46 m

A

36 m

A park has a new slide 46 metres long.
The foot of the slide is 36 metres from the
metal support pole.

Calculate the size of the angle (**A**), between
the slide and the ground.

5. At low tide, passengers have to disembark
from the ship, up a gangway, to the dockside.

The water level is 17 feet below the top edge
of the dockside and the gangway is at an
angle of 22° to the water.

Calculate the length of the gangway.

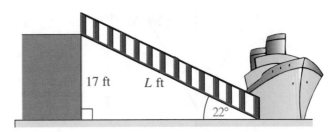

17 ft L ft

22°

6.

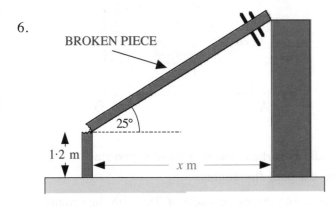

BROKEN PIECE

25°

1·2 m

x m

A telegraph pole was 9 metres in height before it
snapped during a storm and toppled over.

The top of the pole came to rest on a wall as shown.

(a) Use the information in the diagram to write
down the length of the broken piece.

(b) Now calculate how far the base of the pole was
from the wall.

7. In a school hall, the stage is lit by a
spotlight fixed to a wall.

The spotlight is 4·62 metres up the wall and is
set to shine on a spot on the stage at a downward
angle of 70°, as shown.

Calculate the length of the beam of light.

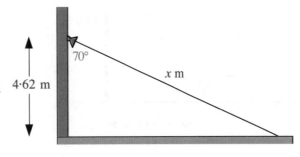

70°

4·62 m

x m

8.

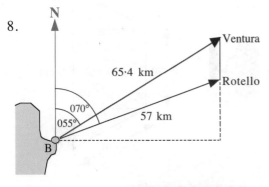

N

Ventura

65·4 km

Rotello

070°
055°

57 km

B

Two ships, the Ventura and the Rotello, set sail from Barlow
Harbour.

• the Ventura sails for 65·4 km on a bearing 055°.

• the Rotello sails for 57 km on a bearing 070°.

At that point, the Ventura was directly North of the Rotello.

How far apart were the two ships ?

9.   The owners of Kingston Hall Manor erected an accessible
     entrance ramp at the main front entrance.

     Local building regulations stated that ramps
     had to be built at an angle of not more
     than 13·8° to the horizontal ground.

     A side view of the ramp which
     was actually erected is shown.

     Did this ramp satisfy the local building regulations ?

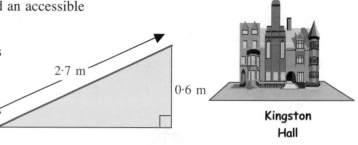 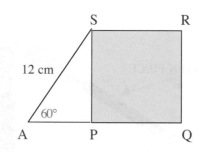

Kingston
Hall

10.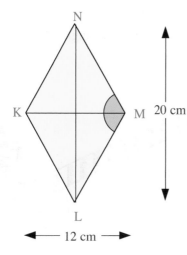

     KLMN is a rhombus.

     Its diagonals LN and KM are 20 centimetres
     and 12 centimetres long respectively.

     Calculate the size of the shaded angle NML.

11. The figure shows a square PQRS with a right angled
     triangle APS attached.

     AS = 12 centimetres,   ∠SAP = 60°.

     Calculate the **area** of square PQRS.

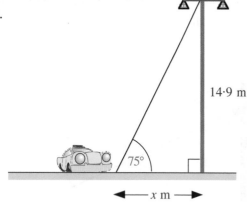

12.

     A taxi is parked next to a cable supporting
     the car park floodlights.

     This cable makes an angle of 75° with the ground.

     The height from the ground to the lights is
     14·9 metres.

     How far away is the foot of the cable from
     the base of the floodlight pole ?

13. The design of a wheel for a wheelbarrow is shown.
     The safety requirements state that angle (x) must
     be greater than 35°.

     Part of this design has its measurements as shown.

     Do these measurements satisfy the safety requirements ?

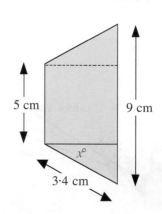

1. Calculate the value of x in each case, to 1 decimal place :-

(a)

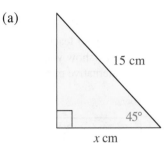

15 cm

45°

x cm

(b)

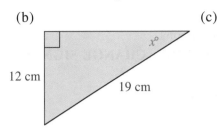

$x°$

12 cm

19 cm

(c)

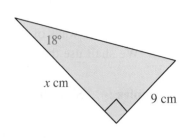

18°

x cm

9 cm

In Questions **2, 3 and 4**, it will be of some help to draw an appropriate diagram.

2. A 15 metre ladder, resting against a wall, is secured 6·5 metres from the foot of the wall.

   Calculate the angle the ladder makes with the ground.

3. A boy who is 1·2 metres tall flies a kite on a string of length 36 metres.

   The string of the kite makes an angle of 62° with the horizontal.

   What is the **height** of the kite above the ground ?

4. Two mountains are 1140 metres and 1262 metres high.

   A climber standing on the summit of the lower one looks up through an angle of elevation of 22° to see the summit of the taller one.

   Calculate the horizontal distance between the summits.

5. A camera is positioned at the top of a 90 metre high tower.

   Two cars are viewed from the camera with angles of depression of 31° and 47°.

   (a) How far is each car from the base of the tower ?

   (b) How far apart are the cars ?

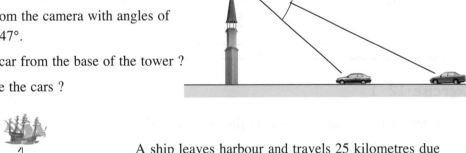

6.

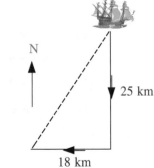

N

25 km

18 km

A ship leaves harbour and travels 25 kilometres due South and then 18 kilometres due West.

On what **bearing** must it travel to return to harbour ?

(*to the nearest degree*).

4 cm

7. A glass has a **radius** of 4·5 centimetres.

   The red straw in the glass makes an angle of 72° with the base and protrudes 4 centimetres above the rim of the glass.

   How long is the straw ?

72°

radius 4·5 cm

Solving Equations

There are various ways of solving equations.

We shall use the "**CHANGE SIDE - CHANGE SIGN**" method. *

* your teacher may show you an alternative method

Examples :-   Solve the following :-

Move the +7 to the other side ... change it to −7

$$x + 7 = 11$$
$$\Rightarrow \quad x = 11 - 7$$
$$\Rightarrow \quad x = 4$$

Move the × 4 to the other side and change to ÷ 4

$$4x = 22$$
$$\Rightarrow \quad x = 22 \div 4$$
$$\Rightarrow \quad x = 5\tfrac{1}{2}$$

Move the −7 to the other side and change to +7

Move the × 2 to the other side and change to ÷ 2

$$2x - 7 = 11$$
$$\Rightarrow \quad 2x = 11 + 7$$
$$\Rightarrow \quad 2x = 18$$
$$\Rightarrow \quad x = 9$$

Move the 3x to the left side and change to −3x

Move the −2 to the right side and change to +2

Move the × 5 to the other side and change to ÷ 5

$$8x - 2 = 3x + 28$$
$$\Rightarrow \quad 8x - 3x = 28 + 2$$
$$\Rightarrow \quad 5x = 28 + 2$$
$$\Rightarrow \quad 5x = 30$$
$$\Rightarrow \quad x = 6$$

Multiply out the brackets

Double Change side
Change sign
Tidy up

Divide by 7

$$2(4x + 1) = x + 16$$
$$\Rightarrow \quad 8x + 2 = x + 16$$
$$\Rightarrow \quad 8x - x = 16 - 2$$
$$\Rightarrow \quad 7x = 14$$
$$\Rightarrow \quad x = 2$$

Multiply out brackets
(Watching −ve × −ve)
Tidy up

Double Change side
Change sign
Tidy up

Divide by 2

$$3(2x + 4) - 2(x - 2) = 2x + 36$$
$$\Rightarrow \quad 6x + 12 - 2x + 4 = 2x + 36$$
$$\Rightarrow \quad 4x - 2x = 36 - 16$$
$$\Rightarrow \quad 2x = 20$$
$$\Rightarrow \quad x = 10$$

Exercise 12·1

1.   Copy each equation and solve to find the value of x :-

   (a) $x + 7 = 9$ (b) $x + 15 = 15$ (c) $x - 4 = 8$

   (d) $x - 17 = 0$ (e) $x - 80 = 70$ (f) $x + 7 = 5$

   (g) $x + 14 = 0$ (h) $7 + x = 12$ (i) $3 + x = 2$

   (j) $5 + x = 5$ (k) $20 + x = 13$ (l) $11 + x = -9$

2.   Copy each equation and solve to find the value of the letter :-

   (a) $2x = 14$ (b) $5a = 40$ (c) $3b = 27$

   (d) $8p = 8$ (e) $4e = 6$ (f) $7c = 0$

   (g) $6d = 3$ (h) $3y = 150$ (i) $6r = 27$

   (j) $4q = 11$ (k) $5s = 28$ (l) $7t = 20$

   (m) $10k = 35$ (n) $5n = 4$ (o) $8h = 2$

3. Find the value of x in the following equations   *(Show each step of working carefully)*.

(a) $2x + 1 = 9$ (b) $3x + 4 = 19$ (c) $5x + 3 = 33$

(d) $4x + 8 = 16$ (e) $8x - 1 = 31$ (f) $6x - 4 = 14$

(g) $8x - 9 = 47$ (h) $7x - 7 = 0$ (i) $10x - 8 = 72$

(j) $5x - 10 = 45$ (k) $2x + 14 = 20$ (l) $7x - 1 = 69$

(m) $2x + 3 = 1$ (n) $12x + 12 = 0$ (o) $2x - 9 = 0$

(p) $4x + 20 = 4$ (q) $4x + 5 = 14$ (r) $6x - 8 = 19$

4. Copy and complete :-

(a) $7x + 2 = 3x + 14$
=> $7x - 3x = 14 - ....$
=> $4x = ...$
=> $x = ...$

(b) $4x - 5 = x + 16$
=> $4x - ... = ... + ...$
=> $3x = ...$
=> $x = ...$

5. Solve these equations using the same method as shown in Question 4 :-

(a) $3x + 1 = x + 7$ (b) $4x + 5 = 2x + 15$ (c) $6x + 1 = 3x + 13$

(d) $7x - 6 = 3x + 22$ (e) $8x - 1 = 2x + 29$ (f) $10x - 2 = 6x + 24$

(g) $9x - 1 = 7x + 14$ (h) $10x - 2 = 5x + 29$ (i) $12x - 12 = 2x + 11$

6. These equations look a little "**different**", but solve them in the same way as Question 5 :-

(a) $4x = 3x + 9$ (b) $6x = 2x + 28$ (c) $6x = 3x + 21$

(d) $7x = 5x + 3$ (e) $8x = 4x + 30$ (f) $7x - 44 = 5x$

(g) $4x - 27 = x$ (h) $9x + 8 = 7x$ (i) $3x - 55 = -7x$

7. Solve these equations by multiplying out the brackets first :-

(a) $2(x + 3) = 12$ (b) $3(x + 5) = 27$ (c) $4(x - 5) = 32$

(d) $7(x + 1) = 56$ (e) $10(x - 2) = 50$ (f) $2(x - 1) = 11$

(g) $5(x - 9) = 0$ (h) $8(x - 6) = 8$ (i) $3(x + 4) = -6$

8. Solve these equations :-

(a) $2(2x + 1) = 18$ (b) $3(4x - 8) = 36$ (c) $6(5x - 1) = 24$

(d) $2(3x + 4) = 20$ (e) $4(2x - 3) = 4x + 12$ (f) $2(1 + 5x) = 3x + 51$

(g) $6(3x - 5) = 13x$ (h) $11(2x - 3) = 15x + 2$ (i) $10(x + 13) = -3x$

9. Solve :-

(a) $2(x + 4) - x - 6 = 11$ (b) $3(x + 2) + 3x - 3 = 21$

(c) $5(x - 1) + 4x = 13$ (d) $2x + 5 + 6(x - 1) = 31$

(e) $3(x - 2) + 2(x + 4) = 17$ (f) $5(2x + 1) + 6(1 - 2x) = 1$

(g) $2(3x + 1) + 3(x - 4) = 4x + 5$ (h) $4(3x - 6) + 5(x + 1) = 5x + 5$

(i) $4(x + 5) - 2(x + 1) = 30$ (j) $2(4x + 1) - 3(x - 3) = x + 35$

10. Dave bought 5 bags of toffee. His friend Jan, bought 1 bag, but she already had 120 loose toffees.

They then discovered that had **exactly** the same number of toffees.

(a) Make up an equation to show this information.
(Let x represent the number of toffees in 1 bag).

(b) Solve the equation to determine how many toffees there were in each bag.

Further Equations with Brackets

Example 1 :-

Solve :- $x(x + 7) = (x + 3)(x + 1)$

$\Rightarrow \quad x^2 + 7x = x^2 + 4x + 3$

$\Rightarrow \quad x^2 + 7x - x^2 - 4x = 3$

$\Rightarrow \qquad\qquad 3x = 3$

$\Rightarrow \qquad\qquad\;\; x = 1$

Example 2 :-

The rectangle and the square are **equal** in area.
Form an equation and solve it to find their dimensions.

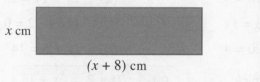

x cm

$(x + 8)$ cm

$(x + 3)$ cm

$x(x + 8) = (x + 3)^2$

$\Rightarrow \quad x^2 + 8x = x^2 + 6x + 9$

$\Rightarrow \quad x^2 + 8x - x^2 - 6x = 9$

$\Rightarrow \qquad\qquad 2x = 9$

$\Rightarrow \qquad\qquad\;\; x = 4 \cdot 5$

Dimensions :- **Rectangle** .... 4·5 cm by 12·5 cm

                Square .... 7·5 cm by 7·5 cm

Exercise 12·2

1. Multiply out the brackets and solve :-

   (a) $x(x + 4) = x^2 + 20$

   (b) $x(x + 5) = x^2 - 35$

   (c) $x(3x + 6) = 3(x^2 - 10)$

   (d) $(x + 5)(x - 3) = x(x - 1)$

   (e) $x(x + 10) = (x + 4)(x - 2)$

   (f) $(x + 4)^2 = x(x + 6)$

   (g) $(x - 2)^2 = x(x + 4)$

   (h) $(x + 1)^2 = x(x + 3)$

   (i) $(x + 1)^2 = (x - 2)^2$

   (j) $x^2 - x(x - 1) = 5$

   (k) $x^2 - x(5 + x) + 20 = 5$

   (l) $x^2 - (x - 4)^2 + 4 = 0$

2. The pictures in each pair below have the same **area**. (*All sizes are in centimetres*).

   (i) Make up an equation for each pair of pictures.

   (ii) Solve the equation to find the dimensions of each picture.

(a)

x

$x + 8$

$x + 4$

$x + 3$

(b)

x

x

$x - 3$

$x + 6$

(c)

$x + 5$

$x + 8$

x

$x - 1$

(d)

$x - 4$

$x - 8$

$x - 2$

$x + 4$

Equations with Fractions

Fractions are a complication in equations we could well do without.

But we can remove the fractions quite easily ....

> **Rule :-** Always **ELIMINATE** the fractions at the very beginning .....
>
> by **MULTIPLYING every term** by the l.c.m. of all the fractional denominators.

Example 1 :-

Multiply BOTH sides by **2** to eliminate the fraction $\frac{1}{2}$

$$\frac{1}{2}x + 5 = 9$$

$$2 \times \frac{1}{2}x + 2 \times 5 = 2 \times 9$$

$$=> \quad x + 10 = 18$$

$$=> \quad x = \boxed{8}$$

* note - every term must be multiplied by 2

Example 2 :-

Multiply BOTH sides by **20** to eliminate the two fractions, since the l.c.m. of 4 and 5 is **20**

$$\frac{3}{4}x + \frac{2}{5} = 1$$

$$20 \times \frac{3}{4}x + 20 \times \frac{2}{5} = 20 \times 1$$

$$=> \quad 15x + 8 = 20$$

$$=> \quad 15x = 12$$

$$=> \quad x = \frac{12}{15} = \frac{4}{5}$$

Exercise 12·3

1. Copy and complete the following two equations :-

(a)
$$\frac{1}{3}x + 2 = 6$$
$$3 \times \frac{1}{3}x + 3 \times 2 = 3 \times 6$$
$$=> \quad x + ... = ...$$
$$=> \quad x = ...$$

(b)
$$\frac{4}{5}x - 5 = \frac{1}{2}x + 1$$
$$10 \times \frac{4}{5}x - 10 \times 5 = 10 \times \frac{1}{2}x + 10 \times 1$$
$$=> \quad 8x - ... = ...x + ...$$
$$=> \quad ...\, x = ...$$
$$=> \quad x = ...$$

2. Solve each of these equations, by first multiplying every term by the l.c.m. of all the fractional denominators.

   This should help eliminate the fractions.

(a) $\frac{1}{2}x - 1 = 4$

(b) $\frac{1}{4}x + 5 = 6$

(c) $\frac{1}{8}x - 2 = 0$

(d) $\frac{2}{3}x - 4 = 6$

(e) $3 + \frac{3}{5}x = 9$

(f) $\frac{3}{8}x + 10 = 19$

(g) $\frac{3}{4}x - \frac{1}{2} = 1$

(h) $\frac{1}{2}x + \frac{1}{5} = 4$

(i) $\frac{2}{5}x - \frac{1}{3} = 3$

(j) $\frac{1}{2}x - 4 = \frac{1}{4}$

(k) $\frac{2}{3}x + 3 = \frac{1}{3}$

(l) $\frac{3}{4}x - 1 = \frac{1}{5}$

(m) $\frac{1}{2}x + 2 = \frac{1}{3}x + 5$

(n) $\frac{3}{4}x - 4 = \frac{3}{5}x + 2$

(o) $1 + \frac{3}{8}x = \frac{1}{3}x + 2$

(p) $\frac{1}{2}x + \frac{1}{3} = \frac{1}{4}$

(q) $\frac{1}{4}x + \frac{1}{2} = \frac{2}{5}$

(r) $\frac{1}{2}x - \frac{1}{3} = \frac{2}{5}x + \frac{1}{4}$

More Equations with Fractions (harder)

Example 1 :-

$$\frac{x+1}{3} + 2 = 8$$

Multiply both sides by **3** to eliminate the **3** in the denominator

$$\cancel{3} \times \frac{x+1}{\cancel{3}} + 3 \times 2 = 3 \times 8$$

$$\Rightarrow \quad x + 1 + 6 = 24$$

$$\Rightarrow \quad x = 24 - 7$$

$$\Rightarrow \quad x = \boxed{17}$$

Example 2 :-

$$\frac{3}{4}(2x - 1) + \frac{1}{3}x = 1$$

Multiply both sides by **12** to eliminate the two denominators, **4 & 3**

$$\overset{3}{\cancel{12}} \times \frac{3}{\cancel{4}}(2x - 1) + \overset{4}{\cancel{12}} \times \frac{1}{\cancel{3}}x = 12 \times 1$$

$$\Rightarrow \quad 9(2x - 1) + 4x = 12$$

$$\Rightarrow \quad 18x - 9 + 4x = 12$$

$$\Rightarrow \quad 22x = 21$$

$$\Rightarrow \quad x = \boxed{\frac{21}{22}}$$

Exercise 12·4

1. Copy and complete the following two fractional equations :-

(a)
$$\frac{x-2}{5} - 3 = 7$$

$$\cancel{5} \times \frac{x-2}{\cancel{5}} - 5 \times 3 = 5 \times 7$$

$$\Rightarrow \quad x - ... - ... = 35$$

$$\Rightarrow \quad x = ... + ... + ...$$

$$\Rightarrow \quad x = ...$$

(b)
$$\frac{2}{5}(2x + 1) - \frac{1}{3}x = 2$$

$$\overset{3}{\cancel{15}} \times \frac{2}{\cancel{5}}(2x + 1) - \overset{5}{\cancel{15}} \times \frac{1}{\cancel{3}}x = 15 \times 2$$

$$\Rightarrow \quad 6(2x + ...) - ...x = 30$$

$$\Rightarrow \quad 12x + ... - ...x = 30$$

$$\Rightarrow \quad 7x = ...$$

$$\Rightarrow \quad x = \frac{...}{7}$$

2. Multiply each term by the l.c.m. of the denominators to eliminate the fractions and solve :-

(a) $\dfrac{x+2}{5} = 4$

(b) $\dfrac{x+7}{4} = 5$

(c) $\dfrac{x-9}{2} = 3$

(d) $\dfrac{x+4}{3} - 1 = 2$

(e) $\dfrac{3x-4}{5} + 2 = 9$

(f) $5 + \dfrac{x-2}{4} = 0$

(g) $\frac{2}{3}(2x + 4) - 2 = 0$

(h) $\frac{3}{4}(3x - 1) - 1 = 2$

(i) $\frac{5}{8}(x + 3) - \frac{1}{2}x = 2$

(j) $\frac{2}{5}(2x + 3) - \frac{1}{3}x = 4$

(k) $\frac{5}{6}(2x + 1) = \frac{3}{4}x + 7$

(l) $8 + \frac{3}{10}(3x + 2) = \frac{1}{3}x + 1$

(m) $\frac{2}{3}(2x + 5) + \frac{1}{2}(x - 2) = 5$

(n) $\dfrac{x}{2} + \dfrac{x+2}{4} = 5$

(o) $\dfrac{x+2}{3} + \dfrac{x+3}{4} = 1$

(p) $\dfrac{2x-1}{5} + \dfrac{x+2}{10} = 3$

(q) $\dfrac{x-1}{2} - \dfrac{x-2}{5} = 1$

(r) $\dfrac{3x-5}{6} - \dfrac{x-7}{3} = 4$

Inequalities

$3x + 1 = 9$ and $7(x + 2) = 5x + 11$ are two examples of **equations**.

Inequalities are similar, except the "=" sign is replaced with one of "<", ">", "≤" or "≥".

Solving an inequality is almost identical to solving the corresponding equation.

equation	inequality
$2x - 5 = 11$	$2x - 5 < 11$
$2x = 11 + 5$	$2x < 11 + 5$
$2x = 16$	$2x < 16$
$x = 8$	$x < 8$

The solution this time is
"x can be any number
'smaller' than 8"
(not just $x = 8$)

equation	inequality
$2(2x - 1) = x + 7$	$2(2x - 1) \geq x + 7$
$4x - 2 = x + 7$	$4x - 2 \geq x + 7$
$4x - x = 7 + 2$	$4x - x \geq 7 + 2$
$3x = 9$	$3x \geq 9$
$x = 3$	$x \geq 3$

The solution this time is
"x can be any number
'bigger' than or equal to 3"
(not just $x = 3$)

Remember :-   " < " - means "less than".

" > " - means "greater than"

" ≤ " - means "less than **or** equal to"

" ≥ " - means "greater than **or** equal to"

Example 1 :-

$$3(x + 1) - 10 \geq x$$
$$\Rightarrow \quad 3x + 3 - 10 \geq x$$
$$\Rightarrow \quad 3x - x \geq 10 - 3$$
$$\Rightarrow \quad 2x \geq 7$$
$$\Rightarrow \quad \boxed{x \geq 3 \cdot 5}$$

Example 2 :-

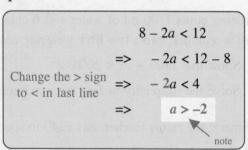

$$8 - 2a < 12$$
$$\Rightarrow \quad -2a < 12 - 8$$

Change the > sign to < in last line
$$\Rightarrow \quad -2a < 4$$
$$\Rightarrow \quad \boxed{a > -2}$$

note

Note *   **If you have to divide by a negative number, you must reverse the inequality symbol.**

Exercise 12·5

Solve each of the inequalities in questions 1 – 3.

1. (a) $x + 2 > 4$ (b) $y + 6 < 5$ (c) $p + 5 > 9$ (d) $t - 2 < 0$

   (e) $v + 6 \geq 7$ (f) $g + 7 \leq -7$ (g) $d - 8 \geq 0$ (h) $e - 4 > -3$

   (i) $q - 5 \geq 2$ (j) $k + 12 \leq 12$ (k) $b + 7 \leq 5$ (l) $m + 21 < 18$

2. (a) $2x > 8$ (b) $5y < 20$ (c) $7m > 14$ (d) $3p < -12$

   (e) $5b < -5$ (f) $7n \leq 49$ (g) $10k \geq -40$ (h) $2u \leq -11$

3. (a) $2x + 1 > 5$ (b) $3a - 4 < 8$ (c) $5b - 2 < 23$ (d) $7c + 7 > 0$

     (e) $4d + 5 < 21$ (f) $8e + 2 > 10$ (g) $6g + 3 \leq 0$ (h) $9h + 9 \geq 9$

     (i) $4k - 2 \leq 0$ (j) $10y - 20 \geq -50$ (k) $6p + 7 \leq -23$ (l) $\frac{1}{2}r + 6 < -1$

     (m) $3r + 7 > 1$ (n) $2c - 9 > -12$ (o) $11y + 11 \leq -33$ (p) $\frac{1}{3}w - 1 \geq 9$

4. By solving each inequality, find the **smallest whole number** which makes it true.

     (a) $2x + 6 > 8$ (b) $5x - 7 \geq 14$ (c) $3x + 9 \geq 20$ (d) $8x - 2 > 0$

5. By solving each inequality, find the **largest whole number** which makes it true.

     (a) $4x + 5 < 17$ (b) $4x + 5 \leq 17$ (c) $7x - 2 < 40$ (d) $6x - 1 \leq 3$

     Solve the following inequalities.   (*Watch for the inequality sign requiring to be reversed !*)

6. (a) $-x > 4$ (b) $-a < 2$ (c) $-b < -6$ (d) $-2c > -11$

     (e) $-3d < 18$ (f) $1 - g > 2$ (g) $9 - h \geq 4$ (h) $12 - n \leq -1$

7. (a) $3x + 3 > x + 9$ (b) $5x + 8 < 3x + 18$ (c) $7x - 3 > 3x + 29$ (d) $7x + 1 \geq 13 - x$

     (e) $13 - 2x \leq 3x - 7$ (f) $24 - 3x \geq x + 12$ (g) $x - 1 \leq 9x - 57$ (h) $15 - 7x \geq 12 - x$

8. (a) $2(x + 3) + 3 > 17$ (b) $2(p + 5) - 1 > 3$ (c) $5(2y - 1) + 7 \leq 3$

     (d) $8 - 2(r - 2) \geq 20$ (e) $9 - (1 - k) < 4$ (f) $1 - 3(m - 5) \geq -2$

     (g) $3(1 - 2x) \leq 27$ (h) $2(5x - 1) > 0$ (i) $-\frac{1}{2}(4x - 5) \leq -2$

     (j) $-6(x + 2) \leq 3x + 24$ (k) $2(2x + 4) \geq 36 - 6x$ (l) $3(1 - 2x) < 13 - 5x$

     (m) $2(5x + 10) > 10(2x + 1)$ (n) $2(4x - 7) \leq 3x - 14$ (o) $9(2x + 2) < 22x$

9. A gardener pours 1100 ml of water and 6 cups of weedkiller, each holding x ml of weedkiller, into a **two litre** watering can.

     (a) Show that $1100 + 6x \leq 2000$.

     (b) Solve the inequality to find the maximum volume of water each cup can hold.

10. Mrs Emery, the maths teacher, has £240 to spend on **Teejay** Maths Books which cost £9 each.

     The delivery charge is £8. She orders y books.

     Make up an inequality and solve it to find the **maximum** number of books she can buy.

11. A village fayre costs £320 to run. A raffle, held locally, raised £70 towards the cost of the fayre.

     x entry tickets were sold, priced at £2·50 each.

     Form an inequality and solve it to find the **minimum** number of tickets that had to be sold to avoid a loss.

                                                       TAYLOR'S TENTS

                                                            £12

12. (a) Write down the hire cost for d days with each hire company.   **PLUS**

                                                             £5 per DAY

     (b) Make an inequality if Taylor's cost is known to be **less** than Camper's for the d days, and solve it.   *CAMPER TENT HIRE*

                                                             £5

     (c) Suggest a reason why most people hire their tents from Taylor's.   **PLUS**

                                                            £12 per DAY

Remember Remember.....?

1.   Copy each equation and solve to find the value of x :-

   (a) $17 + x = 12$ (b) $6x = 9$ (c) $2x + 8 = 19$

   (d) $6x - 2 = 40$ (e) $8x + 4 = 2x - 8$ (f) $10x - 3 = 5x + 17$

   (g) $10x = 3x + 56$ (h) $2(x - 5) = 20$ (i) $4(2x - 3) = 4x + 30$

   (j) $3(x - 3) + 2(x + 5) = 16$ (k) $2(6x + 1) - 3(x - 4) = x + 34$ (l) $2(5x - 3) - 3(4x - 6) = 0$

2.   Multiply out the brackets and solve :-

   (a) $x(x + 5) = x^2 - 45$ (b) $7x(x - 2) = 7x^2$ (c) $x(4x + 8) = 4(x^2 - 1)$

   (d) $(x + 3)(x - 1) = x(x - 6)$ (e) $x(x + 10) = (x + 8)(x - 3)$ (f) $(x + 7)^2 = (x + 1)^2$

3.   The photographs shown have the **same area**.

   Form an equation, and solve it to find the
   dimensions of each photograph.

x

$x - 4$

$x + 8$

x

4.   Solve :-

   (a) $\frac{1}{2}x - 1 = 5$ (b) $\frac{2}{5}x - \frac{1}{4} = 1$ (c) $\frac{2}{3}x - 1 = \frac{3}{4}x + 2$

   (d) $\frac{1}{4}x - \frac{1}{2} = \frac{4}{5}$ (e) $\frac{x + 2}{5} = 3$ (f) $1 + \frac{x - 2}{4} = 0$

   (g) $\frac{2}{5}(2x + 3) - 4 = 0$ (h) $\frac{5}{6}(2x + 2) = \frac{1}{4}x + 3$ (i) $\frac{x + 1}{3} + \frac{x + 4}{4} = 2$

   (j) $\frac{2x - 1}{3} + \frac{x + 2}{6} = 1$ (k) $\frac{x - 1}{5} - \frac{x - 2}{2} = 9$ (l) $\frac{7x - 1}{8} - \frac{x - 2}{4} = 3$

5.   Solve these inequalities :-

   (a) $a + 7 < 8$ (b) $b - 11 \geq 0$ (c) $5c \leq -45$

   (d) $2d + 1 > 12$ (e) $2e - 9 > -17$ (f) $1 - f > -14$

   (g) $7g + 1 \geq 13 - g$ (h) $38 - 3h \geq h + 6$ (i) $2(i + 1) + 5 > 25$

   (j) $11 - (1 - j) \geq -2$ (k) $2(2k + 7) \geq 19 - 6k$ (l) $2(1 - l) \leq 3(2l - 2)$

6.   To rent a DVD movie from **Electroshow** costs :-

   •   membership free   •   then £4 per DVD.

   To rent from **Moviebuster**, the charge is :-

   •   £3 for membership   •   but their DVD's are cheaper to rent at £2·50 each.

   (a)   Take x as the number of DVD's rented and make an inequality showing
         that Electroshow is **dearer** than Moviebuster for renting movies.

   (b)   Solve the inequality and make a recommendation about which shop
         you should go to rent :-

         (i)   1 DVD   (ii)   2 DVD's   (iii)   3 DVD's.

Bar Charts & Line Graphs

Data can be represented in many different ways, so that information can be more easily understood.

The **Comparative Bar Graph** below shows the gender of three second year classes.

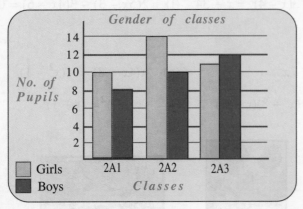

This **Comparative Line Graph** shows the sales of two car companies.

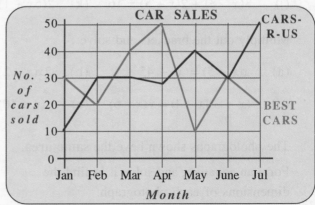

There are 8 boys in 2A1.

There are 18 pupils altogether in 2A1.

Best Cars sold 20 cars in February.

Cars-R-Us sold 10 cars in January.

Exercise 13·1

1. Look at the bar graph directly above.

   (a) How many boys are there in 2A2 ?

   (b) How many girls are there in 2A3 ?

   (c) How many pupils are there in 2A3 ?

   (d) How many more girls than boys are there in total in all three classes ?

2. Construct a **Comparative Bar Graph** showing the gender of the three First Year classes listed below.

	1A1	1A2	1A3
Boys	10	16	11
Girls	14	7	13

3. Construct a **Comparative Bar Graph** showing the number of medals won in an inter-schools competition .

	Swimming	Athletics	Gymnastics
Clyde High	5	4	3
Ayr High	2	4	3
Oban High	3	2	4

4. Look at the line graph above.

   (a) How many cars did **Cars-R-Us** sell in :–

   (i) March   (ii) May   (iii) July ?

   (b) **Estimate** how many cars were sold in April by **Cars-R-Us.**

   (c) How many cars were sold by Best Cars from January to July **inclusive** ?

5. Construct a **Comparative Line Graph** showing these two companies' house sales.

	Jan	Feb	Mar	Apr	May
Scot Homes	10	40	30	50	55
Brit Estates	5	20	35	35	50

6. Construct a **Comparative Line Graph** showing the average rainfall (in mm) in the three towns.

	May	June	July	Aug	Sept
Ayton	100	40	10	30	50
Beeton	80	60	20	20	25
Ceeton	45	35	30	25	35

Exercise 13·2

1. The pie chart shows the results of a class survey into *favourite school canteen food.*

   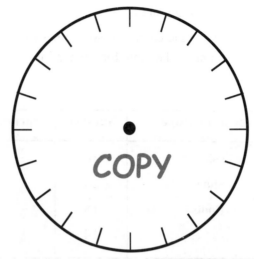

   (a) What fraction of the class chose :-

   (i) Burger ($\frac{?}{10}$)   (ii) Salad

   (iii) Pizza   (iv) Soup ?

   (b) List the foods in order, from **most** popular to **least** popular.

2. The pie chart shows the results of a year-group analysis into hair colour.

   (a) What percentage of the year-group had :-

   (i) dark brown ?

   (ii) light brown ?

   (iii) blonde hair ?

   (b) If 300 pupils were in the year-group, **how many** of them :–

   (i) had blonde hair ?

   (ii) did **not** have black hair ?

3. This pie chart shows the type of houses the people at a political meeting live in.

   (a) What percentage of the people live in a :–

   (i) bungalow   (ii) semi-detached

   (iii) flat   (iv) detached villa ?

   (b) There are 500 people at the meeting. **How many** people live in a :–

   (i) flat   (ii) semi-detached ?

4. (a) Copy or trace the blank pie chart below.

   COPY

   (b) Use the information from this table to complete your blank pie chart.

Football	-	50%
Rugby	-	20%
Tennis	-	5%
Hockey	-	15%
Netball	-	10%

   Copy or trace the blank pie chart above to help you draw pie-charts to represent the following :-

5. In a bowl of minestrone soup, the ingredients were as follows :–

   - 35% pasta
   - 40% carrots
   - 15% tomato
   - the rest was celery.

   Draw a **pie chart** to show the information above.

6. The information below shows the most popular pets in third year at Greenby High school.

   - 40% owned dogs.
   - 30% owned cats.
   - of the others, half owned fish and the other half owned mice.

   Draw a **pie chart** to show this information.

7. Of the 40 000 people at a football match, 20 000 of them were season ticket holders, 10 000 of them were tickets sales, 6000 of them were juvenile ticket holders and the rest held concessionary tickets.

   Draw a **pie chart** to show this information.

Constructing Harder Pie Charts

The table of data shows the number of different types of footwear bought from *Sandy's Shoe Shop* one day.

When drawing a pie chart, it is sometimes easier to add columns to the table for calculations.

Type of Footwear	No. Sold
Trainers	34
Shoes	24
Boots	18
Slippers	14

Type of Footwear	Number	Fraction	Angle
Trainers	34	$\frac{34}{90}$	$\frac{34}{90} \times 360 = 136°$
Shoes	24	$\frac{24}{90}$	$\frac{24}{90} \times 360 = 96°$
Boots	18	$\frac{18}{90}$	$\frac{18}{90} \times 360 = 72°$
Slippers	14	$\frac{14}{90}$	$\frac{14}{90} \times 360 = 56°$
TOTAL	**90**	**1**	**360°**

step 1	**add** all the "numbers" together to get a total (**in this case - 90**).
step 2	express each "number" as a **fraction** of this total. (e.g. $\frac{34}{90}$).
step 3	find this **fraction of 360°** each time (e.g. $\frac{34}{90} \times 360 = 136°$).
step 4	draw the pie chart showing these angles using a **protractor**.

Exercise 13.3

1. (a) **Copy** and **complete** the table which shows the favourite type of pizza chosen by a group of 180 people.

   (b) Construct a pie chart using compasses, a protractor and the table information.

Type of Pizza	Number	Fraction	Angle
Hawaiian	20	$\frac{20}{180}$	$\frac{20}{180} \times 360 = 40°$
Four Seasons	90	$\frac{90}{180}$	$\frac{90}{180} \times 360 = \ldots°$
Americano	10	$\frac{}{180}$	$\frac{}{180} \times 360 = \ldots°$
Hot & Spicy	60	$\frac{}{180}$	$\frac{}{180} \times 360 = \ldots°$
TOTAL	**180**	**1**	**360°**

2. The table shows the favourite T.V. programmes of a group of women.

   (a) **Copy** and **complete** the table.

   (b) Construct an accurate pie chart showing this information.

Programme	Number	Fraction	Angle
Comedy	5	$\frac{5}{45}$	$\frac{5}{45} \times 360 = 40°$
Soap	20	$\frac{20}{45}$	....
Sport	18	$\frac{}{45}$	....
Educational	2	.....	....
TOTAL	**45**	**1**	**360°**

3. (a) Copy and complete the table showing the hair colour of a class of S3 pupils.

Hair colour	Number	Fraction	Angle
Brown	10	$\frac{10}{30}$	$\frac{10}{30} \times 360 = \ldots.°$
Black	12		$\times 360 = \ldots..°$
Blonde	7		$\times 360 = \ldots..°$
Red	1		$\times 360 = \ldots..°$
TOTAL	30		$\ldots..°$

(b) Construct an accurate **pie chart** showing this information.

4. Copy each of the following tables, add new columns to show what calculations you are performing, then construct an accurate **pie chart** to represent the information.

(a)

Super Hero	Number
Rat-Man	36
Chat-Woman	20
Sider-Man	4
Souper-Man	12
TOTAL	....

(b)

Favourite Sport	Number
Football	20
Tennis	8
Snooker	5
Netball	3
TOTAL	....

(c)

Height (cm)	Number
150 - 154	400
155 - 159	240
160 - 164	70
165 - 169	10
TOTAL	....

5. The four main blood groups are **A**, **B**, **AB** and **O**.

This table shows the results of the fourth year biology students who tested their individual blood groups.

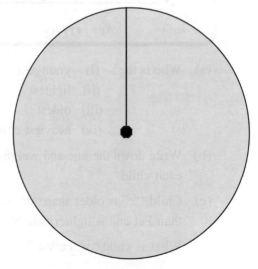

(a) **Copy** and **complete** the table below :–
  (*add any columns you might need to help you make a pie chart*)

Blood Group	Tally Mark	Number
A		
B		
AB		
O		

(b) Construct an accurate pie chart for this information.
  (*Copy or trace the pie chart shown*).

Scattergraphs

A **Scattergraph** is a statistical graph which makes comparisons of two sets of data.

Example :- This scattergraph displays the **heights** and **weights** of the players in a Netball team.

- Joy weighs 40 kg.
- Jo is 160 cm tall.
- Jan is 130 cm tall. She weighs 25 kg.

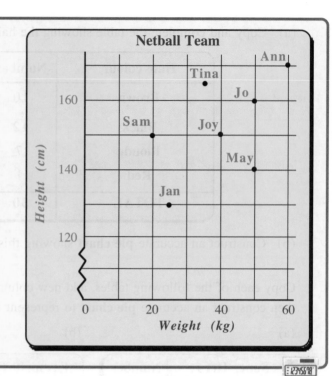

Netball Team

Exercise 13.4

1. For the scattergraph above, write down the **height** and **weight** of each player.

2. The scattergraph below shows the **ages** and **weights** of several children.

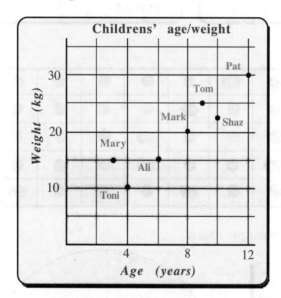

Childrens' age/weight

   (a) **Who is the :–** (i) youngest
                 (ii) lightest
                 (iii) oldest
                 (iv) heaviest child ?

   (b) Write down the **age** and **weight** of each child.

   (c) Child "*x*" is older than Ali, younger than Pat and is lighter than Shaz.

   What is child "*x*" called ?

3. Draw a scattergraph to show the **weights** (*in kg*) and the **shoe sizes** of a group of pupils.

	Mat	Bill	Fred	Jan	Tam
Weight	20	15	30	25	35
Shoe size	4	3	6	6	10

4. For both (a) and (b) below, construct a scattergraph to represent each set of data.

(a)	May	Zak	Jack	Tippi	Guy
Height (cm)	120	115	130	145	135
Weight (kg)	40	30	60	75	80

(b)	Jan	Feb	Mar	Apr	May
Car Sales	25	20	30	55	45
Profit (£1000)	25	30	35	60	50

5. Construct a scattergraph from the **Maths** and **English** grades of the ten pupils below.

Name	Eng	Maths
Tom	1	2
Dick	1	3
Bill	2	4
Jerry	3	4
Nick	6	7

Name	Eng	Maths
Neil	3	3
Iain	2	3
Jack	2	2
Ewan	6	6
Bob	4	5

Scattergraphs - Correlation

In this example, we again show the Standard Grade **Maths** and **English** Grades for 10 pupils.

Name	Eng	Maths
Tom	1	2
Dick	1	3
Bill	2	4
Jerry	3	4
Nick	6	7

Name	Eng	Maths
Neil	3	3
Iain	2	3
Jack	2	2
Ewan	6	6
Bob	4	5

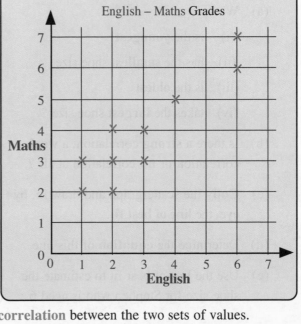

Each pair of grades is plotted on a **Scattergraph**.

Can you see there is a **fairly strong connection** between the two sets of grades ?

If two sets of values are so strongly connected that it is possible to make a fairly accurate estimate of one of the values, knowing the other, we say there is a strong **correlation** between the two sets of values.

Can you see that this is the case - there is indeed a fairly strong **positive correlation** between the Maths and the English Grades ?

       (*Positive because the grouping of pairs of values is "sloping upwards" from left to right*).

Line of Best Fit

The correlation in this example is good enough to allow us to draw a "**best-fitting line**" through the group.

Though the line is only an "estimate", it should :-

- go through as many points as possible
- split the group up so there are roughly as many points above the line as there are below it.

Shown is a good estimate of the **line of best fit**.

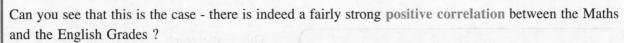

Equation of the Line of Best Fit

In Chapter 6 of Maths 1, you learned that almost every line drawn on an *x, y* diagram has its equation :-

$$y = mx + c.$$

where $(0, c)$ gives the *y*-intercept and *m* is the gradient.

In our example, the *y*-intercept is at ($c =$) 1 and by drawing a small triangle we find the gradient (*m*) is 1.

=> the equation of the above line of best fit is :- $y = x + 1.$

We can also use the line (or its equation) to make further **estimates**.

If an eleventh boy, Harry, is known to have scored 5 in English, the equation of the line tells us that a fair estimate for his Maths Grade would be $y = (5) + 1 = 6$. i.e. he got a **6** for Maths.

Exercise 13·5

1. This scattergraph shows the ages and the shoe sizes of several children.

   (a) Who :–

      (i) is the **youngest**

      (ii) has the **smallest** shoe size

      (iii) is the **oldest**

      (iv) takes the **largest** shoe size ?

   (b) Is there a **strong** correlation, a **weak** correlation or **no** correlation at all ?

   (c) **Copy** the scattergraph and draw in, by eye, the **line of best fit**.

   (d) Determine the **equation** of this line.

   (e) Use the line of best fit to estimate the shoe size for Stephen who is aged 6.

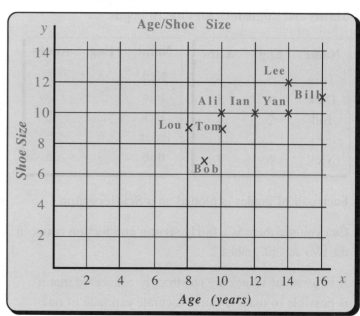

2.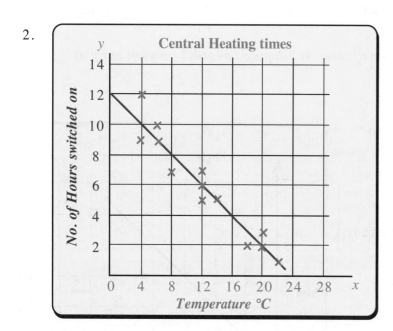

   This scattergraph shows the number of hours a lady had her central heating on each day, plotted against the average daily temperature on each of those days.

   This graph shows a **strong negative correlation** since all the points lie roughly on a straight line going **downwards** from left to right.

   The **line of best fit** is also shown.

   (a) Determine the equation of the line.

   (b) Use your line to estimate how many hours she would expect to run her central heating for, if the average temperature one day was 16°C.

3. Write down whether you think there will be a **correlation** between :–

   (a) the temperature and the sales of ice-cream in June.

   (b) the temperature and the number of people on a beach each day.

   (c) the depth of rain falling and the sale of umbrellas.

   (d) the ages of a group of children and the number of coins in their pockets.

   (If there is a correlation, say whether it is **positive** or **negative**).

4. Write down two of your own examples of pairs of measurements where there would be a :–

   (a) a **positive** correlation   (b) **negative** correlation   (c) **no** correlation between the pairs.

5. Mr. Jones recorded the number of times 11 pupils came up for lunchtime help in the run-up to their Maths exam. He also listed the pupils' actual exam scores.

The results are shown in the table below.

No. lunchtimes	1	2	3	4	5	6	7	9	10	11	12
Maths Score	30	35	35	40	35	45	55	50	50	55	55

(a) Construct a **scattergraph** from the data recorded.

(b) Draw a **line of best fit** on your scattergraph.

(c) Determine the equation of **the line of best fit**.

(d) **Estimate** the Maths score of a 12th pupil who came up 8 times for lunchtime tutorials.

6. Dan was very much overweight. His doctor put him on a strict diet in January and Dan kept a note at the end of each month of how much weight he had lost (in total).

Month	1	2	3	4	5	6	7	8	9	10	11	12
Total loss (kg)	3·5	4	4	5	5·5	5·5	7	8	6·5	8	9	9

(a) Draw up a set of axes as shown and plot the 12 pairs of pieces of data from the table above.

(b) Draw a line of best fit on your scattergraph.

(c) Determine its equation (in the form $y = mx + c$).

(d) Estimate what his total weight loss might be after 15 months.

(e) Dan actually gained weight at one point. During which month ?

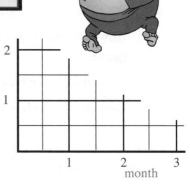

7. For each set of data below :–

- construct a scattergraph.
- show a best line of fit.
- determine the equation of the line.
- use your line to estimate the missing piece of data.

(a) The data below shows the age and the height of a tree planted in a garden.

age (years)	1	2	3	4	5	6	7	8	9	10
height (m)	4	5	6	10	10	14	16	16	?	21

(b) The data shows the number of rats still alive in a warehouse, after poison was put down.

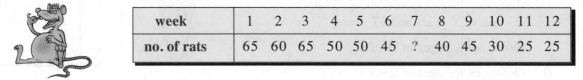

week	1	2	3	4	5	6	7	8	9	10	11	12
no. of rats	65	60	65	50	50	45	?	40	45	30	25	25

(c) A group of eight pupils compared their French and English marks in two tests.

French	10	35	60	24	56	17	42	49
English	23	57	88	40	85	33	62	?

Stem and Leaf Diagrams

A **stem and leaf** diagram is another way of displaying information.

This stem and leaf diagram shows the ages of people waiting in a queue at the bank.

The **key** explains what each number in the diagram represents.

The first line reads 24, 25 and 29 years of age.

Age in Years

2	4	5	9			
3	1	7	8			
4	3	3	5	6	8	9
5	0	1	4	8		
6	2	3	6	8	9	

stem   leaves

Key :–
2 | 4 means 24

Exercise 13.6

1. The 2nd line of the above graph reads 31, 37 and 38 years of age.

   (a) Write the ages given by the 3rd, 4th and 5th lines in the diagram above.

   (b) How old was the youngest person in the queue ?

   (c) How old was the oldest person ?

   (d) How many people were in the queue ?

2. The ages of a group of people waiting in a shop queue were recorded and put into the stem and leaf diagram shown.

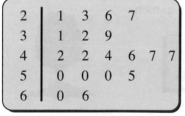

Age in years

2	1	3	6	7	
3	1	2	9		
4	2	2	4	6	7	7
5	0	0	0	5	
6	0	6			

Key :–
2 | 1 means 21

   (a) The first line (*level 2*) reads 21 years, 23 years, 26 years and 27 years.

   Write out the ages in level 3.

   (b) Write out the ages of level 4.

   (c) How old was the youngest person ?

   (d) How old was the oldest ?

   (e) Were most of the people in their 20's, 30's, 40's, 50's or 60's ?

3. S3 pupils were asked how many minutes each day they spent on their Maths homework.

   The results are shown in the stem and leaf diagram below.

Homework times

Key :–
1 | 2 means 12

1	0	2	3	6	8
2	0	1	2		
3	0	0	0	5	6	6
4	2				
5	0	1			

   (a) List the amount of time each pupil spent.

   (b) Which level has the most data ?

   (c) Which time period appears most often ? (*i.e. the mode*).

   (d) How many pupils were surveyed ?

4. The table shows the time it took in seconds for anchor boys to tie a specific knot to a cleat.

Knot Time

0	8				
1	2	5	7	7	
2	0	1	3	3	3	6
3					
4	2	3			

   (a) Write a **key** for this stem and leaf diagram.

   (b) How many pupils took more than 24 seconds to complete the knot ?

   (c) Find the **modal** time (*mode*).

   (d) Determine the **median** time.

5. The graph below, which is **not** in order, shows the results of the times, in minutes, of the competitors in a tortoise race.

Tortoise Race

```
0 | 9
1 | 5 1 2 4 6 1 4 1
2 | 6 1 0 2 0
3 |
4 | 2 0
```

(a) Construct an **ordered** stem and leaf graph.

(b) Write a **key** for this graph.

(c) How many tortoises raced ?

(d) What was the time of the winner ?

(e) What was the difference between first and second ?

(f) What does the empty space at 3 mean ?

(g) Find the **modal** time.

(h) Determine the **median**.

6. The data given shows the distance, in kilometres, that home made model aeroplanes flew on 100 ml of petrol.

10, 11, 7, 3, 7, 21, 30, 1, 19, 14

(a) Copy and complete the ordered stem and leaf diagram.

Flight distance

```
0 |
1 |
2 |
3 |
```

(b) Find the **mode**.

(c) Find the **median**.

7. For each set of data shown :–

• Construct an **ordered** stem and leaf diagram, showing your **key**.

• Find the **mode** and **median**.

(a) Shown are the times taken (*in minutes*), for some cadets to complete an obstacle course.

8	13	18	20	31	23	13	11
22	18	10	15	15	18	27	18

(b) Shown are the lengths, in centimetres, of worms found at the sea-side.

0·4	1·5	2·0	4·2	5·4	6·1	5·3	4·5
3·8	2·7	4·0	1·8	4·5	5·5	4·8	3·8
1·7	4·5	5·5	5·4	4·5	2·4	5·6	2·6
5·2	3·5	3·0	1·4	2·2	1·2	4·0	2·6
2·3	1·5	5·3	3·4	2·7	5·2	4·6	0·3

8. Shown below is a back-to-back stem and leaf diagram, giving the age and gender of people at a 50th birthday party.

Age of People

Male		Female
9 8 7 1	1	5
5 1 0	2	0 2 3
9 5 3 3 2	3	6 7 7 8 9
8 6 6 6 6	4	0 2 4 4 4
3 1 0	5	2 4 9

(a) How many **males** at the party are aged :–

(i) 33   (ii) 46   (iii) 54 ?

(b) Find the **modal** age and **median** age of

(i) the males.   (ii) the females.

9. The information below gives the ages of men and women who took part in a competition.

Men	23	35	45	32	19	23	33	37
Women	22	18	19	23	27	27	30	29

(a) Draw an **ordered back to back** stem and leaf diagram to represent this information.

(b) Find the **modal** and **median** ages of :–

(i) the men.   (ii) the women.

10. (a) Draw an **ordered back to back** stem and leaf diagram showing information about the weights (*in kilograms*) of a group of children given below.

Boys	24	19	18	26	34	26	25	30
Girls	40	23	34	21	25	29	30	25

(b) Find the **modal** and **median** ages of :–

(i) the girls.   (ii) the boys.

Dot Plot

A **dot plot** is another way of displaying information, and is similar to a bar graph.

This dot plot shows the ages of children playing in a playground.

> There are 3 children aged four.
> Four children are aged eleven.

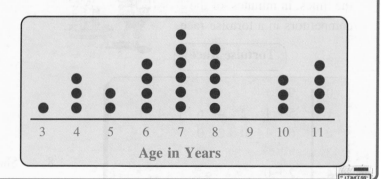

Age in Years

Exercise 13.7

Use the dot plot above to answer questions 1 and 2.

1. Write down the number of children aged :–

    (a) 6   (b) 7   (c) 9 ?

2. (a) How many children were **under** seven ?

    (b) How many children were playing in the playground ?

3. This dot plot shows the time, in minutes, for each call recorded on a mobile phone one day.

    (a) How many calls lasted 5 minutes ?

    (b) How many lasted 9 minutes ?

    (c) How many lasted **more** than 8 minutes ?

    (d) Find the **modal** time.

    (e) Find the **median** time.

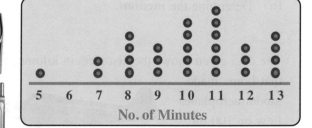

No. of Minutes

4. This dot plot shows the daily rainfall, (*to the nearest millimetre*), that fell during February.

    (a) 1 millimetre fell on 4 separate days. On how many days did 6 millimetres of rain fall ?

    (b) What is the **modal** daily rainfall ?

    (c) Find the **median**.

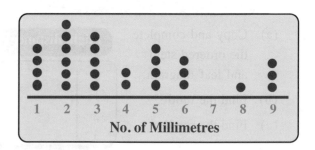

No. of Millimetres

5. For each set of data below, construct a **dot plot**.

    (a)

Week	1	2	3	4	5	6	7	8	9	10	11	12
Rain (mm)	3	4	4	5	2	1	0	3	4	2	5	7

    (b)

Day	1	2	3	4	5	6	7	8	9	10
Staff absence	0	1	4	5	8	8	5	3	3	3

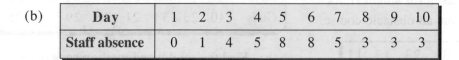

Remember Remember..... ?

1. Use this table to construct a **Comparative Bar Graph** showing the sex of a group of pupils in three senior Maths classes.

	5M1	5M2	5M3
Boys	12	14	11
Girls	14	8	13

2. Use this table to construct a **Comparative Line Graph** to show the sales of TV sets in two television shops last week.

	Wed	Thu	Fri	Sat	Sun
Commet	6	8	4	12	10
Dixies	4	6	10	11	12

3. (a) **Copy** and complete the table showing how a group of third year pupils travel to school.

   (b) Construct a **pie chart** to represent the information shown.

Transport	No.	Fraction	Angle
Bus	20	$\frac{20}{60}$	$\frac{20}{60}$ × 360 = ...°
Train	14		× 360 = ...°
Walk	24		× 360 = ...°
Taxi	2		× 360 = ...°
TOTAL	...		360°

4. The ages and weights of a group of young people are recorded in the table.

Age	10	10	11	12	13	14	15	16	16	17	18	19
Weight (kg)	30	20	30	35	45	35	45	60	50	75	65	?

   (a) Construct a **scattergraph** to represent this information.

   (b) Write a sentence to explain the **correlation** in this example.

   (c) Draw a **Line of best fit** on your scattergraph.

   (d) Estimate, using your line, the weight of the 19 year old.

5. A platoon of soldiers was given a series of training exercises and graded out of a possible 70 marks. The platoon's results were tabulated as shown.

   (a) Construct an ordered **stem and leaf diagram** for this.

   (b) Find the **modal** mark.

   (c) Find the **median** mark.

   (d) Soldiers who score above 50 are given a two day pass.

   How many soldiers receive a pass ?

11	22	27	49	61	68	60	52
45	34	47	25	52	62	65	45
24	52	62	61	52	31	63	33
59	42	37	21	29	19	47	34
30	22	60	41	34	59	53	10

6. Shown is a **dot plot** representing the number of shots a group of golfers took at a par five.

   (a) How many golfers shot a par 5 ?

   (b) How many golfers took :–

       (i) more than 5   (ii) less than 5 ?

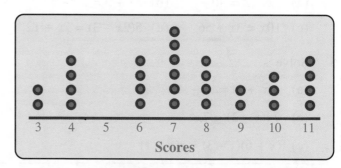

Scores

1. Calculate the values of x and y in the following right angled triangles.

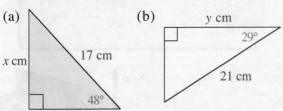

(a)   (b)

2. Calculate the value of s and t in the following right angled triangles.

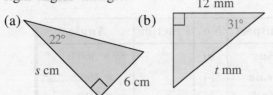

(a)   (b)

3. Calculate the size of the angles marked c and d in the following right angled triangles.

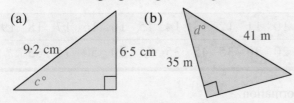

(a)   (b)

4. Shown is a trapezium ABCD with a line of symmetry (shown dotted).

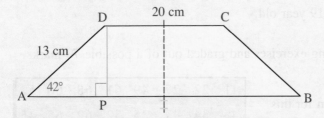

By considering right angled $\triangle$APD, calculate the length of the line AP, and hence determine the **perimeter** of the trapezium.

5. Solve the following equations, showing each step of your working :-

(a) $7x - 2 = 40$ (b) $8x + 3 = 2x - 9$

(c) $10x = 3x + 56$ (d) $5(2x - 3) = 7x + 12$

6. Solve :-

(a) $x(x + 5) = x^2 - 45$

(b) $7x(x - 2) = 7x^2$

(c) $(x + 6)(x - 3) = x(x + 1)$

7. Solve, showing **ALL** working :-

(a) $\frac{3}{5}x - \frac{2}{3} = 2$ (b) $\frac{2x - 3}{7} = 3$

(c) $\frac{x+1}{3} + \frac{x-2}{4} = 1$

8. Solve the following inequalities :-

(a) $25 + 3x \geq x + 37$

(b) $10 + (3 - 2x) \geq 1$

9. The table shows the number of men and women who passed their driving test first time with ROY's School of Motoring, over a 6 week period.

Week	1	2	3	4	5	6
Men	4	6	8	5	2	3
Women	6	9	10	7	1	5

Show the above statistics in a neatly labelled **Comparative Bar Graph**.

10. The table shows the number of hours four part-time female workers were employed last week.

Name	Hours	Fraction	Angle
Julie	24	$\frac{24}{...}$	$\frac{24}{...} \times .. = ..$
Mandy	20		
Norma	16		
Li Ming	30		
TOTAL	...		....

(a) Copy and complete the above table.

(b) Now draw a neat labelled **pie-chart** to represent the above information.

11. The table shows the age and shoe size of a group of young children.

Age	1	7	4	5	3	9	5	2	10	8
Shoe size	2	10	5	8	6	12	5	4	12	9

(a) Draw a neat **scattergraph** to show this.

(b) Draw the **line of best fit** on your graph.

(c) Estimate the shoe size of Sam, aged 6.

Turn off that Calculator...

1. Set down and find the following :-

   (a) $(23)^2$ (b) $8\overline{)5864}$ (c) $25 - 10 \times 2$ (d) $5000 - 297$

   (e) 415×300 (f) $15600 \div 600$ (g) 2^6 (h) $\dfrac{8 \times 15}{12 \times 6}$

2. Set down and find :-

   (a) $53 \cdot 4 + 8 \cdot 956$ (b) $\begin{array}{r} 32 \\ \times\ 24 \\ \hline \end{array}$ (c) $74 \div 5$ (d) $\dfrac{3 \times 6 \cdot 97}{100}$

3. $58 \cdot 56$ litres of milk is poured equally into 8 buckets. How many litres must there be in each bucket ?

4. Change :– (a) 48 m to km   (b) 2 tonnes 75 kg to kg

   (c) $\frac{4}{5}$ litre to millilitres   (d) 500 seconds to minutes and seconds

5. Simplify :–   (a) $\dfrac{35}{105}$ (b) $\dfrac{49}{63}$ (c) $\dfrac{84}{91}$

6. Find :–   (a) $5\frac{1}{2} - 3\frac{1}{2}$ (b) $\frac{4}{5} - \frac{2}{5}$ (c) $\frac{2}{3} \times 240$

   (d) $6 \times 2\frac{1}{2}$ (e) $4\frac{3}{4} - 1\frac{1}{2}$ (f) $\frac{3}{4}$ of $(12\frac{1}{2} + 11\frac{1}{2})$

7. Find :–   (a) 20% of £12   (b) 15% of £4·40   (c) 90% of 600

   (d) 7% of £4   (e) 1% of 3200   (f) $12\frac{1}{2}$% of 240

8. Sally saw a coat costing £120. In a sale a 15% reduction was offered.
   Calculate the reduction and find what Sally would then pay for the coat.

9. Find :–   (a) $29 - 43$ (b) $(-17) - 43$ (c) $(-39) + 18$

   (d) $(-24) - (-18)$ (e) $(-7) \times 11$ (f) $(-17) \times (-3)$ (g) $(-30)^2$

   (h) $63 \div (-9)$ (i) $(-115) \div (-5)$ (j) $\dfrac{(-4) \times (-9)}{-6}$ (k) $-\frac{1}{3} \times (-51)$

10. Draw a neat set of coordinate axes and plot :- A(–7, –1), B(–3, 6) and C(5, 5).
    Find the 4th point (D) such that ABCD is a **rhombus**.

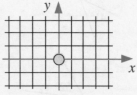

11. Write in 24 hour format :–

    (a) 20 to midnight   (b) 25 to 3 in the afternoon   (c) $\frac{1}{4}$ to 11 in the morning

12. How long is it from :–   (a) 10·48 am to 1·15 pm   (b) 0855 to 1420 ?

13. Which of these were leap years :–   (a) 1968   (b) 1994   (c) 2004 ?

Basic Revision Work - a Reminder !

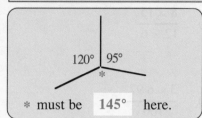

The angles round a point always add to give **360°**.

120° 95°

*

* must be **145°** here.

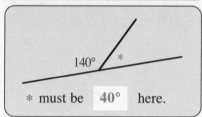

Two angles making a straight line always add to give **180°**.

140° *

* must be **40°** here.

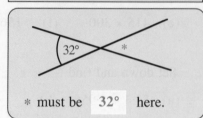

Angles opposite each other at a cross **are equal.**

32° *

* must be **32°** here.

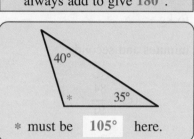

The 3 angles of every triangle always add to give **180°**.

40°

*   35°

* must be **105°** here.

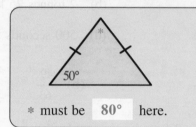

Two of the angles in an **isosceles** triangle are equal.

*

50°

* must be **80°** here.

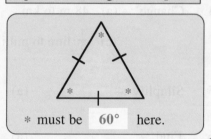

All three of the angles in an equilateral triangle **are equal**.

*

*   *

* must be **60°** here.

Exercise 14·1

1. Calculate the sizes of the angles marked a, b, ...

2. Calculate the sizes of the angles marked m, n, ...

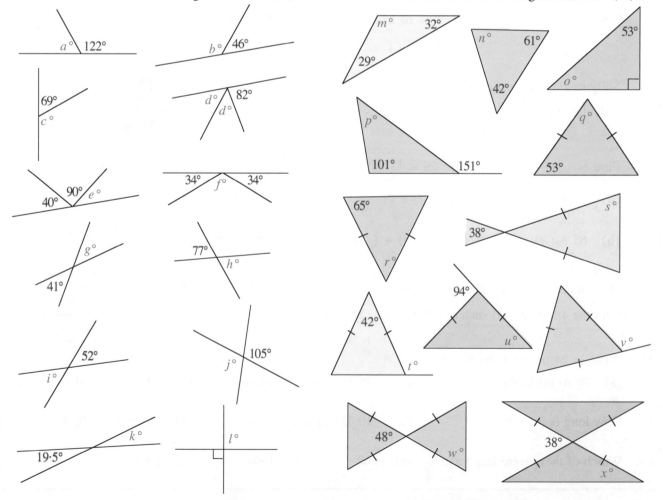

Parallel Lines and Angles

The following should also be known :-

- e is **corresponding** to a and must be 65°.   **F** angles

- c is **(vertically) opposite** a and must be 65°.   **X** angles

- b must be 115°, (**it adds to 65 to give 180**).   **Y** angles

- h is **alternate** to b and must be 115° also.   **Z** angles

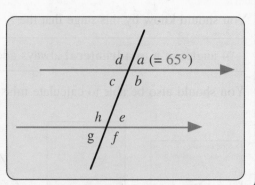

3. **Copy** each diagram neatly and fill in the sizes of **every** angle.

(a)

(b)
61°

(k)
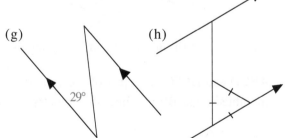
290°

(l)
146°
112°

(c)
42°
105°

(d)
43°
110°

(m)
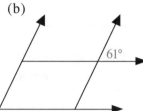
113°

(n)
32°

(e)
40°

(f)
136°

(o)
115°
93°

(p)
70°

(g)
29°

(h)
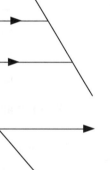

(q)
32°
112°

(r)
278°
29°

(i)
125°
35°

(j)
63°
75°

(s)
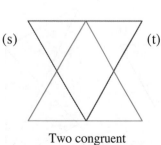
Two congruent
equilateral triangles

(t)
86°
32°
Parallelogram

Quadrilaterals - A Reminder

You should know by this stage that the :-

"4 angles of a **quadrilateral** always add to give **360°**."

$a + b + c + d = 360$

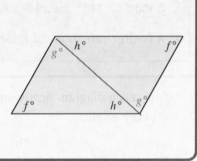

You should also be able to calculate missing angles in any of the 5 main quadrilaterals.

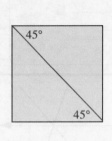 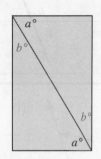 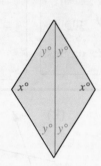 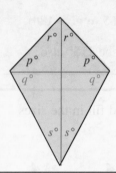

Exercise 14·2

1. **Sketch** the following quadrilaterals, name them and mark in the sizes of all the angles :-

(a)

(b)

51°

126°

(c)

43°

108°

(d)

31°   50°

(e)

48°

(f)

29°

(g)

64°   53°

(h)

39°
30°
76°

2. This shape consists of a rectangle with a trapezium on top and it has 1 **vertical** line of symmetry.

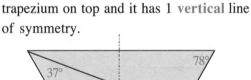

78°
37°
25°

Sketch it and fill in **ALL** the missing angles.

3. This shape is made from a rhombus and a kite.

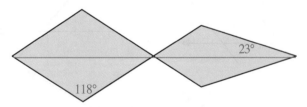

23°
118°

Sketch it and fill in **ALL** the missing angles.

4. ABCD and DEFG are a pair of **congruent** rhombuses and BF is a line of symmetry.

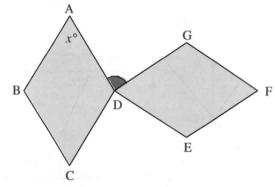

A
x°
G
B   F
D
E
C

Let ∠BAD = x°. Prove that ∠ADG = 90°.

Remember Remember..... ?

Topic in a Nutshell

1. **Copy** each figure and fill in the sizes of **all** the missing angles.

(a)

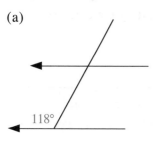

118°

(b)

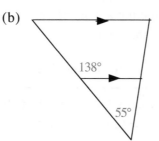

138°   55°

(c)

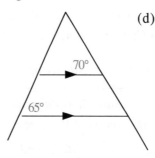

70°   65°

(d)

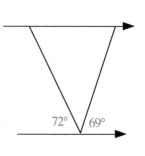

72° 69°

(e)

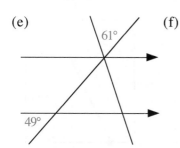

61°   49°

(f)

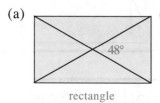

109°

(g)

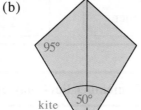

95°   61°

(h)

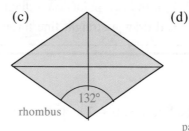

84°   106°

2. **Copy** each figure and fill in the sizes of **all** the missing angles.

(a)

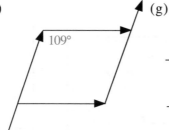

48°

rectangle

(b)

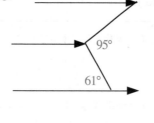

95°   50°

kite

(c)

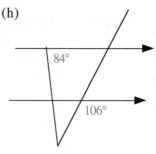

132°

rhombus

(d)

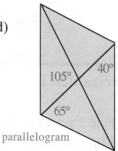

105° 40°   65°

parallelogram

3. This shape consists of two congruent
   rectangles (ABCD and PQRS) and
   trapezium BPSC.

   The dotted line is a line of symmetry.

   Copy the diagram and fill in **ALL** the
   missing angles.

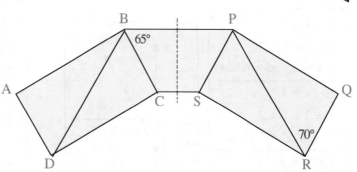

4.

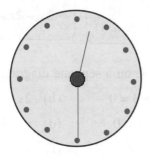

Calculate the size of the smaller angle between the
two hands at half past 12.

5. Repeat question 4 for the time "quarter to 5".

Sketching Straight Lines

Earlier, we practiced **drawing** straight lines by constructing a table of values, plotting the corresponding coordinate points on a Cartesian Diagram and joining them up.

When **sketching** a straight line we really only need **two points** on the line.

Substituting **three x-values** into the equation is usually the easiest if the line is of the form $y = mx + c$, but if the line is of the type $y - 2x + 2 = 0$, the easiest points to find are the **axes** points.

i.e.   (when $x = 0 \Rightarrow (0, ?)$ and when $y = 0 \Rightarrow (?, 0)$)

Example :-   Sketch the line $y - 2x + 4 = 0$.

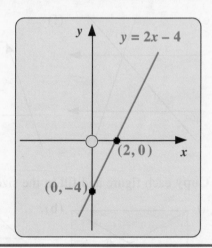

Step 1 Let $x = 0$ $y - 2 \times 0 + 4 = 0$

$y = -4 \Rightarrow (0, -4)$

Step 2 Let $y = 0$ $0 - 2x + 4 = 0$

$2x = 4$

$x = 2 \Rightarrow (2, 0)$

Step 3 Plot the two points on a diagram and draw a straight line through them.

Exercise 15·1

> **Remember lines may be expressed differently.**

1. Find 3 points on the line $y = 2x - 2$ and sketch it.
    Copy and complete :–

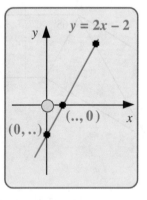

Let $x = 0$

$y = 2 \times 0 - 2$

$y = ... \Rightarrow (0, ...)$

Let $x = 1$

$y = 2 \times 1 - 2$

$y = ... \Rightarrow (1, ...)$

Let $x = 3$

$y = 2 \times 3 - 2$

$y = ... \Rightarrow (3, ...)$

2. Find 3 points on each of these lines, plot them and sketch each line (*on a separate diagram*).

(a) $y = 2x - 6$ (b) $y = 2x + 4$

(c) $y = x + 2$ (d) $y = 4x - 4$

(e) $y = 2x + 1$ (f) $y = 3x - 1$

(g) $y = 5x + 20$ (h) $y = 4x - 16$

(i) $y = 3 - x$ (j) $y = 5 - 4x$

3. Sketch the line $2y - 2x - 4 = 0$.
    Copy and **complete** :–

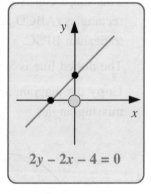

Let $x = 0$

$2y - 2 \times 0 - 4 = 0$

$2y - 4 = 0$

$y = ...$ gives $(0, ...)$

Let $y = 0$

$2 \times 0 - 2x - 4 = 0$

$- 2x - 4 = 0$

$x = ...$ gives $(..., 0)$

4. Sketch each line on a separate diagram.

(a) $3y - 6x + 3 = 0$ (b) $2y - 2x + 2 = 0$

(c) $4y + 8x - 8 = 0$ (d) $y - 4x + 4 = 0$

(e) $2x - 4y = 12$ (f) $x + y = 3$

(g) $2x + y = 5$ (h) $x + y = -1$

(i) $3x + 4y = -12$ (j) $3x = 2y$

Solving Simultaneous Equations - Graphically

If we are given the equations of two lines, for example $y = 2x - 4$ and $y = 5 - x$, we can find the point where they meet (**intersect**) by drawing both lines on the same diagram.

This is referred to as the "**simultaneous**" solution and the equations $y = 2x - 4$ and $y = 5 - x$ are called **simultaneous equations**.

Example :-   Find the coordinates of where the lines $y = 2x - 4$ and $y = 5 - x$ intersect.

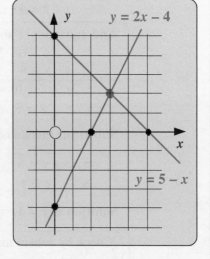

Step 1 Find any 3 points on the line $y = 2x - 4$.

      e.g.   Let $x = 0 \Rightarrow y = -4$ $(0, -4)$

              Let $x = 2 \Rightarrow y = 0$ $(2, 0)$

              Let $x = 4 \Rightarrow y = 4$ $(4, 4)$

Step 2 Find any 3 points on the line $y = 5 - x$.

      e.g.   Let $x = 0 \Rightarrow y = 5$ $(0, 5)$

              Let $x = 2 \Rightarrow y = 3$ $(2, 3)$

              Let $x = 4 \Rightarrow y = 1$ $(4, 1)$

Step 3 Plot and join each set of points on a Cartesian diagram.

         Read off the point of intersection. $(3, 2)$

This process is called solving simultaneous equations **graphically**.

Exercise 15·2

1.   Find the coordinates of the point where the lines $y - x + 4 = 0$ and $y - 8 + x = 0$ intersect.

    (a) **Copy** and complete :–

> $y - x + 4 = 0$ Let $x = 0$, $y = ...$ $(0, ...)$
>
>   Let $y = 0$, $x = ...$ $(..., 0)$
>
> $y - 8 + x = 0$ Let $x = 0$, $y = ...$ $(0, ...)$
>
>   Let $y = 0$, $x = ...$ $(..., 0)$

    (b) Plot each pair of points on one diagram.

    (c) Draw a straight line through each pair.

    (d) Write down the intersection point.

2.   Solve each pair of simultaneous equations. (*Find 3 points on each line, plot the points, draw the lines and find the point of intersection*).

    (a) $y = 2x - 5$ (b) $y = 3x - 1$

          $y = x - 1$ $y = 2x - 3$

    (c) $y = x - 1$ (d) $y = 4x + 6$

          $y = 2 - 2x$ $y = 5 + 3x$

    (e) $y = 3x - 2$ (f) $y = 6x - 4$

          $y = 4x - 1$ $y = -2x$

(*From now on, you decide which method you wish to use to help you draw the lines*).

3.   Solve each pair of simultaneous equations graphically.

    (a) $y + 2x = 2$ (b) $y + 2x = 14$

          $y - x = 2$ $4y + x = 14$

    (c) $y + x = 5$ (d) $2y + 3x = 12$

          $2x - 3y = 10$ $y - 2x = -8$

    (e) $y + x = -1$ (f) $3x + 2y = 12$

          $3x - 2y = 12$ $2x - 2y = 18$

4.   Solve graphically these pairs of equations.

    (a) $y + 2x + 1 = 0$ and $2y - x - 8 = 0$

    (b) $3y - 2x - 6 = 0$ and $y + x - 2 = 0$

    (c) $y = 3x + 1$ and $y + 2x - 6 = 0$

    (d) $y = 4x - 1$ and $y - 2x = -3$

5.   Explain why there are no solutions to the following pair of simultaneous equations.

           $y = 3x + 4$ and $2y - 6x + 8 = 0$

    (*Hint : drawing the graph might help*).

Solving Simultaneous Equations - by Elimination

A pair of simultaneous equations can be solved graphically (as before) or **algebraically**.

If we start with 2 equations in 2 variables (letters), and manage to combine both equations to form one new equation and **eliminating** one of the variables - we can easily solve this single remaining equation.

Example 1 :- Solve this pair of equations.

$$x + y = 6 \quad \text{........ } 1$$
$$x - y = 4 \quad \text{........ } 2$$

Add equations 1 and 2.

$$x + y = 6$$
$$x - y = 4$$
$$\overline{ 2x = 10} \quad \text{(the } y \text{ disappears)}$$
$$\Rightarrow \quad x = 5$$

Substitute this value into equation 1.

$$\Rightarrow \quad 5 + y = 6$$
$$\Rightarrow \quad y = 1$$

Solution is $y = 1$, $x = 5$ (5, 1)

> Check by substituting the values for x and y into equation 2.

Example 2 :- Solve this pair of equations.

$$3x + 2y = 5 \quad \text{........ } 1$$
$$-3x + y = 1 \quad \text{........ } 2$$

Add equations 1 and 2.

$$3x + 2y = 5$$
$$-3x + y = 1$$
$$\overline{ 3y = 6} \quad \text{(the } x \text{ disappears)}$$
$$\Rightarrow \quad y = 2$$

Substitute $y = 2$ into eqn 1

$$3x + 2 \times 2 = 5$$
$$\Rightarrow \quad 3x = 1$$
$$\Rightarrow \quad x = \tfrac{1}{3}$$

Solution is $x = \tfrac{1}{3}$, $y = 2$ $(\tfrac{1}{3}, 2)$

> Check

This process of solving simultaneous equations is called **elimination**.

Exercise 15·3

1. Solve this pair of simultaneous equations.

$$2y + 3x = 16 \quad \text{..... } 1$$
$$4y - 3x = 14 \quad \text{..... } 2$$

> Copy and complete :–
>
> **Add** 1 and 2
>
> $$2y + 3x = 16$$
> $$4y - 3x = 14$$
> $$\overline{ 6y = ...} \quad \text{(the } x \text{ disappears)}$$
> $$\Rightarrow \quad y = ...$$
>
> Substitute $y = 5$ into equation 1.
>
> $$2 \times 5 + 3x = 16$$
> $$\Rightarrow \quad 3x = ...$$
> $$\Rightarrow \quad x = ...$$
>
> Solution is $x = ...$ and $y = ...$ (..., ...)

2. Solve this pair of simultaneous equations.

$$3y + 2x = 11 \quad \text{..... } 1$$
$$y - 2x = 1 \quad \text{..... } 2$$

3. Solve each pair of simultaneous equations.

(a) $5y + 4x = 14$
    $3y - 4x = 2$

(b) $5y + 4x = 13$
    $9y - 4x = 1$

(c) $y + 7x = 24$
    $4y - 7x = -9$

(d) $6y + 2x = 38$
    $4y - 2x = 12$

(e) $7x - 3y = 2$
    $4x + 3y = 20$

(f) $x - 8y = -16$
    $3x + 8y = 16$

(g) $5y - 2x = 11$
    $2y + 2x = -4$

(h) $3x + 4y = -21$
    $2y - 3x = 3$

4. Re-arrange the second of these simultaneous equations so that x and y are on the left hand side, and then solve.

$$2x + 3y = 13$$
$$5x = 3y + 1$$

5. Solve each pair of simultaneous equations.

(a) $2x + y = 7$
    $4x = y + 11$

(b) $5x - 2y = 1$
    $x = 2y - 7$

(c) $4y = 8 - 2x$
    $8 = 2x - 3y$

(d) $2y + 3x + 1 = 0$
    $y - 4 = 3x$

Solving Simultaneous Equations by Elimination – harder

Example :- Solve this pair of simultaneous equations

$$5y + 4x = 13 \quad \text{........ } 1$$
$$3y - x = 5 \quad \text{........ } 2$$

Can you see that if we try adding equations 1 and 2, the new equation we get is no simpler ?

We must "**work**" on one of the equations first.

Step 1 **Multiply** equation 2 **by 4** to form a new equation (call it equation 3).
Step 2 Notice we can now eliminate x by **adding** 1 and 3.
Step 3 Proceed as before.

$$5y + 4x = 13 \quad \text{........ } 1$$
$$3y - x = 1 \quad \text{........ } 2$$
$$4 \times 2 \Rightarrow 12y - 4x = 4 \quad \text{....... } 3$$

Now we can **add** 1 and 3.

$$5y + 4x = 13 \quad \text{........ } 1$$
$$12y - 4x = 4 \quad \text{........ } 3$$
$$1 + 3 \Rightarrow 17y = 17$$
$$\Rightarrow y = 1$$

Substitute $y = 1$ into equation 1.

$$5 \times 1 + 4x = 13$$
$$\Rightarrow 4x = 8$$
$$\Rightarrow x = 2$$

Solution is $x = 2$, $y = 1$.   (2, 1)

Check by substituting x and y into equation 2.

Exercise 15·4

1. Solve this pair of simultaneous equations.

$$2y + 3x = 12 \quad \text{..... } 1$$
$$5y - x = 13 \quad \text{..... } 2$$

Copy and complete :–

$$2y + 3x = 12 \quad \text{..... } 1$$
$$5y - x = 13 \quad \text{..... } 2$$
$$3 \times 2 \Rightarrow 15y - 3x = \text{....} \quad \text{..... } 3$$

Add equation 1 and 3

$$2y + 3x = 12 \quad \text{..... } 1$$
$$15y - 3x = \text{....} \quad \text{.... } 3$$
$$\overline{17y = \text{...}}$$
$$\Rightarrow y = \text{...}$$

Substitute $y = \text{...}$ in equation 1

$$2 \times \text{...} + 3x = 12$$
$$\Rightarrow 3x = \text{...}$$
$$\Rightarrow x = \text{...}$$

Solution is $x = \text{...}$, $y = \text{...}$ (..., ...)

[**Check**]

2. Solve each pair of simultaneous equations.

$$4x + 2y = 14 \quad \text{....... } 1$$
$$2x - y = 5 \quad \text{....... } 2$$

(Hint : multiply equation 2 by 2)

3. For each pair of simultaneous equations :–

• label each equation 1 and 2.
• decide which equation to multiply.
• decide what multiplier to use.
• solve for x and y.

(a) $2x + 6y = 36$ (b) $3x + 4y = 25$
    $3x - 2y = -1$ $x - 2y = 5$

(c) $3x + 2y = 11$ (d) $3x + 4y = 22$
    $2x - y = -2$ $8x - 2y = 8$

(e) $3x - 2y = 11$ (f) $x - y = 3$
    $7x + 8y = 51$ $3x + 5y = 1$

(g) $4y + 9x = -27$ (h) $2y + 3x = -12$
    $8y - 3x = 9$ $y - x = -1$

(i) $12y + 8x = -34$ (j) $4x + 3y = 14$
    $2y - 2x = 6$ $2x - y = -3$

Example :-

Solve this pair of simultaneous equations.

$$5y + 2x = 12 \quad .... \ 1$$
$$3y - 3x = 5 \quad .... \ 2$$

This time **both** equations need to be multiplied.

$$5y + 2x = 12 \quad .... \ 1$$
$$4y - 3x = 5 \quad .... \ 2$$

$3 \times 1 \Rightarrow \qquad 15y + 6x = 36 \quad .... \ 3$

$2 \times 2 \Rightarrow \qquad \underline{8y - 6x = 10} \quad ...... \ 4$

$3 + 4 \Rightarrow \qquad 23y \qquad = 46$

$\Rightarrow \qquad\qquad\quad y = 2$

Substitute $y = 2$ in equation 1

$$5 \times 2 + 2x = 12$$
$$\Rightarrow \qquad 2x = 2$$
$$\Rightarrow \qquad x = 1$$

Solution is $x = 1$, $y = 2$. $\qquad (1, 2)$

---

4. Solve this pair of simultaneous equations.

$$5y + 4x = 18 \quad ..... \ 1$$
$$4y - 3x = 2 \quad ..... \ 2$$

Copy and complete :–

$$5y + 4x = 18 \quad ..... \ 1$$
$$4y - 3x = 2 \quad ..... \ 2$$

$3 \times 1 \Rightarrow 15y + 12x = 54 \quad .... \ 3$

$4 \times 2 \Rightarrow \underline{16y - 12x = ...} \quad .... \ 4$

$3 + 4 \Rightarrow 31y \qquad = ...$

$\Rightarrow \qquad\quad y = ...$

Substitute $y = ...$ in equation 1

$$5 \times ... + 4x = 18$$
$$\Rightarrow \qquad 4x = ...$$
$$\Rightarrow \qquad x = ...$$

Solution is $x = ...$, $y = ...$ $\qquad (... , ...)$

Check

5. Solve this pair of simultaneous equations.

$$2y + 5x = 15 \quad .... \ 1$$
$$3y - 2x = 13 \quad .... \ 2$$

Hint   • *multiply equation 1 × 2*

and   • *multiply equation 2 × 5.*

6. Solve this pair of simultaneous equations.

$$4x + 3y = 22 \quad .... \ 1$$
$$2x - 2y = 4 \quad .... \ 2$$

7. Label each equation and solve simultaneously.

(a) $3x + 4y = 10$ (b) $4x + 2y = 14$
    $2x - 3y = 1$ $7x - 3y = 5$

(c) $2x + 5y = 13$ (d) $6x + 7y = 27$
    $3x - 2y = 10$ $5x - 2y = -1$

(e) $5x - 6y = -11$ (f) $2x - 3y = -1$
    $4x + 4y = 0$ $5x + 4y = -14$

(g) $2x + 3y = 19$ (h) $4x + 8y = 2$
    $6x - 2y = -9$ $3x - 6y = -4·5$

8. Solve each pair of simultaneous equations.

(a) $2x + y = 5 \qquad .... \ 1$
    $x + y = 3 \qquad .... \ 2$
    (This time you must multiply eqn 2 by -1)

(b) $4x + 3y = 15 \qquad .... \ 1$
    $x + y = 4 \qquad .... \ 2$
    (This time you must multiply eqn 2 by -3)

(c) $7x + 3y = 22 \qquad .... \ 1$
    $4x + 2y = 14 \qquad .... \ 2$
    (This time you must multiply eqn 1 by -2)
    $\qquad$ and multiply eqn 2 by ...)

(d) $7x + 4y = 36 \quad .... \ (\times ...)$
    $2x + 3y = 14 \quad .... \ (\times -4)$

(e) $6y + 3x = 9 \quad .... \ (\times 2)$
    $5y + 2x = 8 \quad .... \ (\times -...)$

(f) $2x + 4y = -6$ (g) $4x + 7y = 10$
    $3x + 3y = -3$ $2x + 6y = 10$

(h) $5x + 2y = -19$ (i) $6x + 4y = -5$
    $4x + 3y = -18$ $8x + 3y = -2$

9. Solve :–

(a) $3y + 2x = -10$ (b) $8x - 8y = -16$
    $2y + 5x = -14$ $5x - 3y = -28$

(c) $6y + 6x = 0$ (d) $8x + 6y = -8$
    $7y + 5x = -1$ $2x + 11y = -2$

(e) $3x = 2y - 5$ (f) $2y = 5x + 16$
    $4x - 3y + 8 = 0$ $3y - 5x - 19 = 0$

(g) $2x - 3y - 13 = 0$ (h) $2x + y - 5 = 0$
    $3x + 2y = 0$ $3x - 4y - 13 = 0$

Solving Problems using Simultaneous Equations

Many everyday problems can be solved using simultaneous equations.

Example :-   **Bob** bought 5 balls and 2 teddies which cost him £11.   **Jill** paid £9 for 3 balls and 2 teddies.

Total Cost £11

Total Cost £9

How much does it cost for a ball and how much for a teddy ?

First we must set up two equations to represent **Bob** and **Jill**'s purchases.

Let cost of one ball   = £x,
and cost of one teddy = £y.

Bob : $5x + 2y = 11$ 1
Jill : $3x + 2y = 9$ 2

Now we solve these equations simultaneously.

$5x + 2y = 11$ 1
$3x + 2y = 9$ 2

$-1 \times 2 \Rightarrow$ $-3x - 2y = -9$ 3

add 1 & 3 $\Rightarrow$ $2x = 2$
$\Rightarrow$ $x = 1$

Substitute $x = 1$ in 2.
$3 \times 1 + 2y = 9$
$\Rightarrow$ $2y = 6$
$\Rightarrow$ $y = 3$

One ball cost £1. One Teddy costs £3.

Check your answer by substitution.

Exercise 15·5

1.   Reg paid 17 pence for four sweets and a lolly.

Jen paid 13 pence for three sweets and a lolly.

What is the cost of each sweet and each lolly ?

Copy and complete :–

Let cost of one sweet = x p
and cost of one lolly = y p

Reg : $4x + y = 17$ 1
Jen : $3x + y = 13$ 2

$-1 \times 2 \Rightarrow$ $-3x - y = -...$ 3

$1 + 3 \Rightarrow$ $x = ...$

Substitute $x = ...$ in equation 1

$4 \times ... + y = 17$

$\Rightarrow$ $y = ...$

One sweet costs .... p. One lolly costs ...p.

2.   Sally bought 4 hamburgers and 2 hotdogs at a cost of £14.

Fred paid £20 for 7 hamburgers and 2 hotdogs.

(a)   Set up two equations to represent this information.

(b)   Find the cost of one hamburger.

(c)   Find the cost of one hotdog.

(d)   How much would Bill have to pay for three hamburgers and two hotdogs ?

3. Cheri pays £11 for 2 grow-bags and one plant.
   Ali pays £15 for 3 grow-bags and one plant.

   Find the cost of each grow-bag and each plant.

4. Shez buys 2 coffees and 2 donuts for £3.

   Jeri pays £4 for 3 coffees and 2 donuts.

   Baz bought one coffee **and** one donut.

   How much did Baz have to pay ?

5. Sara purchased three identical blouses and four skirts costing £60.

   May paid £33 for three blouses and one skirt.

   Find the cost of each blouse.

6. Mike and Fran went to the local pet shop.

   Mike bought three mice and a lizard for £16.

   Fran paid £27 for two mice and three lizards.

   Find the cost of each mouse and each lizard.

7. The weight of six VCR players and two DVD players is 22 kg.

   Four VCR's and one DVD player weighs 14 kg.

   Find the weight of a DVD player.

8. Three steak meals and two fish dishes cost £43.
   Five steak meals and five fish dishes cost £85.

   (a) How much would it cost for a steak meal ?

   (b) If I bought two fish dishes and a steak meal, how much change would I receive from £30 ?

9. Mr. Forbes paid £60 for five adults and four children's puppet show tickets.

   Mrs. Rae paid £21 for two adults and one child.

   (a) Write down two equations to represent this information.

   (b) Find the cost of :–
       (i) an adult ticket   (ii) a child's ticket.

   (c) Mr. Allison bought four adult and five childrens' tickets.

       How much did he pay for the tickets ?

10. Miss Spencer bought 3 packs of white paper and 2 packs of coloured paper and found she had 1200 sheets of paper.

    Mr. Lott had 2300 sheets from 4 packs of white and 5 coloured packs.

    How many sheets were in each pack ?

11. A group of teachers and pupils went on a school trip.

    The teachers hired three tandems (2-seater bikes) and four bicycles which cost £27.

    If they had hired four tandems and two bicycles it would have cost them £26.

    How much would the hire charge have been for five tandems ?

12. The *PHOTO-Shop* produce high quality photographic posters.

    Alex paid £255 for four A3 sized posters and three A2 sized posters, Sean paid £240 for five A3 posters and two A2 posters and Tariq bought two A3 and one A2 poster.

    How much did Tariq have to pay ?

13. Tara spent £13·54 on 11 litres of petrol and 3 litres of oil for her car.

    It cost Jake £15·39 for 15 litres of petrol and 2 litres of oil.

    Find the cost of a litre of oil.

14. Four large jugs and three small cups can hold
    a maximum of 2250 millilitres of milk.

    Six large jugs and two small cups can hold a
    maximum of 3·2 litres.

    Can five large jugs hold two and a half litres ?

    (*Explain your answer fully*).

15. Jason does circuit training every day.
    On Monday he trains continuously for 20 minutes.
    On a Tuesday, he does 30 minutes of continuous training.

    His training on a Monday consists of 300 sit-ups and
    200 squat jumps.

    Tuesday consists of 150 sit-ups and 500 squat jumps.

    On Wednesday, Jason does 100 sit-ups and 100
    squat jumps.

    How long, in minutes and seconds, does Jason's
    training last on a Wednesday ?

16. Jennifer uses identical circles and identical squares to make both patterns below.

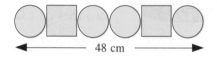 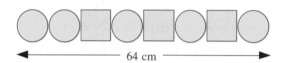

    Calculate :–

    (a) the **diameter** of one circle.   (b) the **area** of one square.

17. An advertising campaign uses two different size square posters to fit billboards.

    Billboard 1   **Billboard 2**   **Billboard 3**

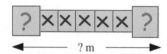

    (a) Calculate the **total** length of the seven posters used in Billboard 3.

    (b) Calculate the **total** area of all the posters used in Billboard 3.

18. Freda bought 4 oranges and 3 pears weighing 590g at a cost of £2·30.
    June paid £2·55 for 3 oranges and 5 pears weighing 690g.

    (a) Write down two equations involving the number
         of apples and pears and their **cost**.

    (b) Solve these equations simultaneously.

    (c) Find also the weight of a single pear.

    (d) Eddie bought ten oranges and a dozen pears.

         What was the total cost and weight of his purchase ?

1. Sketch each line below on a separate diagram.

   (a) $y = 2x + 3$

   (b) $3x + 6y = 12$

2. Solve **graphically** these simultaneous equations.

   $$y = 3x + 2 \quad .... 1$$
   $$y = 4 - x \quad .... 2$$

3. Solve each pair of simultaneous equations using **elimination**.

   (a) $3x + 4y = 13$
   $2x - 4y = 2$

   (b) $4x + 2y = 10$
   $7x - 2y = 12$

   (c) $3x + 5y = 13$
   $4x - y = 2$

   (d) $5x + 4y = 13$
   $x - 2y = -3$

   (e) $3y + 2x = 5$
   $2y + 5x = 7$

   (f) $8x - 8y = -8$
   $5x - 3y = 1$

   (g) $2y + 3x = 9$
   $5y + 2x = 17$

   (h) $2x - 7y = 24$
   $3x - 2y = 19$

   (i) $8y + 2x = 42$
   $3y + 7x = 47$

   (j) $8x - 8y = -56$
   $5x - 3y = -19$

4. **Re-arrange** this pair of simultaneous equations and then solve.

   $$2x + 3y - 10 = 0$$
   $$4x = 3y + 20$$

5. 3 chairs and a table weigh 16 kg.
   5 chairs and a table weigh 22 kg.

   What is the weight of one chair ?

6. Percy bought eight lemonades and three cokes costing £3·60.

   Marion spent £3·30 on seven lemonades and three cokes.

   (a) Set up two equations to represent this information.

   (b) Solve these equations to find the cost of one coke.

   (c) How much would it cost for five lemonades and two cokes ?

7. The Concert Hall staged "Swan Lake".

   Jake paid £76 for 3 stalls tickets and 2 circle tickets.

   Milo paid £122 for 5 stalls tickets and 3 circle tickets.

   Jeri bought 4 stalls tickets and 4 circle tickets.

   How much did Jeri pay for her tickets ?

8.  Two hamburgers and three fries cost £5.

   Five hamburgers and two fries cost £8·10.

   How much does a hamburger cost ?

9. Eight identical trucks and four identical cars were parked bumper to bumper and the total length of all 12 vehicles was 58 metres.

   Six trucks and five cars measured 50·5 metres.

   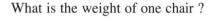

   Calculate the length of two trucks and two cars.

10. Three towers, built from rectangular bricks, are shown below.

    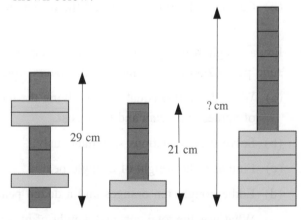

    29 cm

    21 cm

    ? cm

    Find the height of the tallest tower.

What is a Fraction ?

A fraction consists of 2 parts.

$\dfrac{3}{5}$ ← the numerator
     ← the denominator

It may be possible to **simplify** a fraction by dividing top and bottom by a particular number.

$\dfrac{9}{12}$ becomes $\dfrac{9 \div 3}{12 \div 3} = \dfrac{3}{4}$

Mixed fractions

A fraction, like, $\dfrac{23}{4}$, where the **numerator** is bigger than the **denominator** is a "**top-heavy**" fraction.

A number consisting of "whole" part and a "fraction" part, like $1\frac{2}{3}$, is called a **mixed fraction**.

Example 1 :- Changing a top-heavy fraction to a mixed fraction :-

note *

=> $\dfrac{23}{4}$ means $(23 \div 4) = 5$ (remainder 3) $= 5\frac{3}{4}$

Example 2 :- Changing a mixed fraction back to a top-heavy fraction :-

=>   To change $6\frac{2}{3}$ into "thirds"

- Step 1 - multiply the 6 by the 3
- Step 2 - now add on the 2 (thirds).

$6 \times 3 = 18 + 2 = 20$ => $\dfrac{20}{3}$

Exercise 16·1

1. Copy and complete the following :-

(a) $\dfrac{17}{2}$ means $17 \div 2$ => $2\overline{\smash)17} = 8\frac{?}{2}$.

(b) $\dfrac{29}{6}$ means $29 \div 6$ => $6\overline{\smash)29} = 4\frac{?}{6}$.

(c) $\dfrac{17}{9}$ means $17 \div ...$ => $...$ $= ...$

2. In a similar way, change the following top-heavy fractions to **mixed numbers** :-

(a) $\dfrac{10}{3}$ (b) $\dfrac{19}{4}$ (c) $\dfrac{31}{6}$

(d) $\dfrac{11}{2}$ (e) $\dfrac{37}{5}$ (f) $\dfrac{51}{8}$

3. (a) Five girls decide to share 13 bars of tablet evenly. What will each girl receive, (*as a mixed number*) ?

3. (b) 23 kg of onions are packed evenly into 6 bags. What weight of onions goes into each bag ?

(c) A container holds 27 litres of water. An equal quantity of water is poured into 5 cups such that each holds the same amount. How much water will be in each cup ?

4. Copy and complete :-

$\dfrac{26}{6} = 26 \div 6 = 4\frac{2}{6} = 4\frac{?}{3}$ (<— simplified).

5. Change each of the following to mixed numbers and simplify where possible :-

(a) $\dfrac{21}{6}$ (b) $\dfrac{14}{4}$ (c) $\dfrac{26}{8}$

(d) $\dfrac{42}{10}$ (e) $\dfrac{21}{9}$ (f) $\dfrac{30}{8}$

6. This diagram represents $2\frac{3}{4}$ pies.

   (a) How many "$\frac{1}{4}$" pie slices do you get from 1 pie ?

   (b) How many "$\frac{1}{4}$" pie slices do you get from 2 pies ?

   (c) How many "$\frac{1}{4}$" pie slices do you get from $2\frac{3}{4}$ pies ?

7. These pizzas have been cut into "thirds".

   (a) From the 3 whole pizzas, you get ... thirds ?

   (b) From the $\frac{2}{3}$ pizza, you get ..... thirds ?

   (c) How many thirds is this altogether ?

   (d) Write this as $3\frac{2}{3} = \frac{?}{3}$.

8. Copy and complete :–

   $4\frac{3}{5} = ((4 \times 5) + 3)$ "fifths" $= 23$ "fifths" $= \frac{?}{5}$

9. Copy and complete :–

   (a) $3\frac{2}{3} = ...$ (b) $5\frac{3}{7} = ...$ (c) $6\frac{4}{5} = ...$

10. Change each of the following mixed numbers to top heavy fractions :–

   (a) $2\frac{1}{2}$ (b) $3\frac{3}{4}$ (c) $10\frac{3}{5}$

   (d) $6\frac{1}{8}$ (e) $9\frac{2}{3}$ (f) $2\frac{7}{10}$

11. How many $\frac{1}{2}$ pizza slices can I get from :–

   (a) 3 pizzas   (b) 7 pizzas

   (c) $4\frac{1}{2}$ pizzas (d) $9\frac{1}{2}$ pizzas ?

12. How many $\frac{1}{3}$ litre glasses can be filled from :–

   (a) 2 litres   (b) $2\frac{2}{3}$ litres   (c) $4\frac{1}{3}$ litres ?

13. How many $\frac{1}{4}$ kg bags can be filled from :–

   (a) 5 kg   (b) $2\frac{1}{4}$ kg   (c) $3\frac{3}{4}$ kg ?

14. To add $3\frac{3}{5} + 2\frac{4}{5}$ you change them to "$\frac{1}{5}$'s".

   Copy and complete :–

$$3\frac{3}{5} + 2\frac{4}{5}$$
$$= \frac{?}{5} + \frac{?}{5}$$
$$= \frac{?}{5} \quad = 6\frac{?}{5}.$$

Adding and Subtracting Fractions – Basic

Simple Rule :–   You can only add (or subtract) two fractions if :-

    =>   **THEY HAVE THE SAME DENOMINATOR.**

Example 1
$$\frac{2}{9} + \frac{5}{9}$$
$$= \frac{7}{9}$$

Example 2
$$\frac{5}{8} - \frac{3}{8}$$
$$= \frac{2}{8}$$
$$= \frac{1}{4}$$

Example 3
$$3\frac{3}{5} + 2\frac{4}{5}$$
$$= 5\frac{7}{5}$$
$$= 6\frac{2}{5}$$

Example 4
$$4\frac{5}{6} - 1\frac{1}{6}$$
$$= 3\frac{4}{6}$$
$$= 3\frac{2}{3}$$

Exercise 16·2

1. Copy and complete the following :-

   (a) $\frac{1}{5} + \frac{3}{5}$
$$= \frac{?}{5}$$

   (b) $\frac{7}{9} - \frac{5}{9}$
$$= \frac{?}{9}$$

   (c) $\frac{9}{10} - \frac{3}{10}$
$$= \frac{?}{10} = \frac{?}{5}$$

   (d) $\frac{3}{16} + \frac{3}{16}$
$$= \frac{?}{16} = \frac{?}{8}$$

2. Copy the following and simplify :-

(a) $\frac{5}{7} + \frac{4}{7}$ (b) $\frac{1}{9} + \frac{7}{9}$ (c) $\frac{5}{8} - \frac{3}{8}$

(d) $\frac{3}{5} + \frac{3}{5}$ (e) $\frac{9}{11} - \frac{4}{11}$ (f) $\frac{3}{10} + \frac{1}{10}$

3. Copy the following and simplify :-

(a) $4\frac{1}{2} + 2\frac{1}{2}$ (b) $7\frac{3}{4} - 3\frac{1}{4}$ (c) $5\frac{1}{3} + 1\frac{1}{3}$

(d) $3\frac{7}{9} + 2\frac{4}{9}$ (e) $9\frac{3}{4} - 5\frac{1}{4}$ (f) $3\frac{2}{7} + 8\frac{3}{7}$

4. Of the $\frac{7}{10}$ km to her school, Davida had walked $\frac{3}{10}$ km. How much further had she to go ?

5. Hat sizes go up in $\frac{1}{8}$'s of an inch at a time.

Jeff wears hat size $6\frac{7}{8}$.
Luke's hat is 3 sizes bigger than this.

What is Luke's hat size ?

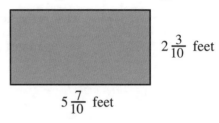

6. Nick mixes $5\frac{4}{5}$ kg of sand with $3\frac{3}{5}$ kg of cement.

What is the total weight of the mixture ?

7. (a) A piece of rope was $6\frac{5}{8}$ metres long.

A piece measuring $3\frac{3}{8}$ metres was cut off.

What length of rope remained ?

(b)  2 jugs of water were poured into an empty basin.

The first jug held $2\frac{3}{4}$ litres and the second held $1\frac{3}{4}$ litres.

How much water was in the basin in total ?

(c) Of the $9\frac{5}{7}$ kilometres from her house to the shops, Jan has cycled $2\frac{2}{7}$ km.

How much further has Jan to cycle to reach the shops ?

7. (d) Steve ate $\frac{3}{8}$ of a pie, Harry ate $\frac{3}{8}$ and Mandy ate $\frac{1}{8}$.

How much had they eaten altogether ?

(e) Lizzie weighed $41\frac{4}{5}$ kilograms. She went on a diet and lost $3\frac{3}{5}$ kilograms.

What is Lizzie's new weight ?

8. A table was $5\frac{7}{10}$ feet long by $2\frac{3}{10}$ feet wide.

$2\frac{3}{10}$ feet

$5\frac{7}{10}$ feet

(a) By how much is the length bigger than the breadth ?

(b) Calculate the **perimeter** of the table top.

9. A lorry weighs $4\frac{5}{8}$ tonnes.

Crates are loaded onto the lorry.

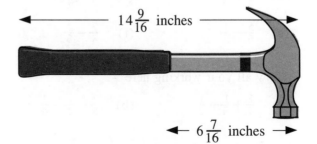

TeeJay Publishers Ltd.

Unladen weight - $4\frac{5}{8}$ tonnes

$\frac{3}{8}$ tonne

Each crate weighs $\frac{3}{8}$ tonne.

What is the total weight of the lorry carrying a load with :-

(a) 1 crate   (b) 2 crates   (c) 3 crates ?

10. Look at the picture of the hammer.

Calculate the length of the rubber handle.

$14\frac{9}{16}$ inches

$6\frac{7}{16}$ inches

Adding and Subtracting Fractions (Harder Examples)

Remember the Golden Rule :– The denominators **MUST** be the same if you wish to add or subtract.

> **Question :-** What do we do if the denominators are not the same ?
>
> **Answer :-** Change each fraction so that they **DO HAVE THE SAME** denominator.

Example 1 :- Find :- $\frac{2}{3} + \frac{1}{2}$. – note :- this does **not** add to give the answer $\frac{3}{5}$ ✗

• the denominators **3** and **2** are **not** the same.

=> what is the l.c.m. (lowest common multiple) of 3 and 2 ? —> answer is **6**.

=> we must change the $\frac{2}{3}$ and the $\frac{1}{2}$ into $\frac{1}{6}$'s.

$$\frac{2}{3} + \frac{1}{2}$$
note —> $$\frac{4}{6} + \frac{3}{6}$$ <— note
$$= \frac{7}{6} = 1\frac{1}{6}$$

$(\frac{2}{3} = \frac{?}{6})$ —> ? = 4

$(\frac{1}{2} = \frac{?}{6})$ —> ? = 3

Example 2 :-

(8 and 5 go into 40)

$$\frac{5}{8} - \frac{1}{5}$$
$$\frac{?}{40} - \frac{?}{40}$$
$$= \frac{25}{40} - \frac{8}{40}$$
$$= \frac{17}{40}$$

$\frac{5}{8} \quad \times 5$ / $\times 5$

$\frac{1}{5} \quad \times 8$ / $\times 8$

Example 3 :-

(6 and 4 go into 12)

$$\frac{5}{6} + \frac{3}{4}$$
$$\frac{?}{12} + \frac{?}{12}$$
$$= \frac{10}{12} + \frac{9}{12}$$
$$= \frac{19}{12} = 1\frac{7}{12}$$

$\frac{5}{6} \quad \times 2$ / $\times 2$

$\frac{3}{4} \quad \times 3$ / $\times 3$

Exercise 16·3

1. Copy and complete the following :-

   (a) $\frac{3}{4} + \frac{1}{3}$
   $= \frac{9}{12} + \frac{?}{12}$
   $= \frac{?}{12} = 1\frac{?}{12}$

   (b) $\frac{4}{5} - \frac{2}{3}$
   $= \frac{?}{15} - \frac{?}{15}$
   $= \frac{?}{15}$

   (c) $\frac{7}{8} - \frac{3}{4}$
   $= \frac{?}{8} - \frac{?}{8}$
   $= \frac{?}{8}$

   (d) $\frac{6}{7} + \frac{2}{3}$
   $= \frac{?}{21} + \frac{?}{21}$
   $= \frac{?}{21} = 1\frac{?}{21}$

2. Simplify the following :-

   (a) $\frac{2}{5} + \frac{1}{3}$

   (b) $\frac{1}{2} - \frac{1}{4}$

   (c) $\frac{3}{8} + \frac{2}{3}$

   (d) $\frac{3}{5} + \frac{1}{4}$

   (e) $\frac{5}{6} - \frac{1}{2}$

   (f) $\frac{7}{8} - \frac{2}{3}$

   (g) $\frac{3}{10} + \frac{4}{5}$

   (h) $\frac{5}{9} - \frac{1}{2}$

3. Show all your working here :-

   (a) $\frac{1}{4} + \frac{1}{3} + \frac{1}{2}$

   (b) $\frac{7}{8} - \frac{1}{2} - \frac{1}{4}$

   (c) $\frac{1}{3} + \frac{4}{5} - \frac{1}{2}$

   (d) $\frac{3}{4} + \frac{2}{5} - \frac{1}{3}$

Mixed Fractions

Deal with the **whole numbers first** – then the fractions.

Example 4 :-

$3\frac{3}{4} + 2\frac{2}{3}$

$= 5(\frac{3}{4} + \frac{2}{3})$

$= 5(\frac{9}{12} + \frac{8}{12})$

$= 5\frac{17}{12} = 6\frac{5}{12}$

Example 5 :-

$6\frac{5}{8} - 4\frac{1}{3}$

$= 2(\frac{5}{8} - \frac{1}{3})$

$= 2(\frac{15}{24} - \frac{8}{24})$

$= 2\frac{7}{24}$

Example 6 :-

$3\frac{3}{5} + \frac{5}{6}$

$= 3(\frac{3}{5} + \frac{5}{6})$

$= 3(\frac{18}{30} + \frac{25}{30})$

$= 3\frac{43}{30} = 4\frac{13}{30}$

4. Copy and complete the following :–

(a) $5\frac{2}{3} + 3\frac{1}{2}$

(b) $4\frac{3}{4} - 1\frac{2}{3}$

(c) $7\frac{5}{8} - 3\frac{1}{4}$

(d) $5\frac{1}{2} + 3\frac{4}{5}$

(e) $3\frac{5}{6} - 1\frac{3}{5}$

(f) $2\frac{1}{3} + 1\frac{3}{8}$

(g) $5\frac{5}{9} + 1\frac{1}{2}$

(h) $6\frac{9}{10} - 2\frac{3}{4}$

5. Copy and complete the following :–

(a) $7 - 3\frac{1}{4}$

$= 4 - \frac{1}{4}$

$= 3\frac{?}{4}$

(b) $6 - 1\frac{3}{5}$

$= 5 - \frac{3}{5}$

$= 4\frac{?}{5}$

6. Use the above method to find :–

(a) $3 - 1\frac{1}{3}$

(b) $7 - 2\frac{7}{9}$

7. From a 6 metre length of cable, the engineer cut off a piece which was $3\frac{3}{8}$ metres long.

What was the length of the piece of cable remaining ?

8. It is exactly 12 miles from Brum to Dyer.

Davie and Bob left Brum and jogged for $7\frac{3}{5}$ kilometres before stopping for a rest.

How much further had they still to jog to get to Dyer ?

A Problem with Subtraction :– $4\frac{1}{3} - 1\frac{3}{5}$?

- **Step 1 –** Subtract whole numbers first —> $3(\frac{1}{3} - \frac{3}{5})$

- **Step 2 –** Change both fractions to $\frac{1}{15}$'s => $3(\frac{5}{15} - \frac{9}{15})$

  (* you cannot take $\frac{9}{15}$ from $\frac{5}{15}$!!!! *)

- **Step 3 –** Take 1 whole number from the 3 and write it as $\frac{15}{15}$ (= 1)

  —> $3(\frac{5}{15} - \frac{9}{15})$

  becomes $2 + \frac{15}{15} + (\frac{5}{15} - \frac{9}{15}) = 2 + \frac{20}{15} - \frac{9}{15}$

  $= 2\frac{11}{15}$

One More Example :-

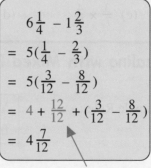

$6\frac{1}{4} - 1\frac{2}{3}$

$= 5(\frac{1}{4} - \frac{2}{3})$

$= 5(\frac{3}{12} - \frac{8}{12})$

$= 4 + \frac{12}{12} + (\frac{3}{12} - \frac{8}{12})$

$= 4\frac{7}{12}$

change 1 (of the 5) to $\frac{12}{12}$

9. Copy and complete the following :–

(a) $5\frac{2}{5} - 1\frac{1}{2}$

$= 4(\frac{2}{5} - \frac{1}{2})$

$= 4(\frac{4}{10} - \frac{5}{10})$

$= 3 + \frac{10}{10} + (\frac{4}{10} - \frac{5}{10})$

$= 3\frac{?}{10}$

(b) $4\frac{3}{8} - 2\frac{3}{5}$

$= 2(\frac{3}{8} - \frac{3}{5})$

$= 2(\frac{15}{40} - \frac{?}{40})$

$= 1 + \frac{?}{40} + (\frac{15}{40} - \frac{?}{40})$

$= 1\frac{?}{40}$

10. Show all your working here :–

(a) $4\frac{1}{5} - 1\frac{1}{2}$

(b) $6\frac{3}{5} - 1\frac{5}{6}$

(c) $4\frac{1}{4} - 2\frac{1}{2}$

(d) $6\frac{3}{8} - 4\frac{3}{4}$

(e) $10\frac{1}{3} - 7\frac{1}{2}$

(f) $6\frac{1}{7} - 1\frac{1}{2}$

(g) $8\frac{1}{3} - 3\frac{7}{10}$

(h) $8\frac{1}{6} - 5\frac{2}{5}$

Multiplying Fractions

The rule for multiplying two basic fractions is very simple.

To multiply $\frac{3}{5} \times \frac{4}{7}$ —> multiply the numerators
—> multiply the denominators —> $\frac{3}{5} \times \frac{4}{7} = \frac{3 \times 4}{5 \times 7} = \frac{12}{35}$

Example 1 :-

$$\frac{3}{4} \times \frac{3}{5}$$
$$= \frac{3 \times 3}{4 \times 5}$$
$$= \frac{9}{20}$$

Example 2 :-

$$\frac{4}{5} \times \frac{5}{6}$$
$$= \frac{20}{30} \; (\substack{\div 10 \\ \div 10})$$
$$= \frac{2}{3} \; (simplified)$$

Example 3 :-

$$\frac{8}{9} \times \frac{3}{4}$$
$$= \frac{24}{36} \; (\substack{\div 12 \\ \div 12})$$
$$= \frac{2}{3}$$

Exercise 16·4

1. Copy each of the following and complete :-

   (a) $\frac{2}{3} \times \frac{4}{5}$ (b) $\frac{5}{6} \times \frac{1}{3}$

   $= \frac{2 \times 4}{3 \times 5}$ $= \frac{5 \times 1}{6 \times 3}$

   $= \frac{?}{15}$ $= \frac{?}{?}$

2. Multiply the following fractions and simplify (where possible) :-

   (a) $\frac{2}{5} \times \frac{2}{3}$ (b) $\frac{5}{6} \times \frac{3}{5}$

   (c) $\frac{3}{7} \times \frac{4}{9}$ (d) $\frac{3}{10} \times \frac{5}{6}$

2. (e) $\frac{3}{8} \times \frac{4}{5}$ (f) $\frac{7}{12} \times \frac{4}{7}$

   (g) $\frac{11}{16} \times \frac{2}{5}$ (h) $\frac{2}{9} \times \frac{9}{10}$

3. Calculate the **area** of a rectangular sheet of metal measuring $\frac{5}{6}$ metre by $\frac{3}{8}$ metre.

4. I spent $\frac{3}{4}$ of my pocket money in a shop. Of that, $\frac{2}{5}$ of it went on comics.

   What fraction of my money was spent on comics ? (i.e $\frac{2}{5} \times \frac{3}{4}$)

Dealing with Mixed Fractions :- $(4\frac{3}{4} \times 1\frac{1}{3})$

Example 4 :-

Simple Rule :– You **MUST CHANGE** any mixed fraction into a **top-heavy fractions**

$$4\frac{3}{4} \times 1\frac{1}{3}$$
$$= \frac{19}{4} \times \frac{4}{3}$$
$$= \frac{76}{12}$$
$$= \frac{19}{3} = 6\frac{1}{3}$$

5. Copy and complete the following :–

   (a) $1\frac{1}{2} \times 2\frac{1}{3}$ (b) $5\frac{2}{3} \times 1\frac{1}{4}$

   $= \frac{3}{2} \times \frac{7}{3}$ $= \frac{17}{3} \times \frac{5}{4}$

   $= \frac{21}{6}$ $= \frac{85}{12}$

   $= 3\frac{?}{6} = 3\frac{?}{?}$ $= 7\frac{?}{?}$

6. Do the following in the same way :-

   (a) $2\frac{1}{3} \times 2\frac{1}{2}$ (b) $4\frac{1}{5} \times 2\frac{1}{2}$

6. (c) $5\frac{1}{3} \times 3\frac{3}{4}$ (d) $1\frac{2}{7} \times 4\frac{2}{3}$

   (e) $6\frac{1}{4} \times 1\frac{3}{5}$ (f) $2\frac{5}{6} \times 5\frac{1}{2}$

   (g) $1\frac{3}{10} \times 4\frac{1}{3}$ (h) $1\frac{1}{2} \times 7\frac{2}{5}$

   (i) $3\frac{2}{3} \times 1\frac{3}{4}$ (j) $5\frac{1}{2} \times 4\frac{4}{5}$

   (k) $10\frac{1}{2} \times \frac{6}{7}$ (l) $6\frac{1}{2} \times \frac{4}{5}$

Division of Fractions tricky !!

It is almost impossible to do fraction calculation like $(\frac{2}{3} \div \frac{3}{5})$ by actually **dividing**.

What we do instead, is change a "**division**" to a "**multiplication**" (*which is easier*) as follows :-

RULE* :-
- Leave the first fraction (*the left hand one*) as it is.
- Turn the second fraction (*the right hand one*) "**upside down**".
- Change the division sign (÷) to a multiplication (×) and **multiply**.

$$\rightarrow \quad \frac{2}{3} \div \frac{3}{5} \text{ becomes } \quad \frac{2}{3} \times \frac{5}{3} = \frac{10}{9} = 1\frac{1}{9}.$$

Example 1 :-
$$\frac{5}{6} \div \frac{2}{3}$$
$$\Rightarrow \frac{5}{6} \times \frac{3}{2}$$
$$\Rightarrow \frac{15}{12} = 1\frac{1}{4}$$

Example 2 :-
$$\frac{7}{8} \div \frac{3}{4}$$
$$\Rightarrow \frac{7}{8} \times \frac{4}{3}$$
$$\Rightarrow \frac{28}{24} = 1\frac{1}{6}$$

Example 3 :-
$$4\frac{4}{5} \div 1\frac{1}{3}$$
$$\Rightarrow \frac{24}{5} \div \frac{4}{3}$$
$$\Rightarrow \frac{24}{5} \times \frac{3}{4}$$
$$\Rightarrow \frac{72}{20} = 3\frac{3}{5}$$

* - Your teacher will explain the rule and how it works.

Exercise 16·5

1. Copy each of the following and complete :-

(a)
$$\frac{3}{4} \div \frac{3}{5}$$
$$= \frac{3}{4} \times \frac{5}{3}$$
$$= \frac{?}{12} = \frac{?}{4} = 1\frac{?}{4}$$

(b)
$$\frac{5}{6} \div \frac{1}{3}$$
$$= \frac{5}{6} \times \frac{3}{1}$$
$$= \frac{?}{6} = 2\frac{?}{6}$$

2. Divide the following and simplify :-

(a) $\frac{2}{5} \div \frac{2}{3}$

(b) $\frac{5}{6} \div \frac{7}{12}$

(c) $\frac{3}{7} \div \frac{6}{7}$

(d) $\frac{3}{10} \div \frac{4}{5}$

(e) $\frac{3}{8} \div \frac{5}{6}$

(f) $\frac{7}{12} \div \frac{7}{8}$

(g) $\frac{11}{16} \div \frac{5}{8}$

(h) $\frac{2}{9} \div \frac{1}{6}$

(i) $\frac{7}{10} \div \frac{3}{5}$

(j) $\frac{7}{16} \div \frac{3}{10}$

(k) $\frac{8}{9} \div \frac{3}{4}$

(l) $\frac{1}{5} \div \frac{1}{7}$

3. How many $\frac{2}{5}$'s are there in $\frac{3}{10}$'s ?

4. How many pieces of cloth $\frac{1}{8}$ metre long, can I cut from a piece $\frac{2}{3}$ metre long ?

5. Copy and complete the following :–

(a)
$$2\frac{1}{4} \div 1\frac{1}{5}$$
$$= \frac{9}{4} \div \frac{6}{5}$$
$$= \frac{9}{4} \times \frac{5}{6}$$
$$= ..... = ...$$

(b)
$$4\frac{2}{3} \div 1\frac{2}{5}$$
$$= \frac{14}{3} \div \frac{7}{5}$$
$$= \frac{14}{3} \times \frac{?}{?}$$
$$= ..... = ...$$

6. Divide the following fractions in the same way (*simplify if possible*) :–

(a) $3\frac{1}{3} \div 1\frac{1}{2}$

(b) $2\frac{1}{5} \div 1\frac{1}{2}$

(c) $4\frac{1}{3} \div 2\frac{3}{4}$

(d) $1\frac{2}{7} \div 2\frac{2}{3}$

(e) $4\frac{1}{4} \div 3\frac{3}{5}$

(f) $6\frac{1}{2} \div 2\frac{1}{4}$

(g) $1\frac{3}{5} \div 4\frac{2}{3}$

(h) $7\frac{1}{2} \div 1\frac{3}{7}$

(i) $6 \div 1\frac{1}{2}$

(j) $8 \div 2\frac{2}{3}$

7. $2\frac{1}{4}$ laps of the park took Tommy Muir, walking his dog, $12\frac{1}{2}$ minutes.

How long, on average did 1 lap take ?

Remember Remember..... ?

1. Change to a mixed number :-
       (a) $\frac{29}{5}$
       (b) $\frac{46}{8}$
       (c) $\frac{76}{10}$

2. Re-write as a top-heavy fraction :-
       (a) $5\frac{2}{3}$
       (b) $6\frac{3}{5}$
       (c) $10\frac{7}{9}$

3. How many $\frac{1}{3}$ pizza slices can by sold from $4\frac{2}{3}$ pizzas ?

4. Copy and complete :-

   (a) $\frac{5}{7} + \frac{1}{7}$
       (b) $\frac{3}{4} - \frac{1}{2}$
       (c) $\frac{5}{8} - \frac{1}{8}$
       (d) $2\frac{2}{5} + 3\frac{4}{5}$

   (e) $\frac{5}{6} - \frac{1}{4}$
       (f) $4\frac{4}{5} + 1\frac{2}{3}$
       (g) $5\frac{7}{8} - 2\frac{3}{5}$
       (h) $3\frac{1}{2} - 1\frac{2}{3}$

5. Copy and complete :-

   (a) $\frac{1}{2} \times \frac{3}{5}$
       (b) $\frac{7}{9} \times \frac{2}{3}$
       (c) $3\frac{1}{2} \times 1\frac{1}{5}$
       (d) $\frac{3}{4} \div \frac{1}{4}$

   (e) $\frac{5}{6} \div \frac{1}{3}$
       (f) $\frac{9}{10} \div \frac{2}{5}$
       (g) $2\frac{2}{3} \div 1\frac{1}{5}$
       (h) $5\frac{1}{4} \div 3\frac{1}{2}$

6. Before going on his diet, Sam weighed $14\frac{1}{2}$ stones.

   He lost $3\frac{3}{4}$ stones on his diet.

   What did Sam then weigh ?

7. 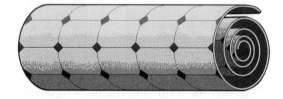 A 1 metre length of this linoleum weighs $3\frac{3}{5}$ kg.

   What will the weight of a $2\frac{3}{4}$ metre length be ?

8. An empty wooden crate weighs $3\frac{3}{8}$ kg.

   It holds 6 bags of ready mix cement.

   Each bag weighs $2\frac{3}{4}$ kg.

   Calculate the total weight of the crate and the 6 bags.

9. 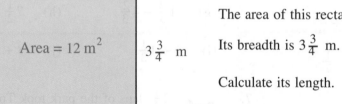 The area of this rectangular lawn is 12 m^2.

   Area = 12 m^2 $3\frac{3}{4}$ m

   Its breadth is $3\frac{3}{4}$ m.

   Calculate its length.

10. Find :- $\frac{2}{3} \times \frac{3}{4} \times \frac{4}{5} \times \frac{5}{6} \times \frac{6}{7} \times \frac{7}{8} \times \frac{8}{9} \times \frac{9}{10}$.   *(This should only take about 10 seconds !).*

1. Calculate the value of *x*, *y* and *z* :-

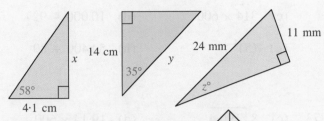
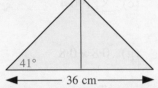
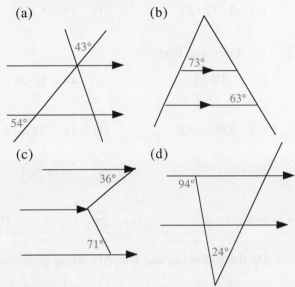

2. Calculate the **area** of this isosceles triangle.

3. Solve the following equations. (*Show working*).

   (a) $12x + 15 = 9x$ (b) $10 - 2(x - 6) = 12$

   (c) $\frac{3}{4}x - \frac{2}{3} = \frac{1}{2}$ (d) $\frac{x+2}{5} - \frac{x-4}{3} = 2$

4. Solve $3(x + 2) - 5(x - 1) \geq 3$.

5. A parking attendant logged how many vehicles she stuck tickets on one Monday morning.

Vehicle	Number	Fraction	Angle
Cars	50	$\frac{50}{...}$	$\frac{50}{...} \times .. = ..$
Vans	35		
Lorries	25		
Motorbikes	10		
TOTAL	...		....

   (a) Make a **copy** of the table and complete it.

   (b) Draw a neat labelled **pie chart** to show the above information.

6. Janice knows what her "ideal" weight was.

   She kept a note of the **number of hours** spent in the gym each week and the number of kilograms **overweight** she was at the end of the corresponding week.

Hours in Gym	2	4	5	6	10	10	12	13	14
Overweight		7	8	7	6	6	5	5	4	5

   (a) Draw a neat **scattergraph** to show the above.

   (b) Draw a **line of best fit** on your scattergraph.

   (c) Last week she did 8 hours in the gym.
       Estimate how much overweight she was then.

7. Sketch each of these and fill in the sizes of **all** the missing angles :-

   (a)   (b)

   (c)   (d)

   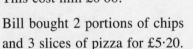
   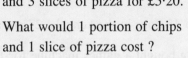

8. Solve each pair of simultaneous equations, showing every step of your working :-

   (a) $3x + 4y = 2$ (b) $8x + 5y = 14$
       $4x - y = 9$ $5x - 3y = 21$

9. Bob bought 3 portions of chips and 2 slices of pizza.
   This cost him £6·00.

   Bill bought 2 portions of chips and 3 slices of pizza for £5·20.

   What would 1 portion of chips and 1 slice of pizza cost ?

10. Do the following, showing all your working :-

    (a) $\frac{4}{5} + \frac{1}{4}$ (b) $\frac{5}{6} - \frac{1}{8}$

    (c) $4\frac{2}{3} + 2\frac{3}{5}$ (d) $6\frac{1}{2} - 2\frac{7}{8}$

    (e) $\frac{2}{5} \times \frac{3}{4}$ (f) $4\frac{1}{2} \times 2\frac{2}{3}$

    (g) $\frac{9}{10} \div \frac{3}{4}$ (h) $4\frac{2}{3} \div 1\frac{2}{5}$

11. Find the following, showing each step of your working clearly :-

    $$4\frac{1}{2} \times (7\frac{1}{8} - 2\frac{3}{5}).$$

1. Set down and find :-

   (a) $(41)^2$ (b) $5173 \div 7$ (c) 314×600 (d) $10\,000 - 927$

   (e) $9\,\overline{)12\,132}$ (f) $19 - 5 \times 3$ (g) $(5)^4$ (h) $54\,400 \div 80$

2. Set down and find :-

   (a) $\begin{array}{r} 19{\cdot}73 \\ \times\ 7 \\ \hline \end{array}$ (b) $49 + 16{\cdot}78 + 0{\cdot}873$ (c) $8\,\overline{)190{\cdot}4}$ (d) $19{\cdot}14 \times 600$

   (e) $828 \div 600$ (f) $35 - 14{\cdot}247$ (g) $0{\cdot}8 \times 0{\cdot}8$ (h) $7{\cdot}38 \div 3000$

3. Find :-   (a) $\frac{5}{9}$ of 504   (b) $\frac{7}{8}$ of £10·40   (c) $\frac{5}{6}$ of £9

4. Simplify :-   (a) $\frac{65}{85}$ (b) $\frac{32}{56}$ (c) $\frac{17}{51}$ (d) $\frac{66}{121}$

5. Do the following and simplify where possible :-

   (a) $\frac{2}{5} + \frac{3}{4}$ (b) $5\frac{1}{4} + 2\frac{2}{3}$ (c) $\frac{5}{8} \times \frac{12}{13}$ (d) $4\frac{2}{5} - 1\frac{3}{4}$

   (e) $7 - 3\frac{1}{5}$ (f) $\frac{7}{10} \div \frac{4}{5}$ (g) $5\frac{2}{5} \times 1\frac{1}{9}$ (h) $4\frac{4}{5} \div 2\frac{2}{3}$

6. Write as mixed numbers :-   (a) $\frac{21}{9}$ (b) $\frac{47}{7}$ (c) $\frac{103}{8}$

7. Express as a simple fraction :-   (a) $87\frac{1}{2}\%$ (b) 36% (c) $6\frac{1}{4}\%$

8. Find :-   (a) 40% of £170   (b) 5% of £12   (c) 75% of 1040

   (d) $33\frac{1}{3}\%$ of 264   (e) 7% of 500   (f) $17\frac{1}{2}\%$ of 240

9. (a) Of the 45 dogs in the kennels, 27 are male. What percentage is this ?

   (b) Having bought a games machine for £240, I sold it later for £192.
   Express my loss as a percentage of the cost price.

10. Find :-   (a) $34 - 76$ (b) $(-79) + 36$ (c) $(-34) - 26$ (d) $(-16) - (-18)$

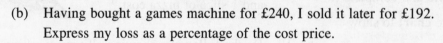

   (e) $(-13)^2$ (f) $(-8) \times (-6) \div (-4)$ (g) $\frac{(-12) - 6}{(-3) - 3}$ (h) $15 - 4 \times (-3)$

   (i) $17 \div (-2)$ (j) $(-1005) + 995$ (k) $-4(-5 - (-9))$ (l) $\frac{5 - (-7)}{(2) - (-2)}$

11. (a) Today is the 24th May. How many days till my mum's birthday on July 6th ?

    (b) Today is September 8th. My parent's anniversary was 3 weeks ago. What was that date ?

12. (a) Convert a speed of 20 metres per second to kilometres per hour.

    (b) Convert a speed of 180 km/hr to metres per second.

Statistics - a Definition

Statistics is the branch of Mathematics which analyses information and data gleaned from surveys, questionnaires or reports. Its purpose is to present this information in a more understandable form, either graphically, as can be seen in Chapter 13, or in some numeric format.

"Average" and "Spread"

Imagine we had a set of numbers to analyse - for example, the ages of those on a Sunday School trip to the beach.

2,   6,   6,   7,   7,   7,   7,   8,   8,   8,   10,   10,   11,   13,   25.

There are basically two "numerical" aspects you might wish to look at.

- • The AVERAGE age - this is a measure of where the "centre" of the group lies.

- • The SPREAD of ages - this gives you an idea of what "range" of ages there are.

Averages - Mean, Median and Mode (partial revision)

In Level E, you learned how to calculate an average of a set of values - namely, the mean.

You will now learn that there are two further measures of average, called the median and the mode.

MEAN -   "Add" all the data together and "divide" by the number of pieces of data.

$$\frac{2 + 6 + 6 + 7 + \quad .... + 13 + 25}{15} = \boxed{9}$$

MEDIAN - The "middle" number, (as long as the numbers are in "order").

2, 6, 6, 7, 7, 7, 7, 8, 8, 8, 10, 10, 11, 13, 25.

median = $\boxed{8}$

MODE -   The number that occurs "most".

2, 6, 6, 7, 7, 7, 7, 8, 8, 8, 10, 10, 11, 13, 25.

mode = $\boxed{7}$

Exercise 17·1

1. Calculate the **mean** for each set of data :–

   (a)   2, 3, 4, 5, 6, 7, 8, 9, 10

   (b)   8, 9, 12, 13, 13, 18, 22, 25

   (c)   21, 22, 24, 27, 27, 29

   (d)   0·3, 0·5, 0·6, 0·7, 0·8, 0·9, 1·1

   (e)   121, 123, 123, 126, 136, 181

   (f)   25, 35, 19, 33, 45, 17, 35, 23, 25, 7.

2. Find the **median** for each set of data :–
   (*Remember to put the numbers in order first*)

   (a)   6, 9, 5, 3, 2, 7, 3, 10, 8

   (b)   41, 51, 44, 16, 57, 39, 45

   (c)   2·7, 3·3, 2·4, 3·5, 2·1, 2·8, 3·3

   (d)   122, 133, 76, 184, 155, 130, 168.

   If there is not a single middle number :–
   take the **mean of the middle two numbers**.

   Example :–   2, 2, 4, 5, 6, 7, 8, 10

   The **median** is   (5 + 6) ÷ 2 = 5·5

3. Find the **median** for each of the following :-
   (a) 14, 21, 17, 18, 22, 17
   (b) 9, 13, 15, 31, 7, 35, 25, 17, 21, 19
   (c) 111, 107, 108, 106, 104, 107, 103, 110
   (d) 0·6, 0·7, 0·1, 1·0, 1·6, 0·9, 0·2, 0·3
   (e) −6, −6, −3, −1, 1, 3, 5, 10
   (f) 2, $2\frac{1}{2}$, $2\frac{1}{2}$, $4\frac{1}{2}$, $5\frac{1}{2}$, $5\frac{1}{2}$, $5\frac{1}{2}$, 7.

4. Find the **mode** for each set of data :–
   (a) 2, 3, 4, 5, 6, 7, 8, 8, 9
   (b) 21, 32, 23, 64, 21, 23, 41, 20, 23
   (c) 1·4, 1·8, 2·0, 1·1, 1·8, 5·7, 2·5
   (d) 2, 0, 2, 0, 2, 0, 2, 0, 2, 0, 2
   (e) 1131, 1210, 1113, 1124, 1021, 1120, 1124
   (f) $\frac{3}{4}$, $\frac{1}{4}$, $\frac{2}{3}$, $\frac{1}{2}$, $\frac{3}{4}$, $\frac{4}{5}$, $\frac{1}{4}$, $\frac{3}{4}$.

A Measure of Spread - The Range (revision)

The **RANGE** is a mathematical tool used to measure how widely spread a set of numbers are.

=> **Range = Highest score – Lowest score**

Example :- For the set of numbers :-   3, 3, 4, 6, 7, 7, 8, 11, 13, 13,

=> **Range = 13 – 3 = 10**

---

5. Calculate the **range** for each set of data in :–
   (a) question 3 (b) question 4.

6. Look at this data set :-

   5, 7, 2, 9, 10, 2, 3, 4, 57

   (a) Find the **range**.
   (b) Find the **mean**, **median** and **mode**.
   (c) Which average is best suited here ?
   (d) Explain why you think the other two averages are less suitable.

7. Calculate the **mean**, **median**, **mode** and **range** for each set of data below : –
   (a) 2, 3, 3, 3, 5, 9, 17
   (b) 6·7, 3·3, 5·4, 5·4, 6·1, 5·4, 4·8
   (c) 307, 106, 293, 314, 307, 299
   (d) 40, 42, 33, 51, 65, 46, 37, 40
   (e) 65, 65, 63, 64, 67, 66, 67, 67
   (f) 13 000, 10 000, 15 000, 10 000, 19 000.

8. The weights of six women are shown :–

   45 kg,   55 kg,   68 kg,   45 kg,   52 kg,   54 kg.

   (a) Find the **range** of their weights.
   (b) Calculate the **mode** and **median** weights.
   (c) Choose which is the better average of the two and explain why.

9. Rory buys 10 Easter Eggs.

   The number of chocolates in each is listed below :-

   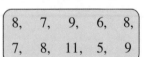
   | 8, | 7, | 9, | 6, | 8, |
   | 7, | 8, | 11, | 5, | 9 |

   (a) Calculate the **mean**, **median** and **mode**.
   (b) How many eggs have **less** than the **mean** number of chocolates ?

10. (a) Calculate the **mean** and the **range** of the first ten **prime** numbers.
    (b) Calculate the **mean** and the **range** of the first ten **square** numbers.

11. The heights of six children are shown opposite.

Bob says, " the average height is 1·23 m."

Bill says, " the average height is 1·57 m."

Ben says, " the average height is 1·47 m"

> 1·23 m, 1·23 m, 1·56 m
>
> 1·58 m, 1·59 m, 1·63 m

(a)   Explain why, technically, all three could be correct.

(b)   Which of the three would be least likely to be used ?

12.  The mean weight of two tyres is 12 kilograms.

If one of the tyres weighs 13·5 kg, what must the weight of the other tyre be ?

13. The mean age of five children is 13 years old.
Four of the childrens' ages are 10, 10, 12 and 16.

What is the age of the fifth child ?

14.  When a family of seven visit "gran", their mean age is 22.

When gran is included in the group, the mean age of the eight goes up to 29.

How old must gran be ?

15.  Billy owns a corner sweet shop and buys in 10 jars of lollies.

He discovers that the jars contain the following number of lollies : –

> 59, 61, 57, 60, 58, 59, 58, 58, 61, 59.

(a)   Is the statement on the jar correct ? (*explain*).

(b)   An eleventh jar is examined. How many lollies would need to be in that jar in order for the sweet manufacturer's claim to **then** be 100% accurate ?

16. Ten people threw 3 darts at a dartboard and recorded their scores.
The mean for the the first nine, (all men), was 33.
The 10th contestant, a woman, pushed the mean score up to 39.

What must the woman have scored with her three darts ?

17. On a putting green, the mean score for the 4 children for a round was 54.
The mean score of the 3 adults with them was 61.

Calculate the mean score of all 7 in the group.

18. Freddy's dad said he would buy him a new bike if he could get a mean score of at least 75% for his **six** science tests.

In his first **five** tests Freddy scored : 72%, 69%, 83%, 65% and 60%.

Can Freddy possibly do well enough to get the bike ? (Explain !!)

Mean, Median and Mode from a Frequency Table

When you are given a frequency table, you will find that adding a third column helps you to find the total number of items and hence the **mean**.

This table shows the number of make-up items found in the purses of a group of women.

No. of items x	Freq f	$f \times x$
1	8	$1 \times 8 = 8$
2	2	$2 \times 2 = 4$
3	1	$3 \times 1 = 3$
4	4	$4 \times 4 = 16$
5	1	$5 \times 1 = 5$
TOTALS	16	36
	Total purses	Total items

=> **Mean** number of items $= \dfrac{36}{16} = 2\cdot25$

=> **Mode** is the no. of items which occur most $= 1$

=> **Median** is the middle no. of items (*between the 8th and 9th*) $= 1\cdot5$

the 8th is a 1 and the ninth is a 2.

=> median $= \dfrac{1+2}{2}$

Exercise 17·2

1. This table shows the results from a group of third year pupils who were asked how many textbooks they carried to school one day.

    (a) **Copy** and complete the table.

    (b) How many pupils were asked ?

    (c) How many textbooks in total were there ?

    (d) Calculate the **mean** number of textbooks.

    (e) What is the **modal** number of books ? (*the mode*).

    (f) What is the **median** ?

No. of books x	Freq f	$f \times x$
0	2	$0 \times 2 = 0$
1	6	$1 \times 6 = \ldots$
2	11	$2 \times .. = \ldots$
3	7	$.. \times .. = \ldots$
4	4	$.. \times .. = \ldots$
	30	...

2.

No. of passes x	Freq f	$f \times x$
2	3	
3	7	
4	9	
5	4	
6	2	
...	...	

The table shows the number of Credit Grade passes gained by the top maths class in 4th year.

(a) **Copy** and complete the frequency table.

(b) Find the total number of pupils.

(c) Find the total number of Credit passes.

(d) Calculate the **mean** number of passes.

(e) What is the **modal** number of passes ?

(f) What is the **median** ?

3. (a) **Copy** and complete each of the following tables, add a **third** column and calculate the **mean**.

    (b) For each table, calculate the **mode** and the **median**.

(i)

No. of passengers x	Freq f
2	5
3	12
4	7
5	2
6	4

(ii)

No. of teams x	Freq f
2	1
4	9
6	2
8	6
10	1
12	1

(iii)

No. of coins x	Freq f
3	3
4	6
5	2
6	7
7	0
8	1
9	0
10	1

4. Look at the tables in question 3.

    Table (i) has **range** $(6 - 2) = 4$.

    Find the **range** for 3 (ii) and 3 (iii).

5. A group of people were each asked 10 questions in a quiz.

    Two points were given for a correct answer.

    (a) How many people took part in the quiz ?

    (b) Find the **range** of scores.

    (c) Find the **mean** score for the group.

    (d) Find the **median** from this table.

    (e) Write down the **modal** score.

What is half of 99 ?

Test score x	Freq f
8	2
10	3
12	9
14	6
16	5

6. A group of 18 year old boys were asked how old they were when they went out on their first date.

    The results are shown in this bar graph.

    (a) Make up a frequency table from the information in the bar graph.

    (b) Calculate the : –

    (i) **mode**

    (ii) **range**

    (iii) **mean**

    (iv) **median**.

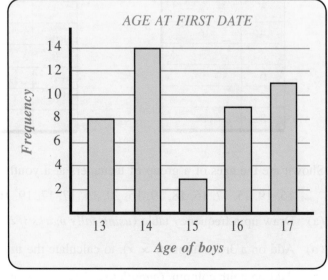

AGE AT FIRST DATE

Frequency

Age of boys

Cumulative Frequency

It is sometimes handy to show a table which **"totals up"** the frequencies **"to date"**, (*to accumulate the frequencies*).

Example :- A group of rail passengers were asked to note how many £1 coins they had in their pockets.

The ***22** in the Cumulative Frequency simply tells you that 22 passengers had "**3 or fewer** £1 coins".

No. of £1 coins x	Freq f	Cumulative Frequency
1	5	5
2	7	12 *(5 + 7)*
3	10	*** 22 *(12 + 10)*
4	8	30 *(22 + 8)*
5	1	31 *(30 + 1)*
Total £1 coins	31	

It is quite easy to find the **median** from the **Cumulative Frequency** column.

There were **31** passengers - the median must be the **16th** passenger.

=> Since 12 passengers had 2 or fewer coins and 22 had 3 or fewer => the **median** is $\boxed{3}$ coins.

Exercise 17·3

1. A school recorded the number of new absences of First Year pupils, (*due to a flu epidemic*), over a 7 week period.

   The results are shown in the frequency table.

   (a) **Copy** and complete the table.

   (b) How many new absences **in total** were there over the 7 week period ?

   (c) How many new absences had there been altogether by the end of week 5 ?

   (d) During which week was the infection at its worst ?

Week	Frequency (new cases)	Cumulative Freq (total so far)
1	5	5
2	10	15
3	12	...
4	25	...
5	17	...
6	8	...
7	3	...

2. For each frequency table :– • add a **cumulative frequency** column • find the **median**.

   (a)
TV's	Frequency
2	1
3	10
4	16
5	7
6	3
7	2
8	1

   (b)
Shots	Frequency
3	2
4	6
5	8
6	20
7	42
8	14
9	8

   (c)
Age	Frequency
5	4
10	2
15	7
20	11
25	19
30	7
35	1

3. Shown are the ages of a group of teenagers at a youth club :-

   16, 19, 15, 17, 16, 18, 19, 15, 20, 15, 17, 17, 19, 16, 18, 16, 15, 17, 17, 19, 15, 15, 18, 19, 16.

   (a) Draw up a frequency table (*using tally marks if it helps*) to show all the ages.

   (b) Add on a 3rd column, ($f \times x$), to calculate the **mean** age.

   (c) Add on a 4th column, (*cumulative frequency*), and from it, calculate the **median** age.

The Semi-Interquartile Range - A new Measure of Spread

Let us look back at the example on page 181 - the ages of a group on a Sunday school trip.

2, 6, 6, 7, 7, 7, 7, 8, 8, 8, 10, 10, 11, 13, 25.

If we use the only measure of **spread** we have - the **range** - there is a slight problem.

> **Range** = Highest – Lowest = 25 – 2 = **23**.

- can you see that most of the children are aged 6 to 13 ?
- the Sunday school teacher is aged 25 and has her 2-year old son with her.
- the range of **25** gives a false impression of "how widely spread" the actual ages are.
- the **range** only concentrates on the two "end" ages and disregards **all** of the other ages.

We need a new measure of **SPREAD** which takes into account more of the numbers in the distribution.

Such a measure of spread exists - the **semi-interquartile range**, which we will study soon.

The Quartiles of a set of Numbers

The **MEDIAN** is the value that splits a distribution of **ordered** numbers into two equal bits.

2, 6, 6, 7, 7, 7, 7, (8,) 8, 8, 10, 10, 11, 13, 25.

←——— 7 values ———→ median ←——— 7 values ———→

The **QUARTILES** are the 3 values that split a distribution of **ordered** numbers into **four** equal bits.

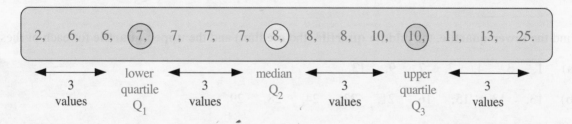

2,   6,   6, (7,)   7,   7,   7, (8,)   8,   8,   10, (10,) 11,   13,   25.

| 3 values | lower quartile Q_1 | 3 values | median Q_2 | 3 values | upper quartile Q_3 | 3 values |

Can you see that, for the above group of ages,

> the **lower quartile** (Q_1) = 7,   the **middle quartile** (Q_2) = 8,   the **upper quartile** (Q_3) = 10 ?

* the **middle quartile** (Q_2) is just another name for the **median** ?

> The **quartiles** must split up a distribution of ordered numbers in such a way that there are an equal number of values in each of the 4 "quarters" of the distribution.

Quartiles - continued

Example :-   Find the quartiles for the set :- 2, 3, 3, 4, 5, 5, 9, 10, 10, 10, 11, 12, 15, 17, 17, 19, 20

Step 1   There are 17 values in the question.

This means that the **median** must be the 9th value.   => median = **10**.

2,   3,   3,   4,   5,   5,   9,   10,   (10,)   10,   11,   12,   15,   17,   17,   19,   20.

Step 2   This now leaves 8 values in each half of the distribution.

The **middle of the LEFT set** is between the 4th and 5th value (up) => $Q_1 = \dfrac{4+5}{2} = 4.5$.

The **middle of the RIGHT set** is between the 4th and 5th value (down) => $Q_3 = \dfrac{15+17}{2} = 16$.

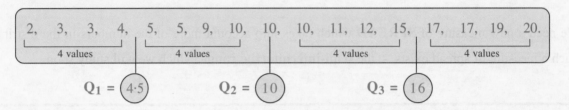

$Q_1 =$ (4·5) $Q_2 =$ (10) $Q_3 =$ (16)

Exercise 17·4

1. (a) Copy the following 11 numbers. (*you should try to space them fairly widely and fairly evenly*).

8,   8,   9,   10,   10,   11,   11,   11,   12,   13,   14,

(b) Circle the **middle** value - the **median**.

(c) Forgetting this number, how many numbers are there in each of the left and the right halves ?

(d) Find the middle of the left set of numbers - the **lower quartile** - Q_1.

(e) Find the middle of the right set of numbers - the **upper quartile** - Q_3.

2. Find the **lower quartile**, the **middle quartile** (the **median**) and the **upper quartile** for each of these :-

(a) 1,   3,   4,   7,   7,   9,   13.

(b) 13,   13,   15,   16,   21,   23,   24,   28,   29.

(c) 3·2,   3·5,   3·6,   3·8,   3·8,   4·0,   4·4,   4·4,   4·7,   5·3,   5·4,   5·9.

(d) 48,   51,   54,   54,   58,   64,   67,   71,   73,   78.

(e) 34,   31,   25,   35,   35,   23,   23,   40,   37,   27,   21,   29,   39.   (*order ?*)

3. Mrs Jones weighs the 65 children in Primary 7 and writes them all down in order.

Their weights, (in kilograms), are :-   34, 34, 35, 36, 36, 36, 37, ..., 50, 50, 51.

(a) Of the 65, which child's weight should be given as the **median** weight. (*the 30th, 31st, 32nd..*) ?

(b) Which of the 65 children's weights will give the **lower quartile** and which will give the **upper** ?

Quartiles - The "divide by 4" Rule

As you found in question 3, it is difficult at times, especially with large numbers of values, to know which values to look to for the median and quartiles. Here is a simple rule to help you :-

Step 1	Divide the **number** of values by 4. Note how many times 4 goes into it and the **remainder**.
	Examples :- 17 values => $17 \div 4 = 4$ remainder **1**.
	31 values => $31 \div 4 = 7$ remainder **3**.
Step 2	When you divide by 4, the answer tells you how many values are placed in each **quarter**.
Step 3	The **remainder** tells you how many extra values have to be considered $(0, 1, 2$ or $3)$

Example 1

8 numbers   2, 4, 5, 6, 8, 8, 9, 11.

$8 \div 4 = 2 \; r \; 0$ => 2 values in each quarter and **0** extra values to fit in.

2, 4, | 5, 6, | 8, 8, | 9, 11   => $Q_1 = 4 \cdot 5$, $Q_2 = 7$, $Q_3 = 8 \cdot 5$.

Example 2

9 numbers   3, 5, 6, 7, 9, 9, 10, 12, 15.

$9 \div 4 = 2 \; r \; 1$ => 2 values in each quarter and **1** extra value to fit in **symmetrically**.

3, 5, | 6, 7, | 8, 8, 10, | 12, 15   => $Q_1 = 5 \cdot 5$, $Q_2 = 8$, $Q_3 = 11$.

Example 3

10 numbers   4, 6, 7, 8, 10, 10, 11, 13, 13, 16.

$10 \div 4 = 2 \; r \; 2$ => 2 values in each quarter and **2** extra values to fit in **symmetrically**.

4, 6, 7, 8, 10, | 10, 11, 13, 13, 16   => $Q_1 = 7$, $Q_2 = 10$, $Q_3 = 13$.

Example 4

11 numbers   1, 3, 4, 5, 7, 7, 8, 10, 10, 12, 14.

$11 \div 4 = 2 \; r \; 3$ => 2 values in each quarter and **3** extra values to fit in **symmetrically**.

1, 3, 4, 5, 7, 7, 8, 10, 10, 12, 14 => $Q_1 = 4$, $Q_2 = 7$, $Q_3 = 10$.

4.   (a)   Copy the following **18 numbers**. (*Try to space them fairly widely and fairly evenly*).

3,	3,	4,	5,	5,	6,	6,	6,	7,	8,	9,	9,	10,	10,	11,	12,	13,	15.

    (b)   Divide 18 by 4 => $18 \div 4 = \ldots$ remainder **2**.

    (c)   How many of the 18 values should be placed in each of the 4 quarters ?

    (d)   Decide where the remaining **2** values should be to maintain symmetry.

    (e)   Use this to determine the **lower quartile** (Q_1), **upper quartile** (Q_3) and **median** (Q_2).

5.   Use the above method to find the **quartiles** and **median** for this set of 25 test marks :-

      5, 5, 5, 6, 6, 7, 8, 10, 10, 11, 12, 12, 12, 12, 13, 15, 16, 17, 17, 18, 20, 20, 21, 24, 25.

The Semi-Interquartile Range

Let us look once more at the example on page 181 - the ages of a group on a Sunday school trip.

$$2, \ 6, \ 6, \ 7, \ 7, \ 7, \ 7, \ 8, \ 8, \ 8, \ 10, \ 10, \ 11, \ 13, \ 25.$$

We found the **quartiles** and these are shown below :-

$$2, \quad 6, \quad 6, \quad \boxed{7,} \quad 7, \quad 7, \quad 7, \quad \boxed{8,} \quad 8, \quad 8, \quad 10, \quad \boxed{10,} \quad 11, \quad 13, \quad 25.$$

lower quartile Q_1 median   upper quartile Q_3

RANGE :- You learned on page 183 that the range was a simple measure of spread.

Range = highest − lowest = 25 − 2 = 23 (but this gave too "**big**" an answer).

If we now find the **difference** => upper quartile − lower quartile, and **halve** this answer,

we end up with a new measure of spread, called the **semi-interquartile range**. (S.I.Q.R.)

$$\text{Semi-Interquartile Range} \ = \ \frac{\text{Upper Quartile} - \text{Lower Quartile}}{2}$$

$$\text{S.I.Q.R} \ = \ \frac{Q_3 - Q_1}{2} \ = \ \frac{10 - 7}{2} \ = \ \boxed{1.5}$$

* In many instances, this measure of spread is preferable to the range. It does not simply rely on the two end values, the "highest" and "lowest" – rather, it takes into account more of the numbers in the distribution.

Exercise 17·5

1. Calculate the **median** and **lower** and **upper quartiles** for each of the following sets of values. Hence, calculate the **semi-interquartile range** of each.

   (a) 13, 13, 15, 19, 23, 23, 24, 26, 27.

   (b) 2·4, 2·6, 2·9, 2·9, 3·1, 3·1, 3·3, 3·6, 3·6, 3·8, 4·1, 4·1, 4·5, 4·7, 4·9, 5·0.

   (c) 101, 108, 109, 112, 112, 115, 120, 121, 125, 131, 131, 134, 135, 138, 140.

2. A group of 25 third year pupils were asked to say how many cousins they had.

   3, 1, 4, 2, 3, 4, 5, 2, 2, 4, 5, 1, 0, 6, 8, 2, 4, 4, 6, 2, 3, 1, 0, 9, 6.

   (a) Re-arrange them in order starting with the lowest.

   (b) Calculate the **mean**, **median** and **modal value**.

   (c) Determine the **lower** and **upper quartiles**.

   (d) Calculate the **range** and the **S.I.Q.R.**

3. A shoe shop assistant took a note of the sizes of a popular make of trainers that were sold in her shop last week.

   $$1, \ 4, \ 4, \ 4\tfrac{1}{2}, \ 5, \ 5, \ 5, \ 5\tfrac{1}{2}, \ 5\tfrac{1}{2}, \ 6, \ 6, \ 6, \ 6\tfrac{1}{2}, \ 6\tfrac{1}{2}, \ 10.$$

   Calculate the **range** and the **S.I.Q.R.** and say why the S.I.Q.R. would be a better indicator of the true spread of the shoe sizes sold last week.

Box-Plots - 5 Point Diagrams

Let us look once more at the example on page 181 - the ages of a group on a Sunday school trip.

$$2, \ 6, \ 6, \ 7, \ 7, \ 7, \ 7, \ 8, \ 8, \ 8, \ 10, \ 10, \ 11, \ 13, \ 25.$$

We found that $Q_1 = 7$, $Q_3 = 10$, the **median** = 8, the **lowest** value is 2 and the **highest** is 25.

This can be represented on a **box–plot** (*or 5-point summary*) as shown below.

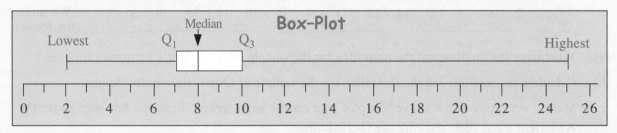

Box-Plot

Box–Plots are very useful diagrams, particularly when you wish to compare 2 or more sets of values.

They are also sometimes referred to as **box-whisker** diagrams for obvious reasons.

Exercise 17·6

1. James rolled two die, (*plural of dice*), twelve times, and noted the **total** score each time.

    $$3, \quad 5, \quad 6, \quad 7, \quad 7, \quad 7, \quad 8, \quad 9, \quad 9, \quad 10, \quad 10, \quad 12.$$

    (a) Calculate the **median** as well as the **upper** and **lower quartiles**.

    (b) **Copy** this scale and draw a neat **box-plot** to represent the above scores.

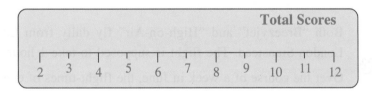

2. A group of pupils took part in a sun-flower growing competition and they all planted their sun-flower seed at the same time.

    Eight weeks later, the heights of the plants were measured (*to the nearest 5 cm*).

    $$35, \quad 35, \quad 40, \quad 40, \quad 40, \quad 50, \quad 50, \quad 55, \quad 60, \quad 70, \quad 85, \quad 85, \quad 95, \quad 105.$$

    (a) Calculate the values of the three quartiles, Q_1, Q_2 and Q_3.

    (b) Draw a suitable scale and show the above heights on a neatly drawn labelled box-plot.

3.

    The weights, (*in kilograms*), of the luggage of the 15 passengers boarding a plane bound for the Orkneys was recorded.

    $$15, \ 18, \ 14, \ 22, \ 19, \ 18, \ 14, \ 25, \ 24, \ 18, \ 10, \ 13, \ 21, \ 18, \ 24.$$

    (a) Re-arrange the weights in order, smallest first and calculate the **median** and the **quartiles**.

    (b) Draw and label a box-plot showing these weights. (*Choose a suitable scale*).

4. Osiris claim that their light-bulbs last longer than Awlbright's bulbs.

A sample of each was tested. **Osiris'** sample is shown below (*in months*).

8, 9, 10, 10, 12, 14, 14, 14, 15, 15, 17, 17, 18.

A box plot was created to represent **Awlbright's** sample and is shown below,

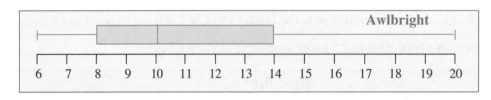

Awlbright

Osiris

We shine for longer

(a) What were the **median** and the **quartiles** for the sample of Awlbright's light-bulb lifetime ?

(b) Calculate the **median** and the **quartiles** for the sample of Osiris' light-bulb lifetime.

(c) Make a neat copy of the above box-plot, and **on the same graph**, draw the box-plot above the Awlbright's box plot, showing the Osiris bulbs.

(d) Write a couple of sentences comparing the two samples.

5. A group of men and a group of women, in a local gym, decided to hold a competition.
They counted how many pull-ups each person could do in a two minute period.

men	7	9	9	11	13	13	15	18	18	20	25
women	5	5	6	7	7	10	12	12	14	14	15	17

(a) Calculate the **medians** and **quartiles** for both the men and the women.

(b) Draw a neat labelled **composite** box-plot diagram to show how the two groups fared.

(c) Write a couple of sentences comparing the men competitors with the women.

6.  Both "Breezyjet" and "High-on-Air" fly daily from Edinburgh to London Stanstead. The flight is supposed to take 1 hour.

Over the course of a week in June, the flight-times of every Breezyjet and High-on-Air plane from Edinburgh to Stanstead was recorded in minutes.

Easyjet -	55	57	61	63	66	66	67	70	70	72	72	75	75	77	80
High-on-Air -	61	61	61	62	63	65	65	65	66	66	68	68	68		

(a) Draw a neat labelled composite box-plot diagram to show the above flight-times.

(b) Make a statement comparing both company's flight-times from Edinburgh to London.

7. Three men hit 15 golf balls on a driving range, each using a number 6 iron.
The box plot diagram shows the distances (in metres) they hit their golf balls.

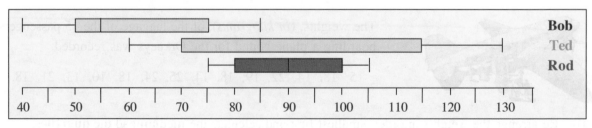

Write a few sentences comparing the three men's driving skills, mentioning their **median** scores, the **spread** of their drives, who was likely to be the novice, who was most erratic and who most consistent.

Standard Deviation - a better measure of Spread

Let us take a final look at the ages of the group on the Sunday School outing.

$$2, \ 6, \ 6, \ 7, \ 7, \ 7, \ 7, \ 8, \ 8, \ 8, \ 10, \ 10, \ 11, \ 13, \ 25.$$

The two measures of **SPREAD** we looked at were the **range** and the **semi-interquartile range**.

Neither of them is particularly satisfactory for the following reasons :-

- the **range** depends solely on the two end-values and totally ignores every other value.
- the **S.I.Q.R.** totally disregards the two end-values.

We require a new measure of spread that takes into account **ALL** the numbers in the distribution, not just the end-values or the quartiles.

This new measure is called the **STANDARD DEVIATION**.

Definition :- For a set of values (for example, the ages of the group above), the **standard deviation** is a measure of how "far away", on average, each of the values is, from the **mean**.

Let us explain exactly what we mean by following through a simpler example :-

Example :- Six pea-pods were opened and the number of peas in each was noted.

$$6, \ 7, \ 9, \ 9, \ 10, \ 13.$$

Calculate the **mean** and the **standard deviation**.

Step 1 Calculate the **mean** first.

A new notation :- If we think of any of the variables, (*the values*), as x's,

then the **mean** = (the sum of all the x's) ÷ (the number of values).

We have a **mathematical** way of expressing this, namely :-

$$\bar{x} = \frac{\sum x}{n}$$

where $\bar{x}$, (reads as "x bar"), is the **mean**.

and $\sum x$ means the "**sum of all the x's**".

and n is the **number** of values used.

In our example, $\bar{x} = \dfrac{\sum x}{n} = \dfrac{6 + 7 + 9 + 9 + 10 + 13}{6} = \dfrac{54}{6} = 9.$ the mean

Step 2 We now draw up a table to show how "far" each of the six values, (6, 7, 9, 9, 10, 13), is "away" from the mean ($\bar{x} = 9$).

x	$(x - \bar{x})$
6	$6 - 9 = -3$
7	$7 - 9 = -2$
9	$9 - 9 = 0$
9	$9 - 9 = 0$
10	$10 - 9 = 1$
13	$13 - 9 = 4$

cont'd ......

To find the "average" of these $(x - \overline{x})$'s, we should really add them together, then divide by 6.

A **problem** :- if we add $(-3) + (-2) + 0 + 0 + 1 + 4 \longrightarrow$ we get 0 !

(*This is because they all "cancel" each other out*).

A **"neat" trick** :- If we "square" these 6 values $((-3), (-2)$, $0, 0, 1, 4)$, all the negative signs disappear.

=> we add on an extra column showing $(x - \overline{x})^2$'s.

x	$(x - \overline{x})$	$(x - \overline{x})^2$
6	-3	$(-3)^2 = 9$
7	-2	$(-2)^2 = 4$
9	0	$(0)^2 = 0$
9	0	$(0)^2 = 0$
10	1	$(1)^2 = 1$
13	4	$(4)^2 = 16$

Step 3 We now find the "average" of the numbers in the last column. $(9 + 4 + 0 + 0 + 1 + 16) \div 6$.

We can use our new notation => $\text{average} = \dfrac{\sum (x - \overline{x})^2}{n} = \dfrac{30}{6} = 5.$ the average is 5

Step 4 But remember − these six numbers, $(9, 4, 0, 0, 1, 16)$, were the **squares** of the $(x - \overline{x})$'s.

=> As a final step, we find the **square root** of this "average", (the 5). => $\sqrt{5}$.

We call this measure of how far away the values are from the mean, the **standard deviation**. We have a special formula for it.

$$\text{standard deviation} = \sqrt{\dfrac{\sum (x - \overline{x})^2}{n}}$$

* this is not exactly the correct formula, but we'll explain this later.

=> In our example, we have $s.d. = \sqrt{\dfrac{\sum (x - \overline{x})^2}{n}} = \sqrt{\dfrac{30}{6}} = \sqrt{5} = \boxed{2 \cdot 236}.$

* The important thing about this measure of **spread** is that it takes into account every one of the six numbers, and gives a "feel" for how far, on average, each value is from the middle of the distribution, (the **mean**).

Exercise 17·7

1. Shown below are the number of touch-downs, made by the Cincinati Crawlers in their last 5 matches.

$$2, \quad 3, \quad 9, \quad 6, \quad 5.$$

Copy the following and calculate the **mean** and the **standard deviation**.

(a) $\text{mean} = \overline{x} = \dfrac{\sum x}{n} = \dfrac{2 + 3 + 9 + 6 + 5}{5} = \ldots..$

(b) **standard deviation** - see table ⟶

$s.d. = \sqrt{\dfrac{\sum (x - \overline{x})^2}{n}} = \sqrt{\dfrac{\ldots}{5}} = \sqrt{\ldots} = \ldots.$

x	$(x - \overline{x})$	$(x - \overline{x})^2$
2	$2 - 5 = -3$	$(-3)^2 = 9$
3	$3 - 5 = -2$	....
9	......	....
6	......	....
5	......	....
	$\sum (x - \overline{x})^2 =$	......

2. The first sentence James read in his new book had eight words in it.

   The number of letters in each word was :- 1, 3, 4, 8, 5, 1, 7, 3.

   Calculate the **mean** number of letters per word and the **standard deviation**.

   Copy and complete the following :–

(a) mean $= \bar{x} = \dfrac{\sum x}{n} = \dfrac{1 + 3 + 4 + 8 + \ldots\ldots}{\ldots} = \ldots\ldots$

(b) **standard deviation** - see table $\longrightarrow$

$$s.d. = \sqrt{\dfrac{\sum(x-\bar{x})^2}{n}} = \sqrt{\dfrac{\ldots}{\ldots\ldots}} = \sqrt{\ldots} = \ldots\ldots$$

x	$(x - \bar{x})$	$(x - \bar{x})^2$
1	$1 - 4 = -3$	$(-3)^2 = 9$
3	......	....
4	......	....
8	......	....
5	......	....
1	......	....
7	......	....
3	......	....

$$\sum(x - \bar{x})^2 = \ldots\ldots$$

Standard Deviation - the Real Formula

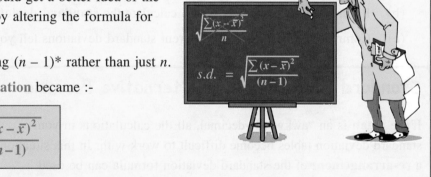

Statisticians discovered that they could get a better idea of the spread of a distribution of values by altering the formula for the standard deviation slightly.

They decided it worked better using $(n - 1)$* rather than just n.

The formula for the **standard deviation** became :-

$$s.d. = \sqrt{\dfrac{\sum(x-\bar{x})^2}{(n-1)}}$$

* the reason for this is too complicated to explain at this stage - wait till you go to University !!!!!

* From now on, use the new formula for standard deviation using $(n - 1)$ rather than n.

3. The weights of the first four letters George weighed in his post office one morning, were :- 30 grams, 41 grams, 48 grams, 29 grams.

   (a) Calculate the **mean** weight in grams.

   (b) Draw up a table and use the formula, $s.d. = \sqrt{\dfrac{\sum(x-\bar{x})^2}{(n-1)}}$,

       to calculate the **standard deviation**.

4.

   The school bus is supposed to arrive at Bromley Primary every day at 3.30 prompt.

   The head teacher noted how many minutes late the driver was last week – 6 mins, 15 mins, 8 mins, 2 mins, 9 mins.

   Calculate the **mean** number of minutes late and the **standard deviation** of the times.

5. The Edinburgh Annual Paper Airplane Making contest was held in June.

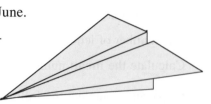

The distances travelled by the planes of the last 8 competitors were :-

22 m, 35 m, 26 m, 28 m, 30 m, 24 m, 36 m, 23 m.

(a) Calculate the **mean** distance travelled by the 8 planes.

(b) Draw up a table and use it, along with the formula, to calculate the **standard deviation** of the distances travelled.

6.
On a field trip, Susan collects 7 worms and measures their lengths.

6·5 cm, 4·7 cm, 10·2 cm, 9·1 cm, 8·8 cm, 12·0 cm, 7·5 cm.

Calculate the **standard deviation**.

7. Two men were playing a "friendly" game of darts.

The scores, for each of their first six darts, are shown below.

Donald	18	22	17	20	15	16
Graeme	3	38	6	30	1	30

(a) Show that both men scored the same **mean**.

(b) By drawing up 2 separate tables, calculate the **standard deviation** of both mens' scores.

(c) Comment on what the two different standard deviations tell you about the men's scores.

Standard Deviation - an Alternative Formula

If the **mean** is an "awkward" decimal, all the calculations in your standard deviation tables become difficult to work with. In this situation, a **re-arrangement** of the standard deviation formula can be used.

$$s = \sqrt{\frac{\sum x^2 - (\sum x)^2 / n}{(n-1)}}$$

Example :- Calculate the mean and standard deviation for the numbers :- 3, 5, 2, 9, 1, 8.

mean :- $\bar{x} = \dfrac{\sum x}{n} = \dfrac{28}{6} = 4\cdot6666...$

s.d. :- $s = \sqrt{\dfrac{\sum x^2 - (\sum x)^2 / n}{(n-1)}}$

$s = \sqrt{\dfrac{184 - 28^2 / 6}{5}} = \sqrt{\dfrac{53\cdot33..}{5}} = \sqrt{10\cdot66..} = 3\cdot27$

x	x^2
3	9
5	25
2	4
9	81
1	1
8	64

$\sum x = 28 \qquad \sum x^2 = 184$

---

8. Use the above formula to calculate the **mean** and the **standard deviation** of the following :-

(a) 4, 12, 9, 6.   (b) 45, 32, 37, 34, 40, 27.

(c) 6·2, 7·3, 9·1, 5·7, 11·4.   (d) 115, 130, 122, 129, 130, 133, 136.

9. Re-calculate the **standard deviation** for the set of numbers :- 4, 12, 9, 6. (see question 8(a) above), using your original formula given on page 195, and check it gives the same value.

Probability

The **Probability** of "something" happening is simply the **likelihood** or **chance** of it happening.

Examples :-   What is the **probability** that :-

> if today is Monday, then tomorrow will be Wednesday ?   (impossible)
>
> it will rain **every day** in June ?   (unlikely)
>
> if I toss a coin, it will land heads ?   (even chance)
>
> if I toss 8 coins, at least one will be tails ?   (likely)
>
> if I put my hand in a fire, I will get burned ?   (certain)

Exercise 17·8 - (Oral exercise)

For each statement below, say whether the probability of it happening is :-

> impossible - unlikely - evens (50-50)
>
> likely - certain.

1.   If today is Monday, yesterday was Thursday.

2.   The next person I see will be male.

3.   No trains will be on time tomorrow.

4.   There will be snow in January.

5.   I will win the lottery jackpot this week.

6.   I will have a birthday this year.

7.   Christmas will be in November next year.

8.   I will blink my eyes today.

Calculating Probability

The **Probability** of an event happening simply means "what **fraction** of the time it will happen".

It is defined as :-

$$\text{Probability} = \frac{\text{number of favourable outcomes}}{\text{number of possible outcomed}}$$

Example :-   This bowl contains 8 **blue** balls and 4 **red** balls.

If I choose a ball at random without looking, what is the **probability** that I will pick a **red** ball ?

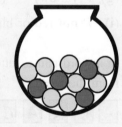

$$\text{Probability of red} = P(\text{red}) = \frac{\text{number of red balls}}{\text{total number of balls}} = \frac{4}{12} = \frac{1}{3}$$

Exercise 17·9

1.   A bag contains 6 black balls and 12 white balls.

If a ball is picked at random, what is the **probability** that it will be **black** ?

(*Use the notation :-*   P(black) = ...)

2.   A bag has 3 red sweets, 6 green sweets and 9 blue sweets.

If a sweet is picked at random, what is the probability that the sweet will be :-

(a)   red   (b)   green

(c)   blue   (d)   orange ?

3.   A dice numbered from 1 to 6, is rolled.

(a)   What is the probability that the dice will end up showing the number 2 on top ?
          (i.e. P(2) = ...)

(b)   Find :-

(i)   P(3)   (ii)   P(odd)

(iii)   P(8)   (iv)   P(smaller than 2).

4. A **duo–decagon** (12 sided) spinner is spun and its number is noted.

   Find :–

   (a) P(less than 4)

   (b) P(multiple of 3)

   (c) P(prime)

   (d) P(factor of 12).

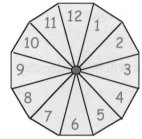

5. A bag contains 20 raffle tickets.

   Four tickets win a cuddly toy, two tickets win £10 and the rest are losing tickets. If you buy a single ticket, find the following probabilities :-

   (a) P(win a toy)   (b) P(losing ticket)

   (c) P(win £10)   (d) P(**not** win £10).

6. A garage forecourt has the following colours of cars :–

   12 blue, 8 green, 6 silver,
   4 white,   3 black, 2 red,
   1 yellow.

   Find the following probabilities :-

   (a) P(blue)   (b) P(green)

   (c) P(silver)   (d) P(white)

   (e) P(black)   (f) P(red)

   (g) P(yellow)   (h) P(red or blue)

   (i) P(**not** red or blue).

7. In a word game, letters are chosen at random from the word :–

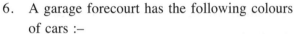

   Find :–

   (a) P(A)   (b) P(R)

   (c) P(vowel)   (d) P(consonant).

8. The probability of an event happening is calculated to be $\frac{3}{7}$.

   What is the probability the event will **not** happen ?

9. Three coins are tossed at the same time.

   (a) Make a neat list of all the possibilities.

       (HHH, HHT, HTH etc....).

   (b) Find :–   (i) P(all heads)   (ii) P(2 tails).

10.  One dart is thrown at a dart-board, numbered 1 – 20.

    If the dart actually lands on the board, find :-

    (a) P(16)   (b) P(over 12)

    (c) P(even)   (d) P(prime).

11. Look at the two bags shown.

    How many **more** green balls do I have to put into bag 2 so that each bag has the same probability of picking, at random, a **green** ball ?

    Bag 1   Bag 2

12. The weathermen reckon that the probability it will rain in Perth tomorrow is 0·25.

    What is the probability it will **not** rain in Perth ?

13. After counting the number of boys and girls in a 3rd year group, the teacher says the following :-

    "If I chose a name at random, from this group, the probability it will be a male is $\frac{3}{5}$".

    The teacher knows there are 60 in the group.

    How many boys and how many girls are there ?

14. A pack of cards consists of 52 cards. There are 13 spades, 13 clubs, 13 hearts and 13 diamonds.

    Each suit has :- Ace, 2, 3, 4, 5, 6, 7, 8, 9, 10, Jack, Queen and King.

    If I shuffle the cards and look at the top one, what are the following probabilities :-

    (a) P(a red card)   (b) P(a spade)

    (c) P(an Ace)   (d) P(King of Hearts)

    (e) P(a face card)   (*Jack, Queen or King*).

15. I roll **two** six-sided dice and add the 2 numbers.

    Make a list of all 36 possible pairings like this :-

        (1, 1), (1, 2), (1, 3).......... (5, 6), (6, 6).

    Calculate the following probabilities :-

    (a) P(total = 3)   (b) P(total = 7)

    (c) P(total = 12)   (d) P(1st no. > 2nd no.).

1. Calculate the **mean**, **median**, **mode** and **range** :-

   15, 18, 13, 14, 18, 15, 18, 17, 22, 25, 12.

2. The **mean** number of chocolates I counted in the first 3 of my Easter eggs was 18.

   After opening the 4th Egg, I discovered that the mean for all 4 was then 22.

   How many eggs were in that last egg ?

3. The frequency table below shows the cost of a tin of P.H. Beans in various shops in and around Aberdeen.

Cost of 1 Tin x	Freq f	$f \times x$
31p	4	1 × 8 = 8
32p	7	2 × 2 = 4
33p	10	3 × 1 = 3
34p	6	4 × 4 = 16
35p	3	5 × 1 = 5

   Total shops   Total cost

   (a) What is the **modal** cost (the mode) ?

   (b) What is the **median** cost ?

   (c) State the **range**.

   (d) **Copy** the table and complete the 3rd column to help determine the **mean** cost.

4. Suzie looked at her telephone bill and wrote down the duration of her last 15 calls (*to the nearest minute*).

   2, 3, 5, 5, 5, 7, 8, 12, 12, 13, 15, 15, 16, 17, 20.

   (a) Calculate the **median** and the **lower** and **upper** quartiles**.**

   (b) Calculate the **semi-interquartile** range.

5. Shown below are the hours worked by the part-timers at Q & B Super-Store :-

   12, 12, 14, 15, 17, 19, 19, 20, 20, 22, 24, 25, 27

   (a) Calculate the **median** and the **quartiles**.

   (b) Draw a neatly labelled **box-plot** to show the distribution of the above hours.

6. 6 brand new Mini's were tested by pouring exactly 1 gallon of petrol into their tanks and carefully measuring how far they travelled before the cars came to a halt.

   The distances, in miles, were :-

   42, 43, 45, 49, 50, 53

   (a) Calculate the **mean** number of miles.

   (b) Calculate the **standard deviation**.

7. Rod and Stan both hit 5 shots with their drivers off the tee.

   Shown below are the distances travelled by each ball, (in yards).

Rod :-	230,	275,	245,	220,	180.
Stan :-	225,	230,	240,	220,	235.

   (a) Show that both Rod and Stan's **mean** driving distance was the same.

   (b) Calculate the **standard deviation** for both golfers and comment on who was the more consistent golfer.

8. There are 52 cards in a deck. If I choose one without looking, what is the probability it will **not** be a face card ?

   (*King, Queen or Jack*).

The Area of a Triangle

Reminder :-

You should already know a formula for finding the area of a triangle given the length of its **base** and its **height**.

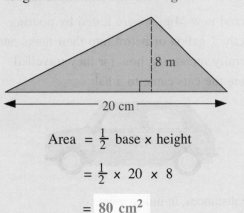

Area $= \frac{1}{2}$ base × height

$= \frac{1}{2} \times 20 \times 8$

$= \boxed{80 \text{ cm}^2}$

What happens when you are **NOT** told the height of the triangle ?

In this case, you are given **two of the sides** and the **angle** between those sides.

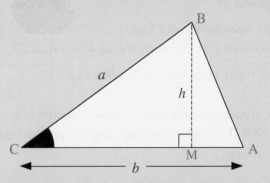

Draw in height BM to make two RAT's.

Let BM = h units.

Using **SOH**CAHTOA in triangle BCM

=> $\sin C = \frac{h}{a}$ => $h = a\sin C$

=> AREA of triangle ABC $= \frac{1}{2}$ base × height

=> Area $= \frac{1}{2} ab \sin C$.

Generally - given **2 sides** of a triangle and the **included angle** (whether acute or obtuse) :-

$$\text{Area of a Triangle} = \frac{1}{2} ab \sin C$$

Example :-

Calculate the **area** of triangle PQR.

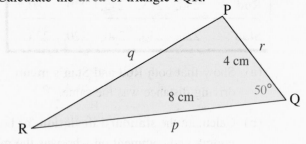

Area $= \frac{1}{2} pr \sin Q$

$= \frac{1}{2} \times 4 \times 8 \times \sin 50°$

$= \boxed{12 \cdot 3 \text{ cm}^2}$ (to 3 sig. figs.)

Exercise 18·1

1.   Calculate the area of each of these triangles, (*to 3 sig. figs.*) :-

(a)
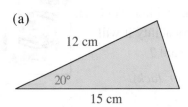

(b)
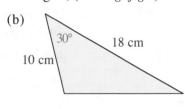

(c)
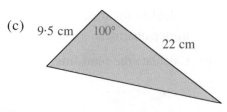

Answer to 3 significant figures unless stated :-

2. Calculate the **area** of each of these triangles :-

(a)

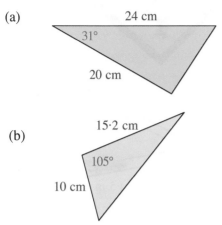

24 cm

31°

20 cm

(b)

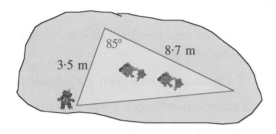

15·2 cm

105°

10 cm

3. Calculate the **area** of the triangular fish pond in the garden.

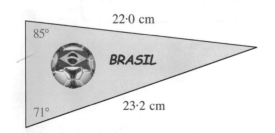

85°

8·7 m

3·5 m

4. A traffic island ABC is shown.

Find the **area** of the traffic island if ;-

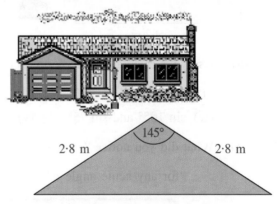

B

C

A

AB = 12·6 metres,
AC = 10 metres and
angle BAC = 58°.

5. This is a replica of Brazil's World Cup soccer pennant.

22·0 cm

85°

BRASIL

71°

23·2 cm

(a) Write down the size of the **third** angle in the triangular pennant.

(b) Calculate the **area** of the pennant.

6. Choose the correct data and calculate the **area** of these triangles :-

(a)

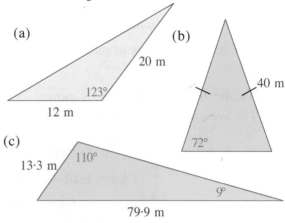

20 m

123°

12 m

(b)

40 m

72°

(c)

110°

13·3 m

9°

79·9 m

7. Calculate the area of this **parallelogram** :-

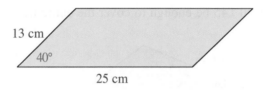

13 cm

40°

25 cm

8. After a very damp winter, the owner of this bungalow decided to protect the brickwork at the front of his garage by coating it with an orange all-weather waterproof sealant.

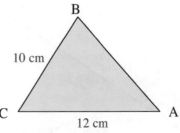

145°

2·8 m   2·8 m

If £15 worth of sealant covers 1 m² of brickwork, calculate how much it will cost him to coat this part of the garage wall with paint.

9. The **area** of this triangle ABC is **54 cm²**.

B

10 cm

C

12 cm

A

AC = 12 cm and BC = 10 cm.

Calculate the size of **acute** angle ACB.

10. An identification tag, made of plastic, is in the form of an isosceles triangle, with dimensions as shown.

The badge is 1·3 millimetres thick.

Calculate the **volume** of plastic required to make one tag.

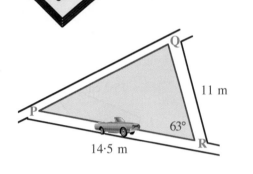

70 mm

30°

1·3 mm

70 mm

11. Another traffic island, PQR, is shown.
The town council decide to lay red chip stones on the island.

RED CHIPS

1 lorry-load - £15·00.

Covers 25 square metres

11 m

P

63°

R

Q

14·5 m

The price of the red chips is shown on the sign above.

Will £45 be enough to cover the entire traffic island ? *Explain fully with working*.

12.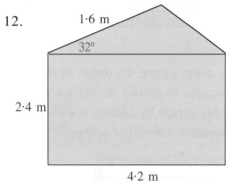

1·6 m

32°

2·4 m

4·2 m

The side wall of a hut, with measurements shown, requires to be painted with green creosote.

The wall consists of a rectangular base with a triangular top.

A litre of paint will cover (*on average*), 3 square metres.

A painter guesses that he will require 4 litres of paint.

Will he have enough paint ? *Justify your answer*.

13. (a) Use your calculator to look up each of the following pairs of **sine** values :-

(i) sin 30° and sin 150°. (ii) sin 50° and sin 130° (iii) sin 10° and sin 170°

(iv) sin 105° and sin 75° (v) sin 175° and sin 5° (vi) sin 63° and sin 117°.

(b) What did you notice ? Copy and complete :-

"for any acute angle $a°$, => **sin** $a°$ = **sin** $(180 – ...)°$".

> Can you see that if you now know the value of the sine of an angle,
> then there are **two possible values** for the actual size of the angle ?
> (*This will be studied later in the course*).

14. The area of **both** triangles below is 78·6 cm².

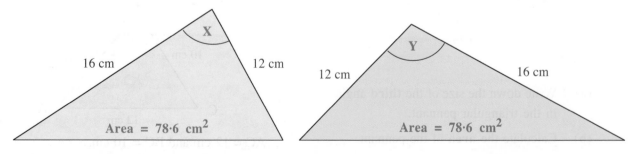

X

16 cm

12 cm

Area = 78·6 cm²

Y

12 cm

16 cm

Area = 78·6 cm²

Calculate the size of acute angle **X** and obtuse angle **Y**.

The Sine Rule - Missing Sides

Look at the (*non right angled*) triangle ABC.

We **cannot** use **SOHCAHTOA** in $\triangle ABC$ since it is not a right angle triangle.

We can draw in altitude CM to create 2 right angled triangles.

Let CM = h units.

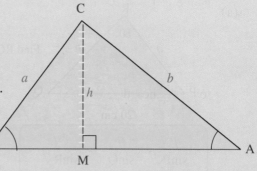

In $\triangle ACM$,

$$\sin A = \frac{h}{b}$$

$$\Rightarrow \quad h = b\sin A$$

In $\triangle BCM$,

$$\sin B = \frac{h}{a}$$

$$\Rightarrow \quad h = a\sin B$$

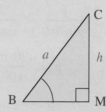

$$\Rightarrow \quad b\sin A = a\sin B$$

$\div$ both sides by sinAsinB

$$\Rightarrow \quad \frac{b\sin A}{\sin A \sin B} = \frac{a\sin B}{\sin A \sin B}$$

By symmetry, it can also be shown that :-

$$\frac{a}{\sin A} = \frac{c}{\sin C}$$

$$\Rightarrow \quad \frac{a}{\sin A} = \frac{b}{\sin B}$$

We now have a tremendously powerful formula that enables us to find missing sides and angles in non-right angled triangles - **the Sine Rule**.

The Sine Rule	in any $\triangle ABC$, $\quad \dfrac{a}{\sin A} = \dfrac{b}{\sin B} = \dfrac{c}{\sin C}$

Example

Calculate the length of side AB in triangle ABC.

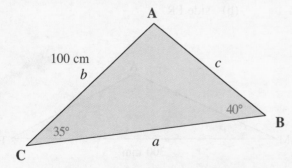

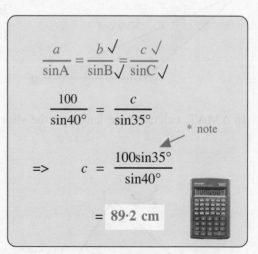

$$\frac{a}{\sin A} = \frac{b \checkmark}{\sin B \checkmark} = \frac{c \checkmark}{\sin C \checkmark}$$

$$\frac{100}{\sin 40°} = \frac{c}{\sin 35°}$$

* note

$$\Rightarrow \quad c = \frac{100\sin 35°}{\sin 40°}$$

$$= 89{\cdot}2 \text{ cm}$$

- Write down all 3 ratios $\dfrac{a}{\sin A} = \dfrac{b}{\sin B} = \dfrac{c}{\sin C}$

- tick the 2 angles and side you are given.

- tick the side you are asked to calculate.

- score out the 1 ratio not required.

1.   Copy and complete the following to find the required length :-

    (a)

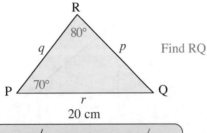

Find RQ

$$\frac{p\checkmark}{sinP\checkmark} = \frac{q}{sinQ} = \frac{r\checkmark}{sinR\checkmark}$$

$$\frac{p}{sin70°} = \frac{20}{sin80°}$$

$$p = \frac{20sin...°}{sin....°}$$

$$p = ... \text{ cm}$$

    (b)

Find ML

$$\frac{k\checkmark}{sinK\checkmark} = \frac{l\checkmark}{sinL\checkmark} = \frac{m}{sinM}$$

$$\frac{k}{sin120°} = \frac{10·5}{sin10°}$$

$$k = \frac{.....sin...°}{sin....°}$$

$$k = ... \text{ cm}$$

2.   Calculate the length of the marked side in each of the following triangles.

    (a)

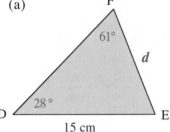

    (b)

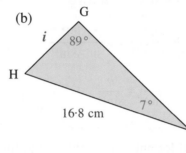

    (c)

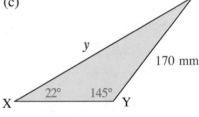

3.   In △ABC, calculate the size of :-

    (a) ∠ACB   (b) side AB.

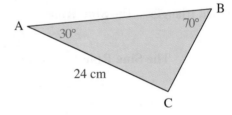

4.

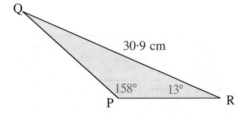

    In △PQR, calculate the size of :-

    (a) ∠PQR   (b) side PR.

5.   In △MAT, calculate the length of the **shortest** side.

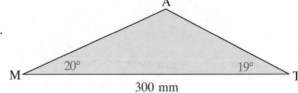

6.

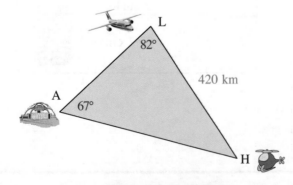

    The diagram shows the positions of an airport (A), a light aircraft (L) and an helicopter (H).

    How far away is the helicopter from the airport ?

7. A yacht sets sail from a jetty, 40 metres from the lighthouse.

   Its course makes an angle of 28° to the coastline.

   Find, (*to the nearest metre*), the distance :-

   (a) from L to D (b) from J to D.

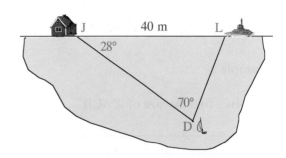

8.

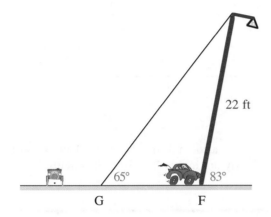

   A road traffic accident resulted in a 22 foot lamp-post ending up at an angle of 83° to the ground.

   To secure the lamp-post a strong wire has been attached to its top and tethered to the ground at G.

   (a) The wire makes an angle of 65° with the ground. Calculate how long the wire is.

   (b) Calculate the distance from G to the foot of the lamp-post.

   (c)   One week later, the Lighting Department restores the lamp-post to its vertical position but leaves a shortened wire (still attached at G) for a few more days.

   How long will this shortened wire have to be ?

9. A canopy is built over the front door of a house.

   To support it, two metal struts, MR and MS, are attached as shown.

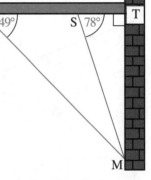

   (a)   Given ∠MRS = 49° and ∠MST = 78°, write down the size of ∠MSR.

   (b)   If strut RM = 150 centimetres, calculate the length of strut SM.

10. H.M.S. Tiger is positioned 100 kilometres **west** of H.M.S. Fearful, when they both receive a distress signal from a yacht (at point Y).

   The bearing of the yacht from H.M.S. Tiger is 045°.

   The bearing of the yacht from H.M.S. Fearful is 310°.

   (a)   Sketch triangle TYF and fill in the sizes of all three angles.

   (b)   Which ship will be closer to the yacht ?

   (c)   Calculate the distance from this ship to the yacht.

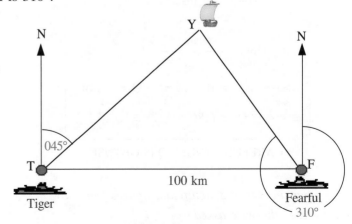

The Sine Rule - Finding an Angle

Example :-

In $\triangle ABC$, find the size of $\angle ACB$.

$$\frac{a\checkmark}{\sin A\checkmark} = \frac{b}{\sin B} = \frac{c\checkmark}{\sin C\checkmark}$$

=> $\dfrac{25}{\sin 60°} = \dfrac{20}{\sin C}$

Now Rearrange

=> $\sin C = \dfrac{20\sin 60°}{25}$

=> $\sin C = 0\cdot 6928$ INV sin

=> $\angle C = \boxed{43\cdot 9°}$ to 3 sig. figs.

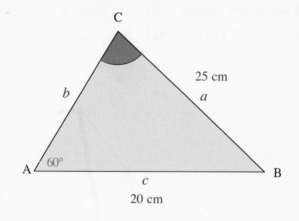

* note $\angle C$ could also, in theory, be $(180 - 43\cdot 9) = 136\cdot 1°$, but obviously not in this case, since it is **acute**.

Exercise 18·3

1.   Copy and complete the following to find the size of angle PQR :-

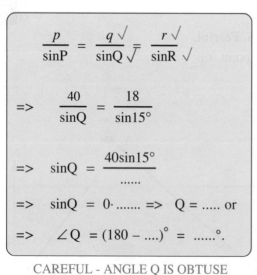

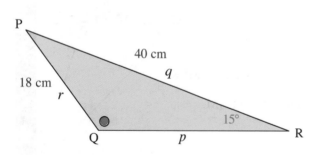

$$\frac{p}{\sin P} = \frac{q\checkmark}{\sin Q\checkmark} = \frac{r\checkmark}{\sin R\checkmark}$$

=> $\dfrac{40}{\sin Q} = \dfrac{18}{\sin 15°}$

=> $\sin Q = \dfrac{40\sin 15°}{......}$

=> $\sin Q = 0\cdot .... $ => Q = ... or

=> $\angle Q = (180 - ....)° = ...°.$

CAREFUL - ANGLE Q IS OBTUSE

Give your answer to 3 significant figures from now on unless otherwise asked.

2.   Copy and complete the following to find the marked angle in each case :-

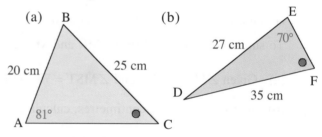

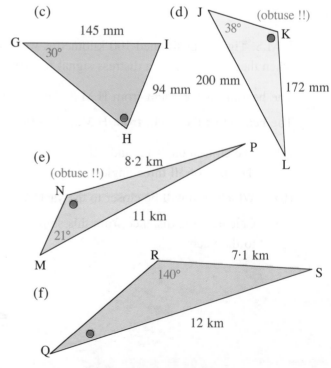

(a)

(b)

(c)

(d) (obtuse !!)

(e) (obtuse !!)

(f)

3. Find the size of obtuse ∠PTN in △PNT.

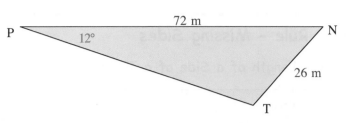

4.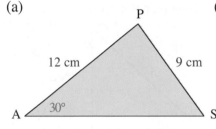

In △ABC, calculate the size of the other **TWO** angles.

5. Calculate the sizes of :-   (i) ∠APS   (ii) ∠FMR   (iii) ∠UDY.

(a)

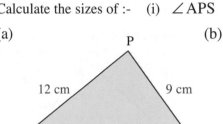

(b)

(c)

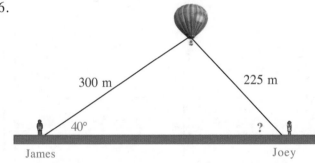

6.

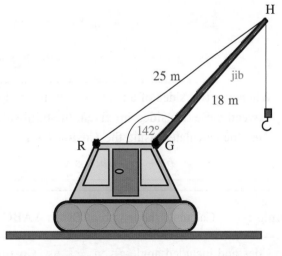

A hot air balloon is hovering above the ground.

From James, the balloon is 300 metres away and its angle of elevation is 40°.

The balloon is 225 metres from where Joey stands.

What is the angle of elevation of the balloon from Joey ?

7. The jib, GH, of a crane is 18 metres long.

The wire, RH, is 25 metres long.

Angle RGH = 142°.

Calculate the sizes of angles GRH and RHG.

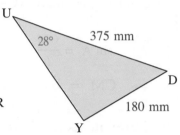

8.

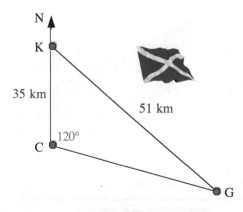

Three radio masts, Colligan (C), Kelty (K) and Glen (G) are situated in the Scottish Highlands.

Colligan is 35 km due south of Kelty.

Kelty is 51 km from Glen.

Glen is on a bearing of 120° from Colligan.

Calculate the bearing of Glen from Kelty.

The Cosine Rule - Missing Sides

Calculating the Length of a Side of a Triangle given Two Sides and the Included Angle.

Look at this **example**.

Calculate the length of AC.

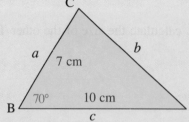

$$\frac{a\sqrt{}}{\sin A} = \frac{b\sqrt{}}{\sin B} = \frac{c\sqrt{}}{\sin C}$$

We **don't** have a group of **FOUR**.

=> We **cannot** use the **Sine Rule**.

We need a new rule to calculate a missing side in a triangle like this when the **Sine Rule** won't work.

Consider right angled $\triangle$CAM formed in $\triangle$ABC by drawing the perpendicular line from C to AB.

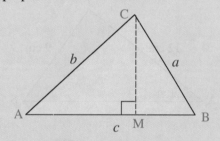

$$\sin A = \frac{CM}{b}$$

=> $CM = b\sin A$

$$\cos A = \frac{AM}{b}$$

=> $AM = b\cos A$

Can you see :- $MB = c - AM$

$$= c - b\cos A$$

By using **Pythagoras' Theorem** in $\triangle$CMB,

$$BC^2 = CM^2 + MB^2$$

=> $\quad a^2 = (b\sin A)^2 + (c - b\cos A)^2$

=> $\quad a^2 = b^2\sin^2 A + c^2 - 2bc\cos A + b^2\cos^2 A$

=> $\quad a^2 = b^2(\sin^2 A + \cos^2 A)* + c^2 - 2bc\cos A$

=> $\quad a^2 = b^2 + c^2 - 2bc\cos A$ ...... which is known as the **Cosine Rule**.

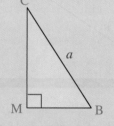

> Whenever two sides of a triangle and the angle between these two sides are given, the third side can be calculated using the **Cosine Rule** :-
>
> $$a^2 = b^2 + c^2 - 2bc\cos A$$

* It is known that $\sin^2 A + \cos^2 A = 1$.

This proof shown above is probably beyond your understanding at this stage - it will be explained later on in the course, when you have more background knowledge.

Example :-   Calculate the length of BC in $\triangle$ABC.

> Two sides and included angle given => use **Cosine Rule**.
>
> $$a^2 = b^2 + c^2 - 2bc\cos A$$
>
> => $\quad a^2 = 23^2 + 15^2 - 2 \times 23 \times 15 \times \cos 25°$
>
> => $\quad a^2 = 128 \cdot 648$
>
> => $\quad a = 11 \cdot 3$ to 3 sig. figs.
>
> BC = $\boxed{11 \cdot 3 \text{ cm}}$

Remember to press $\sqrt{....}$

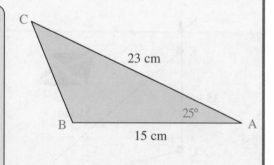

Exercise 18·4   *Answer to 3 significant figures unless otherwise asked.*

1. **Copy and complete** the following to find the length of the third side :-

(a)

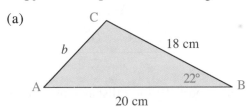

$$b^2 = a^2 + c^2 - 2ac\cos B$$
$$=> b^2 = 18^2 + \ldots^2 - 2 \times \ldots \times \ldots\cos 22°$$
$$=> b^2 = \ldots\ldots$$
$$=> b = \ldots\ldots \quad => AC = \ldots\ldots \text{ cm}$$

(b)

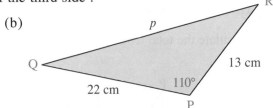

$$p^2 = q^2 + r^2 - 2qr\cos P$$
$$=> p^2 = 13^2 + \ldots^2 - 2 \times \ldots \times \ldots\cos\ldots$$
$$=> p^2 = \ldots\ldots$$
$$=> p = \ldots\ldots \quad => QR = \ldots\ldots \text{ cm}$$

2. Calculate the length of the unknown side in each of the following triangles :-

(a)

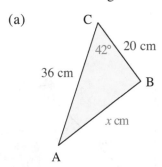

(b)

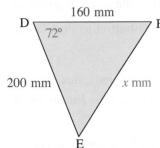

(c)

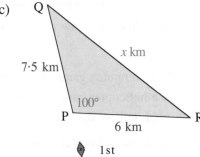

3. A yacht takes part in a race over a triangular course.

Calculate the length of the final stage of the race, from the 2nd buoy to the finishing line.

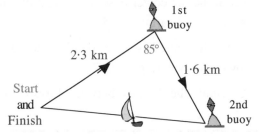

4.

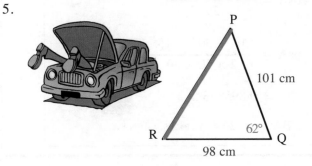

The pair of compasses shown opposite is used to draw a circle.

Calculate the **radius** of the circle.

5.

The bonnet of a car is held open at an angle of 62°, by a metal rod.

PQ represents the bonnet, PR represents the metal rod and QR represents the distance from the base of the bonnet to the front of the car.

Calculate the length of the metal rod.

6. A triangular wall has been built round a compound of igloos.

It has sides measuring 18 metres and 22·5 metres.
The angle between these sides is 105°

Calculate the total length of the **perimeter** wall.

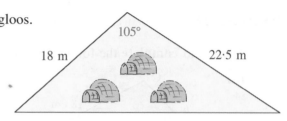

105°
18 m   22·5 m

7.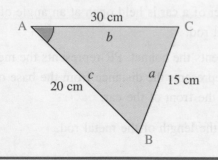

N

P

72 km

055°   25 km

A ship sailed south from a port (P) for a distance of 72 kilometres.

It then sailed on a bearing of 055° for 25 kilometres.

How far is the ship now from port ?

8. The town of Port Greenick is 20 miles north of Longbank and the town of Donburton lies 15 miles north-west of Longbank.

(a) Make a (*rough*) sketch, showing the relative positions of the 3 towns.

(b) Calculate how far it is from Donburton to Port Greenick.

9. The computer game "Dinosaur Islands" indicates the position of a helicopter base in relation to two islands, Juraso and Repto, inhabited by dinosaurs.

From the helicopter base, the island of Juraso is 36 km away on a bearing of 050°.

From the same base, the island of Repto is 22 km away on a bearing of 135°.

Calculate the distance between Juraso and Repto.

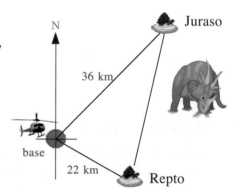

N

Juraso

36 km

base

22 km   Repto

The Cosine Rule - Calculating an Angle

The **Cosine Rule** formula, used to calculate the length of a missing side, can be re-arranged to allow you to calculate the size of a missing angle.

(*As long as you know the lengths of all 3 sides*).

$$a^2 = b^2 + c^2 - 2bc\cos A$$

$$=> \quad 2bc\cos A = b^2 + c^2 - a^2$$

$$=> \quad \cos A = \frac{b^2 + c^2 - a^2}{2bc}$$

Example :-

Calculate the size of ∠BAC.

A   30 cm   C
        b
   c   a   15 cm
20 cm
        B

$$\cos A = \frac{b^2 + c^2 - a^2}{2bc}$$

$$=> \quad \cos A = \frac{20^2 + 30^2 - 15^2}{2 \times 20 \times 30}$$

$$= 0·895833...$$

INV cos

∠BAC = **26·4°**   to 3 sig. figs.

Answer to 3 significant figures unless otherwise asked.

1. In a $\triangle ABC$, to find $\angle C$, we can use the formula :- $\cos C = \dfrac{a^2 + b^2 - c^2}{2ab}$.

    This time we are dealing with $\triangle PQR$. Using the Cosine Rule, write down
    a formula for calculating the size of each of the following angles :-

    (a) $\angle Q$ $(\cos Q = \dots)$ (b) $\angle P$ (c) $\angle R$.

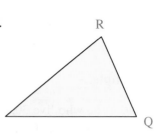

2. Calculate the size of the marked angle in each of the following triangles :-

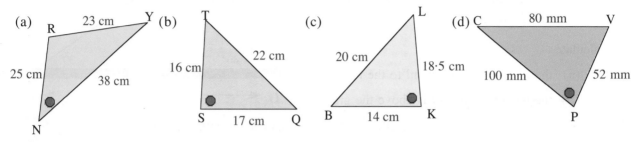

    (a)   (b)   (c)   (d)

3. In $\triangle PLY$, calculate the size of the
    largest angle. (*It is obtuse*).

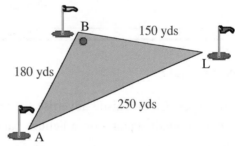

    *note - if the cosine of an angle turns
    out to be **negative**, we will discover
    later that the angle is **obtuse**.

4.   (a) Use the Cosine Rule to show that $\angle RMF = 90°$.

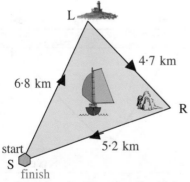   (b) Use the Converse of Pythagoras' Theorem to
                                                     confirm that $\angle RMF$ is a right angle.

5. The diagram shows part of a pitch & putt golf course.
    The lengths of the holes are as stated in the diagram.

    Calculate the size of obtuse angle ABL.

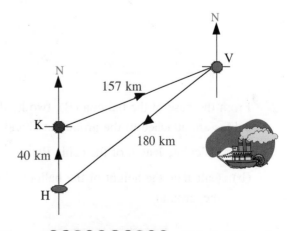

6.   A yacht race, over a triangular course, starts at S,
                                                turns at the lighthouse, sails around the rocks and
                                                finishes back at the starting point.

                                                Calculate the size of the angle LSR.

7. A steamboat leaves H and sails 40 km due north to K.
    It then turns and sails 157 km to V.

    It completes its journey by sailing 180 km back to H.

    (a)   Calculate the **bearing** of V from H.

    (b)   Calculate the **bearing** of V from K.

The Sine Rule, The Cosine Rule and SOHCAHTOA

Sometimes, a "**SOHCAHTOA**" Question is disguised behind the Sine Rule or the Cosine Rule. The following exercise gives you some practice at these types of questions.

Example :-

Two girls, who live 300 metres apart, are looking up at what they believe to be a space rocket.

The angle of elevation of the rocket is 40° from Gemma and 30° from Sammi.

Calculate :-

   (a) the distance from Sammi to the rocket.

   (b) the height the rocket is above the ground.

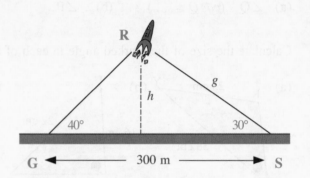

∠GRS is not given, but can be found easily

(a) $\dfrac{g\checkmark}{\sin G\checkmark} = \dfrac{s}{\sin S\checkmark} = \dfrac{r\checkmark}{\sin R\checkmark}$

=> $\dfrac{g}{\sin 40°} = \dfrac{300}{\sin 110°}$

R = 180 − 40 − 30

=> $g = \dfrac{300\sin 40°}{\sin 110°}$

$g = \boxed{205\cdot2 \text{ m}}$

(b) $\sin 30° = \dfrac{h}{205\cdot2}$

$h = 205\cdot2 \times \sin 30°$

$= \boxed{102\cdot6 \text{ m}}$

The rocket is 102·6 m above the ground.

Exercise 18·6

1. Inverness Caley Thistle advertise the return to their football stadium on a helium balloon.

   The distance between the two points C and D on the ground is 110 metres and the angle of elevation from each point is shown on the diagram below.

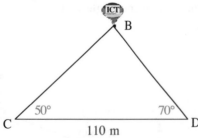

   From the base of the balloon (B), two holding cables are attached to the ground at C and D.

   (a) Calculate length of the cable BC.

   (b) Calculate the height of the balloon above the ground.

2. The path in the diagram below runs parallel to the river.

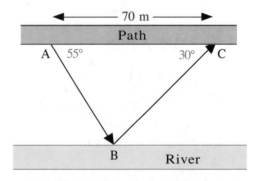

   Colin leaves the path at A, walks to the river for a paddle (B) and rejoins the path further on at C.

   (a) Calculate the distance from A to B.

   (b) Calculate the (shortest) distance between the river and the path.

3. In the diagram shown opposite, PQRS has been split into two triangles, one of which is right angled.

PQ = 20 cm and QR = 60 cm.

∠PQR = 120° and ∠SPR = 50°.

(a) Calculate the length of the line PR.

(b) Calculate the length of the line SP.

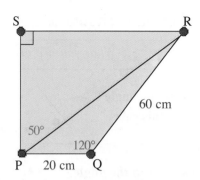

60 cm

50°

120°

P   20 cm   Q

4.

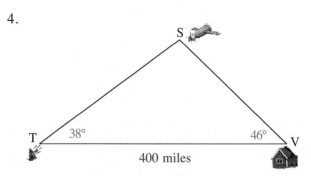

S

T 38°   46° V

400 miles

A TV signal is sent from a transmitter T, via a satellite S, to a village V.
The village is 400 miles from the transmitter.
The signal is sent out at an angle of 38° and is received in the village at an angle of 46°.

Calculate the height of the satellite above the ground.

5. In the shape shown opposite, determine the size of ∠KLM.

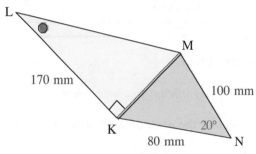

L

M

170 mm

100 mm

K   20°

80 mm   N

6.

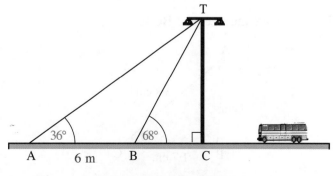

M 81°   85° N

G   ground

An aeroplane is flying parallel to the ground.
Lights have been fitted at M and N as shown in the diagram.

When the aeroplane is flying at a certain height, the beams from these lights meet exactly on the ground at G.

- The angle of depression of the beam of light from M to G is 81°.

- The angle of depression of the beam of light from N to G is 85°.

- The distance MN is 15 metres.

(a) Sketch triangle MGN and mark on all the sizes.

(b) Calculate the **height** of the aeroplane above G.

7. Two support cables, from the top (T) of a motorway light, are attached to the ground at A and B. A is 6 metres away from B.
The angles of elevation are 36° and 68°.

(a) Calculate the sizes of ∠ABT and ∠ATB.

(b) Calculate the length of wire BT.

(c) Calculate the height of pole TC.

T

36°   68°

A   6 m   B   C

Which Formula should I use ?

	What you are given	*What you should use*
A side & the angle opposite this side	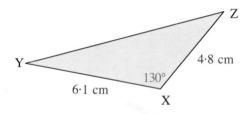 or	**the Sine Rule** $$\frac{a}{\sin A} = \frac{b}{\sin B} = \frac{c}{\sin C}$$
Two sides and the angle between the two sides		**the Cosine Rule** $$a^2 = b^2 + c^2 - 2bc\cos A$$
All three sides		**the Cosine Rule** $$\cos A = \frac{b^2 + c^2 - a^2}{2bc}$$
Two sides and the angle between the two sides (area required)		**Area of a Triangle** $$\text{Area} = \frac{1}{2}ab\sin C$$

Exercise 18·7

Answer to 3 significant figures each time here.

1. Calculate the **area** of these triangles :-

   (a)
   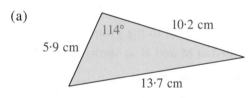
   114°   10·2 cm
   5·9 cm
   13·7 cm

   (b)
   56·5 m
   32°
   30·0 m   88°

2. In △PQR, find the length of the line **PQ**.

   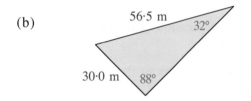
   R
   50 mm
   40°   28°
   P   Q

3. Calculate the size of ∠BCA.

   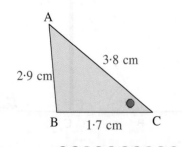
   A
   3·8 cm
   2·9 cm
   B   1·7 cm   C

4. Calculate the length of the line **YZ**.

   Z
   4·8 cm
   Y   130°
   6·1 cm   X

5. Calculate the size of ∠**DEF**.
   (*Think carefully about this one*).

   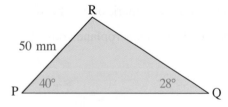
   D
   2·7 km
   10°
   E   7·5 km   F

6. The area of a triangle GTD is 9130 cm².

   GT = 240 cm and TD = 80 cm.

   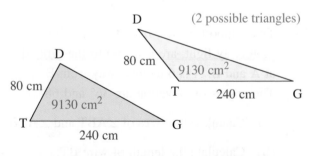
   (2 possible triangles)
   D
   80 cm   9130 cm²
   T   240 cm   G

   D
   80 cm   9130 cm²
   T   G
   240 cm

   (a) Calculate the size of **acute** angle GTD.

   (b) If angle GTD is **obtuse**, calculate its size.

7.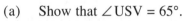

A pulley system is used to raise objects up to the top of a high building. The triangular metal structure, ABC, is used to support the small pulley wheel.

Calculate the length of the bar AC.

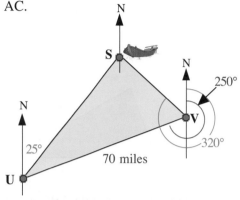

8. Two oil platforms in the North Sea are 70 miles apart. Platform U is on a bearing of 250° from platform V. A rowing boat is spotted on a bearing of 025° from platform U and 320° from platform V.

(a) Show that ∠USV = 65°.

(b) Now calculate how far the boat is from V.

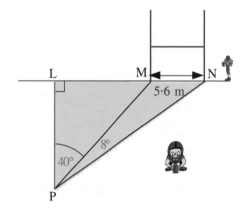

9.

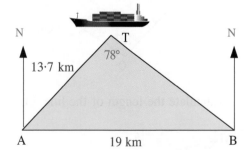

A rescue boat, at R, picks up a distress call from a boat B, 35 km away, on a bearing of 120°.
At the same time, another distress call comes from a yacht Y, which is 17 km away from B and on a bearing of 220° from B.

(a) Prove clearly that ∠RBY = 80°.

(b) Calculate the distance from the rescue ship to the yacht.

10. The diagram opposite shows the goalposts on an American Football field.

LP is perpendicular to the touchline, LN.

∠LPM = 40° and ∠MPN = 8°.

The distance MN between the goalposts is 5·6 metres.

To kick for goal the kicker walks straight out from L to P.

Calculate the distance LP.

(*Hint - find ∠PMN and the side PM first*)

11. A coastguard at A is 19 kilometres due west of a coastguard at B.
In relation to the two coastguards, a tanker is spotted at T, such that ∠ATB = 78°.

The tanker is 13·7 km away from point A.

(a) Calculate the size of ∠TBA, then ∠TAB.

(b) Calculate the bearing of the tanker from A.

(c) Calculate the bearing of the tanker from B.

12. Two ships leave port together.
One sails on a course of 030° at 9 mph.
The other sails on a course of 090° at 12 mph.

Make a neat sketch and calculate how far apart they will be after 5 hours.

Answer to 3 significant figures.

1. Calculate the **area** of these triangles :-

   (a)
   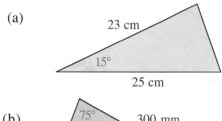
   23 cm
   15°
   25 cm

   (b)
   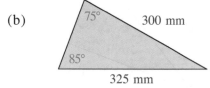
   75°   300 mm
   85°
   325 mm

2. The area of a triangle ABC is 250 cm².

   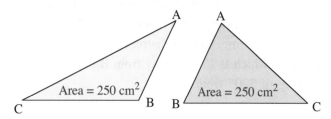

   Area = 250 cm²
   Area = 250 cm²

   AB = 20 cm and BC = 50 cm.

   Calculate **two** possible sizes for angle ABC.

3. Determine the size of obtuse ∠EFD.

   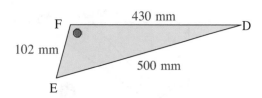
   F   430 mm   D
   102 mm
   500 mm
   E

4. Find the length of the line **PR**.

   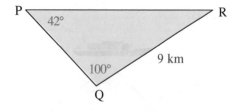
   P   42°   R
   100°   9 km
   Q

5. Calculate the length of the line **TU**.

   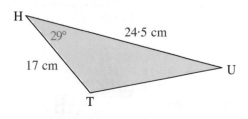
   H
   29°   24·5 cm
   17 cm   U
   T

6. Determine the size of ∠**GBC**.

   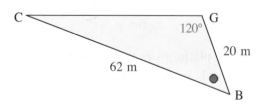
   C   G
   120°
   20 m
   62 m
   B

7. A statue lies directly East of a large palm tree. Treasure is buried **below ground** at an angle of 25° to the palm tree and at an angle of 34° to the statue as shown below.

   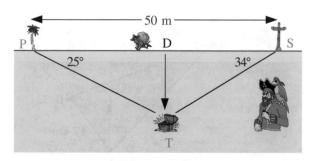
   50 m
   P   D   S
   25°   34°
   T

   The distance from the palm tree to the statue is 50 metres.

   (a) Calculate the distance from P to T.

   (b) Calculate how deep the pirate would have to go if he started at D and dug vertically down to the treasure at T.

8. A ship leaves N and sails to M on a course bearing 070°.

   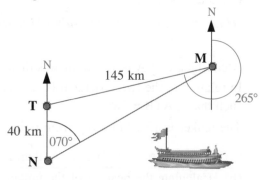
   N
   M
   145 km
   N
   265°
   T
   40 km
   070°
   N

   At M, the ship changes course and sails on a bearing of 265° to T directly North of N.

   (a) Explain why ∠NTM = 95°.

   (b) If NT = 40 km and TM = 145 km, calculate the distance from M to N.

Practice for Maths 2 - N.A.B.

Outcome 1 - Using Trigonometry

Area of a Triangle

1. Calculate the **areas** of the following triangles :-

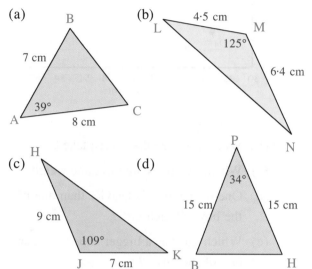

(a)

(b)

(c)

(d)

3. (c)

(d)

Outcome 2 - Simultaneous Equations

Solving Simultaneous Equations Graphically

4. Each of the following equations represent straight lines :–

- Find three points on each line, or find the two axes points.
- Plot your points.
- Draw a straight line through the 3 points.

(a) $y = x$ (b) $y = 2x$

(c) $y = x + 3$ (d) $y = 3x + 1$

(e) $y = 2x - 3$ (f) $x + y = 8$

(g) $x - y = 4$ (h) $3x + y = 0$

Solve Problems using Sine & Cosine Rules

2. Use the Sine rule to calculate the value of x.

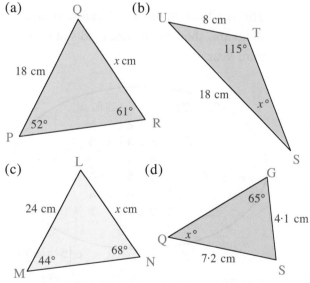

(a)

(b)

(c)

(d)

5. Draw the graphs represented by the following equations on squared paper.

Use the graphs to help solve each pair of simultaneous equations.

(a) $x + y = 10$ (b) $x + 2y = 7$
$x - y = 4$ $x - y = -2$

(c) $y = x + 4$ (d) $x + 3y = 8$
$y = -x + 8$ $x - 3y = 2$

Solve Simultaneous Equations Algebraically

3. Use the Cosine rule to calculate the size of each side marked x cm here.

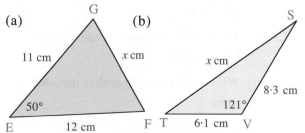

(a)

(b)

6. Solve these simultaneous equations by **eliminating** one of the letters first.

(a) $x + y = 10$ (b) $x + y = 8$
$x - y = 6$ $x - y = -2$

(c) $x + 2y = 6$ (d) $x + 4y = 9$
$x - 2y = 2$ $x - 4y = 1$

(e) $3x + y = 10$
     $3x - y = 2$

(f) $-3x - 4y = 3$
     $3x + y = 6$

7. Solve these simultaneous equations by first multiplying both sides of the equations by suitable numbers.

(a) $2x - 3y = 1$
     $3x + 2y = 21$

(b) $2x + 4y = 4$
     $7x + 3y = 14$

(c) $2x + 3y = 12$
     $5x - 2y = 11$

(d) $7p + 4q = 24$
     $5p + 3q = 17$

(e) $2m - 3n = 3$
     $3m - 4n = 5$

(f) $3x - 8y = 0$
     $4x - 3y = 23$

Outcome 3 - Graphs, Charts & Tables

Construct & Interpret Statistical Graphs

8. The **pie-chart** shows the proportions of people taking part in a survey, who read the 4 popular Scottish Newspapers.

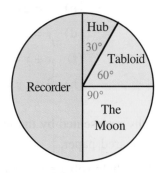

(a) Which is the most popular paper ?

(b) What **percentage** of the sample prefer

    (i) the Moon   (ii) the Tabloid ?

(c) If 1200 people took part in the survey, **how many** of them said they preferred

    (i) the Tabloid   (ii) the Hub ?

9. After growing for 4 weeks, the heights of a sample of tomato plants were measured and recorded.

Height (in cm)	10-19	20-29	30-39	40-49	50-59
No. of Plants	2	10	17	21	30

Draw a neat labelled **bar graph** showing the information.

10. The scatter diagram shows the weight and shoe size of eight students.

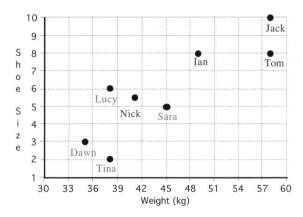

(a) How heavy is **Ian** ?

(b) What shoe size does **Sara** take ?

(c) Which two boys are the same weight ?

(d) One of the girls is heavier than one of the boys. Which girl ?

(e) Which girl has a bigger shoe size than one of the boys ?

(f) What is the **mean** shoe size for the girls ?

(g) A new boy, Alex, weighs 54 kg. Estimate his shoe size from the graph.

11. This is a **back to back ordered stem and leaf diagram**, showing the test marks of two third year classes.

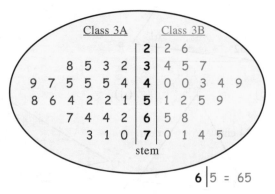

(a) What is the lowest mark scored in :-
    (i) class 3A   (ii) class 3B ?

(b) How many students were there in class 3B ?

(c) What was the highest score gained by a student ?

(d) Which class has the higher **median** mark ?

12. Construct an ordered **stem and leaf diagram** to show the following test marks for Class 3C.

62	65	54	47	84	88	42
56	64	77	40	50	83	83
75	52	66	81	59	60	48
51	74	70	81	69	55	51

13. The table shows how a group of 4th year pupils travelled to school.

Journey to School	Number	Calc^n	Angle
Walked	80	$\frac{80}{\ldots} \times 360°$	......
Cycled	15	$\times 360°$	......
Car	60	......	......
Bus/Train	25	......	......
Total No. =	....	**Total** =	......

(a) Make a **copy** of the table and complete it.

(b) Use compasses and a protractor to construct a neat labelled **pie-chart** to show this information.

14. A head teacher noted the number of pupils in each of the school's classrooms during a particular morning period.

The information is shown in a **dot plot**.

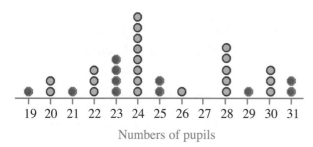

Numbers of pupils

(a) In how many classrooms were there more than 25 pupils ?

(b) Write down the number of pupils in each room, in order, **smallest** first.

(c) Find the **median** and the **mode**.

15. The table shows the weights of a group of people *(in kilograms)*.

Weight (kg)	52	53	54	55	56	57	58	59	60
Number	6	3	5	10	8	7	3	0	2

Draw a **dot plot** to represent the information.

Construct a Cumulative Frequency Table

16. This table shows the scores of the golfers in a local golf competition.

Score in golf competition	Number of golfers
68	1
69	2
70	5
71	10
72	7
73	4
74	6
75	3
76	2

Make a copy of it and add a third column showing the **cumulative frequency**.

From it, say what **fraction** of the competitors scored 75 or less.

17. This table shows the ages of all the students in Stow College's Mechanical Engineering Course.

Ages of Students	Number of Students	Cumulative Frequency
18	12	
19	8	
20	2	
21	7	
22	5	
23	9	
24	4	
25	2	
26	1	

(a) Make a neat copy of the table and fill in the final column showing the **Cumulative Frequencies**.

(b) How many of the students were 21 or under ?

(c) What **percentage** were over 23 ?

Outcome 4 - Using Simple Statistics

The Semi-Interquartile Range

18. For each set of data, find the :-

    RANGE, MEAN, MEDIAN and **MODE** :-

    (a) 11, 9, 5, 12, 10, 10, 8, 8, 14, 5, 11, 8, 9, 6.

    (b) 54, 72, 58, 54, 17, 25, 26, 84, 10,
         14, 11, 36, 18, 43, 21, 54, 67, 83.

    (c) 3·4, 4·9, 7·1, 5·0, 3·8, 2·8, 10·2, 5·8, 3·8.

19. The pupils in Coburn High School measured the lengths of their hands.

    The table shows the results.

Length (cm)	Frequency	Length × Frequency
18	3	
19	4	
20	5	
21	2	
22	10	
23	1	

    (a) How many pupils are in the class ?

    (b) What is the **range** ?

    (c) Calculate the :-
         (i) **mean**   (ii) **median**   (iii) **mode**.

20. Remember :-

    > **Semi-Interquartile Range** $= \frac{1}{2}(Q_3 - Q_1)$

    (Q_1 is the lower quartile and Q_3 is the upper).

    For the following scores, calculate :-

    • the **Upper** and **Lower Quartiles** and

    • the **Semi-Interquartile Range**.

    3, 4, 4, 5, 5, 5, 6, 8, 8, 9, 10, 10, 12, 13, 13.

21. Find the **range** and **semi-interquartile range** for each of the following sets of scores :-

    (a) 32, 30, 28, 35, 31, 33.

    (b) 7·5, 8·5, 9·5, 11·5, 3·5, 2·5, 1·5, 6·5, 10·5, 4·5.

    (c) 318, 318, 320, 311, 320, 321, 314, 314, 315, 317.

22. A group of children were asked to say how many coins each had in his/her pockets.
    The table shows how they replied.

Number of coins	Frequency	Cumulative Freq
0	1	1
1	3	4
2	5	9
3	6	…
4	2	…
5	1	…
6	1	…

    (a) **Copy** the table and complete it showing the **cumulative frequencies**.

    (b) Pick out the **upper** and **lower quartiles**.

    (c) Calculate the **semi-interquartile range**.

23. This table shows the ages of a group of men and women at a fitness centre one night.

Ages (in years)	19	20	21	22	23	24	25	26
Frequency	8	6	3	5	1	4	3	1

    By either constructing a cumulative frequency table or writing all the ages out in full (in order) find the upper and lower quartiles and the semi-interquartile range of the ages.

24. Shown below is a **box plot** indicating the test scores (out of 25) for a 2nd year class.

    10 11 12 13 14 15 16 17 18 19 20 21 22

    (a) What is the lowest and highest scores ?

    (b) What is the **range** of scores ?

    (c) What is the **median** score ?

    (d) What are the upper and lower **quartiles** ?

    (e) Calculate the **Semi-Interquartile Range**.

25. The number of full hours it rained each day between January 2nd and 15th is noted below.

    1, 2, 4, 5, 8, 14, 11, 4, 2, 1, 7, 11, 4, 7

    (a) Rearrange the measurements in order and find the **median** and **quartiles**.

    (b) Show the results as a **boxplot**.

The Standard Deviation

26. Shown are the ages of a group of people out for dinner.

    19, 20, 22, 24, 30, 35.

    (a) Show that the mean age, $\bar{x}$, is 25.

    (b) Copy the table below and use it to calculate the **standard deviation**.

Score x	$(x - \bar{x})$	$(x - \bar{x})^2$
19	$19 - 25 = -6$	$(-6)^2 = 36$
20	$20 - 25 = -5$	$(-5)^2 = 25$
22		

27. Calculate the **mean** and the **standard deviation** for the following set of numbers :-

    5, 6, 11, 9, 8, 10, 5, 2.

The Line of Regression (Line of Best Fit)

28. In this question, sets of values for P and t have been plotted and the **line of best fit** drawn.

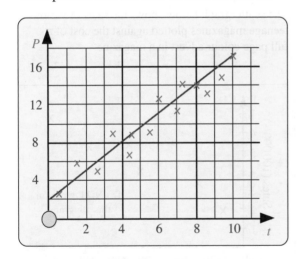

    (a) Find the gradient of the line and state where it cuts the P axis.

    (b) Now write down the equation of the line in the form :- $P = ... t + ... $.

    (*note:– the scales on the axes are not the same*).

29. Repeat question 28 for the set of data shown in the graph at the top of the next column.

    i.e. find the equation of the line of best fit in the form:- $F = ... d + ...$

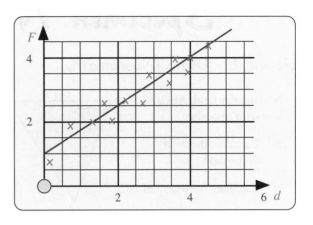

30. (a) Use $\frac{1}{2}$ centimetre squared paper to plot the following sets of points.

    (i)

x	0·5	1·0	1·5	2·0	2·5	3·0	3·5
y	1	2·1	2·5	4·0	5·2	5·6	7·0

    (ii)

x	0	5	10	15	20	25	30
y	12	15	20	22	29	30	37

    (b) Decide if there is a strong enough **correlation** (or connection) between the pairs of points to draw a **line of best fit**.

    (c) Where yes, draw, by eye, the line of best fit.

    (d) Find the equation of your line of best fit.

Probability

31. On a normal six-sided die (numbered 1 to 6), what is the probability of rolling :-

    (a) a three   (b) an even number

    (c) bigger than a 4   (d) a prime number ?

32. There are 49 numbers which can be drawn in the National Lotto. What is the probability that the first number out will be :-

    (a) 14   (b) odd

    (c) a square number   (d) a multiple of 6 ?

33. A letter is chosen at random from the word

    MISSISSIPPI.

    Calculate the probability that the chosen letter will be :–

    (a) an M   (b) the letter P

    (c) a vowel.   (d) the letter D.

Specimen N.A.B. -Maths 2

Outcome 1 - Using Trigonometry

1. A triangular field, ABC, is shown opposite.

   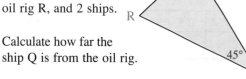

   (a) Calculate the **area** of the field. (3)

   (b) Calculate the length of AC. (4)

2. The diagram shows the position of an oil rig R, and 2 ships.

   Calculate how far the ship Q is from the oil rig. (3)

   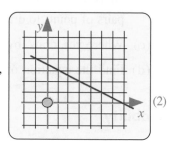

   required to pass - $^7/_{10}$

Outcome 2 - Simultaneous Equations

3. The diagram shows the line $x + 2y = 7$.

   (a) **Copy** the diagram, and on it show the line $x + y = 3$. (2)

   (b) Use your graph to solve the system of equations :-

   | $x + 2y = 7$ |
   | $x + y = 3$ | (1)

4. Solve **algebraically**, the system of equations.

   | $4x + 3y = 15$ |
   | $2x - y = 5$ | (3)

   required to pass - $^4/_6$

Outcome 3 - Graphs, Charts and Tables

5. The marks obtained in a class test are as follows :-

   | 26 | 31 | 41 | 20 | 35 | 24 | 29 | 33 | 37 |
   | 41 | 44 | 26 | 41 | 32 | 33 | 37 | 27 | 40 |

   (a) Find the **maximum, minimum, median** and **quartiles** of this data set. (4)

   (b) Draw a neat labelled **box-plot** to illustrate the data. (2)

6. A survey was done with 90 pupils caught truanting. The table below shows the reason they gave for truanting.

Reason	Number	Calcⁿ	Angle
dislike teacher	16		
work too hard	30		
school boring	44		
total =			

   (a) **Copy** and **complete** the above table. (2)

   (b) Use compasses and a protractor to draw a pie chart representing the above. (2)

   required to pass - $^7/_{10}$

Outcome 4 - Using Simple Statistics

7. Find the standard deviation of this random sample of digits, showing all the necessary working.

   7, 9, 6, 8, 11.

   (*note :- no credit will be given for reading the standard deviation directly from a calculator*). (4)

8. The scattergraph below shows the sales of various teenage magazines plotted against the cost of a full page colour advert in a magazine.

   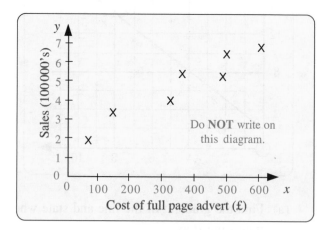

   (a) Copy or trace the scattergraph and draw your estimate of the line of best fit. (1)

   (b) State the equation of this line of best fit. (3)

   (c) Use your equation to estimate the charge for an advert of a magazine with sales of £400 000. (2)

9. The National Lotto has balls numbered 1 to 49.

   What is the probability that a ball, selected at random, has a number less than 20 ? (2)

   required to pass - $^8/_{12}$

Answers to Book 3C

Decimals

1. a 3600 b 9120 c 580 d 12800
   e 210 f 23·7 g 1·76 h 12·3
   i 0·098 j 11·5 k 7·3 l 0·97
2. a 45·63 b 35·16 c 106·08 d 1·73
3. a 0·3 b 0·75 c 0·4
4. a tenths b hundredths c thousandths
5. £14·61
6. a 18·8 b 0·4 c 0·4 d 20·9
7. $14·80   8. 4·08 euros   9. 1·4 kg

Fractions & Percentages

10. a $2/3$ b $4/9$ c $1/3$ d $3/7$
11. a 40 b £90 c 28 kg d 360
12. 20
13. a £80 b £300 c £7 d 12p
    e £16 f £21 g 58 h 12 kg

Ratios

14. a 1 : 2 b 3 : 4 c 2 : 5 d 12 : 5
15. 4 : 3   16. 25 sprained wrists

Patterns

17. a 18, 22, 26,... b 62, 55, 48, ...
    c 36, 49, 64, ... d 21, 34, 55, ...
18. 91   19. 2, 3, 5, 7, 11, 13, 17, 19, 23, 29.
20. a 10, 13, 16
    b bricks = 3 × pattern no. + 1   c 301

Negative Numbers

21. a –12°C b –48°C
22. 25°C   23. 25°C

Algebra

24. a 7 b 3
25. a $x = 15$ b $x = 9$ c $x = 6$ d $x = 6·5$
    e $x = 7$ f $x = 8$ g $x = 0$ h $x = 2·5$
26. a 1, 2, 3 b 5, 6, 7, 8, 9, 10
    c 10 d 1, 2, 3, 4

Measurement & Estimation

27. 12 square metres   28. 70 mm
29. 5000 kg   30. 650 ml
31. 1·15 seconds
32. a $66cm^2$ b $81cm^2$
    c $30cm^2$ d $16·5mm^2$
33. a 92 cm b 44 cm
34. a $96cm^3$ b $125cm^3$ 35. 2 cm

Scale Drawing

36. a 7 cm b 175 m c 500 m
37. 610 metres

Quadrilaterals

38. a parallelogram b rhombus
    c trapezium d kite
39. circumference = 3 × diameter (approx)
40. a square, rhombus b rectagle, rhombus
    c kite, trapezium d square, rectangle

Drawing

41. a – c see drawings
42. a cuboid b triangular prism
    c square based pyramid

Bearings & Rotational Symmetry

44. B, C and D (not A)
45. a A(–3, 2)
    b B(4, –3) and C(–3, –1) plotted correctly
    c 3 boxes
46.

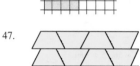

47.

Angles

48. a straight b reflex c obtuse
    d right e acute
49. a 85° b 66° c 116°
50.

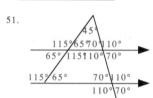

51.

Statistics

52. See bar graph neatly drawn and labelled
53. a 25%
    b

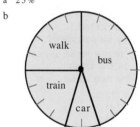

54. mean = £70
55. a trend - fall - rise - fall - rise - fall (none)
    b (i) 22°C (ii) 6°C
    c 6 am and 4 pm
56. a 26 b 50 c 3 d 13
    e 3.6 f 106 g 5 h 2
    i 11 j 7

Exercise 1·1

1. 50   25   75 $33^1/_3$ $66^2/_3$
   $^1/_2$ $^1/_4$ $^3/_4$ $^1/_3$ $^2/_3$
   20   40   60   80   10   30   70   90
   $^1/_5$ $^2/_5$ $^3/_5$ $^4/_5$ $^1/_{10}$ $^3/_{10}$ $^7/_{10}$ $^9/_{10}$
2. a £3.50 b £28 c 90p d 24p
   e £270 f £8 g £1.80 h £140
   i £4800 j £15000 k £140 l 9p
   m £8.40 n 18p o £1.80 p £1
3. 112 pupils
4. a 160 b 120 c 200 d 320
5. a $^{32}/_{100} = 0.32$ b $^{45}/_{100} = ^9/_{20} = 0.45$

c $^{51}/_{100} = 0.51$ d $^{31}/_{100} = 0.31$
e $^{78}/_{100} = ^{39}/_{50} = 0.78$ f $^8/_{100} = 0.08$
g $^1/_8 = 0.125$ h $^1/_{40} = 0.025$

6. a $35\% = ^{35}/_{100} = ^7/_{20}$ b $60\% = ^{60}/_{100} = ^3/_5$
   c $55\% = ^{55}/_{100} = ^{11}/_{20}$ d $90\% = ^{90}/_{100} = ^9/_{20}$
   e $15\% = ^{15}/_{100} = ^3/_{20}$ f $75\% = ^{75}/_{100} = ^3/_4$
   g $4\% = ^4/_{100} = ^1/_{25}$ h $85\% = ^{85}/_{100} = ^{17}/_{20}$
   i $5\% = ^5/_{100} = ^1/_{20}$ j $36\% = ^{36}/_{100} = ^9/_{25}$
   k $2^1/_2\% = ^1/_{40}$ l $150\% = ^{150}/_{100} = ^3/_2$
7. a £3.20 b £12 c £19.20 d £1680
   e £2.70 f £19.80 g £3.80 h £5.60
   i 45p j £42 k £20.40
8. 189mm   9. 825,000 eels
10. £830.70   11. 48.4 sec
12. £153   13. 19250 feet
14. 268.8g
15. a per annum/yearly b £54 c £1254
16. a £112.50 b £56.25   17. £189
18. Brian £104
    Nicole £103.50 so Brian will get 50p more.

Exercise 1·2

1. a 14% b 20% c 24% d 80%
   e 45% f 85% g 92% h 12.5%
   i 36% j 37.5% k 75% l 62.5%
   m 65% n 50%
2. a 80% b 54% c 37.5% d 30%
3. a 80% b 20% 4. 77.8%
5. a 81.3% b 7.1% c 97.6%
6. a Aug 50%   Sep 60%   Oct 65%
   Nov 60%   Dec 70%   Jan 75%
   Feb 90%   Mar 80%   Apr 100%
   May 85%

   b see diagram   c 73.5%

   d Generally, her test marks improve as the year goes on.
7. 49

Exercise 1·3

1. Profit £3 - % profit 20%   2. 15%
3. a 10p, 12.5% b £450, 30%
   c £480, 3% d 60p, 150%
4. £150, 30%
5. a £48, 30% b £2740, 68.5%
   c 70p, 87.5%
6. £7800   7. £5.04

Exercise 1·4

1. Final balance = £1311.27
   Total interest = £111.27
2. £34.19   3. £28529.15   4. £3121.87
5. a 27.68 b £325.12   c £42.74
6. a (i) £6540 (ii) £7128.60 b after 9 years
7. a 1st year £12540   2nd year £13167
   3rd year £13864.85 4th year   4544.23
   b £2544.23   c 21.2%

Exercise 1·5

1. Final value £204.80
2. a £4800 b £3600   c £2700
3. £61560 4. 12459 feet 5. £54950.40
6. a £156 b £162.24   c £168.73
7. a (i) 3% (ii) 4.8%

b   £624   c   £43.26
d   (i)   £30900   (ii)   £32012.40
    (iii)   £33549

8.   During the 5th hour.

Exercise 1·6

1.   £15000   2.   £400   3.   240 ºC

4.   150 cm   5.   50 mph   6.   £200

7.   300   8.   30 ºC   9.   £45000

Exercise 1·7

1.   a   1   b   1   c   2   d   4

2.   a   3   b   3   c   4   d   3
     e   3   f   4   g   2   h   7
     i   1   j   7   k   6   l   2

3.   a   50   b   500   c   6000   d   20000
     e   4000   f   5000   g   2   h   0.4
     i   0.8   j   0.002   k   0.02   l   4000000
     m   0.00008 n   80

4.   a   810   b   7100   c   31000   d   180000
     e   46   f   20   g   7.2   h   0.34
     i   0.0037 j   90

5.   a   5840   b   25100   c   73900   d   482000
     e   15.8   f   12.8   g   0.287   h   0.294
     i   0.00168 j   0.0500

6.   14700 - 15000   7.   £470   8.   £63.20

Remember Remember 1

1.   a   £14   b   £42   c   £40
     d   £400   e   £1800   f   £50

2.   a   £49   b   £329

3.   £508.80   4.   £431.20

5.   a   £115.20   b   £67.20

6.   a   85%   b   81.25%

7.   67.5%   8.   a   £55   b   27.5%

9.   profit = £35   % profit = 43.75%

10.   £282.33   11.   £760.44

12.   £6375   13.   £12

14.   £30

Answers to Chapter 2 Page 17

Introductory Ex 2.0

1.   a   36, 64, 100   b   100   c   check

2.   a   81, 144, 225   b   225   c   check

3.   a   25, 144, 169   b   169   c   check

Exercise 2·1

1.   17 cm   2.   39 cm

3.   a   25 cm b   25 cm   c   12.75

4.   11.66 cm   5.   16.12 cm

6.   18.03 cm   7.   27.80 cm

8.   15.18 cm

9.   a   10.3 cm   b   21.1 cm   c   9.62 cm
     d   13.35 m   e   41.4 mm   f   35.78cm

Exercise 2·2

1.   8.5 m   2.   5.28 m   3.   209.4 km

4.   65.5m   5.   12.9 cm

6.   sloping edge 5.3 cm   p = 26.2

7.   180.5 cm   8.   29.8 m   9.   3.3 m

10.   2.6 m   11.   64 cm   12.   35 m

13.   a   90 cm   b   63 cm

Exercise 2·3

1.   36 cm   2. a   12.7 cm   b   19.7 cm

3.   4.1 m   4.   70.8 m   5.   960 cm²

6.   56.5 cm   7.   90 cm   8.   21.2 cm

Exercise 2·4

1.   a   8.9 cm b   17.9 cm   c   13.5 m
     d   24.3   e   71.0   f   9.2 m

---

2.   Hypotenuse is always the longest side

3.   y = 9.6 is correct as y cannot be greater than
     the hypotenuse.

4.   10.6 mm   5.   3.00 m   6.   442 m

7.   42.7 cm

8.   a   6.6m   b   3.8 m   c   2.8 m

9.   8.8 km   10.   5.3 m

Exercise 2·5

1.   b   5 boxes

2.   a   see diagram   b   13 boxes

3.   8.06 boxes

4.   a   9.49 boxes   b   8.49 boxes

5.   a   5 boxes   b   5 boxes c   yes

6.   MN=14.14   LM=10   LN=10
     since LM = LN —> triangle is isosceles.

Exercise 2·6

1.   PQ² + QR² = 324 + 56.25 = 380.25
     PR² = 380.25,   so right angle

2.   UW² + WV² = 43.56 + 77.44 = 120.96
     UV²= 123.21,   so not right angled

3.   a   shorter sides   84² = 7056 and 35² =1225
         longest = 91² = 8281, so by converse of
         Pythagoras it is right-angled
     b   shorter sides   9.6² = 92.16 and
                            18.0² = 324
         longest = 20.4² = 416.16, so by the
         converse of Pythagoras it is right-angled

4.   shorter   84² = 7056 and 63² = 3969
     longest   105² = 11025 => pitch is square

5.   shorter   10.8² = 116.64 and 8.1² = 65.61
     longest   13.5² = 182.25 => yes, it is vertical

Remember Remember 2

1.   x = 9.90cm   y = 14.3cm
     z = 3.86m   w = 4.24

2.   a   36cm   b   540cm²

3.   672cm²   4.   90cm   5.   7.84m

6.   a   53.4cm b   1060.8cm²

7.   10.3 boxes 8.   11.4 boxes

9.   A. shorter   6.8² = 46.24 and 5.1² = 26.01
         longest   8.3² = 68.89,
         by converse not right angled

     B. shorter   19.2² = 368.64, and 8.0² = 64
         longest 20.8² = 432.64,
         by converse right angled

10.   SR² = 16.5² = 272.25
      PS² = 8.8² = 77.44
      PR² = 18.7² = 349.69

      since SR² + PS² = 349.69, by converse of
      Pythagoras, opposite sides equal so
      rectangle.

Answers to Chapter 3 Page 28

Exercise 3·1

1.   a   18km   b   800km   c   15km
     d   4.375km e   50 miles f   21 miles
     g   42 miles h   135km

2.   a   250 miles b   9 miles c   45 miles
     d   15km   e   20400 miles

3.   a   900 miles b   4.5 miles c   99 miles
     d   90km   e   22km   f   28km

Exercise 3·2

1.   a   50mph   b   23km/h c   62mph

2.   a   18km/h b   70 m/min c   5m/sec
     d   14km/day

3.   a   404mph b   42km/h c   60 km/h
     d   12mph   e   68cm/hour

---

4.   a   4 hours   b   4 hours 30 mins
     c   60 sec   d   1 hour 30 mins

5.   a   2 hours 30 mins b   5 hours 15 mins
     c   3 hours 45 mins d   8 hours 15 mins

6.   a   3.5 hours   b   2.25 hours
     c   5.75 hours   d   0.25 hours

7.   a   1 hour 15 mins   b   1 hour 15 mins

Exercise 3·3

1.   a   37.5 km/h b   3 hours c   116 miles
     d   60 km/h   e   180 m   f   1hour 45 m

2.   a   5400 m/h   b   90 m/min

3.   30 mins   4.   105 km   5.   60 mph

7.   10800 km   8.   a   3 mph b   3 mph faster

Exercise 3·4

1.   a   0.8 hours b   0.3 hours c   0.1 hours
     d   0.9 hours e   0.4 hours f   0.65 hours
     g   0.35 hours

2.   a   0.17 hours   b   0.28 hours
     c   0.33 hours   d   0.87 hours
     e   0.83 hours   f   1.17 hours

3.   a   4.2 hours   b   3.8 hours
     c   4.6 hours   d   2.85 hours
     e   2.95 hours   f   1.2 hours
     g   5.1 hours   4.   48 km

5.   a   9 miles   b   8 miles   c   10.5 km
     d   150 miles e   4 miles

6.   Bob 15 km   Ted 12 km   Bob by 3km

7.   D = 89.6km   8.   a   728 miles b   91 mile

9.   50 km/h

10.   a   70 mph   b   100 km/h c   320 mph
      d   70 mph   e   40 km/h f   70 mph
      g   6000 mph h   60 mph

Exercise 3·5

1.   a   51 min   b   36 min   c   54 min
     d   45 min   e   21 min   f   40 min

2.   3h 54 mins

3.   a   3h 12 mins   b   5h 30 mins
     c   1h 39 mins   d   2h 48 mins
     e   3h 51 mins   f   4h 42 mins
     g   3h 40 mins   h   1h 50 mins
     i   37.5 mins

4.   a   4 hours 45 mins   b   3 hours 36 min
     c   1 hour 20 mins

5.   a   3.3 hours   b   3 hours 18 mins

6.   a   1.7 hours   b   1 hour 42 mins

7.   a   2.3 hours = 2 hours 18 mins
     b   0.33 hours = 20 mins
     c   0.35 hours = 21 mins
     d   1.125 hours = 1 hour 7 mins 30 secs

8.   a   2 hours 15 mins   b   2 hours
     c   6 hours 45 mins

9.   a   7m/s   b   25.2km/h

10.   a   28.8 km/h   b   54 km/h
      c   720 km/h   d   135 km/h
      e   1.8 km/h   f   3600 km/h

Exercise 3·6

1.   a   2 hours b   1 hour   c   1500
     d   (i)   50 km/h (ii) 0   (iii)   20 km/h

2.   a   15 mins b   120 km/h c   80 km/h
     d   slowed him down

3.   a   24 km/h b   72 km/h
     c   1045am d   18km

4.   a   A is the goods train as it is the less steep
         of the 2 lines.
     b   (i) 40 mph   (ii) 80 mph
     c   1100   d   1700

5.   Boppard arrive 11.00 am   leave 11.30 am
     St Goar arrive 12.30 pm   leave 12.50 pm
     Binghen arrive 1.20pm

5. b (i) 24km (ii) 20 km
 c (i) 24 km/h (ii) 16 km/h
 (iii) 40 km/h (iv) 18 km/h
6. a 1 hour 30 mins b 60 mph
 c see diagram

Remember Remember 3

1. a 720 km b 60mph c 1h 15 mins
2. a 0.4h b 0.15h
 c 3.17h d 2.85h
3. a 42mins b 21 mins
 c 5h 18mins d 1h 39 mins
4. a 12mph b Mandy's by 5 mins
5. a 1930 b 24km c 16km/h
 d 45 mins e 30 mins
 f 48km/h g 3 hours

Turn off that calculator - Non-calc. 1

1. a 3811 b 3573 c 825600
 d 1593 e 897 f 2500
 g 950 h 3 i 105
 j 25
2. a 3.293 b 5.543 c 4.86
 d 22.246 e 166.4 f 3.74
 g 0.1778 h 0.00196
3. a 3.72km b 60m
 c 0.54m d 3.096kg
4. a 24 b 1600 c 850
5. a $2/3$ b $5/7$ c $13/15$
6. a $1/4$ b $5 3/4$
 c $2 7/8$ d 16
7. a $4/5$ b $1/8$ c $4/3$
8. a £1200 b £120 c £1.48
 d £60 e £70 f 12p
9. a 15 b 122 c -14
 d -40 e -6 f -41
 g 20 h 4 i 29
 j 1 k -9
10. a -52 b -168 c 42
 d -5 e 121 f -30
 g 5 h -8
11. a 0825 b 1945 c 2345
12. a 6h 35mins b 4h 33mins
13. 7.30pm
14. a 840 miles b 128km/h

Answers to Chapter 4 Page 40

Exercise 4·1

1. 6.4×10^3
2. a 7.3×10^1 b 5.16×10^2
 c 8.54×10^3 d 6.421×10^3
 e 7.0×10^3 f 1.0×10^4
 g 2.9×10^4 h 3.45×10^4
 i 9×10^0 j 6.0×10^1
 k 4.12×10^5 l 6.582×10^5
 m 8.763×10^4 n 5.0×10^6
 o 4.8×10^6 p 3.71×10^6
 q 4.2×10^7 r 5.55×10^7
 s 3.0×10^8 t 4.531×10^8
3. a $3000000 = 3.0 \times 10^6$
 b $2500000 = 2.5 \times 10^6$
 c $6290000 = 6.29 \times 10^6$
 d $9500000 = 9.5 \times 10^6$
 e $3600000 = 3.6 \times 10^6$
 f $15500000 = 1.55 \times 10^7$
 g $7632000 = 7.632 \times 10^6$
 h $44250000 = 4.425 \times 10^7$
 i $50750000 = 5.075 \times 10^7$
 j $£12400000 = £1.24 \times 10^7$
 k $285000 = 2.85 \times 10^5$
4. a 3.56×10^1 b 2.15×10^0
 c 2.501×10^2 d 4.6255×10^2
 e 6.4705×10^3 f 8.27001×10^4
 g 2.000001×10^5 h 3.33333×10^1

5. a 230 b 6,410
 c 800,000 d 77,300
 e 9102 f 60,040
 g 4,913,000 h 110,000
 i 87,100,000 j 214,000
 k 190,000,000 l 355,500
6. a 5,800,000 b 1,750,000,000
 c 2,200,000,000,000
7. 773,000 litres 8. £4,250,000
9. 31,560,000 secs 10. 4,497,000,000
11. £8,105 12. 1,298,000,000
13. £24,300,000

Exercise 4·2

1. a 5.0×10^{-2} b 7.0×10^{-3}
 c 9.0×10^{-1} d 4.0×10^{-4}
 e 6.0×10^{-5} f 1.0×10^{-6}
 g 4.3×10^{-2} h 9.7×10^{-3}
 i 3.5×10^{-4} j 6.6×10^{-5}
 k 1.47×10^{-3} l 3.58×10^{-1}
 m 2.49×10^{-4} n 9.63×10^{-6}
 o 3.0×10^{-9} p 1.8×10^{-11}
2. a 1.2×10^{-3}m b 2.4×10^{-7} Kg
 c 9.9×10^{-2} sec d 7.55×10^{-7} mm
 e 1.14×10^{-4} years f 2.5×10^{-3}
3. a 0.05 b 0.0034
 c 0.0047 d 0.000009
 e 0.000801 f 0.003002
 g 0.000004775 h 0.00006283
 i 0.01111 j 0.005442
 k 0.00000099 l 0.38874
4. 1g less
5. a 0.08 b 0.59
 c 0.000814 d 0.001755
 e 0.000005006 f 0.0000000000065
6. a 0.003 b 700 c 0.025 d 8200
 e 48700 f 0.000603
 g 0.000007123 h 385000
 i 0.00002 j 700900000
7. a 6.0×10^{-4} b 4.9×10^1
 a 9.310×10^3 b 2.0×10^{-2}
 a 3.0×10^{-1} b 8.85×10^5
 a 8.9×10^{-2} b 1.95×10^6
 a 5.5×10^{-7} b 6.9×10^7
8. a 8.295×10^4 $a = 8.295$ $n = 4$
 b 2.17×10^8 $a = 2.17$ $n = 8$
 c 9.0×10^{-5} $a = 9.0$ $n = -5$
 d 6.27×10^5 $a = 6.27$ $n = 5$
 e 4.0×10^{-1} $a = 4.0$ $n = 1$
 f 1.05×10^8 $a = 1.05$ $n = 8$
 g 1.365×10^4 $a = 1.365$ $n = 4$
 h 1.0×10^{-6} $a = 1.0$ $n = -6$
 i 1.65×10^{-5} $a = 1.65$ $n = -5$
 j 9.0×10^{-3} $a = 9.0$ $n = -3$
 k 8.5×10^{-5} $a = 8.5$ $n = -5$
 l 4.435×10^2 $a = 4.435$ $n = 2$
 m (i) 2.0×10^9 (ii) 3.1×10^9
 (iii) 9.6×10^{10} (iv) 1.75×10^{10}

Exercise 4·3

1. a 2.13×10^6 b 1.782×10^9
 c 2.769×10^6 d 1.05×10^5
 e 1.65×10^{-3} f 1.71×10^{-6}
 g 1.71×10^{-7} h 1.628×10^{-2}
2. a 6.44×10^2 b 4.05×10^7
 c 1.63×10^5 d 5.11×10^1
 e 2.36×10^{-4} f 2.67×10^{-8}
 g 7.20×10^2 h 3.04×10^8
3. a $5807 = 5.807 \times 10^3$
 b $15500 = 1.55 \times 10^4$

c $9760 = 9.76 \times 10^3$
d $10.043 = 1.0043 \times 10^1$
e $19.25 = 1.925 \times 10^1$
f $800 = 8.0 \times 10^2$
g $54 = 5.4 \times 10^1$
h $0.1462 = 1.462 \times 10^{-1}$
4. a 2,540,000 b 0.0267
 c 5,280,000,000,000 d 6,250,000,000
 e 754,000,000,000,000,000
 f 233,000,000,000,000,000
5. 1.578×10^8 seconds 6. $£2.8 \times 10^6$
7. $£7.012 \times 10^7$ 8. 2.03×10^{-20} g
9. 6.64×10^{-15} 10. 8mins 12 sec
11. 13mins 12. 1.786×10^{25} stars
13. 7.89×10^{20} atoms 14. 2.23×10^{21} m/s
15. 1340 visitors 16. £101.19 per sec
17. 2.39×10^5 miles

Remember Remember 4

1. 7.83×10^4
2. a 8.6×10^2 b 7.21×10^3
 c 9.52×10^4 d 1.268×10^5
 e 1.682×10^1 f 5.24×10^6
 g 6.0×10^6 h 2.43×10^8
 i 5.5×10^6 j 1.75×10^6
3. 6.23×10^{-4}
4. a 3.6×10^{-3} b 5.21×10^{-2}
 c 7.7×10^{-5} d 8.0×10^{-4}
 e 9.89×10^{-1} f 4.2×10^{-7}
5. a 5,900 b 808,000
 c 4,000,000 d 28,100
 e 710 f 3,200,000,000
 g 10,010,000 h 3,500,000,000,000
6. a 0.0058 b 0.099
 c 0.000062 d 0.23
 e 0.0000003 f 0.0004
7. a 4.2×10^4 b 8.01×10^{-2}
 c 1.37×10^5 d 3.4×10^{-4}
 e 6.5×10^{-6} f 9.5×10^6
 g 3.4×10^7 h 2.0×10^{-5}
8. a 7,300,000 b 0.0049
 c 36,100 d 0.00008
 e 800,000,000 f 0.055
 g 303,000 g 0.42
9. a 5.7×10^{10} b 3.1185×10^{11}
 c 1.35×10^{10} d 1.7×10^{11}
 e 2.9×10^{13} f 1.024×10^{21}
 g 2.197×10^{-12} h 3.5×10^{19}
10. 8.32×10^{11} mm^2
11. a 1.08×10^{12}m b 2.59×10^{13} m
 c 9.45×10^{15}m 12. 1.10×10^{12} km^3

Answers to Chapter 5 Page 47

Exercise 5·1

1. 25.12cm
2. a 31.4cm b 37.68cm c 204.1cm
 d 125.5cm e 1.57cm f 3.14cm
3. a 188.4cm b 62.8mm
 c 314cm d 172.7cm
4. 62.8cm 5. a 18.84cm b 3.14cm
6. a 128.74cm b 9.42m
7. 78.5cm 8. 20.56m 9. 25.7m
10. 7.85m
11. A = 53cm B = 53.38cm B larger perim
12. a 13m b 71.4mm
 c 278.5m d 65.7
13. £59.10 14. £84.55

Exercise 5·2

1. 7cm

2. a 157cm b 11m c 1mm d 770mm

3. a 50cm b 123mm c 2000m d 0.1km

4. a 25cm b 61.5mm c 1000m d 0.05km

5. 75mm 6. 478m

7. a 63.7cm b 2.5cm c 8.0cm
   d (i) 2.9cm (ii) 168.2m

8. a 9.6mm b 6.28mm 9. 777.7cm

Exercise 5·3

1. 50.24cm²

2. a 78.5cm² b 283.4mm²

3. a 2289.06cm² d 86.55cm²

4. a 226.87 b 3.14

5. a 2826cm² b 530.66cm²
   c 3.80m² d 0.20m² e 0.20m²

6. a 1225cm² b 961.625cm²
   c 263.375cm²

7. 3096cm²

8. a 7850cm² b 0.875km²

9. 25.12m² 10. 92.52m² 11. £110.39

Exercise 5·4

1. a 10cm

2. a 9cm b 3m c 13cm d 85cm

3. 14.14cm 4. 40cm

5. a 77.5cm b 51cm 6. 80 biscuits

7. circle would have diameter of 20.3cm and
   square has length of 20cm

8. 12cm 9. 131.88cm

Exercise 5·5

1. a 226.08cm² b 47.5m²
   c 19.625cm² d 0.196m²

2. a (i) 129.12cm² (ii) 46.56cm
   b (i) 114.24cm² (ii) 44.56cm
   c (i) 79.625cm² (ii) 41.85cm

3. 1962.5cm² 4. 383.08cm

5. a 25.7m b 36.54m

6. 95.54cm 7. 82.24cm 8. 117.81

Remember Remember 5

1. a 37.68cm b 34.54cm

2. a 28.27m b 17.85cm c 362.8m

3. a(i) 6.5cm (ii) 1.5km b 52.5mm

4. a 78.5cm² b 113.04cm²
   c 628cm² d 0.785cm²

5. a 706.5cm² b 412.27cm

6. a 1.5m b 1mm 7. 13.76

8. a (i) 33.55cm (ii) 58.875cm²
   b (i) 16.56cm (ii) 12.56cm²

9. 14.13cm² 10. 3.785m² 11. 4.71m²

Answers to Chapter 6 Page 55

Exercise 6·1

1. a $1/12$ b (i) Hill St (ii) New St

2. a Sunny Hill G=$1/8$ Dark Hill G= $1/9$
   b Sunny Hill is steeper

3. 0.24, 0.20, 0.19, 0.16

4. a Ramp 1 G=$2/9$ Ramp 2 G=$5/19$
   b 0.22 and 0.26 c Ramp 2

5. $7/2$

6. Purple ladder/ladder on right

7. 4.63 8. 8m 9. 240m

Exercise 6·2

1. 2

---

2. a $1/3$ b $3/4$

3. Blue = $3/5$ Red = $1/3$ Green = $1/5$

4. a 1 b $1/2$ c 4

5. a (i) (-2, -1) (ii) (4, 3) b $2/3$

6. a $1/4$ b 1

7. a 1 b $1/5$ c 2
   d $1/3$ e 4

8. -$1/2$ 9. a -$1/7$ b -$5/7$

10. a m_{CD} = -$2/3$ m_{EF} = -$1/8$ m_{GH} = 0
    b always 0

11. a m_{PQ} = -$5/2$ m_{RS} = -$5/2$ m_{TV} = -$5/2$
    b parallel lines have the same gradient

12. a (i) $1/2$ (ii) -2 (iii) 2 (iv) -$1/2$
    b m_{EF} =2m_{FG} = -$1/4$ m_{GH}=4 m_{EH}= -$1/3$
    c this is not a parallelogram
       since m_{EH} =m_{FG} and m_{GH} =m_{EF}

13. m_{VT} =7 m_{SU} = -1

14. m_{AB} = -$1/5$ m_{BC} = -$1/5$
    since m_{AB} = m_{BC} and B is common to both
    they lie on the straight line.

Exercise 6·3

1. a
x	-1	0	1	2
y	3	0	3	6

   b see diagram c m=3

2. a (i)
x	-1	0	1	2
y	-4	0	4	8

   (ii) see diagram (iii) m = 4
   b (i)
x	-1	0	1	2
y	-1	0	1	2

   (ii) see diagram (iii) m=1
   c (i)
x	-2	0	2	4
y	-1	0	1	2

   (ii) see diagram (iii) m=$1/2$
   d (i)
x	-1	0	1	2
y	1	0	-1	2

   (ii) see diagram (iii) m=-1

3. a 6 b $1/5$ c -12 d 0.5

4. a
x	-1	0	1	2
y	-2	1	4	7

   b see diagram c m=3 d (0,1)

5. a (i)
x	-1	0	1	2
y	-5	-1	3	7

   (ii) see diagram (iii) m=4 (iv) (0,-1)
   b (i)
x	-1	0	1	2
y	5	3	1	-1

   (ii) see diagram (iii) m=-2 (iv) (0, 3)
   c (i)
x	-2	0	2	4
y	2	3	4	5

   (ii) see diagram (iii) m=$1/2$ (iv) (0, 3)
   d (i)
x	-1	0	1	2
y	-3	-4	-5	-6

   (ii) see diagram (iv) (0, -4)

6. a 5 b (0, 2)

Exercise 6·4

1. a m = 3 (0, 2) b m = 5 (0, -3)
   c m = 1 (0, 1) d m = -2 (0, 5)
   e m = $1/2$ (0, 2) f m = -$1/3$ (0, -1)
   g m = 0.5 (0, 9) h m = -0.1 (0, 2)
   i m = 2 (0, 4) j m = -1 (0, 15)

2. (0 ,0)

3. a y = 2x + 3 b y = 4x - 2
   c y = 4x + 6 d y = -2x + 3
   e y = $1/3$x - 1 f y = 12x

4. a m = 2 b y = 2x + 4

5. a (i) m=$2/9$ (ii) (0,2) (iii) y=$2/9$x+2
   b (i) m=1 (ii) (0,0) (iii) y=x
   c (i) m=$1/9$ (ii) (0,3) (iii) y=$1/9$x+3

---

   d (i) m=-$1/3$ (ii) (0,5) (iii) y=-$1/3$x+5
   e (i) m=$4/5$ (ii) (0,-1) (iii) y=$4/5$x-1
   f (i) m=-2 (ii) (0,-1) (iii) y= -2x-1

6. a 2 b $1/4$ c y=$1/4$x+2

7. a y=$5/4$x+1 b y=-$1/6$x+2
   c y=$1/2$x d y=4

8. a see diagram b m=$1/2$
   c (0,2) d y=$1/2$x+2

9. y = 5x+30

10. graph 1 m=$5/2$ graph2 m=$4/5$
    graph 1 is steeper

11. a y = $3/4$x - 2 b y = $3/5$x + 3
    c y = -x + 4 d y = $1/8$x - 1

12. a B b C c E
    d D e A f F

13. a y = x + 1 b y = $1/6$x + 5
    c y= -4x - 2 d y = 3x - 5

14. both have gradients of $3/2$ thus parallel.

15. m_1=$5/11$ m_2=$11/26$
    gradients different, so not parallel.

16. a y = 5x + 3 b y = -x - 6

17. y = 2x - 2 18. y = $1/2$x + 1

19. a y = 5x - 14 b y =-$1/2$x - $3/2$

Exercise 6·5

1. m=-$2/3$ (0,$1/3$)

2. m=$3/2$ (0,-$3/4$)

3. a m = -$1/2$ (0,-$3/2$) b m = -$1/2$(0,$1/2$)
   c m = 1 (0,-$1/3$) d m = 3 (0,-2)
   e m = -2 (0,16) f m = -3 (0,-1)
   g m = -$1/3$ (0,-1) h m = $1/4$ (0,-4)

4. a y = -2x+4 b see diagram

5. see diagrams 6. m = 1 (0,2)

7. a m = 3 (0,5) b m = $1/2$ (0,-$1/4$)
   c m = -2 (0,5) d m = -2 (0,4)
   e m = -$1/4$ (0,$3/2$) f m = $5/4$ (0,$1/4$)

8. m = $1/2$ (0,-2)

Exercise 6·6

1. a,c,d and f

2. a
hours(h)	0	1	2	3	4
pay(£p)	0	6	12	18	24

   b see diagram c m = 6 (0,0)
   d p = 6h e (i) £48 (ii) £75
   f 12 hours

3. a
hours(h)	0	1	2	3	4
pay(£p)	0	9.50	19	28.50	38

   see diagram b p=9.5h
   c £57 d 23 hours

4. a
Length(Lm)	0	1	2	3	4
Hours(H)	0	3	6	9	12

   see diagram b H=3L c 15 hours

5. a
Time(t)	0	1	2	3	4
Roses(R)	0	7	14	21	28

   see diagram b R=7t t = 5hours

6. a (i)£60 (ii)£115 b 6 hours

7. a (i) £30 (ii) £5 an hour
   b (ii m = 5 (ii) (0,30)
   c C=5t+30 d (i) £65 (ii) £7750
   e 5 hours

8. a C=5h+20 b £45

9. a m=-10 b H = -10s+100
   c 50m d 10 sec

10. a
Days(d)	1	2	3	4
Cost(£C)	25	35	45	55

    b see diagram c C = 10d + 15
    d £85

11.
a
Days(d)	0	1	2	3	4
Cost(£C)	5	11	17	23	29

b see diagram   c $C = 6D+5$, 9 days

12. a $F=20h+60$ b $C=5d+10$
   c $H=-2t+20$ d $T=4h-6$

13. a Hire-a-car

Days(d)	0	1	2	3	4
Cost(£C)	40	50	60	70	80

Car Rent Co.

Days(d)	0	1	2	3	4
Cost(£C)	10	30	50	70	90

b see diagram   c 3 dayd

d Hire-a-car $H=10d+40$
   Car Rent Co. $C=20d+10$

e (i) either   (ii) Hire-a-car

Exercise 6·7

1. $y=\tfrac{1}{2}x+4$
2. a $y=\tfrac{1}{2}x+3\tfrac{1}{2}$ b $y=3x-17$
   c $y=-x+11$ d $y=-\tfrac{3}{8}x+\tfrac{123}{8}$
3. a $y=\tfrac{1}{2}x+1$ b $y=x$
   c $y=-x+2$ d $y=-\tfrac{1}{2}x-1$
4. a $y=\tfrac{5}{7}x+\tfrac{29}{7}$ b $x=-1$
   c $y=-\tfrac{9}{7}x-7\tfrac{1}{7}$ d $y=-16x$
5. a $y=\tfrac{3}{4}x+33$ b $a=-12$

Remember Remember 6

1. $m=\tfrac{3}{12}=\tfrac{1}{4}$
2. skateboard, bike, car, garage
   $\tfrac{1}{2}$, 0.3, 20%, 0.15
3. a $m=\tfrac{3}{4}$ b $m=\tfrac{1}{2}$
   c $m=-\tfrac{1}{2}$ d $m=0$
4. a $m=1$ b $m=-1$
5. a $m=2$ (0,7) b $m=-1$ (0,1)
6. a $y=3x-2$ b $y=-x-2$
   c $y=-5x$
7. a $y=4x-3$ b $y=-\tfrac{1}{2}x-2$
8. $y=x-1$
9. a $m=-3$ (0,1) b $m=-\tfrac{3}{4}$ (0,0)
10. $y=-3x+\tfrac{3}{2}$ see diagram
11. a

Days(d)	0	1	2	3	4
Cost(£)	10	15	20	25	30

b see diagram   c $C=5d+10$

d £45   e 17 days

12. $y=\tfrac{1}{2}x+1$

Turn off that Calculator - Non-calc. 2

1. a 25606 b 627 c 124800 d 900
   e 343 f 5471 g 3 h 722
2. a 24.936 b 26.076
   c 92.62 d 10458
   e 0.19 f 0.721
   g 0.002 h 0.0076
3. a 105 b 240 c 720
4. a $\tfrac{4}{7}$ b $\tfrac{2}{9}$ c $\tfrac{1}{4}$ d $\tfrac{13}{17}$
5. a $\tfrac{2}{3}$ b $5\tfrac{1}{2}$ c $2\tfrac{1}{3}$ d $10\tfrac{2}{5}$
6. a $\tfrac{3}{5}$ b $\tfrac{12}{25}$ c $\tfrac{1}{40}$
7. a £120 b £150 c 9g
   d 30ml e £96 f 99p
8. a 70% b $33\tfrac{1}{3}$%
9. profit £1.20   % profit 40%
10. a 15 b -20 c -11 d 18
   e -7 f 40000 g 8 i 9
   j 5 k 6
11. a $x=-4$ b $x=5$ c $x=2$ d $x=5$
12. a 2h 42 mins b 1h 15mins
13. a 18mins b 2h 27mins
   c 1h 40 mins

Answers to Chapter 7 Page 71

Exercise 7·1

1. a 19 b 37 c 52 d 3
   e 4 f 0 g -5 h -10
   i -16 j 9 k 0 l 11
   m -1 n -3 o -8 p -9
   q -20 r -31 s -14 t -37
   u 30 v -65 w -35 x -6
2. a 5 b 0 c -1 d -2
   e -3 f -8 g -17 h -7
   i -11 j -20 k -17 l -43
   m -20 n -27 o -500 p -80
   q -65 r -28 s -18 t -55
   u -6 v -90
3. a -5 b -8 c 9 d -13
   e -12 f -17 g -40 h -10
   i 10 j -3 k -1 l 0
   m -3 n -1
4. a $10x$ b $-5x$ c $3a$ d $3a$
   e $-4y$ f $-9y$ g $-2m$ h $3m$
   i $-4p$ j $-8p$ k 0 l $-6x$
   m $6x$ n $-2x$ o $-2x$ p $-12x$
   q $5a-3b$ r $5a-b$
   s $5a-4b$ t $-10a-10b$
5. a -3 b 5 c -10 d -6
   e 8 f 2 g -12 h -5
   i -10
6 a(i) 10 (ii) 0 (iii) -5
  b(i) 10m above window
  (ii) level with window
  (iii) 5m below window

Exercise 7·2

1. a 5 b 14 c 10 d 35
2. a -1 b 1 c -3 d 7
   e 5 f -6 g 1 h 0.8
   i 0 j 1 k -1 l 1
3. a $6x$ b $16x$ c $8x$ d $8p$
   e $17q$ f $17m$ g $23y$ h $40y$
   i $5x$ j $5k$ k 0 l w
   m $-7n$ n $5a$ o $4x$ p 0
4. a 6 b -11 c 7 d 3
   e 0 f -14 g -12 h $8x$
   i $22a$ j 6 k 12 l $20b$
   m $11x$ n $7p$ o $15a$ p $-14t$
   q $2c$ r $21e$ s 201 t $-60f$
   u $8t^2$ v $-22t^2$ w -100 x $-16\tfrac{1}{2}$
5. a -4 b 2 c 2
   d -8 e 4 f -6
6. a -2 b 6 c 22 d -9
   e 4 f 0 g -1 h 1
   i -7 j -5 k 5 l 5
7. a $10a$ b c c 0 d $12w$
   e $-3g$ f $-m$ g $3x-y$ h $4p-5q$
   i $4a$ j $2p^2$ k $2x^2+5y^2+7z^2$

Exercise 7·3

1. a -10 b -49 c -27 d -25
   e -32 f -45 g -66 h -30
   i -56 j -8 k -44 l -63
   m $-8a$ n $-20y$ o $-20p$ p $-45x^2$
   q -10 r -9 s -7 t -7
   u -4 v -6 w -8 x $-2a$
2. a 25 b -8 c -24 d -10
   e 21 f -45 g -4 h -27
   i -70 j -1 k -3 l -13
3. a 16 b 12 c 54 d 56
   e 40 f 81 g 17 h 30
   i 1 j 90 k 250 l 2000
   m 5 n 9 o 4 p 5
   q 6 r 7 s 10 t 30
   u 13 v 40 w 80 x 71
4. a -4 b 4 c 70 d 2
   e -3 f 2 g 20 h 45
   i 6 j -36 k $21a^2$ l $-40p^3$
   m 16 n 49 o $100y^2$ p 10
   q -1 r 16 s 1 t 2

---

u 0 v $2p$ w $16a$ x $10ab$
5. a 0 b -1 c 13 d -6
   e 5 f 26 g -19 h 3
   i -5 j 25 k 0 l 2
6. a ab b $-ab$ c $-ab$ d ab
   e y^2 f $6y^2$ g $25x^2$ h p^3
   i w^2 j $40t^2$ k x^2y^2 l w^2y^2
   m $-w^2y^2$ n 5 o -5 p $-6b$
   q $-2a$ r x
7. a £2000   b A loss of £2000
   c 60 passengers

Remember Remember 7

1. a -1 b -18 c 4 d 35
   e -17 f -13 g -33 h 12
   i -10 j 5 k 210 l -610
2. a $13x$ b $-5x$ c $7a$ d $6y$
   e $-8b$ f $9e$ g $-10m$ h $2x$
   i x j $-c$ k $-21w$ l $4a+5b$
3. a -3 b 3 c -8 d 16
   e 9 f -10 g 2 h -10
4. a 8 b 20 c 2 d -6
   e 1 f 0 g $8x$ h $11x$
   i x j $-8x$ k $5x$ l 0
5. a -3 b -1 c 2 d -5
   e 1 f -5 g 5 h -4
6. a -9 b -35 c -9 d 0
   e $-10x$ f $-21y$ g $-6x^2$ h -10
   i $-10x$ j $-2p$ k -5 l -28
   m -48 n -10 o 70 p 200
   q 5 r 10 s 40 t 4
   u $12a^2$ v 49 w 64 x 24
7. a 0 b 3 c 29
   d -10 e 27 f 108
   g 117 h 45 i -21

Answers to Chapter 8 Page 77

Exercise 8·1

1. a $78cm^2$ b $78.5cm^2$
   c $225cm^2$ d $68cm^2$
   e $80m^2$ f $77mm^2$
   g $420cm^2$ h $150cm^2$
2. a $139cm^2$ b $126cm^2$
   c $58.5cm^2$ d $91cm^2$
   e $277cm^2$ f $156cm^2$

Exercise 8·2

1. $350cm^3$ 2. 3cm
3. a $37500cm^3$ b 37500ml c 37.5 litres
4. 3.75 litres
5. a 67200 b 24cm
6. a 480000 b 80 mins
7. 75cm
8. a $1m^3$ b $1,000,000cm^3$
   c $1m^3 = 1,000,000cm^3$
9. a $8,000,000cm^3$ b $8m^3$
10. $9,000,000cm^3 = 9m^3$
11. a $2,067,000cm^3$ b $2.067m^3$
12. a $60cm^2$ b $280cm^2$
13. $792cm^2$ 14. $236cm^2$
15. a $1340cm^2$ b £42.88
16. a 30cm b $2800cm^2$
17. $V= 3000cm^3$ - surface area = $1100cm^2$

Exercise 8·3

1. $144cm^3$ 2. $225cm^3$ 3. $1200cm^3$
4. 8cm 5. 26cm 6. 6cm
7. a $24cm^2$ b $288cm^3$
8. $1800cm^3$ 9. a $20cm^2$ b $240cm^3$
10. 8.5cm

Exercise 8·4

1. 2009.6cm³   2. 1271.7cm³
3. a 6cm   b 2034.72cm³
4. A = 791.28cm³ , B = 785cm³ => A
5. 226080cm³ = 226.08 litres
6. a 62800cm³ = 62.8 litres   b 125 tins
7. Tank = 60000cm³ = 60 litres
   Bucket = 3077.2cm³ = 3.0772 litres
   It can be filled 20 times
8. 9.54 litres
9. a 1.1775cm³ b 22.73g c £418.15
10. 20410cm³   11. 13.74 litres
12. 791.28cm³
13. a 502.4cm³ b 13990.4cm³
14. 353.25cm³   15. 3.26cm

Exercise 8·5

1. 39cm³   2. 50cm³   3. 84cm³
4. 196cm³   5. 732cm³
6. a 5.2cm b 51.9cm³   7. 235.5cm³
8. a 200.96cm³   b 61.23m³
   c 1004.8cm³   d 153.07mm³
9. a 153.86cm³   b 7.8cm
10. 27468.72kg   11. 4.82litres
12. 3709.125cm³
13. a 602.88cm³   b 348.54cm³

Exercise 8·6

1. 502.4cm³
2. 621.72cm³
3. a 20cm   b 7536cm²
4. a 314cm²   b 1004.8cm² c 1632.8cm²
5. 238.64cm² - 188.4cm² - 50.24cm²
6. 6104.16cm²   7. 17.62m²
8. 1075ml

Exercise 8·7

1. 7234.56cm³   2. 33493mm³
3. 523.33cm³
4. a 32708.33cm³   b 32.7litres
5. 197820cm³   6. 26451.36cm³
7. a 1216   b 9764.48g

Remember Remember 8

1. a 648 cm³   b 468 cm²
2. 288 litres
3. a 495 cm³   b 4500 cm³
4. V = 28260cm³ = 28·26 litres
5. a 5000 ml   b 63·7 cm
6. a 768 cm³   b 891 cm³
7. 565·2 cm³
8. 6908 cm²
9. a 113·04 cm²   b 527·52 cm²
   c 753·6 cm²
10. 17·15 m³
11. 28·94 litres
12. 10098·24 cm³

Exercise 9·1

1. a $12m$ b $2p$ c $14x$
   d $2b + 7c$ e $2v$ f $10g - 3r$
   g $a^2 - h^2$ h 0
2. a $15c$ b $18u$ c t^2
   d $6p^2$ e $9s^2$ f $6ky$
   g $32c$ h $30p$ i $54a^2$
   j $42v^2$ k $3h^2$ l $48n^3$
   m $15p^2$ n $64w^2$ o $8k^3$
   p $27f^3$ q $4x^2y^2$ r $27k^3m^3$
   s $16m^4n^4$ t $16v^3w^3$
3. a $8xy$ b $15x^2y$ c $24xy^2$
   d $7xy^2$ e $2x^2y$ f $8x^3y$

g $9xy^3$ h $3x^4y$ i $12x^2y^3$
j $10x^2y^3$ k $6x^3y^2$ l $3x^3y^3$
m $16x^2y^2$ n $6x^3y^3$ o $24x^3y^2$
p $10x^4y^4$
4. a 12 b 3 c $2q$
   d $3g$ e 2 f $10n$
   g $4x$ h $8a^2$ i $8ab$
   j $4ab$ k $4a^2$ l $4a$
   m 4 n $3xy$

Exercise 9·2

1. a $2b + 8$ b $5a + 5$ c $8d - 48$
   d $9 - 9g$ e $3m + 3n$ f $7c - 7e$
   g $33 + 11y$ h $30x-150$ i $18p + 3$
   j $15 - 20q$ k $88x - 56y$ l $ab +7a$
   m $gh - 10g$ n $6x + x^2$ o $3ek + 8gk$
   p $40u^2 - 4uv$ q $12a + 21b + 6$
   r $9p + 9q - 36r$ s $18 - 30f - 12g$
   t $x^2 - xy - 9xz$ u $-5a - 5$
   v $-3x - x^2$ w $-6g^2 + g$
   x $-7xy + 11x^2$
2. a $2q + 11$ b $3e + 9$ c $5t + 22$
   d $6u + 5$ e $4p + 1$ f $3s - 2$
   g $10f + 8$ h $10h + 9$ i $k + 20$
   j $4z + 12$ k $50 + 7c$ l $14b + 14$
   m $17m - 9$ n $13w + 6$ o $19r - 8$
   p $6y - 1$ q $16a + 30p$ r $51g + 20h$
   s $30x - 30y$ t $150v + 10n$
   u $2q + 9$ v $4w - 24e$
   w $2x + 1$ x $22 - 2x$
3. a $7m + 10$ b $7b + 18$ c $11c + 26$
   d $6k + 6$ e $9g$ f $9a + 2$
   g $19 - 4p$ h $12 - 6u$ i $26y + 8$
   j $26t + 16$ k $38 - 2c$ l $21x + 7y$
4. a $3x + 1$ b $x + 2$ c $x + 3$
   d $5x - 2$ e $17x + 4$ f $2x + 30$
   g $3x + 21$ h $30x$ i $4x - 2$
   j $x^2 + 6x - 5$ k $x^2 - 2x - 5$
   l $8x^2 - 8x + 16$
5. a $1 - 2y$ b $12 - 6p$ c $9 - d$
   d $6h + 19$ e $20 - 9c$ f $2u + 10$
   g $10b - 21$ h $10 - 2n$ i $4m - 60$
   j $2x - 100$ k $5k - 22$ l $14w - 2$

Exercise 9·3

1. a $x^2 + 4x + 3$ b $x^2 + 8x + 15$
   c $x^2 + 6x + 8$ d $x^2 + 7x + 12$
   e $p^2 + 10p + 25$ f $p^2 + 7p + 6$
   g $p^2 + 5p + 6$ h $2x^2 + 3x + 1$
   i $3x^2 + 7x + 2$ j $2x^2 + 12x + 18$
   k $4a^2 + 16a + 16$ l $9y^2 + 6y + 1$
   m $8m^2 + 10m + 3$ n $25m^2 + 15m + 2$
   o $16g^2 + 28g + 6$ p $x^2 + 9x + 20$
   q $6x^2 + 21x + 18$ r $100w^2 + 20w + 1$
   s $9x^2 + 24x + 16$ t $4y^2 + 32y + 64$
2. a $x^2 - 5x + 6$ b $x^2 - 3x + 2$
   c $x^2 - 7x + 12$ d $p^2 - 8x + 16$
   e $-p^2 + 10p - 25$ f $p^2 - 2p + 1$
   g $2x^2 - 5x + 6$ h $4x^2 - 10x + 4$
   i $5x^2 - 11x + 2$ j $2x^2 - 9x + 9$
   k $4a^2 - 12a + 9$ l $8a^2 - 14a + 3$
   m $4m^2 - 12m + 5$ n $6c^2 - 22m + 12$
   o $25x^2 - 10x + 1$ p $4w^2 - 4w + 1$
3. a $x^2 + 3x - 10$ b $y^2 + 3y - 4$
   c $a^2 + a - 6$ d $b^2 + b - 2$
   e $m^2 - 2m - 15$ f $-n^2 - 2n + 3$
   g $2x^2 + 5x - 3$ h $5a^2 - 19a - 4$
   i $3u^2 - 2u - 8$ j $9x^2 - 25$
   k $14a^2 - 12a - 2$ l $20h^2 - 7h - 6$
   m $x^2 + 3xy + 2y^2$ n $x^2 - xy - 2y^2$
   o $x^2 + xy - 2y^2$ p $x^2 - 3xy + 2y^2$
   q $3a^2 + 7ab + 4b^2$ r $2p^2 - pq - 2q^2$
   s $2x^2 + 9x + 10$ t $a^2 - 3a + 2$
   u $-2b^2 + 7b + 15$ v $p^2 - q^2$
   w $-9y^2 + 8y + 1$ x $20k^2 - 9k + 1$
4. a $x^3 + 2x^2 + x + 2$ b $x^3 + 3x^2 + 5x + 15$
   c $x^3 - 2x^2 + 3x - 6$ d $2x^3 - 8x^2 + 3x - 12$
   e $2x^3 + x^2 - 4x - 2$ f $10x^3 - 6x^2 +15x- 9$
   g $x^4 + 7x^2 + 12$ h $x^4 + 3x^2 - 10$

i $x^3 + x^2y + xy^2 + y^3$ j $2x^3 - x^2y +2xy^2-y^3$
k $3x^3 + 2x^2y -2xy^2-2y^3$ l $x^4 - y^4$
5. a $(x + 5)(3x + 1) = 3x^2 + 16x + 5$
   b $(5x - 3)(2x - 4) = 10x^2 - 26x + 12$
   c $(x + y)(3x + y) = 3x^2 + 4xy + y^2$
   d $(5a + 2b)(3a - 2b) = 15a^2 - 4ab - 4b^2$
6. a $x^3 + 6x^2 + 9x + 2$ b $x^3 + 6x^2 + 3x - 2$
   c $x^3 - 4x + 3$ d $6a^3 + 13a^2 + 9a +2$
   e $6p^3 - 7p^2 - 10p + 8$ f $8y^3 - 2y^2 - 3y + 15$
7. a $x^2 + 6x + 9$ b $x^2 + 14x + 49$
   c $x^2 + 2xy + y^2$ d $y^2 - 4y + 4$
   e $y^2 - 12y + 36$ f $x^2 - 2xy + y^2$
   g $4x^2 + 4x + 1$ h $9x^2 + 24x + 16$
   i $16a^2 - 8a + 1$ j $4b^2 - 40b + 100$
   k $x^2 + 6xy + 9y^2$ l $a^2 - 14ab + 49b^2$
   m $4x^2 - 12hx + 9h^2$ n $16v^2 - 40vw + 25w^2$
   o $4x^2 + 4x + 4$ p $y^4 - 8y^2 + 16$
   q $p^2 + 2 + 1/p^2$ r $q^2 - 2 + 1/q^2$
   s $4x^2 - 2 + 1/4x^2$ t $25x^2 - 2 + 1/25x^2$
8. a $(3x + 2)^2 = 9x^2 + 12x + 4$
   b $(5x - 1)^2 = 25x^2 - 10x + 1$
   c $(3x + 6y)^2 = 9x^2 + 36xy + 36y^2$

Exercise 9·4

1. a $-6x + 24$ b $7x + 14$
   c $-7a + 25$ d $2b - 2$
   e $x + 10$ f $5x + 1$
   g $8y^2 + 12y$ h $8p^2 + 3p - 1$
   i $13x^2 - 21x + 4$ j $10x^2 - 14x - 11$
   k $20g^2 + 4g + 29$ l $2q^2 + 9q + 3$
   m $4x^2 - 15x - 11$ n $12x^2 + 5x - 7$
   o $3x^2 + 2x - 17$ p $5x^2 - 52x + 20$
   q $10a - 75$ r $6w$
   s $-x^2 +44x + 2$ t $14x^2 - 36x + 21$
2. a $x^3 - 6x^2 + 12x - 8$ b $x^3 + 3x^2 + 3x + 1$
   c $a^3 - 3a^2 + 3a - 1$ d $x^3 + 9x^2 + 27x +27$
   e $k^3 - 9k^2 + 27x - 27$ f $8x^3 + 12x^2 +6x + 1$
   g $27x^3 - 54x^2 + 36x - 8$
   h $3m^3 + 36m^3 + 144m + 192$
   i $2x^3 - 30x^2 + 150x - 250$
   j $a^3 + 3a^2b + 3ab^2 + b^3$
   k $p^3 - 3p^2q + 3pq^2 - q^3$
   l $8x^3 - 24x^2y + 24xy^2 - 8y^3$

Exercise 9·5

1. a $5(a + b)$ b $2(x + 4y)$ c $2(3g + 2h)$
   d $p(q + r)$ e $c(d + 1)$ f $n(m + n)$
   g $v(w^2 + 1)$ h $2a(b + c)$ i $4(2x + 3y)$
   j $8(5b - 2a)$ k $2d(c - 2)$ l $3p(2 + 7p)$
2. a $5(a + 5)$ b $3(x + 4)$ c $9(p - 4)$
   d $11(v + w)$ e $6(p - q)$ f $10(c - 2h)$
   g $7(m - 4)$ h $12(n + 5)$ i $2(2x + 3y)$
   j $7(2u - 3v)$ k $5(4x - 5y)$
   l $4(r - 8u)$ m $3(3s + 8)$ n $11(2u - 1)$
   o $8(3x - 7y)$ p $6(3a + 2c)$
3. a $b(5 + c)$ b $x(7 - v)$ c $p(q + r)$
   d $a(a + 6)$ e $t(8 - t)$ f $c(c - 4)$
   g $4x(m + n)$ h $5a(d - 2a)$ i $17s(r - 1)$
   j $y(3y + 7)$ k $4x(3x - 5y)$ l $q(6q + 1)$
   m $3d(3 + 7d)$ n $a(1 - 13a)$ o $8y(y - 8c)$
   p $8n(3m + 4n)$
4. a $a(a + 4b - 7)$ b $x(8y - 8z + 1)$
   c $p^2(p + 1)$ d $4d(d^2 - 4)$
   e $ac(a + c)$ f $6rs(3s - 5)$
   g $4x(2x - 3a)$ h $0·2h(g + j)$

Exercise 9·6

1. a $(x - 2)(x + 2)$ b $(a - 4)(a + 4)$
   c $(b - 5)(b + 5)$ d $(x - 1)(x + 1)$
   e $(1 - k)(1 + k)$ f $(7 - w)(7 + w)$
   g $(8 - h)(8 + h)$ h $(10 - x)(10 + x)$
   i $(a - b)(a + b)$ j $(w - v)(w + v)$
   k $(2a - 1)(2a + 1)$ l $(1 - 5y)(x + 5y)$
   m $(6 - 7p)(6 + 7p)$ n $(9a - 2b)(9a + 2b)$
   o $(11v - 10w)(11v + 10w)$
   p $(8p - 9q)(8p + 9q)$ q $(1 - 4a)(1 + 4a)$
   r $(5 - 9x)(5 + 9x)$ s $(7 - 2k)(7 + 2k)$
   t $(1 - 12y)(1 + 12y)$
2. a $2(x - 3)(x + 3)$ b $3(p - 1)(p + 1)$
   c $5(a + 4)(a - 4)$ d $6(v - 2)(v + 2)$

e $4(g - 2)(g + 2)$ f $7(x - y)(x + y)$
g $6(v + 5)(v - 5)$ h $10(a - 3b)(a + 3b)$
i $19(x - y)(x + y)$ j $a(w - v)(w + v)$
k $\pi(m - n)(m + n)$ l $k(p - 6q)(p + 6q)$
m $k(p - 3q)(p + 3q)$ n $d(d + 2)(d - 2)$
o $3x(3x - 4)(3x + 4)$ p $(a^2 - 1)(a^2 + 1)$
q $(1 - k^2)(1 + k^2)$ r $(p^2 - q^2)(p^2 + q^2)$
s $(1 - 4y^2)(1 + 4y^2)$ t $3(d^2 - 4)(d^2 + 4)$

3. a Yellow area $= k^2 - 5^2 = (k - 5)(k + 5)$
    b $47.25 cm^2$

Exercise 9·7

1. a $(x + 1)(x + 1)$ b $(a + 2)(a + 1)$
    c $(k + 5)(k + 2)$ d $(d + 7)(d + 2)$
    e $(x - 1)(x - 1)$ f $(b - 3)(b - 3)$
    g $(c - 6)(c - 3)$ h $(w - 3)(w - 8)$
    i $(x + 4)(x - 1)$ j $(n + 3)(n - 2)$
    k $(p + 5)(p - 3)$ l $(q + 6)(q - 3)$
    m $(x - 4)(x + 1)$ n $(r - 7)(r + 1)$
    o $(y - 6)(y + 2)$ p $(h - 10)(h + 2)$

2. a $(x - 6)(x + 1)$ b $(x + 3)(x + 5)$
    c $(x - 5)(x + 10)$ d $(x - 9)(x - 2)$
    e $(y - 5)(y + 3)$ f $(y + 8)(y - 1)$
    g $(y - 7)(y - 2)$ h $(y + 6)(y + 2)$
    i $(a - 7)(a + 7)$ j $(a - 11)(a + 1)$
    k $(a + 6)(a - 5)$ l $(a - 4)(a - 5)$
    m $(c - 5)(c - 3)$ n $(c + 7)(c - 3)$
    o $(c - 9)(c + 3)$ p $(c - 8)(c - 2)$
    q $(k + 10)(k - 1)$ r $(k - 9)(k + 1)$
    s $(k - 7)(k + 5)$ t $(k + 6)(k - 4)$
    u $(v + 4)(v - 2)$ v $(v - 3)(v - 10)$
    w $(v - 4)(v + 3)$ x $(v - 8)(v - 5)$

3. a $(2x + 3)(x + 1)$ b $(2a + 1)(a + 3)$
    c $(3y + 2)(2y + 1)$ d $(3g + 5)(g + 3)$
    e $(6k - 1)(2k - 1)$ f $(2b - 1)(b - 3)$
    g $(4c - 5)(2c - 1)$ h $(3x + 4)(x - 2)$
    i $(3a + 1)(a - 2)$ j $(5p - 1)(p + 1)$
    k $(2m - 1)(m + 1)$ l $(3q + 1)(q - 1)$
    m $(4c + 3)(2c - 1)$ n $(4n - 1)(2n + 3)$
    o $(4w - 5)(3w + 1)$ p $(2c + 3)(2c + 3)$
    q $(4k + 1)(6k - 1)$ r $-(6x + 1)(3x - 1)$
    s $-(2y - 3)(y + 5)$ t $(x + 6y)(x + 2y)$
    u $(p - 12q)(p + 2q)$ v $(b + 2c)(b + c)$
    w $(a - 7b)(a + 2b)$ x $(2u + v)(u - 3v)$
    y $(3g + 4)(3g - 2)$ z $(3\sin - 2)(3\sin - 2)$

Exercise 9·8

1. $6(x + 6y)$ 2. $(p + 7)(p - 7)$
3. $(y + 3)(y + 3)$ 4. $k(k - 1)$
5. $(v - 3)(v + 2)$ 6. $(1 - a)(1 + a)$
7. $d(e + h - j)$ 8. $3(c - 2)(c + 2)$
9. $m(m - 8)$ 10. $(q - 1)(q - 1)$
11. $(b - 1)(b + 1)$ 12. $b(b - 1)$
13. $(b - 2)(b + 1)$ 14. $2(t - 3)(t + 3)$
15. $2x(x - 16)$ 16. $a^2(a - 1)$
17. $(2p + 5)(p - 1)$ 18. $(3n + 1)(3n + 1)$
19. $(9 - x)(9 + x)$ 20. $2(5 - c)(5 + c)$
21. $6y(3 - y)$ 22. $(9 - 2b)(9 + 2b)$
23. $(2k + 1)(k - 1)$ 24. $14(x^2 + 3y^2)$
25. $14(m - 2n)(m + 2n)$ 26. $(4x - 1)(4x - 1)$
27. $3pq(p - 3q)$ 28. $(u - 1)(u - 1)$
29. $3x(x - 3)(x + 3)$ 30. $(3a - 2)(2a + 3)$
31. $4(x + 2)(x - 1)$ 32. $10w(1 - 2w)(1 + 2w)$
33. $a(k - m)(k + m)$ 34. $(2x + 3)(x - 5)$
35. $p^5(p^2 - p - 1)$ 36. $(x + 3)(x - 3)(x^2 + 9$

Remember Remember 9

1. a $24x$ b g^2 c $32ab$ d $50p^2$
    e $4m^2n$ f $3xq^3$ g 20   h $4x^2$
2. a $5a + 10$ b $8 - 24r$ c $9a + a^2$
    d $-6x^2 + 12xy$
3. a $3x + 10$ b $y + 36$ c $16 - 3q$
    d $9w + 14$ e $18 - 8d$ f $3q + 2$
    g $5 - 5u$ h $2k + 6$ i $14m - 2$
4. a $a^2 + 9x + 14$ b $b^2 - 9b + 18$
    c $c^2 + 7c - 18$ d $12d^2 + 20d + 3$
    e $6e^2 - 17e + 5$ f $14y^2 + 19y - 3$
    g $4k^2 - 20k + 25$ h $m^2 + 4 + 4/m^2$
    i $n^3 + 3n^2 + 3n + 1$ j $8s^3 - 36s^2 + 54s - 27$
    k $7x$ l $5x^2 - 12x + 1$
    m $6y^3 + 5y^2 - 10y + 3$

---

5. a $4(a + 6)$ b $7(3x - 4b)$ c $c(d + g)$
    d $2b(b - 5)$ e $n^2(n - 1)$ f $12kh(2k + 3h)$
    g $(r - 10)(r + 10)$ h $5(q - 2)(q + 2)$
    i $(w - 8)(w - 2)$ j $(2m + 3)(m + 2)$
    k $(5b - 2)(b - 5)$ l $(x - 2y)(x + y)$
    m $(3x - y)(2x + 3y)$ n $(x - 7y)(x - 7y)$
    o $(1 - 5a)(1 + 5a)$ p $(9n + 9)(n - 2)$
    q $3p(p - 16)$ r $7ab(a^2 - 3)$
    s $17st(t - u)(t + u)$ t $(x^2 - y^2)(x^2 - y^2)$

6. a $2k + 3$ b $k + 2$
    c $(2k + 3)(k + 2) = 2k^2 + 7k + 6$
    d $2k^2 + 6k + 14$

Turn off that Calculator - Non-calc. 3

1. a 6575   b 837   c 360   d 27360
    e 12500   f 6300000   g 880   h 7036
2. £2220
3. a 4·75   b 6·716   c 10·251   d 0·18
    e 70   f 115·644   g 23·444   h 2·168
4. a 264   b 63   c 600
5. a $^2/_3$ b $^8/_9$ c $^2/_3$ d $^1/_4$
6. a $1^1/_4$ b $4^3/_4$ c 9   d $^1/_4$
7. 100 pupils
8. a £282   b £23·50   c £42·30
9. a £1·60   b £4·20   c 96p
    d £9   e £75   f £30
10. £1632
11. a 7   b −29   c −17   d 40
    e −60   f −45   g 121   h −5
    i −45   j −6   k −18   l 35
12. 36°
13. 23rd May

Exercise 10·1

1. 5·5 cm
2. a 12·56 cm   b 11·78 cm
    c 6·98 cm   d 18·84 cm
3. a 25·12 cm   b 19·63
    c 18·14   d 37·68 cm
4. a 18·84 mm   b 54·95 cm
    c 39·08 m   d 52·33 cm
5. a 41·8 cm   b 74·89 mm
6. 16·28 cm

Exercise 10·2

1. 39·25 cm²
2. a 26·17 cm²   b 42·39 cm²
3. a 274·75 cm²   b 52·33 cm²
4. a 43·96 cm²   b 802·44 cm²
    c 83·41 cm²   d 54·51 cm²
    e 128·22 cm²   f 69·32 cm²
    g 163·54 cm²

Exercise 10·3

1. a (i) 55·8 cm   (ii) 1116·44 cm²
    b (i) 12·95 mm   (ii) 35·62 mm²
2. 1395·56 cm²
3. 157 cm²
4. 24·42 cm
5. a 115·13 m   b 105·54 m
6. 11·6 m
7. a 29·34 cm   b 53·22 cm²
8. a 113·04 cm²   b 72 cm²   c 41·04
9. 182·18

Exercise 10·4

1. 45°
2. a 120°   b 240°
3. 180°

---

4. a 147·4°   b 169·8°   c 223°   d 107·5°
5. a 330°   b 5077·38 mm²

Exercise 10·5

1. 45°   2. a 115·6°   b 238·9°
3. 300·4°
4. a 120·0°   b 156·0°   c 107·5°   d 301·0°
5. a 202·5°   b 63·6 cm

Exercise 10·6

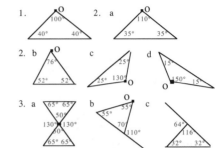

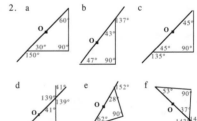

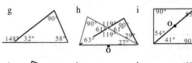

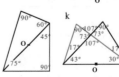

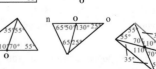

4. 3
5. a 89 mm   b 32 mm
6. a 6·3 mm   b 17·3 mm
7. 530·66 cm²
8. a 9 cm   b 6 cm
9. 11·87 m
10. a 18·3 cm   b 45·3 cm
11. a 48 cm   b 68 cm

Exercise 10·7

1. a 30°   b 17°   c 48°   d 34°
    e 48°
2. a   b   c
    d   e   f
    g   h   i
    j   k   l
    m   n   o
3. 13 cm

---

4. a 21·54 cm b 13·42 mm
c 12·49 cm d 21·56 cm

5. 17·6 cm 6. 907·46 mm^2

7. 6·3 m 8. 8·28 m

9. (longest)^2 = (shortest)^2 = 72·25 by converse of Pythagoras T lies on circumference.

10. a 40 cm b 24 cm c 872 cm

Exercise 10·8

1. a 90° b 55°

2. a 38 b 75° c 15° d 60°
e 45° f 47° g 32°

3.

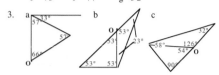

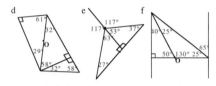

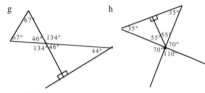

4. 15·5 cm

5. a 9·2 cm b 3·4 cm

6. 346·185 cm^2 7. 21·2 cm

8. 2·4 cm

9. a 18 cm b 22·6 cm

10. 8·9 cm 11. 62·1 cm

Exercise 10·9

1. a 125°

2. ∠AOB = 138° ∠CAO = 90° ∠CBO = 90°

3. a 24° b 132° c 66° d 24°

4. 22·4 cm

5. 706·5 cm^2

6. a (i) 10 cm (ii) 28 cm b 26·2 cm

7. 60·9 cm

Remember Remember 10

1. a 11·8 m b 41·9 mm

2. a 88·3 m^2 b 209 mm^2

3. a 135° b 100° c 300° d 160°

4. a x = 44° b y = 50°
c z = 50° d w = 37·5°

5. a 6 cm b 7·81 m c 20·6 mm

6. a 10·6 cm^2 b 19·39 m

7. 26·37 m b 40·03 m^2

Maths 1 NAB Practice Page 114

Outcome 1

1. a £16 b £8·75 c 94p
d £1·50 e £560 f £80

2. 1·35 m

3. a 655·64 b £1255·83

4. £102960 5. £50494·25

6. £4050

7. a 4000 b 30000 c 40 d 700

8. a 4300 b 44000 c 530 d 860

9. a 8180 b 64700 c 6090 d 147000

10. a 6·86 b 19·3 c 0·235 d 0·0570

Outcome 2

11. a 120 cm^3 b 42·5 cm^3
c 495 cm^3 d 150·5 cm^3

12. a 960 cm^3 b 98 cm^3

13. a 804 cm^3 b 4850 cm^3

14. 43·96 litres

15. a 565·2 cm^3 b 220·8 mm^3

Outcome 3

16. a 523 cm^3 b 56520 cm^3

17. a $^7/_3$ b $^2/_3$

18. a $^2/_3$ b 2

19. a −2 b $-^2/_7$

20. a −1 b −4 c 1

21. a m = 2 (0, 3) b m = 3 (0, −1)
c m = 1 (0, −5) d m = 1/2 (0, 2)
e m = −2 (0, −1) f m = −4 (0, 1)

22. a m = 2 (0, 0) $y = 2x$
b m = 2 (0, −2) $y = 2x - 2$
c m = $^1/_2$ (0, 2) $y = {}^1/_2 x + 2$
d m = −2 (0, 1) $y = -2x + 1$
e m = $-^2/_3$ (0, 3) $y = -{}^2/_3 x + 3$
f m = −1 (0, 3) $y = -x + 3$

Outcome 4

23. a $8x + 40$ b $5p + 10$
c $3a - 18$ d $9w - 27$
e $18n - 12$ f $df + 6d$
g $4g^2 + 5gh$ h $31w - 3w^2$

24. a $4a + 4b - 12$ b $y^3 + 4y$
c $5e - 5f + 55$ d $3d - d^3$

25. a $x^2 + 8x + 15$ b $x^2 + 10x + 16$
c $x^2 + 6x - 7$ d $h^2 + h - 12$
e $k^2 - 10k + 25$ f $q^2 - 4q - 21$

26. a $8x^2 - 14x - 15$ b $12e^2 + 8e - 15$
c $9e^2 + 9e - 10$ d $a^2 - 11a + 30$
e $-2w^2 + 17x + 30$ f $5r^2 - 16r + 3$

27. a $w^2 - 4w + 4$ b $e^2 + 20e + 100$
c $9x^2 + 6x + 1$ d $25a^2 - 20a + 100$
e $9x^2 + 6x + 1$ f $25a^2 - 20a + 4$
g $9a^2 + 12ab + 4b^2$ h $16t^2 - 8ts + s^2$

28. a $8(a + b)$ b $5(t + s)$
c $10(u - v)$ d $3(3d - 2e)$
e $5(2a + 3b)$ f $4(3m - 2n)$
g $b(e + u)$ h $x(n - m)$

29. a $(x - 5)(x + 5)$ b $(a - 9)(a + 9)$
c $(6 - w)(6 + w)$ d $(e - f)(e + f)$

30. a $(x + 5)(x + 2)$ b $(w + 8)(w + 2)$
c $(g + 9)(g + 2)$ d $(w - 2)(w - 2)$
e $(d - 4)(d - 4)$ f $(m - 6)(m - 2)$
g $(b - 4)(b - 9)$ h $(y - 1)(y - 1)$
i $(e - 10)(e - 5)$ j $(f + 15)(f + 1)$
k $(r - 5)(r + 2)$ l $(e - 6)(e + 2)$
m $(z + 5)(z - 4)$ n $(c + 7)(c - 2)$

31. a 4·99 cm b 42·52 cm

32. a 99·15 cm^2 b 181·1 cm^2

33. a 31° 59° b 114° 24°

34. x = 4·5 cm

35. a m = 58° b n = 115°

36. 11·4 cm

37. 55°

Answers to Chapter 11 Page 120

Exercise 11·1

1. a 0·424 b 1·072 c 1·376 d 11·430
e 1·428 f 0·287 g 0·070 h 2·050
i 8·144 j 1·000 k 2·174 l 0·061

2. Yes, it is !

3. a 16 cm b 10 cm c 1·6 d 1·6

Exercise 11·2

1. 32·2 cm

2. a 10·0 b 7·4 c 5·7
d 78·6 e 7·7 f 20·8 (all cm)

3. 56 m 4. 8·1 m 5. 15·5 m

6. 125 m 7. 41·3 m 8. 51·2 ft

Exercise 11·3

1. a 25° b 56° c 14° d 6°
e 45° f 38° g 22° h 12°
i 66° j 85°

2. 21·8° 3. a 24·0° b 32·1°

4. a 38·7° b 45·0° c 71·6°
d 20·7° e 28·1° f 52·4°

5. 31·7° 6. 70·7° 7. 13·6°

8. a 10·3° b 100·3°

Exercise 11·4

1. a 0·766 b 0·500 c 0·866 d 0·995
e 0·122 f 0·477 g 0·339 h 0·951
i 0·99.. j 1·000

2. a 23·6° b 12·4° c 26·4° d 73·7°
e 7·2° f 10·5° g 30·0° h 14·5°
i 19·5° j 36·0°

3. a 17·8 b 8·8 c 105·0
d 207·4 e 2·4 f 17·8 (all cm)

4. 1·75 m 5. 0·92 m 6. 1·5 km 7. 6·3 m

8. a 60° b 8·7 m c 8·7 m same !

9. a 23·6° b 41·8° c 10·8°
d 56·4° e 58·8° f 38·7°

10. 53·1° 11. 13·7° 12. 15·5° 13. 14·9°

Exercise 11·5

1. a 0·766 b 0·174 c 0·500
d 0·866 e 0·996 f 0·609

2. a 36·9° b 69·1° c 83·6°
d 32·9° e 79·5° f 29·0°

3. a 4·2 cm b 5·7 cm c 4·2 cm

4. 22·3 cm 5. 2·71 m 6. 27·5 cm 7. 10·6 cm

8. 39·7° 9. a 33·6° b 56·4° 10. 81·1°

Exercise 11·6

1. a 6·7 b 50·5 c 172·9 (all cm)

2. 8·12 m

3. a 37·1cm b 8·1cm c 247·2 mm

4. 3·1 m

5. a 20·9cm b 19·9cm c 306·7 mm

6. 15·8 cm 7. 51·6 cm 8. 10·3 cm

Exercise 11·7

1. a 5·1 b 15·1 c 10·0
d 14·0 e 10·1 f 24·2 (all cm)

2. a 57·3° b 39·9° c 11·7°
d 35·7° e 64·6° f 30·0°

3. 39·4 m 4. 38·5° 5. 45·4 ft

6. a 7·8 m b 7·1 m 7. 13·5 m

8. 18·0 km 9. 12·8° Yes, ok

10. 118° 11. 108 cm^2 12. 3·99 m

13. 36° - Yes, ok

Remember Remember 11

1. a 10·6 cm b 39·2° c 27·7 cm

2. 64·3° 3. 33 m

4. 302 m

5. a 149·8 m & 83·9 m b 66 m

6. 036° 7. 33·1 cm

Answers to Chapter 12 Page 136

Exercise 12·1

1. a $x = 2$ b $x = 0$ c $x = 12$

d $x = 17$ e $x = 150$ f $x = -2$
g $x = -14$ h $x = 5$ i $x = -1$
j $x = 0$ k $x = -7$ l $x = -20$
2. a $x = 7$ b $a = 8$ c $b = 9$
d $p = 1$ e $e = 1\frac{1}{2}$ f $c = 0$
g $d = \frac{1}{2}$ h $y = 50$ i $r = 4\frac{1}{2}$
j $q = 2\frac{3}{4}$ k $s = 5\frac{3}{5}$ l $t = 2\frac{6}{7}$
m $k = 3\frac{1}{2}$ n $n = \frac{4}{5}$ o $h = \frac{1}{4}$
3. a $x = 4$ b $x = 5$ c $x = 6$ d $x = 2$
e $x = 4$ f $x = 3$ g $x = 7$ h $x = 1$
i $x = 8$ j $x = 11$ k $x = 3$ l $x = 10$
m $x = -1$ n $x = -1$ o $x = 4.5$ p $x = -4$
q $x = 2\frac{1}{4}$ r $x = 4\frac{1}{2}$
4. a $x = 3$ b $x = 7$
5. a $x = 3$ b $x = 5$ c $x = 4$
d $x = 7$ e $x = 5$ f $x = 6.5$
g $x = 7.5$ h $x = 6\frac{1}{5}$ i $x = 2.3$
6. a $x = 9$ b $x = 7$ c $x = 7$
d $x = 1.5$ e $x = 7.5$ f $x = 22$
g $x = 9$ h $x = -4$ i $x = 5.5$
7. a $x = 3$ b $x = 4$ c $x = 13$
d $x = 7$ e $x = 7$ f $x = 6.5$
g $x = 9$ h $x = 7$ i $x = -6$
8. a $x = 4$ b $x = 5$ c $x = 1$
d $x = 2$ e $x = 6$ f $x = 7$
g $x = 6$ h $x = 5$ i $x = -10$
9. a $x = 9$ b $x = 3$ c $x = 2$
d $x = 4$ e $x = 3$ f $x = 5$
g $x = 3$ h $x = 2$ i $x = 6$
j $x = 6$
10. a $5x = x + 120$ b $x = 30$

Exercise 12·2
1. a $x = 5$ b $x = -7$ c $x = -5$
d $x = 5$ e $x = -1$ f $x = -8$
g $x = 0.5$ h $x = 1$ i $x = 0.5$
j $x = 5$ k $x = 3$ l $x = 1.5$
2. a $x(x + 8) = (x + 3)(x + 4)$, 12 x 20 15 x 16
b $x^2 = (x + 6)(x - 3)$, 6 x 6, 12 x 3
c $x(x + 5) = (x + 8)(x - 1)$, 4 x 9, 3 x 12
d $(x - 2)(x - 4) = (x + 4)(x - 8)$,
18 x 16 and 24 x 12

Exercise 12·3
1. a $x = 12$ b $x = 20$
2. a $x = 10$ b $x = 4$ c $x = 16$
d $x = 15$ e $x = 10$ f $x = 24$
g $x = 2$ h $x = 7.6$ i $x = 8\frac{1}{3}$
j $x = 8.5$ k $x = -4$ l $x = 1\frac{3}{5}$
m $x = 18$ n $x = 40$ o $x = 24$
p $x = -\frac{1}{2}$ q $x = -\frac{2}{5}$ r $x = 5\frac{5}{6}$

Exercise 12·4
1. a $x = 52$ b $x = \frac{24}{7}$
2. a $x = 18$ b $x = 13$ c $x = 15$
d $x = 5$ e $x = 13$ f $x = -18$
g $x = -\frac{1}{2}$ h $x = 1\frac{2}{3}$ i $x = 1$
j $x = 6$ k $x = \frac{74}{11}$ l $x = -\frac{288}{17}$
m $x = \frac{16}{11}$ n $x = 6$ o $x = -\frac{5}{7}$
p $x = 6$ q $x = \frac{11}{3}$ r $x = 15$

Exercise 12·5
1. a $x > 2$ b $y < -1$ c $p > 4$ d $t < 2$
e $v \geq 1$ f $g \leq -14$ g $d \geq 8$ h $e > 1$
i $q \geq 7$ j $k \leq 0$ k $b \leq -2$ l $m < -3$
2. a $x > 4$ b $y < 4$ c $m > 2$ d $p < -4$
e $b < -1$ f $n \leq 7$ g $k \geq -4$ h $u \leq -5.5$
3. a $x > 2$ b $a < 4$ c $b < 5$ d $c > -1$
e $d < 4$ f $e > 1$ g $g \leq -\frac{1}{2}$ h $z \geq 0$
i $k \leq \frac{1}{2}$ j $y \geq -3$ k $p \leq -5$ l $r < -14$
m $r > -2$ n $c > -\frac{3}{2}$ o $y \leq -4$ p $w \geq 30$
4. a 2 b 5 c 4 d 1
5. a 2 b 3 c 5 d 0
6. a $x < -4$ b $a > -2$ c $b > 6$ d $c < 5.5$

e $d > -6$ f $g < -1$ g $h \leq 5$ h $n \geq 13$
7. a $x > 3$ b $x < 5$ c $x > 8$ d $x \geq 1.5$
e $x \geq 4$ f $x \leq 3$ g $x \geq 7$ h $x \leq 0.5$
8. a $x > 4$ b $p > -3$ c $y \leq 0.1$ d $r \leq -4$
e $k < -4$ f $m \leq 6$ g $x \geq -4$ h $x > 0.2$
i $x \geq 2\frac{1}{4}$ j $x \geq -4$ k $x \geq 2.8$ l $x > -10$
m $x < 1$ n $x \leq 0$ o $x \geq 4.5$
9. a Proof b 150 ml
10. $9y + 8 \leq 240$ 25 books
11. $2.5x + 70 \geq 320$ 100 tickets
12. a $5d + 12$, $12d + 5$ b $5d + 12 < 12d + 5$ $d > 1$
c Over 1 day hire Taylors always cheaper

Remember Remember 12
1. a $x = -5$ b $x = 1.5$ c $x = 5.5$
d $x = 7$ e $x = -2$ f $x = 4$
g $x = 8$ h $x = 15$ i $x = 10.5$
j $x = 3$ k $x = 2.5$ l $x = 6$
2. a $x = -9$ b $x = 0$ c $x = -0.5$
d $x = \frac{3}{8}$ e $x = -\frac{44}{5}$ f $x = -4$
3. $x^2 = (x + 8)(x - 4)$ $x = 8$ 8 x 8 16 x 4
4. a $x = 12$ b $x = 3\frac{1}{8}$ c $x = -36$
d $x = 5\frac{1}{5}$ e $x = 13$ f $x = -2$
g $x = 3.5$ h $x = \frac{16}{17}$ i $x = \frac{8}{7}$
j $x = \frac{6}{5}$ k $x = -\frac{82}{3}$ l $x = 4\frac{1}{5}$
5. a $a < 1$ b $b \geq 11$ c $c \leq -9$
d $d > 5.5$ e $e > -4$ f $g < 15$
g $g \geq 1.5$ h $h \leq 8$ i $i > 9$
j $j \geq -12$ k $k \geq \frac{1}{2}$ l $l \geq 1$
6. a $4x > 2.5x + 3$
b $x > 2$ (i) Electro (ii) Either (iii) Movie

Answers to Chapter 13 Page 144

Exercise 13·1
1. a 10 b 11 c 23 d 5
2. See Graph 3. See Graph
4. a (i) 30 (ii) 40 (iii) 50 b 27 c 200
5. See Graph 6. See Graph

Exercise 13·2
1. a i $\frac{4}{10}$ ii $\frac{1}{10}$ iii $\frac{2}{10}$ iv $\frac{3}{10}$
b burger, soup, pizza, salad.
2. a i 40% ii 30% iii 20%
b i 60 ii 270
3. a i 25% ii 40% iii 15% iv 20%
b i 75 ii 200
4-7 See Pie-charts

Exercise 13·3
1. a 40° 180° 20° 120°
b Pie chart with angles listed above. Check
2. a 40° 160° 144° 16°
b Pie chart with angles listed above. Check
3. a 120° 144° 84° 12°
b Pie chart with angles listed above. Check
4. a 180° 100° 20° 60°
Pie chart with angles listed above. Check
b 200° 80° 50° 30°
Pie chart with angles listed above. Check
c 200° 120° 35° 5°
Pie chart with angles listed above. Check
5. a A - 9 B - 8 AB - 8 O - 15
b Pie chart with angles listed below :-
A - 81° B - 72° AB - 72° O - 135°

Exercise 13·4
1. Jan 25 kg 130 cm May 50 kg 140 cm
Sam 20 kg 150 cm Joy 40 kg 150 cm
Tina 35 kg 165 cm Jo 50 kg 160 cm
Ann 60 kg 170 cm
2. a i Mary ii Toni
iii Pat iv Pat

b See ages and weights
c Mark
3. See Scattergraph 4. See Scattergraph
5. See Scattergraph

Exercise 13·5
1. a i Lou ii Bob iii Bill iv Lee
b strong
c Line passing from 3 on y-axis,
on through Toni & Yan.
d $y = \frac{1}{2}x + 3$ (various answers) e 6(ish)
2. a $y = -\frac{1}{2}x + 12$ b 4 hours
3. a yes b yes c yes d no
4. Own Answers
5. a/b/c $y = 2\frac{1}{2}x + 28$ (various answers)

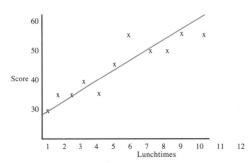

d 48 (various answers)
6. ab Scattergraph with rising line of best fit.
c $y = \frac{1}{2}x + 3$ d $10\frac{1}{2}$kg e 9
7. a $y = 2x + 1$ (approx - various answers)
b $y = -4x + 75$ (various answers) 47 rats
c $y = \frac{4}{3}x + 8$ Eng 74 (approx)

Exercise 13·6
1. a 3rd 43 43 45 46 48 49
4th 50 51 54 58
5th 62 63 66 68 69
b 24 c 69 d 21
2. a 31 32 39
b 42 42 44 46 47 47
c 21 d 66 e 40's
3. a 10 12 13 16 18 20 21 22 30 30
30 35 36 36 42 50 51
b 30's
c 30 mins d 17
4. a various eg 2/3 = 23
b 3 c 23 secs d 21 secs
5. a
```
0 | 9
1 | 1 1 1 2 4 4 5 6
2 | 0 0 1 2 6
3 |
4 | 0 2
```
b various eg 2 | 6 = 26
c 16 d 9 cm e 6 cm
f No 30's g 11 cm h 15·5 cm
6. a
```
0 | 1 3 7 7     b 7     c 10·5
1 | 0 1 4 9
2 | 1
3 | 0
```
7. a
```
0 | 8                          1/5 = 15
1 | 0 1 3 3 5 5 8 8 8 8
2 | 0 2 3 7
3 | 1        mode = 18.  median = 18
```
b
```
0 | 3 4                        3/8 = 38
1 | 2 4 5 5 7 8
2 | 0 2 3 4 6 6 7 7
3 | 0 4 5 8 8
4 | 0 0 2 5 5 5 5 6 8
5 | 2 2 3 3 4 4 5 5 6
6 | 1
```
Mode 4·5 Median 3·8
8. a i 2 ii 4 iii 0
b i mode = 46 median = 33

b ii mode = 44   median = 39

9. a
Men		Women
	0	
9	1	8 9
3 3	2	2 3 7 7 9
7 5 3 2	3	0
5	4	

b i   mode = 23   median = 32·5
b ii mode = 27   median = 25

10. a
Boys		Girls
9 8	1	
6 6 5 4	2	1 3 5 5 9
4 0	3	0 4
	4	0

b i   mode = 25   median = 27
b ii mode = 26   median = 25·5

Exercise 13·7

1. a 4   b 6   c 0
2. a 10   b 28
3. a 1   b 3   c 21
    d 11 m e 10 m
4. a 3   b 2 mm   c 13 mm
    See dot-plot
5. a/b see dot-plots

Remember Remember 13

1. See Bar Graph
2. See Line Graph
3. a 120°   84°   144°   12°
    b Pie chart with angles listed above. Check
4. a Scattergraph b strong - older, so heavier.
    c shown   d 70 - 75 kg
5. 1 | 0 1 9   b 52   c 45   d 16
   2 | 1 2 2 4 5 7 9
   3 | 0 1 3 4 4 4 7
   4 | 1 2 5 5 7 7 9
   5 | 2 2 2 2 3 9 9
   6 | 0 0 1 1 2 2 3 5 8
6. a 0   b i 23   ii 6

Turn off that Calculator - Non-calc. 4

1. a 529   b 733   c 5   d 4703
    e 124500 f 26   g 64   h 1²/₃
2. a 62·356 b 768   c 14·8   d 0·2091
3. 7·32 litres
4. a 0·048   b 2075   c 800   d 8 m 20 s
5. a 1/₃   b 7/₉   c 12/₁₃
6. a 2   b 2/₅   c 160
    d 15   e 3¹/₄   f 18
7. a £2·40   b £0·66 c £540
    d £0·28   e 32   f 30
8. £18, £102
9. a −14   b −60   c −21   d −6
    e −77   f 51   g 900   h −7
    i 23   j −6   k 17
10. a see diagram b   D(1, −2)
11. a 2340   b 1435   c 1045
12. a 2 hr 27 mins   b 5 hr 25 mins
13. Only 1968 and 2004 were leap years.

Answers to Chapter 14 Page 158

Exercise 14·1

1. a 58°   b 134°   c 111°   d 49°
    e 50°   f 112°   g 41°   h 77°
    i 52°   j 105°   k 19·5°   l 90°
2. m 119°   n 77°   o 37°   p 50°
    q 74°   r 50°   s 71°   t 111°
    u 47°   v 120°   w 66°   x 19°

3.
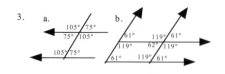
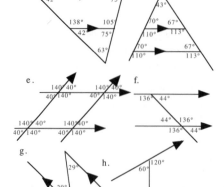
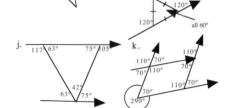
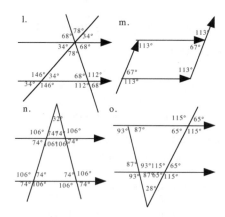
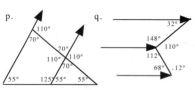
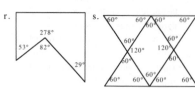
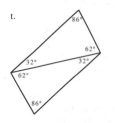

Exercise 14·2

1.
a.
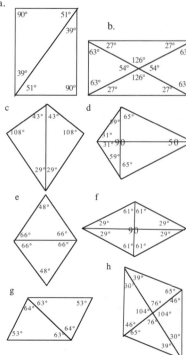
b.

c
d
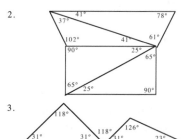
e
f
g
h

2.
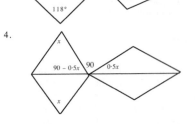

3.

4.

Exercise 14·3

1. a 360°   b 360 ÷ 12 = 30°
2. a 60°   b 90°   c 120°
    d 150°   e 180°   f 90°
3. a 105°   b 165°   c 165°
4. a 135°   b 15°   c 75°
    d 15°   e 135°   f 105°
5. a 82·5° b 337·5° c 80°
6. 10¹⁰/₁₁ minutes past 2.

Remember Remember 14

1. a   b
    c   d
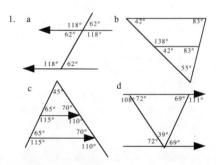

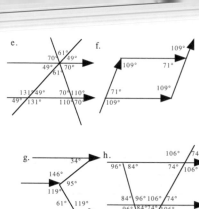

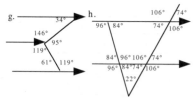

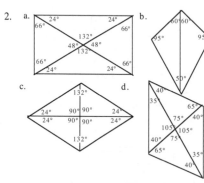

2. a. 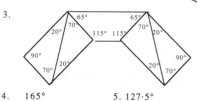 b.

c. d.

3.

4. 165°   **5.** 127·5°

Answers to Chapter 15 Page 162

Exercise 1

1.   **2. (a)**   **(b)**

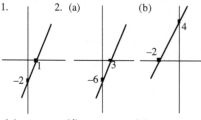

(c)   **(d)**   **(e)**

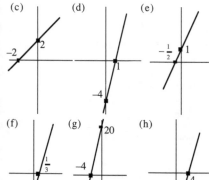

(f)   **(g)**   **(h)**

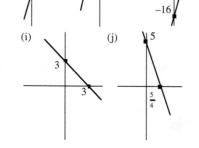

(i)   **(j)**

---

3.   **4. (a)**

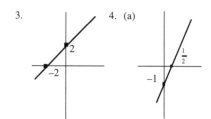

4. (b)   **(c)**   **(d)**

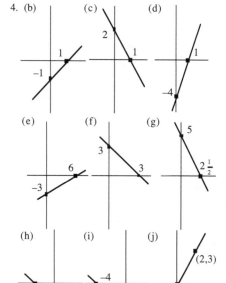

(e)   **(f)**   **(g)**

(h)   **(i)**   **(j)**

Exercise 15.2

1. (6, 2)
2. a (4, 3) b (−2, −7) c (1, 0)
   d (−1, 2) e (−1, −5) f (0·5, −1)
3. a (0, 2) b (6, 2) c (5, 0)
   d (4, 0) e (2, −3) f (6, −3)
4. a (−2, 3) b (0, 2) c (1, 4) d (−1, −5)
5. Lines are parallel.   6. Coordinates too large.

Exercise 15.3

1. (2, 5)   2. (1, 3)
3. a (1, 2) b (2, 1) c (3, 3) d (4, 5)
   e (2, 4) f (0, 2) g (−3, 1) h (−3, −3)
4. (2, 3)
5. a (3, 1) b (2, 4·5) c (4, 0) d (−1, 1)

Exercise 15.4

1. (2, 3)   2. (3, 1)
3. a (3, 5) b (7, 1) c (1, 4) d (2, 4)
   e (5, 2) f (2, −1) g (−3, 0) h (−2, −3)
   i (−3·5, −0·5)   j (0·5, 4)
4. (2, 2)
5. (1, 5)
6. (4, 2)
7. a (2, 1) b (2, 3) c (4, 1) d (1, 3)
   e (−1, 1) f (−2, −1) g (0·5, 6) h (−0·5, 0·5)
8. a (2, 1) b (3, 1) c (1, 5)
   d (4, 2) e (−1, 2) f (1, −2)
   g (−1, 2) h (−3, −2) i (0·5, −2)
9. a (−2, −2) b (−11, −9) c (0·5, −0·5) d (−1, 0)
   e (1, 4) f (−2, 3) g (2, −3) h (3, −1)

Exercise 15.5

1. Sweet 4p. Lolly 1p
2. a 4x + 2y = 14,   7x + 2y = 20
   b £2   c £3   d £12
3. Grow-bag £4. Plant £3   4. £1·50
5. £8   6. Mouse £3. Lizard £7
7. 2 kg   8. a £9   b £5

---

9. a 5a + 4c = 60,   2a + c = 21
   b (i) £8   (ii) £5   c £57
10. White 200 sheets. Coloured 300 sheets.
11. £25   12. £165   13. £1·47
14. No. 5 jugs needs 2·55 litres.
15. 500 secs. (8 mins 20 secs)
16. a 8 cm   b 64 cm^2
17. a 9 m   b 13 m^2
18. a 4x + 3y = 2·30,   3x + 5y = 2·55
    b Orange 35p. Pear 30p.
    c 90g   d 1880g. £7·10.

Remember, Remember 15

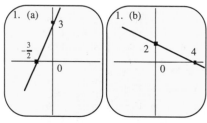

1. (a)   1. (b)

2. ($\frac{1}{2}$, $3\frac{1}{2}$)
3. a (3, 1) b (2, 1) c (1, 2) d (1, 2)
   e (1, 1) f (2, 3) g (1, 3) h (5, −2)
   i (5, 4) j (1, 8)
4. (5, 0)   5. 3 kg
6. a 8x + 3y = 3·60,   7x + 3y = 3·30
   b 40p c £2·30
7. £120   8. £1·30 9. 18 m   10. 43 cm

Answers to Chapter 16 Page 171

Exercise 16.1

1. a 8^1/$_2$ b 4^5/$_6$ c 18/$_9$
2. a 3^1/$_3$ b 4^3/$_4$ c 5^1/$_6$
   d 5^1/$_2$ e 7^2/$_5$ f 6^3/$_8$
3. a 2^3/$_5$ b 3^5/$_6$ kg c 5^2/$_5$ l
4. 4^1/$_3$
5. a 3^1/$_2$ b 3^1/$_2$ c 3^1/$_4$
   d 4^1/$_5$ e 2^1/$_3$ f 3^3/$_4$
6. a 4   b 8   c 11
7. a 9   b 2   c 11   d 1^1/$_3$
8. 23/$_5$ 9. a 1^1/$_3$ b 38/$_7$ c 34/$_5$
10. a 5/$_2$ b 15/$_4$ c 53/$_5$
    d 49/$_8$ e 29/$_3$ f 27/$_{10}$
11. a 6   b 14   c 9   d 19
12. a 6   b 8   c 13
13. a 20   b 9   c 15   14. 6^2/$_5$

Exercise 16.2

1. a 4/$_5$ b 2/$_9$ c 3/$_5$ d 3/$_8$
2. a 12/$_7$ b 8/$_9$ c 1/$_4$
   d 1^1/$_5$ e 5/$_{11}$ f 2/$_5$
3. a 7   b 4^1/$_2$ c 6^2/$_3$
   d 6^2/$_9$ e 4^1/$_2$ f 1^{15}/$_7$
4. 2/$_5$ km   5. 7^1/$_4$ 6. 9^2/$_5$ kg
7. a 3^1/$_4$ m   b 4^1/$_2$ l
   c 7^3/$_7$ km d 7/$_8$ e 3 8^1/$_5$ kg
8. a 3^2/$_5$ ft   b 16 ft
9. a 5 tonnes b 5^3/$_8$ tonnes   c 5^3/$_4$ tonnes
10. 8^1/$_8$ inches.

Exercise 16.3

1. a 1^1/$_{12}$ b 2/$_{15}$ c 1/$_8$ d 1^{11}/$_{21}$
2. a 11/$_{15}$ b 1/$_4$ c 11/$_{24}$ d 17/$_{20}$
   e 1/$_3$ f 5/$_{24}$ g 11/$_{10}$ h 1/$_{18}$
3. a 1^1/$_{12}$ b 1/$_8$ c 19/$_{30}$ d 49/$_{60}$

Int-2-Maths 3C   this is page 233   Answers

4. a $9\frac{1}{6}$ b $3\frac{1}{12}$ c $4\frac{3}{8}$ d $9\frac{3}{10}$
 e $2\frac{7}{30}$ f $3\frac{17}{24}$ g $7\frac{1}{18}$ h $4\frac{3}{20}$

5. a $3\frac{3}{4}$ b $4\frac{2}{5}$ 6. a $1\frac{2}{3}$ b $4\frac{2}{9}$

7. $2\frac{5}{8}$ m 8. $4\frac{2}{5}$ km

9. a $3\frac{9}{10}$ b $1\frac{31}{40}$

10. a $2\frac{7}{10}$ b $4\frac{23}{30}$ c $1\frac{3}{4}$ d $1\frac{5}{8}$
 e $2\frac{5}{6}$ f $4\frac{9}{14}$ g $4\frac{19}{30}$ h $2\frac{23}{30}$

Exercise 16.4

1. a $\frac{8}{15}$ b $\frac{5}{18}$

2. a $\frac{4}{15}$ b $\frac{1}{2}$ c $\frac{4}{21}$ d $\frac{1}{4}$
 e $\frac{3}{10}$ f $\frac{1}{3}$ g $\frac{11}{40}$ h $\frac{1}{5}$

3. $\frac{5}{16}$ m^2 4. $\frac{3}{10}$

5. a $3\frac{1}{2}$ b $7\frac{1}{12}$

6. a $5\frac{5}{6}$ b $10\frac{1}{2}$ c 20 d 6
 e 10 f $15\frac{7}{12}$ g $5\frac{19}{30}$ h $11\frac{1}{10}$
 i $6\frac{5}{12}$ j $26\frac{2}{5}$ k 9 l $5\frac{1}{5}$

Exercise 16.5

1. a $1\frac{1}{4}$ b $2\frac{1}{2}$

2. a $\frac{3}{5}$ b $1\frac{3}{7}$ c $\frac{1}{2}$ d $\frac{3}{8}$
 e $\frac{9}{20}$ f $\frac{2}{3}$ g $1\frac{1}{10}$ h $1\frac{1}{3}$
 i $1\frac{1}{6}$ j $1\frac{11}{24}$ k $1\frac{5}{27}$ l $1\frac{2}{5}$

3. $\frac{3}{4}$ 4. $5\frac{1}{3}$ 5. a $1\frac{7}{8}$ b $3\frac{1}{3}$

6. a $2\frac{2}{9}$ b $1\frac{7}{15}$ c $1\frac{19}{33}$ d $\frac{27}{56}$
 e $1\frac{13}{72}$ f $2\frac{8}{9}$ g $\frac{12}{35}$ h $5\frac{1}{4}$
 i 4 j 3

7. $5\frac{5}{9}$ mins.

Remember Remember 16

1. a $5\frac{4}{5}$ b $5\frac{3}{4}$ c $7\frac{3}{5}$

2. a $\frac{17}{3}$ b $\frac{33}{5}$ c $\frac{97}{9}$ 3. 14

4. a $\frac{6}{7}$ b $\frac{1}{4}$ c $\frac{1}{2}$ d $6\frac{1}{5}$
 e $\frac{7}{12}$ f $6\frac{7}{15}$ g $3\frac{11}{40}$ h $1\frac{5}{6}$

5. a $\frac{3}{10}$ b $\frac{14}{27}$ c $4\frac{1}{5}$ d 3
 e $2\frac{1}{2}$ f $2\frac{1}{4}$ g $2\frac{2}{9}$ h $1\frac{1}{2}$

6. $10\frac{3}{4}$ 7. $9\frac{9}{10}$ 8. $19\frac{7}{8}$ kg

9. $3\frac{1}{5}$ m 10. $\frac{1}{5}$

Non-Calculator 5

1. a 1681 b 739 c 188 400 d 9073
 e 1348 f 4 g 625 h 680

2. a 138·11 b 66·653 c 23·8 d 11 484
 e 1·38 f 20·753 g 0·64 h 0·00246

3. a 280 b £9·10 c £7·50

4. a $\frac{13}{17}$ b $\frac{4}{7}$ c $\frac{1}{3}$ d $\frac{6}{11}$

5. a $\frac{13}{20}$ b $7\frac{11}{12}$ c $1\frac{15}{26}$ d $2\frac{13}{20}$
 e $3\frac{4}{5}$ f $\frac{7}{8}$ g 6 h $1\frac{4}{5}$

6. a $2\frac{1}{3}$ b $6\frac{5}{7}$ c $12\frac{7}{8}$

7. a $\frac{7}{8}$ b $\frac{9}{25}$ c $\frac{1}{16}$

8. a £68 b £0·60 c 780
 d 88 e 35 f 42

9. a 60% b 20%

10. a −42 b −43 c −60 d 2
 e 169 f −12 g 2 h 27
 i −8·5 j −10 k −16 l 3

11. a 43 b 18th August

12. a 72 km/hr b 50 m/sec.

Answers to Chapter 17 Page 181

Exercise 17.1

1. a 6 b 15 c 25
 d 0·7 e 135 f 26·4

2. a 6 b 44 c 2·8 d 133

3. a 17·5 b 18 c 107
 d 0·65 e 0 f 5

4. a 8 b 23 c 1·8
 d 2 e 1124 f 0·75

5. (i) a 8 b 28 c 8
 d 1·5 e 16 f 5
 (ii) a 7 b 44 c 4·6
 d 2 e 189 f 0·55

6 a 55 b Mean = 11, Med = 5, Mode = 2
 c Median
 d Only one value > mean. Mode - lowest.

7. a Mean 6 Median 3 Mode 3
 b Mean 5·3 Median 5·4 Mode 5·4
 c Mean 271 Median 303 Mode 307
 d Mean 44·25 Median 41 Mode 40
 e Mean 65·5 Median 65·5 Mode 67
 f Mean 13 400 Med - 13 000 Mode 10 000

8. a 23 b Mode 45 Median 53
 c Median, since mode is the lowest value.

9. a Mean = 7·8, Med = 8, Mode = 8 b 4

10. a 12·9, 27 b 38·5, 99

11. a Each uses mean, median and mode.
 b Mean indicates more "central" value.

12. 10·5 kg 13. 17 14. 78

15. a No. Mean, median and mode all 59. b 70

16. 93 17. 57

18. Not possible. Score needed is 101%!

Exercise 17.2

1. a 0, 6, 22, 21, 16 => Total = 65
 b 30 c 65 d 2·2 e 2 f 2

2. a 6, 21, 36, 20, 12 => Total = 95
 b 25 c 95 d 3·8 e 4 f 4

3. a (i) 10, 36, 28, 10, 24 => Total = 108
 Mean = 3·6, Mode = 3, Median = 3
 (ii) 0, 6, 22, 21, 16 => Total = 65
 Mean = 6, Mode = 4, Median = 5
 (iii) 9, 24, 10, 42, 0, 8, 0, 10, Tot = 103
 Mean = 5·2, Mode = 6, Median = 5

4. (ii) 10 (iii) 7

5. a 25 b 8 c 12·7 d 12 e 12

6. a 104, 196, 45, 144, 187 => Tot = 676
 b Mode 14, Range 4, Mean 15, Median 15

Exercise 17.3

1 a CF = 5, 15, 27, 52, 69, 72, 80
 b 80 c 69 d 4

2. a CF = 1, 11, 27, 34, 37, 39, 40, med = 4
 b CF = 2, 8, 16, 36, 78, 92, 100, med = 7
 c CF = 4, 6, 13, 24, 43, 50, 51, med = 25

3. a 15(6), 16(5), 17(5), 18(3), 19(5), 20(1)
 b (90 + 80 + 85 + 54 + 95 + 20) ÷ 25 = 17·0
 c CF = 6, 11, 16, 19, 24, 25, med = 17

Exercise 17.4

1. b 11 c 5 d 9 e 12

2. a Q1 : 3 Q2 : 7 Q3 : 9
 b Q1 : 14 Q2 : 21 Q3 : 26
 c Q1 : 3·7 Q2 : 4·2 Q3 : 5
 d Q1 : 54 Q2 : 61 Q3 : 71
 e Q1 : 24 Q2 : 31 Q3 : 36

3. a 33rd
 b Q1 - between 16th & 17th
 Q3 - between 49th and 50th.

4. b 4 c 4 d 4th/5th & 14th/15th
 e Q1 : 5 Q2 : 7·5 Q3 : 10·5

5. Q1 : 7·5 Q2 : 12 Q3 : 17·5

Exercise 17.5

1. a Med 23, Q1 = 14, Q3 = 25, SIQR = 5·5
 b Med 3·6, Q1 = 3, Q3 = 4·3, SIQR = 0·65
 c Med 121, Q1 = 112, Q3 = 134, SIQR = 11

2. a 0,0,1,1,2,2,2,2,2,3,3,3,4,4,4,4,4,5,5,6,6,6,8,9
 b Median 3 Mean 3·5 Mode 2 or 4
 c Q1 2 Q3 5 d Range 9 SIQR 1·5

3. Range 9, SIQR 0·75

Exercise 17.6

1. a Median 7·5 Q1 : 6·5 Q3 : 9·5
 b
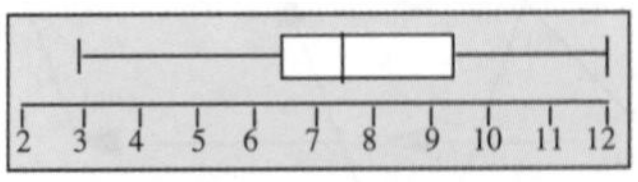

2. a Q1 : 40 Q2 : 52·5 Q3 : 85
 b
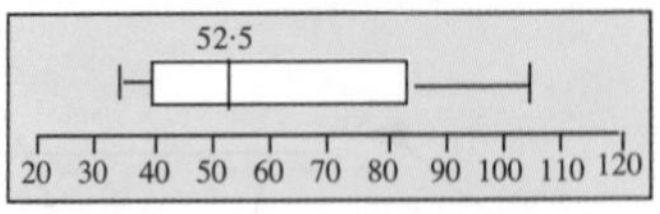

3. a Q1 : 14 Q2 : 18 Q3 : 22
 b
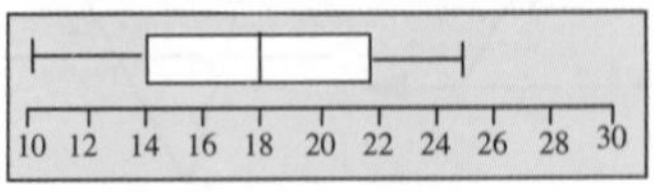

4. a Awlbright Q1 : 8 Q2 : 10 Q3 : 14
 b Osiris Q1 : 10 Q2 : 14 Q3 : 16
 c
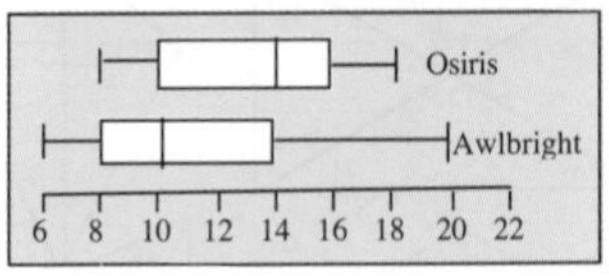

 d Osiris has a higher mean- will last longer.

5. a Men Q1 : 9 Q2 : 13 Q3 : 18
 Women Q1 : 6·5 Q2 : 11 Q3 : 14
 b
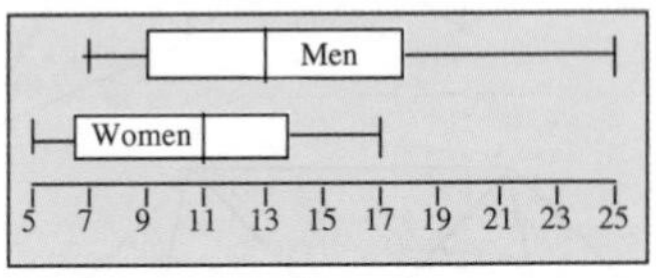

 c The men have a higher median, therefore on average can do more pull-ups.

6. a
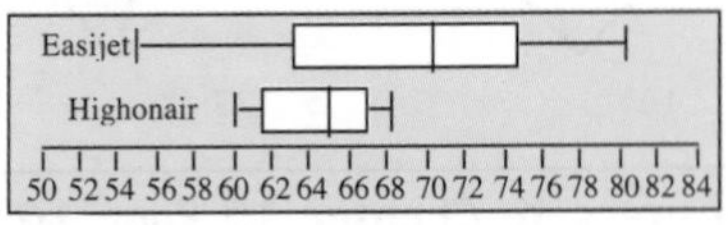

 b High-on-air times are more grouped therefore more consistant.
 They have a shorter mean time therefore shorter average flight time.

7. Rod's hits are more grouped so more consistant. He also has a higher mean therefore on average his hits go further.
 Ted can hit further but is very inconsistant and has a lower mean than Rod.
 Bob with his lowest mean is the novice.

Exercise 17.7

1. a 5 b 2·45 2. a 4 b 2·398

3. a 37 b 9·13 4. a 8 b 4·74

5. a 28 b 5·138 6. 2·41

7. a Both means are 18
 b Donald : 2·61 Graeme : 16·41
 c Donald's s.d. is lower => more consistant.

8. a Mean - 7·75, s.d. : 3·5
 b Mean - 35·8 s.d. : 6·31
 c Mean - 7·94 s.d. : 2·33
 d Mean - 127·857 s.d. : 7·11

9. 3·5

Exercise 17.8 - oral replies

Exercise 17.9

1. $\frac{1}{3}$

2. a $\frac{1}{6}$ b $\frac{1}{3}$ c $\frac{1}{2}$ d 0

3. a $\frac{1}{6}$
 b (i) $\frac{1}{6}$ (ii) $\frac{1}{2}$ (iii) 0 (iv) $\frac{1}{6}$

4. a $\frac{1}{4}$ b $\frac{1}{3}$ c $\frac{5}{12}$ d $\frac{1}{2}$

5. a $\frac{1}{5}$ b $\frac{7}{10}$ c $\frac{1}{10}$ d $\frac{9}{10}$

6. a $\frac{1}{3}$ b $\frac{2}{9}$ c $\frac{1}{6}$ d $\frac{1}{9}$
 e $\frac{1}{12}$ f $\frac{1}{18}$ g $\frac{1}{36}$ h $\frac{7}{18}$
 i $\frac{11}{18}$

7. a $\frac{5}{11}$ b $\frac{2}{11}$ c $\frac{5}{11}$ d $\frac{6}{11}$

8. $4/7$

9. a HHH, HHT, HTH, THH, TTT, TTH, THT, HTT b (i) $1/8$ (ii) $1/8$

10. a $1/20$ b $2/5$ c $1/2$ d $2/5$

11. 3 12. 0·75

13. Boys 36, Girls 24.

14. a $1/2$ b $1/4$ c $1/13$ d $1/52$ e $3/13$

15. a $1/18$ b $1/6$ c $1/36$ d $5/12$

Remember Remember 17

1. Mean 17 Median 17
   Mode 18 Range 13

2. 34

3. a 33p b 33p c 4p d 32·9

4. a Med = 12, Q1 = 5, Q3 = 15 b SIQR = 5

5. a Med = 19 Q1 = 14·5 Q3 = 23

   b [box plot: 10 12 14 16 18 20 22 24 26 28 30]

6. a 47 b 4·34

7. (a) mean = 220, (b) Rod = 34·8, Stan = 7·9

8. $10/13$

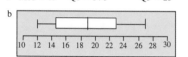

Answers to Chapter 18 Page 200

Exercise 18.1

1. a 30·8cm² b 45 cm² c 102·9cm²

2. a 124 cm² b 73·4 cm²

3. 15·2 m² 4. 53·4

5. a 24° b 104 cm²

6. a 101 m² b 470 m² c 465m²

7. 210 cm² 8. £33·73 9. 64·2°

10. 1590 mm² 11. No. £2·12 short.

12. Yes - area = 71m² and £45 buys 75m²

13. a (i) 0·5 (ii) 0·766 (iii) 0·174 (iv) 0·966 (v) 0·087 (vi) 0·891

   b Sin a = sin (180 - a)

14. X = 55° Y = 125°

Exercise 18.2

1. a 19·1 cm b 52·4 cm

2. a 8·05 cm b 2·05 cm c 260 mm

3. a 80° b 25·2 cm

4. a 9° b 12·9 cm

5. AM = 155 mm 6. 452 km

7. a 20·0 m b 42·2 m

8. a 24·1 ft b 7·50 ft c 23·2 ft

9. a 102° b 116 cm

10. a [triangle Y 95°, T 45° 40° F] b Tiger c 64·5 km

Exercise 18.3

1. 145°

2. a 52·2° b 46·5° c 50·5° d 134° e 151° f 22·4°

3. 145°

4. ∠ACB = 42·8°, ∠CBA = 57·2°

5. a 108° b 127·7° c 79°

6. 59° 7. 11·7° 8. 156°

Exercise 18.4

1. a 7·51 cm b 29·1 cm

2. a 25·0 cm b 214 mm c 10·4 km

3. 2·68 km 4. 5·60 cm 5. 103 cm

6. 72·7 m 7. 61·2 km

8. a see sketch b 14·2 miles 9. 40·5 km

Exercise 18.5

1. a $CosQ = \dfrac{p^2 + r^2 - q^2}{2pr}$ b $CosP = \dfrac{q^2 + r^2 - p^2}{2qr}$

   c $CosR = \dfrac{p^2 + q^2 - r^2}{2pq}$

2. a 35·9° b 83·6° c 74·5° d 52·7°

3. 117° 4. Proof 5. 98·1°

6. 43·6° 7. a 049·5° b 119°

Exercise 18.6

1. a 119 m b 91·4 m

2. a 35·1 m b 28·8 m

3. a 72·1 km b 46·4 cm

4. 178 miles 5. 12·3°

6. b 61·0 m

7. a 112° & 32° b 6·66 m c 6·18 m

Exercise 18.7

1. a 27·5 m² b 734 m²

2. 98·7 mm 3. 46·3° 4. 9·89 cm

5. 141° 6. a 72° b 108°

7. 2·56 m 8. a Proof b 54·6 m

9. a Proof b 362 km 10. 20·6 m

11. a ∠TBA = 45° ∠TAB = 57° b 033° c 315°

12. 54·1 miles

Remember Remember 18

1. a 74·4 cm² b 16 700 mm²

2. 30° or 150° 3. 129° 4. 13·2 km

5. 12·7 km 6 43·8°

7. a 32·6 m b 13·8 m

8. a Proof b 154 km

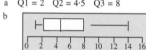

Maths 2 NAB Practice Page 217

Outcome 1

1. a 17·6cm² b 11·8cm² c 29·8cm² d 69·9cm²

2. a 16·2 cm b 23·8° c 18·0 cm d 31·1°

3. a 9·76 cm b 12·6 cm c 16·4 cm d 4·34 cm

Outcome 2

4 (a) [graph (2,2), (1,1)] (b) [graph (2,4), (1,2)] (c) [graph 3, (1,4), (2,5)]

(d) [graph 1, (2,7), (1,4)] (e) [graph (2,1), (1,-1), -3] (f) [graph 8, (2,6), (4,2)]

(g) [graph -4, (2,-2), (1,-3)] (h) [graph 0, (1,-3), (2,-6)]

5. a (7, 3) b (1, 3) c (2, 6) d (5, 1)

Outcome 3

6. a (8, 2) b (3, 5) c (4, 1) d (5, 1) e (2, 4) f (3, -3)

7. a (5, 3) b (2, 0) c (3, 2) d (4, -1) e (3, 1) f 8, 3)

Outcome 3

8. a Recorder b (i) 25% (ii) 16·7% c (i) 200 (ii) 100

9. See Bar Graph

10. a 49 kg b 5 c Jack & Tom d Sara e Lucy f 4 g about 8

11. a (i) 2 (ii) 22 b 20 c 3 A

   d 22, 26, 34, 35, 37, 40, 40, 43, 44, 48, 51, 52, 55, 59, 65, 68, 70, 71, 74, 75.

12. See Stem-and-leaf diagram

13. a 160°, 30°, 120°, 50°. b see pie-chart

14. a 12 b med = 24, mode = 24

15. See dot-plot

16. C.F. 1, 3, 8, 18, 25, 29, 35, 38, 40. —> $19/20$

17. a C.F. 12, 20, 22, 29, 34, 43, 47, 49, 50. b 29 c 14%

Outcome 4

18. a Range 9, Mean 9, Median 9, Mode 8
    b Range 74, Mean 41·5, Med 39·5, Mode 54
    c Range 7·5, Mean 5·2, med 4·9, Mode 3·8

19. a 25 b 5 c (i) 20·6 (ii) 21 (iii) 22

20. Q1 : 5 Q2 : 8 Q3 : 10 SIQR : 2·5

21. a Range = 7 SIQR = 1·5 b Range = 10 SIQR = 3 c Range = 10 SIQR = 3

22. a C.F. 1, 4, 9, 15, 17, 18, 19 b Q3 = 3 Q1 = 2 c 0·5

23. Q1 : 19 Q3 : 24 SIQR : 2·5

24. a 11, 21 b 10 c 16 d Q1 : 13 Q3 : 20 e 3·5

25. a Q1 = 2 Q2 = 4·5 Q3 = 8
    b [box plot: 0 2 4 6 8 10 12 14 16]

26. b 6·26 27. Mean : 7 s.d. : 3·02

28. a Gradient = $3/2$ cuts at (0,2) b P = $3/2\,t + 2$

29. F = $3/4\,d + 1$

30. See Scattergraphs d (i) $y = 2x$ (ii) $y = 3/5\,x + 12$ (various)

31. a $1/6$ b $1/2$ c $1/3$ d $1/2$

32. a $1/49$ b $25/49$ c $1/7$ d $8/49$

33. a $1/11$ b $2/11$ c $4/11$ d 0